Eng^d by H.B.Halls Sons, New York

M. Simpson

THE LIFE

OF

BISHOP MATTHEW SIMPSON

OF THE METHODIST EPISCOPAL CHURCH

BY

GEORGE R. CROOKS, D.D.

ILLUSTRATED

NEW YORK

HARPER & BROTHERS, FRANKLIN SQAURE

1891

PREFACE.

In the preparation of this life I have been placed under many obligations by friends of Bishop Simpson who have supplied me with materials. I desire especially to thank the Rev. George B. Smith, of Cadiz, Ohio, for aid given me at the time of my visit to that town; also to Professor Hamnet, of Allegheny College, Meadville, Pennsylvania, and Professor James R. Weaver, of De Pauw University for help when I was in those places searching for information. I am also indebted to Ex-Governor A. G. Porter, and Dr. T. A. Goodwin, of Indianapolis, for their accounts of life in Greencastle, when the university was under the direction of President Simpson. Mr. John H. Nicolay, of Washington, the biographer of President Lincoln, very kindly made a search among the Lincoln papers for letters. And I beg also to thank Bishop Bowman, General Clinton B. Fisk, Dr. John Lanahan, Professor Joseph Tingley, President W. F. Warren, of Boston University, Mr. George H. Stuart, and other correspondents for reminiscences of the bishop which have greatly enriched this volume.

It ought to be said that I have found among the papers placed in my hands no trace of the bishop's opinions upon public questions, or of his estimates of public men. His familiar correspondence is in the main with his family, and is wholly of a domestic nature. On this I have drawn freely, for it shows his character in a most amiable light. I have looked for letters which contain expressions of his judgments upon public affairs, but have looked in vain. The bishop has put his thinking into his public addresses, and there is nothing remaining that can be added to these sources of information.

GEORGE R. CROOKS.

DREW THEOLOGICAL SEMINARY,
   MADISON, NEW JERSEY,
     February 26, 1890.

CONTENTS.

CHAPTER IV.

HIS EARLY MINISTRY.

CHAPTER V.

INCIDENTS OF HIS EARLY MINISTRY.

CHAPTER VI.

PROFESSOR IN ALLEGHENY COLLEGE AND VICE-PRESIDENT.

CHAPTER X.

BISHOP SIMPSON'S THEORY OF PREACHING.

CHAPTER XI.

DELEGATE TO THE GENERAL CONFERENCE, 1844, 1848, 1852.

CHAPTER XII.

EDITOR OF THE " WESTERN CHRISTIAN ADVOCATE."

CHAPTER XIII.

FIRST EPISCOPAL TOURS.

CHAPTER XIV.

AN EPISCOPAL TOUR THROUGH CALIFORNIA AND OREGON.

CHAPTER XV.

AN EPISCOPAL TOUR TO TEXAS.—JOURNEY TO EUROPE.

CHAPTER XVI.

JOURNEY TO THE EAST.—ILLNESS AND RECOVERY OF HEALTH.

CHAPTER XVII.

THE CIVIL WAR.

CHAPTER XVIII.

LAY DELEGATION.

CHAPTER XIX.

THE YEARS OF PEACE.

CHAPTER XX.

LAST DAYS.

APPENDIX.

ILLUSTRATIONS.

LIFE OF MATTHEW SIMPSON.

INTRODUCTION.

BISHOP SIMPSON was born in the town of Cadiz, Ohio, of which his father, James Simpson, was one of the first settlers. Cadiz is now the county-seat of Harrison County, and was usually reached from the Ohio River, in the days of the bishop's boyhood, by the way of Steubenville or Wheeling. The site of the town, and the region roundabout, are underlaid with coal; the soil is fertile, and the farms are rich in wool and grain, their chief products. Of the first settlement the following account is given in Howe's history of Ohio: "Cadiz was laid out in 1803–4 by Messrs. Briggs and Beatty. Its site was then, like most of the surrounding country, a forest, and its location was induced by the junction there of the road from Pittsburgh by Steubenville, with the road from Washington, Pennsylvania, by Wellsburg, Virginia, from whence the two united by Cambridge to Zanesville; and previous to the construction of the national road through Ohio was travelled more than any other road northwest of the Ohio River. In April, 1809, it contained the following-named persons with their families: Jacob Arnold, inn-keeper, Andrew McNeely, hatter, and justice of the peace; Joseph Harris, merchant; John

1

Jamison, tanner; John McRea, wheelwright; Robert Wilkens, brickmaker; Connell Abdill, shoemaker; Jacob Myers, carpenter; Nathan Pritchard, blacksmith; Nathan Adams, tailor; James Simpson, reedmaker; William Tingley, school-teacher, and old Granny Young, midwife and baker, who was subsequently elected justice of the peace by the citizens, in a fit of hilarity, but, women not being eligible to office in Ohio, was obliged to forego the pleasure of serving her constituents."

The town has been, in former days, and no doubt is still, noted for the brilliant talents of the members of its bar. Here Edwin M. Stanton, Lincoln's secretary of war, and John A. Bingham, the prosecutor of Lincoln's murderers (still living in a green old age), practised their profession. Here, too, Bishop Simpson's maternal uncle, William Tingley, was clerk of the county court for the long period of thirty years. His minute handwriting, as exact and as finished as copper-plate engraving, is still to be found in the records of the court, and of itself is enough to silence the suggestion that the first settlers of Cadiz were rude bordermen. From this town, too, the bishop's paternal uncle, Matthew Simpson, was sent to the Ohio legislature, where, in the state senate, he took high rank as a clear-sighted and logical debater. Of the old times in Ohio, fifty or sixty years ago, the recollections are passing away, chiefly from the lack in the local historians of the pictorial power which can produce a clear image of the past out of the materials which it has left us. We catch some glimpses of the state of society in that period from the recent life of Ben Wade.* The supreme judges were of high quality; justice travelled with them on wheels, visiting every county-seat in a twelve-month. "Judge Peter Hitchcock," says Riddle, "used to drive a sorrel horse in a wooden-springed light wagon, painted yellow, annually over the state for many years."

---

* "Life of Benjamin F. Wade." By A. G. Riddle, Cleveland, 1886.

When Wade went to the county-seat of Ashtabula, he found "a muddy, sodden little town, largely of log buildings. The woods were very near walling it in all round. They still covered the whole country, with stumpy and muddy roads through them leading to it; the wide swampy lands were traversed on log-ways of sections of trees, twelve or eighteen inches through, laid side by side, sometimes for miles in extent." Like all pioneers, these Ohio people were litigious; "to go to a law-suit between others was a great thing. To be called as a juror gave a man importance; he not only heard the lawyers, they talked to *him*. He was a part of the tribunal; ever after a man of note in the neighborhood."* Not only were these borderers litigious, they were acute polemics in theology. In no part of the land was theological debate so rife as in the valley of the Ohio from 1800 to 1840. Thought was free. New religious sects, unknown to former times, had sprung up on the soil; the historic churches had chosen what appeared to be eligible positions, and were competing for ascendency. I doubt if the Bible was ever more used for debating purposes than in the states of Ohio, Indiana, and Illinois during this period. The traveller on horseback might often stop on a Saturday, at a log school-house, and find the rustic combatants battling with each other on "the five points," the divinity of Christ, or baptism, with all the energy of Luther and Eck at Leipsic.

Into the midst of such a community Bishop Simpson was born, in the early part of this century. It was a virtuous community; religious feeling was intense, and religious zeal active. The public-school system of Ohio did not then exist, and the schools taught by his uncle Matthew, of which we shall hear, were maintained by subscriptions. The house in which the bishop was born is no longer standing; its site is now occupied by a hotel and other business buildings.

---

* "Life of B. F. Wade," pp. 75, 76.

THE SIMPSON HOME IN CADIZ, OHIO.

The house in which the family lived, for some years after his father's death, is still to be found, though now removed from its original place. It was a plain one story and a half structure, and most likely of the style of the majority of the homes of his native town. "It was," says Professor Joseph Tingley, the bishop's cousin, "a small, unpainted plain frame house, of four or five rooms, one of which was used for a schoolroom by Uncle Matthew. This last was an addition, probably built for the purpose." Born and reared under these conditions, Bishop Simpson, laying hold of such helps as he could find, acquired as much knowledge of the Latin and Greek classics as was attainable in Ohio in that generation, studied and practised medicine, became a college professor and then a college president, administered the office of a bishop for thirty-two years, was, during the civil war, a recognized power in national affairs, and left a fame for pulpit eloquence throughout the English-speaking world. It will be our task to trace the successive steps of this progress, and to show the means by which it was accomplished; and we first offer to the reader his own brief narrative of his early life.

I.

LIFE IN CADIZ.

AUTOBIOGRAPHIC.

I.

I was born in Cadiz, Harrison County, Ohio, June 21, 1811. Of my paternal ancestry I know comparatively little. My grandfather by the father's side was Thomas Simpson, who was from England, and had been in the service of the government as a horse dragoon for a few years, then emigrated to Ireland and settled in Tyrone County. Of his people I have had little information. He died in middle life of a strain received in attempting to raise a huge pole upon a building, and left a family of five sons and one daughter. The sons were Andrew, John, William, Matthew, and James, and the daughter was Mary, who was married to a Mr. Eagleson.

In 1793 the family, including my father's mother, emigrated to the United States, sailing from Londonderry to Baltimore. On their way, not far from the American coast, they were taken by a French vessel—France being then at war with England—and stripped of nearly everything they had. Landing at Baltimore, they removed to Huntingdon County, Pennsylvania, and afterwards to Western Pennsylvania and Ohio. Andrew Simpson settled near Chillicothe, and has left a large family. John settled on Stillwater Creek, in Harrison County, Ohio, when the population was small, raised a large family of sons and daughters, the most of whom are now in Illinois. William settled near Waterford, Erie County, Pennsylvania, and died in the prime of life, leaving several sons. Mary Eagleson settled in Harrison County, Ohio, and brought·up a large family of sons and daughters, all of whom, except two daughters, died without children.

James, my father, the youngest of the family, was a man of great personal energy, and unusual business tact. From exposure to the weather he caught a severe cold, which produced a sciatic affection and made him lame for several years, and finally ended in an affection of the lungs. In consequence of his enfeebled health, he entered a store in Pittsburgh as a clerk. Afterwards he began the business of manufacturing weavers' reeds, and, with my uncle Matthew, who had no family, but lived with him, set up this business in Cadiz, and connected with it a store, in which they were in partnership with Mr. Wrenshall, of Pittsburgh.

He was married, in 1806, to Sarah Tingley, with whom he had formed an acquaintance when living, for a short time, at Short Creek, Jefferson County, Ohio. They removed to Cadiz immediately after marriage. He bought property in the centre of the town, and was very successful in business until, his health failing, in 1811, he moved to Pittsburgh for medical advice, and there died, at his home on Fourth Street, between Market and Ferry, June 15, 1812.

Being of Scotch Presbyterian descent, my grandmother Simpson educated her family very strictly in the faith of the Irish Presbyterian Church, but shortly after being left a widow, she heard Mr. Wesley preach, on one of his visits to Ireland. Her heart was touched; she attended class and joined the Methodist Society, and from that time forward her children attended Methodist meetings, and, at an early age, all of them united with the Methodist Church. She was a woman of more than ordinary intellect. Left a widow in narrow circumstances, she trained a large family in habits of industry and economy, and had the satisfaction of living to see every one of them occupying a respectable position in life. She had a wonderful memory. Often, when a boy, did I listen to her reminiscences of Scotch and Irish life, the persecution of Protestants by the Catholics; and often have I, in the long winter evenings, listened to stories of fairy and elf and ghost, the common traditions of the North of Ireland, until I found my hair standing on end, and I was almost afraid to leave the little circle in which I sat enchanted. She was happy at ninety, with her old-fashioned spinning-wheel and her hymn-book, singing the hymns she loved, and was a devout and constant attendant at the church as long as she was able to visit it.

My mother, Sarah Tingley, was born in New Jersey, some twenty miles from South Amboy, near Stony Brook; but in her childhood was taken to the neighborhood of Amboy. Her father's name was Jeremiah Tingley. During the war of the Revolution he was drafted and served a term in the army, and then, as the war continued, he enlisted for an additional term, and was present at several battles, though not actively engaged. At the close of the war he received a soldier's claim for lands in Western Virginia, and purposed to move west, but the agent who pretended to locate his land deceived him, and he never recovered it. On his way west, in 1790, he was taken ill at Winchester, Virginia, and, after recovering, remained a number of years in that region. He was brought up, as was my mother's mother, a Baptist, but on removing to Winchester, there being no Baptist church near them, my mother attended Methodist preaching, and was awakened and converted. In 1801 the family removed to Ohio and settled on Short Creek, near Hopewell, where Grandfather Tingley died, and where, June 10, 1806, my mother was married. She was the first member of the family who joined the Methodists, but the entire family followed her example.

My mother was born May 23, 1781. In our family there were three children: Hettie, the eldest, was born April 3, 1807, and was married, in 1829, to Mr. George McCullough, for many years a merchant in Cincinnati. My second sister, Elizabeth, was born February 2, 1809. She was of delicate health, but a woman of clear intellect and more than ordinary genius. She was married to a physician named

Scoles, who became a Methodist minister. She gave birth to one son, a very promising boy, who lived to be about five years of age. In 1833 she died, a devoted and lovely Christian. Never shall I forget how calmly and peacefully she passed away near sunset one summer evening. She now rests in the cemetery of Cadiz. I was the third child, and was born, as already stated, June 21, 1811.

From the time of the marriage of my father and mother and of their beginning housekeeping, both of them being members of the Methodist Episcopal Church, their house was a home for travelling preachers, and, in the lack of church accommodations, the place of class-meetings and occasional preaching. At the time of my birth my father was in feeble health. Both he and my mother consecrated me to God, and their prayer was that if he should see fit to call me, I might be made a minister of the gospel. Passing westward in 1811, Bishop Asbury stopped at my father's house, and Father Boehm, in his reminiscences, states that he remembers Bishop Asbury's baptizing the little boy, though I remember to have heard my mother say that she was not clear who had baptized me. She was in such trouble on account of my father's sufferings and approaching death that these things passed from her mind. She remained in Pittsburgh only a short time after my father's decease, and then the family returned to their former home in Cadiz, where I was brought up.

Of my early childhood I have heard but little. My mother thought me exceedingly active, and hence, unusually troublesome; and during my father's illness, when I was not yet a year old, and when she was harassed with cares, at every opportunity I would make for the open door or stairway and go tumbling down the stairs or the stone door-steps, and was often picked up with scarcely breath remaining in me. She one day said to a friend, who afterwards playfully twitted her about it, that it would be a mercy if I should die, as she did not believe, if spared, I would ever have any sense. She often spoke of one peculiarity—my delight in noise and excitement; in the fiercest storm I was anxious to have the door open, and would laugh with childish glee at the thunder and lightning.

I was not sent to school, but, seeing my sisters with their books, I was anxious to read also; and beginning of my own accord, I learned the alphabet and some spelling, and at three years of age could read. My memory, which extends to about that period, finds no trace of the time when I could not read. I can well remember when from four to six years of age, if ministers staying at the house asked me if I could read, how astonished I was at such questions. In the same way I learned early the elements of arithmetic, and I recollect, on a removal of the family from one house to another, when I was between four and five years of age, finding an old copy of the multiplication table which had once been set for me, and my running it over as a reminiscence of a matter which seemed long past. There were then a few places in the table that were a little difficult for me, and at which I hesitated, and in after-life I have occasionally found myself hesitating at the same places that troubled me then.

In my early years I was rather restrained from than urged to my books, for my health was delicate. When about seven years of age, I attended school for a few months, learning arithmetic and the elements of grammar. Between nine and ten I attended a select school for two short periods, studying grammar and geography; this was all the time spent in school until I attended an academy to learn the classic languages. From my earliest childhood I had an intense desire to read. In Cadiz a public library had been opened, to which I had access, and between five and ten years of age I had read a large number of its volumes of travels, history, and biography.

As a boy, while I disliked writing, I had a still stronger repugnance to declamation, which was one of the duties enjoined while studying grammar. I could easily commit to memory, but I disliked exceedingly to stand up and repeat some other person's thoughts; and this repugnance, joined with a feeble voice and an entire indifference to the study of elocution, made my schoolmates say that I could study, but that I could not speak. At that time the practice in all the schools was to recite in classes and to trap, and in all exercises which were of that character my ambition made me eager to be at the head, a place which I very generally succeeded in keeping; or, if I was not first, I was very near first. This imparted an interest to spelling; and there were occasionally given by the teacher spelling-schools, as they were called, or evenings when the young people, meeting, would choose sides, and beginning with comparatively easy words, would go on until, finally, one by one, they were spelled down, and one side or the other was declared victor. I think that partly from an attachment to these exercises I acquired a great accuracy in spelling at a very early age.

From the earliest period of my memory religious ideas were deeply impressed upon my mind. The instructions I received from my mother and from my uncle, and the religious services at which I was present, so influenced my heart that I had a deep reverence for God; and often, if I was conscious of any error or act of impropriety, did I in early childhood pass through seasons of severe mental suffering. Many times have I lain awake at night thinking of divine truths, and especially of that question which all hearts will turn over, "What must I do to be saved?" "And how to come to Jesus?" What I was to believe, and how I was to believe, were questions that deeply moved me. The habit of prayer, which my mother taught me, I never forsook; and while guilty of many childish indiscretions and youthful follies, such was the influence of parental instruction and of God's holy word (which I read regularly from my childhood up), and such the influence of God's house, which I attended, that I can say, to the praise of God's grace,

I seldom, if ever, committed any outward act which would have brought censure upon me as a member of the Christian Church. With a heart as prone to evil as any other, I was restrained from every word or act of either profanity or licentiousness, and never engaged in what are termed by Christians sinful amusements, though exceedingly fond of all boyish sports. In running, jumping, wrestling, shooting with a bow and arrow, flying kites, and all exercises which boys in town or in country then engaged in, I tried to excel, and as these tended to develop my body or to occupy my mind, I was encouraged in most of them by my friends.

My taste for arithmetic was very decided. At school I felt it to be a drudgery to write down in a book, as was then the custom, what are termed the "sums," in order to preserve them for reference. It seemed to me that working a problem or finding the solution of a question once, I was able to master it again. But while I disliked the labor of writing, I was fond of working out the longest, the most intricate and perplexing problems, and often, at home, I spent all my leisure time for days in working at them, rather than ask for the slightest assistance from those who were more skilled. In this way I mastered perfectly the entire arithmetical course, and laid the foundation for whatever accuracy and skill in computations I afterwards gained. A work on surveying, embracing the elements of geometry and trigonometry, was put into my hands when quite a boy, and gave me special delight, and was mastered without a teacher except occasional suggestions from my uncle, who was a superior mathematician, and from whom, at home, I could receive all the benefits to be expected from the most capable instructor in college. When about eight years of age, at that time being pretty well acquainted with English grammar, I wished to study German. My uncle had a German Bible and an old German grammar, and without the aid of a dictionary, but by comparing the English Bible with the German, I managed to read the German Bible through and to gain a knowledge of the elements of that language. In family worship every morning I was expected to read the German copy, while my uncle, or, in his absence, my mother, read in the English, and, after the close of worship, to note whatever differences I might find in the texts. This was continued for several years.

My father, at his death, had left a little property finely situated in the town, but the maintenance and education of a young family had exhausted a part of his resources. Diligent industry and strict economy were required of each member of the family. I enjoyed, in addition to our library, which was not of large dimensions, but well selected, the advantages of the public library to which I have referred, and access to the libraries of several friends who had collections of choice works. To ministers of our church, lodging at my mother's, I early listened, not only for the news affecting the Church, but for information upon general literary and theological topics; sometimes I had the privilege of hearing discussions between them and my uncle. Some of them were men of very superior minds and of much general information, though, in that day, few of them had enjoyed the advantages of exact scientific or literary culture. In addition to this my uncle, under whose care I was educated, was somewhat in political life, having been for a number of years one of the judges of the county court, and, for some ten years, a member of the Senate of the State of Ohio; while another uncle, in the same town, my mother's brother, was clerk of the court for thirty years, and in constant association with the members of the bar. Still another brother of my mother was for several years the editor and publisher of our county paper. These associations gave me unusual opportunities for coming into contact with the best minds of that part of the country. When but a little boy I usually attended the sessions of the court, and closely watched the order of business and listened to the pleadings of the lawyers. Such men as Tappan, Wright, Hammond, Goodenough were in their prime, and I have never, in any part of the country, seen a court, I think, whose attorneys were equal orators. In listening to the judges, I acquired a knowledge of the general principles of law upon almost all points, a knowledge which I have since found to be of great service to myself, though I scarcely knew how I had acquired it.

With the fondness of boyhood for trying everything new, I familiarized myself with all the details of printing, learned to set type and to perform all parts of the work as then practised in a small office, until I gained an expertness that led to my being called upon for help when any emergency arose. This, too, came to my assistance when, in later life, I was called to conduct one of our Church periodicals. In reading works of history and literature, I found quotations from the Latin and Greek, and I longed to understand these languages. But my friends thought these were needful only for the few who have wealth and time for study, or who wish to enter a profession, but that for one in humble circumstances and with ordinary prospects a purely business education was enough. There was an academy in our town, and I often looked upon the boys who went to and from it with envy, wishing I could enjoy advantages like theirs. When between eleven and twelve years of age events occurred which very unexpectedly opened my way to classical studies. My uncle had kept up the manufacture of weavers' reeds, but, as his health was poor, he was unable to work much at the business, although he had invented and erected special machinery for the purpose. A partner was taken about a year before this time, and, young as I was, I not only shared in the labor, as I had strength, but chiefly kept the accounts. This partner had taken in as boarders two young men who were attending the academy and studying Latin. I frequently visited their room, turned over the leaves of their Latin books, talked with them about the study, and tried my hand at rendering Latin into English, as I had done with the German. Finding me able to comprehend the principles of language, these students urged my friends to allow me to begin the Latin, but the way did not open.

In the latter part of November, however, just as my uncle was about leaving for Columbus, to attend the sessions of the Senate, of which he was then a member, the wife of the partner was taken suddenly ill, and, at their earnest request, these young students were taken into our family for a short time, until she should recover. The request of the young men that I should study was renewed, one of them promising his assistance. I obtained the privilege of spending my spare time in study on condition of my first doing every day the half of a man's work in the shop. This condition I accepted gladly. My uncle left home, as I have said, the last of November, and returned the middle of February. In that time, in addition to performing my daily tasks, which were never omitted, I had studied Ross's "Latin Grammar," read "Historia Sacra," four books of Cæsar, and a large part of Sallust's "Catiline," and found myself sitting side by side with the young men who had begun some eighteen months before me. On his return home my uncle wished to know what I had learned, and called upon me to read, and finding I could render Latin so easily, I was permitted to attend the academy. During the following summer and winter I did so, and finished the Latin course and also studied the Greek Grammar. It became evident that I could have but one summer term at the academy for my Greek, and this was a short term of a little over four months. In the vacation I had read, for my own pleasure, a number of chapters in the Greek Testament, and was put with a classmate commencing the "Græca Minora." He was a boy of moderate ability, pleasant disposition, rich parentage, and a brother-in-law of the Presbyterian minister in our place. He was fonder of amusement than of his studies. Knowing it to be my last session, I was exceedingly anxious to advance rapidly, and finding he would not exert himself I begged to be permitted to proceed alone. The teacher of the academy at that time was John McBean, then studying medicine and nearly prepared to practice, a man of fine education and of more than ordinary talents. He at first refused, as my plan would increase his labor, but after two or three weeks he yielded.

The practice was to write compositions on every Saturday, and though I disliked the exercise, yet becoming deeply interested in my favorite project, I on one Saturday prepared a composition representing two boys who set out to climb the Hill of Knowledge. They had an able and experienced guide who tied them both together. One of them was earnest to see all that could be seen on the hill, and anxious to breathe the pure air upon the top. The other was easily tired and disposed to rest by the way, thinking he had time enough by and by to look at its sights. The one who was anxious to gain the top pleaded often with his guide to let him go on, but the guide refused, advising him to hunt for choice pebbles or to gather some flowers by the way while his mate was resting. After the reading of the composition the teacher smiled, called me to him, and said I might recite on Monday as far as I chose. The result was that in the remainder of that summer session I finished the " Græca Minora," read the first volume of the " Græca Majora,"* a part of the poetry of the second volume, and a number of books of Homer, completing what was then marked out in the neighboring colleges as the entire Greek course. At the examination, the minister whose brother-in-law I had succeeded in leaving thought, and, perhaps, very naturally, that I must be exceedingly superficial, and he would test my knowledge. This I believe he did to his full satisfaction, as in a most rigorous examination I happened to pass through without mistake, though in one or two instances he challenged the rendering I gave, but in each case I was sus-

---

* These old collections of Greek prose and poetry were in all the colleges of that time. The "Majora" bristled with Latin notes, some of them as tough for a boy as the Greek text itself.

2

tained by my teacher. The work, however, was such as I would not recommend to any other young student. I had confined myself closely at an age when I was growing rapidly. The study of the Greek at that time was wholly through the Latin; my lexicon, an old Schrevelius, was printed in very small type and on very poor paper, and the result was, I was troubled with inflammation of the eyes and a pain in the head for several years afterwards.

In order to improve my health as far as possible, I spent much of the next two or three years in the open air, especially in the summer, in planting and ploughing and harvesting. I still worked in the shop, and the partnership which I have mentioned being dissolved, I had the management of what business was done. In addition to my regular labor I studied algebra, the elements of which I had learned some years before, began the study of French, read French somewhat extensively, and also did something with Spanish and Italian. To these I added the study of botany, beginning with Barton's large work, and the study of chemistry and geology. At the request, also, of my uncle, who was clerk of the court, I practised penmanship and made such improvement that I became his assistant in making up the court records.

When about fifteen years of age, my uncle Simpson opened a select school in which were taught both the elementary and higher branches. Here I assisted him, teaching grammar, geography, arithmetic, and some higher studies, and, in his absence, taking the entire management of the school. Thus working part of the time in the shop, occasionally writing in the county clerk's office, assisting in the school, and pursuing some branch of study, I spent my life until the summer of 1828, when I was a little more than seventeen years of age. About that time the Rev. Doctor Charles Elliott, who was professor in Madison College, at Uniontown, Pennsylvania, a small institution then under the control of the Pittsburgh Conference of the Methodist Episcopal Church, visited Cadiz and lodged at our house.

He was deeply interested in promoting higher education in the Church, and finding that I had enjoyed some advantages and was thirsting for knowledge, he urged me to come to Madison College. Finding what my attainments were, and that I had practical experience as a teacher, and, though young, was both thoughtful in my manner and regular in my habits, he offered me a position as an assistant teacher for some classes. Dr. Homer J. Clark, also of the Ohio Conference, was then acting as agent, and about the same time passed through our town. He was trying to raise money for the college, and he likewise urged that I should try to pursue a collegiate course. They were the first ministers of our Church whom I had met with who were finely educated. A number of years before Valentine Cook had spent a little time in our home, and in family prayer, as was his custom, read out of the Greek Testament, which he always carried with him, translating as he read. With this exception, I had met with no classical scholar in our ministry, nor do I believe there was any one in all that region of country, connected with the Church, who had enjoyed any classical advantages. When it was proposed that I should go to college, the inquiry was raised among many of my friends, what purpose I had in view, and what profession I designed to enter. About the first of November, however, I was ready to start. Uniontown was over ninety miles from Cadiz. There was no stage-road through our town, nor was there any public conveyance, and my means were so narrow that I judged it best to make the journey on foot. So, tying up what clothes I needed and a few books in a little bundle which I carried, I set out for college with eleven dollars and twenty-five cents in my pocket. I made the whole journey on foot, travelling in the most economical way, and arrived at Uniontown on the afternoon of the third day.

My ideas of college life were somewhat exalted. I ex-

pected to find young men of superior minds and large attainments, professors who had mastered the whole range of science
and would take me by the hand as a giant would lead a
little child. I shall never forget the feelings with which I
approached the town, and my meeting some of the students
and wondering what kind of a reception I should have. I
was cordially welcomed by Dr. Elliott, and invited to board
in his family. I began the study of Hebrew, or, rather,
joined a class reviewing, having prosecuted its study at
home; entered a class with Dr. Fielding, reviewing geometry; and assisted Dr. Elliott with his classes in the languages, and when he was absent from home, sometimes for
two or three weeks, I took charge of his entire department.

There were some four or five boarders in his family,
among whom was his brother, Simon Elliott, afterwards a
distinguished minister in the Pittsburgh Conference, and
also an older brother. These and one or two others read
the Bible in family prayer, and the plan was adopted of
each one's reading from a Bible in a different language
from the rest—the Vulgate, the Septuagint as well as the
Hebrew, and the French, and German. After prayer, the
various readings of the several versions were a subject of
more or less extended conversation. Being of a timid disposition, I associated very little with the students, except in
the classes in which I recited or taught, and formed very
few acquaintances in the town. At that time Dr. Bascom
was nominally professor of belles-lettres and intellectual
philosophy, but there were no regular classes in these
studies, and he simply, being on the circuit, occasionally
visited the college and delivered a few lectures on mental
philosophy. Professor Fielding had charge of the mathematics, and was one of the clearest and ablest teachers in that department I ever knew. He inspired his students with an earnest love for their work, and took special interest in such as showed aptitude. A young man
who was studying law in the town was acting as tutor.

He afterwards became a judge in the city of Pittsburgh. As he was about finishing his course he resigned the tutorship, to take place at the close of the fall term. On the recommendation of the Faculty, I was elected tutor for the rest of the year. Returning to Cadiz, however, during the holidays—walking again the whole length of the way—I found such a change in the circumstances of the family as seemed to make it necessary that I should remain at home. I was obliged reluctantly to give up my college pursuits and the tutorship to which I had been promoted.

My stay at the college was very short, only two months, and yet it gave me what I had long coveted—a knowledge of college life. I found that professors, while they were men of learning, were yet but men. My college life and the views which I then entertained were sketched in a letter addressed to my uncle, dated November 30, when I had been not quite four weeks in the institution. I give the following extract :

"Here, at Mr. Elliott's, I have good boarding, and find both himself and Mrs. Elliott quite agreeable. I pay for everything but my board ; to wit: coal, candles, washing; room with four or five students, some of whom are quite agreeable in their manners, others not quite so much so. At the college, on account of the shortness of the days and the inclemency of the weather, there is but one session in the day, beginning at nine and ending at three. Mr. Elliott's work in the school consists, first, of grammatical exercises, including Latin and Greek Grammar and "Mair's Introduction;" then, four classes in reading: to wit, "Græca Majora," Virgil, Cicero, and Greek Testament. Of these, he attends to the grammatical exercises and also my Hebrew, "Græca Majora," and Virgil. He gets through about twelve or one, and leaves me to attend to Cicero and the Greek Testament. Upon rainy days or when he is from home, I have the management of the whole of his department, and he has been several days from home since I came here. He advised me to read over the current lessons, and in what time I could spare from that and Hebrew to read Livy, and if I found any difficulty to bring it to him. I did so, and found what was difficult to me was not less so to him. I have read Livy about one half through, and Tacitus is the only work required to be read, which I have not studied. Mr. Elliott says that I will need no instruction from him in Latin or Greek. About a week since, on Mr. Fielding's invitation, I entered a class beginning to review Euclid. We have now finished the first two books, and will finish the rest by the time of examination."

While debating the question whether to accept or decline the position of college tutor, he writes to his uncle for advice. The letter is thoughtful, especially for a youth of seventeen, and shows how closely he was compelled to compute income and resources before determining what was best to do. With great affectionateness he decides the case by the probable effect of his choice upon the welfare of the loved ones at home.

We give the letter:

" Madison College, Uniontown, November 30, 1828.

" The examination will commence the twenty-second day of December, and continue three days; during that time the tutor will be appointed, and I must have, if possible, an answer to this letter before then. The session will not be over until the first of January, but I think it is likely I shall go home immediately after the examination, especially if I be appointed tutor. I think that there is very little doubt that I can be appointed. If the present one desires continuance he will get it, but Mr. Elliott thinks he will not want to be continued. And now the question is, whether I shall apply for the office or not; and upon this I desire you to send me a letter, and let me know what is your judgment upon that subject. If you think that it would be better for me to continue here, so send me word, and if you think not, let me know that, and also send Mr. Elliott a letter stating as a reason for my non-continuance, disappointment in circumstances at home, so that he may not think hard of me. You can now better judge how you can make out in my absence, having had the trial of it, than you could when I was with you. The advantages to be derived from being tutor are, improvement in Latin and Greek, and probably in eighteen months I could get a diploma, and perhaps this might open the way to some preferment. Upon the other hand, the expenses will be considerable, and I am afraid more than you can spare, and be comfortably situated at home. I could enjoy myself here very well, if you and the rest could be comfortably situated; but I could not without that were the case. And also after having spent the time and money here, I should run the risk of being no nearer the attainment of any business than I now am. The tutor's fees will be one hundred dollars, including tuition, that is eighty dollars clear, which is eight dollars a month. Boarding here is, on account of the price of grain, one dollar and fifty cents per week, washing twenty-five cents, so that counting four and a half weeks to the month, that will be seven dollars and eighty-seven and a half cents per month, leaving only twelve and a half cents for incidental expenses, such as shoe-blacking, mending, etc. So that the whole expense of my clothing will come upon you, except what I could earn in the two months of the vacation. Remember, in estimating this, to count everything—shoes, hat, stockings, coat, pantaloons, vests (handkerchiefs, pocket and neck), shirts, etc. I may be mistaken, but I think that the expense will be about fifty dollars per year; but of this you can judge better than I can.

"I also think that if I had a good common school, with a few Latin or Greek scholars, I would advance as much in real learning as I would here and be tutor. These facts I submit to you to form what opinion upon them you may think proper. For my own part, if you think that, taking all things into consideration, it is better for me to leave this at the end of the session, and not to apply for the tutorship, I will not think that my time here has been misspent; but, upon the contrary, I shall think that I have received very important advantages. I have paid good attention here to all their forms and rules, and I think that by the practice I have now had and will have this session, I shall be more competent to teach, and also shall have more confidence in my own ability. But I am comfortably situated here, and therefore am well satisfied to stay, if you can be also comfortably situated at home. But my happiness will be dependent on yours, and therefore if it will incommode you for me to be here I cannot enjoy myself and be here. I wish you among you to consult upon these things and do what you think best, and if I am to stay, so write, and if not, besides writing to me, write also to Mr. Elliott, as I before stated. But write as decisively as the nature of the circumstances will permit, and also let me know how matters are at home, how business comes on, etc., also whether Hetty officiated at that wedding, etc. Tell her that I will try to have the French pronunciation before I come home. Giving my respects to grandmother and all friends,

"I remain your affectionate and obedient nephew,

"M. SIMPSON."

"Mr. Matthew Simpson."

One or two hundred dollars more at this critical moment of his life would have—not changed his destiny—but changed its complexion for a term of years. It seems a pity that all the means of culture he could reach were only such as were afforded by a college in its most rudimentary stage, imperfectly organized, imperfectly equipped, and that even these could be enjoyed for no longer time than a few months. Here was a youth with an insatiable hunger for knowledge, and with very unusual capacity for its acquisition. Brave, hopeful as he was, he could not by any arithmetic he knew make one hundred dollars do the work of one hundred and fifty. Uncle and mother he must not burden, rather he must be helpful to them. So he turns his face homeward, walking again over the roads by which he came; but " where there is a will, there is a way," and *he had the will*.

We now resume his own narrative:

Shortly after my return home, my eldest sister, who had been assisting my uncle in teaching, was married, and my services were needed to keep up the school. It was also thought best to transfer it from a private room to the academy which I had formerly attended, and higher classes were added. I devoted to it the greater part of my time.

The Conference sat that summer in Wheeling, in the month of July, and, anxious to see the professors from Uniontown, I visited Wheeling. On Sunday I listened in the morning to a sermon by Bishop Soule, and in the afternoon to an ordination sermon of remarkable power, preached by Dr. Elliott, which made a deep impression upon my mind. On Monday morning I attended the conference session and listened to some very beautiful remarks from Bishop McKendree. He was then quite advanced in years, was growing frail, spoke in a voice low but exceedingly sweet and musical. He gave a little narrative of the work in the conferences which he had visited, of some precious revivals that were in progress in different parts of the country, of his personal experience, which was clear and joyful, and urged the ministers to entire devotion to their ministry. He referred, in giving a narrative of his journey, to the fact that it was not necessary to say so much on those subjects now as formerly, since the *Christian Advocate and*

Journal had been started, which would inform the preachers of what was in progress. From the address I received the impression that before the establishment of our church papers the bishops were in the habit of giving to the different conferences they visited information respecting the Church at large. I enjoyed a pleasant interview with Dr. Bascom and Dr. Elliott, and had the satisfaction of learning that quite a number of the youth with whom I had been associated had been the subjects of a powerful revival, and gave promise both of deep piety and of great usefulness. In all this I rejoiced, although I was not then a member of the Church.

A few weeks after this a camp-meeting was held in Dickerson's neighborhood, some three miles from Cadiz. I attended on Sabbath and returned home on the same evening, but one of my sisters desiring to remain, I promised to return on Monday evening, after the close of school, and accompany her home. Returning on Monday evening to the camp-ground, I found that a remarkable religious interest had appeared during the day, and that several boys and young men, some of whom had been very wild, were awakened. My sister was anxious to stay until after evening service, and I consented. Some of these young men I saw, and with some of them I conversed, and immediately felt anxious that, by some means, proper influences should be thrown around them to preserve them from the temptations to which I knew they would be exposed. I attended the evening service, but was not specially interested until, at the close of the service, those who were seeking religion were invited forward. A large number went, and, among them, some of these whom I have mentioned. I felt deeply interested in the scene, and wondered why I, who had been so religiously educated and whose life had been so guarded by Christian influences, should not experience the same religious emotions as they. I drew near to the railing and was standing absorbed in thought, when I saw a short distance from me, standing near the railing, a young man of religious family with whom I had formed a pleasant acquaintance, but who, like myself, was not a professed Christian. The thought suddenly occurred to me that possibly while I was not being benefited he might be, and, making my way through the crowd to him, I laid my hand gently on his shoulder and asked him if he would not like to go forward for prayer.

His head immediately dropped, the tears started from his eyes, and he said to me that he would go if I would go with him. I led him forward, found a place where he could kneel, and I knelt down beside him. There was much excitement, and while I purposed to be religious, still, being of a cooler temperament than many, while others wept and prayed earnestly I could not but listen to all that occurred around me. I was sincere, wished to be a servant of Christ, but did not feel any special earnestness of spirit. The young man was shortly after converted, and lived, and I believe died, a faithful member of the Church. At the close of the meeting I returned home, said but little about my determination, but was firmly resolved from that day that, at the next opportunity, I would unite with the Church, which I did. About four weeks from this time, at the first visit of our minister, I went to a morning class, as I had resolved to act without excitement, and in the class-room gave my name for membership in the Church. Having done so, I became intensely anxious to benefit in every possible way the young men who were the subjects of the revival. I proposed a young men's prayer-meeting; there having been previously only one young man a member of the Church, we applied to him to be our leader. This meeting was kept up for some time, and was productive of great good. As I did not enjoy any consciousness of my acceptance with God, it was a cross for me to engage in the exercises of a prayer-meeting, and yet I felt it to be a duty. The first evening I thought I would prepare a form of prayer and write it out, but failed to commit it properly to memory, and when called on to lead in prayer my prepared words all escaped me and I was worse troubled than if I had not attempted any preparation. It was the first and last prayer I ever attempted to write for delivery.

I thought that a Sunday - school ought to be opened in the town; for, at that time there was none. Two or three efforts had been made the year before to start a general Sunday-school in some school-house; this was well attended for two or three Sabbaths, but was abandoned in a few weeks. I conversed with two or three young men, and we resolved to start a school in the fall—a thing then thought to be wholly impracticable. We pledged ourselves to each other that we would attend whether we had any scholars or not. We asked the use of the Methodist church, a small frame building, but found great difficulty in getting permission. Some members of the church thought that day-schools were sufficient, that teaching was not proper work for Sunday, that the church would be soiled by the children and rendered unfit for service; but we at last succeeded in getting the use of it, and started our school. It began with some half-dozen scholars, but has not been abandoned from that day to this. The next spring a Sunday-school was started in another church, and it was found that several could be held without interfering with each other. My Uncle Tingley took a deep interest in the school, and I was anxious to procure a Sunday-school library. At that time our Book Concern published but few Sunday-school books proper, but they offered to Sunday-schools at cheap rates the old magazines, half-bound, and other religious books generally a little below the ordinary price. My uncle headed the subscription list with ten dollars, and by going to citizens, though it cost me many a pang, for it was the first subscription of any kind I ever attempted to raise— my first attempt to ask money for the Church—I succeeded in securing something over sixty dollars, purchased the whole set of magazines, and Question and other books for the school, and thus helped it to get a permanent foothold.

In the summer of 1830, I found my health seriously affected—from close application to study, from attending night meetings (and oftentimes with cold, damp feet), and meetings of literary associations in which I took an interest—with a severe pain in the head, attended with inflammation of the eyes, the most unpleasant symptom being a sense of occasional dizziness and fulness in the head. By a rigid course of treatment these symptoms were partially removed, but I felt that instead of devoting myself to general study without any special object, it became my duty to select some profession for life. I had thought of the law, being familiar with court methods, but having some doubt how far a Christian might engage in ordinary practice, and having also the conviction that I never could make a popular public speaker, I selected the profession of medicine, and entered as a student in the office of Dr. McBean, my former teacher in the classics. Under his direction I spent about three years in study, at the same time supporting myself chiefly by my pen in the clerk's office, and also pursuing, as far as my health would permit, other studies. During these three years I practised writing to some extent in order to form a style. I had never taken pleasure in composition, but, believing it my duty to turn my attention to it, I attempted poetical and occasionally humorous and other pieces in order to give myself facility of expression. Some of these youthful attempts were published in the county paper, its editor being one of my friends, and I having, also, access to the office, and, not unfrequently, in his absence, charge of the editing.

In April, 1833, I completed the study of medicine, having read all the works prescribed, and passed my examination before the medical board, organized under the laws of Ohio. At that time very few medical students attended lectures, but read under preceptors, and enjoyed such facilities as their practice afforded. Dr. McBean left Cadiz shortly after I began reading with him and removed to Freeport. Before finishing my course I spent a few weeks in Freeport making a final review and undergoing re-examinations. During this time, one morning, Dr. Elliott, then on a visit to his friends in Ohio, rode up to the hotel opposite the doctor's office and alighted for breakfast. The hour of his stay I spent very pleasantly with him talking over former associations. Our conversation turned especially upon the educational facilities which ought to be afforded to our youth, and the doctor urged me to engage in some specific literary work, but before the conversation ended asked me if I did not think I was called to preach. I said to him frankly that I had had thoughts upon the subject, but that I had in my own conscience decided to obey the action of the Church; I intended to do what I could; I had devoted my life to the service of God, but I designed simply following the openings of his providence. If the Church desired me to preach I believed the way would be opened without any agency of mine.

I had been licensed a few weeks before as an exhorter, and had spoken in the Church at Cadiz on a few occasions. On his return, in a short time, through Cadiz he had an interview with the minister, and I received a notification that I had been recommended for license as a local preacher, and that I was desired to attend the next Quarterly Conference, which sat at New Athens, for examination. I attended the quarterly meeting, and, on Saturday, the presiding elder, Rev. Mr. Brown, asked me to preach, which I declined to do. He insisted that it was necessary for the members of the conference to know my qualifications as a speaker before they would license me. I said to him that if he could show me any rule in the Discipline authorizing persons to preach before they were licensed, I would yield, but otherwise he must excuse me, as I had determined that I would take no step towards the ministry unless called out by the Church. As he could not show me any rule in the Discipline requiring a trial sermon he ceased importuning me, but said it was probable the Quarterly Conference would not license me. To this I replied, that would be very agreeable to me. The Quarterly Conference, however, met, and my case was laid before it. I was examined upon doctrine and discipline, and retired. In the discussion which came up upon my case, as I subsequently understood, fears were expressed that my health, which was very delicate, would not be at all adequate to the work of the ministry, and that it was doubtful whether I would ever be a sufficiently able speaker to be of service to the Church. Others, who had known me from childhood, said I had always been a child of Providence, and they thought it best to license me, for the reason that possibly God had a work for me to do. Without my having ever attempted to preach, I was licensed, and recommended by the Quarterly Conference for admission to the Pittsburgh Annual Conference.

II.

LIFE IN CADIZ.

1811–1834.

Personal Appearance.—Bashfulness.—The Old Home.—Helps in the Shop and Teaches in the School.—Passages from his Diary, 1831–1834.—Reads Medicine with Dr. McBean.—Is Admitted to Practice as a Physician.—Great Variety of his Occupations.—Verse-Making.—Distrust of his Ability to Become a Public Speaker.—Makes Known to his Mother his Purpose to Preach.—Her Answer.—Consecrated from his Birth to the Christian Ministry.

II.

BESIDES the bishop's account of his boyhood and youth, we have accounts from surviving friends, who were much with him in those days. As well as he might know what he purposed to do, and what he did, he could not know how he appeared to others. We can look at his early life from another point of view, and we shall find features which are not to be found in his picture, and of much of which he was wholly unconscious. "He was very awkward," says one informant, "when nearly grown up, even uncouth, stooped in the shoulders, but was an earnest reader of books." Another: "We were always glad, when he took his uncle's place in the schoolroom, for we were all fond of him as a teacher;" of his bashfulness, not unmixed, however, with manly courage, "I have it from his own lips," says one informant, "that he was often driven to dodge down a by-street to avoid meeting certain persons, or even passing the doorways occupied by them. He was especially timid in the presence of ladies, not acquaintances." I have already spoken of the small frame house in which the family lived. Professor Joseph Tingley, his cousin, says still further of it and the life there: "It was a small, unpainted, plain frame house of four or five rooms, one of which was used for a schoolroom by 'Uncle Matthew.' This last was an addition, probably built for the purpose. Upon the same lot, and fronting on another street, was built a neat frame by his sister Hetty's husband, George McCullough, and occupied by them as a home and place of business for the manufacture and sale of neckwear. The fashion in those days was the high "stock," a necktie from three to four inches wide, stiffened with bristles and

3

buckling behind. Uncle Matthew was very apt in mechanics, especially in invention, and at Hetty's suggestion contrived for her an ingenious machine for weaving the bristles into the required form. It was a great success, and the manufacture of stocks became quite brisk and remunerative. Uncle Matthew had previously perfected a successful invention for manufacturing weavers' reeds, which was not patented, but for a long time kept secret. It embraced contrivances for splitting and shaping the half-round wooden strips for the frame work, splitting the canes and dressing them to the required thickness, and for tying them in place. The weavers' reeds thus produced were far superior to those made wholly by hand, and found a ready sale. All the male members of the family, including uncle, the future bishop, Curtis Scoles (the husband of his sister " Betsy "), and others, found occasional employment in this private factory.

" I was one of Uncle Matthew's pupils during the active period of the factory, and from the window of the schoolhouse beheld Cousin Matthew daily busied in turning the crank which drew the long, pliant strips of wood through the shaping-machine, or, at times, occupied in the lighter, but more particular, work of dressing the split canes. Both cousin and uncle varied their work by teaching in the school, the latter during school hours, and the former during the recitation of certain classes assigned him. These were the higher mathematics and advanced classes in grammar and rhetoric. He was my own preceptor in these branches, and to his superior instruction in applied mathematics I attribute my own subsequent fondness for geometrical studies. He was a successful and much-beloved teacher, and attracted many adult pupils into the unpretentious private school in which he was only occasionally and temporarily employed. Concerning this school of Uncle Matthew's I can truthfully say, after much experience and observation, that I have not since seen it excelled, in its line. It was of necessity an ungraded school, but, as such, it was a *model* school. I have seen no "normal principle," so called, that had not its prototype in this. Uncle Matthew was apt in illustration, a good disciplinarian, kind and gentle with his pupils, though at times seemingly severe with the unruly. His corporal punishment was a stroke or two upon the open palm with the flat side of a light pine " ruler," aptly named. "Cousin Matthew " was never under the necessity of administering punishment. He was too greatly feared and respected, and, moreover, his mode of instruction forbade inattention by reason of its absorbing interest."

We are aided, too, in getting a complete knowledge of this Cadiz life by the entries, very brief for the most part, made in a diary begun by young Simpson in the year 1831. His college career was already two years overpast, and he was looking out upon life with a sense of uncertainty, not to say hopelessness. His health was broken, no doubt from over-exertion, and he was persuaded that he would meet an early death. I will copy a few passages, enough to show his spirit and manner of life. Some of them touch, and very sweetly, upon his inner, spiritual state; others show the unusually wide range of his occupations. They reveal, too, the every-day occupations of a democratic community slowly consolidating :

"*Jan.* 21, 1831.—This day I am twenty. The one fifth of a century has elapsed since I was born. In that period I have but been acquiring necessary information for a journey which I shall probably never take. Though I am young, I feel in myself the shafts of death. But since the future is hid from our view, and we are commanded to improve our talents while here, in what manner can I best fulfil the purposes of my creation? Surely not by repining, surely not by sitting down in despondence, and closing my eyes ere their light shall have departed."

Evidently he is resolved to make a brave fight for life, fills his hands with work, both in-doors and out-of-doors, teaches, studies medicine, works in the county clerk's office, helps the editor of the village newspaper, takes his turn at harvesting, and what not. On the whole we must say that, for a young man supposing himself to be dying, he is tremendously energetic. He has already tried precise plans for the distribution of time, with the usual result of failure, and already, at twenty, has become cautious. "Could I accustom myself to it, I would wish to adopt rules like the following: Rise at four, spend one hour in exercise and devotion · then read, or pursue lawful business, etc. But, alas! I have often endeavored for a time to do something like this, yet I always gave way. I forbear laying down any more until I try rising regularly at four o'clock in the morning."

And so the young man puts on himself the yoke of John Wesley's daily regimen, and finds, as his fathers had found before him, that he cannot bear it, and in time wisely casts it off.

"*Friday, June* 25.—The doctor thinks that, by strict care and active exercise, I may recover.

Wednesday, June 29. — This evening prayer-meeting was at our house; pretty large meeting. The pain in my side better, though not well.

Tuesday, July 5.—Dismissed my scholars for harvest. Expect to go in the country to take fresh air.

Saturday, July 9.—Wrote half the day for [county] clerk. Read some. Six-o'clock prayer-meeting.

Tuesday, July 12.—Went to McD., where I tried harvesting. Able to stand more than I expected.

Wednesday, July 13.—At Uncle John's. Tried reaping, etc. Still better than I expected, but caught a little cold.

Thursday, July 14.—Reaped some, and read Mr. Fletcher's letters. They are worthy to be perused by every Christian, and will afford both pleasure and profit.

Saturday, July 16.—Cool, but pleasant. In the evening put plugs in two teeth for Curtis, which is the first I have done. [Medical practice included dentistry in those days.]

Tuesday, July 19.—Reaped oats. I stood labor beyond my expectations. Thankfulness should fill my heart when I reflect on what the Lord has done and is still doing for me.

Friday, July 22.—Hetty's symptoms still unfavorable. O, may the Giver of all consolation fill her heart with love, and place in her such a sense of his goodness as will calm every emotion and repress every rising murmur. How striking a difference exists between the religious and the thoughtless. She, although racked with pain, although a fever preys upon her vitals, is calm and collected. She feels that Jesus is her friend and support.

Tuesday, July 26.—Wrote in clerk's office, and read some.

Friday, July 29.—Wrote in clerk's office. Evening, went to the woods to take fresh air.

Saturday, July 30.—Wrote in the forenoon as before; afternoon, working in the air, which is the most wholesome for me.

Monday, Aug. 1.—Court began its session. I attended to see what was to be seen, and hear what was to be heard.

Tuesday, Aug. 2.—Same. This evening Dr. McBean was with us, and directed me to read Cooper's 'Surgery' next.

Wednesday, Aug. 3.—Attended court, and read some.

Thursday, Aug. 4.—Purchased Hufeland 'On Scrofula.' Court some. Read some.

Friday, Aug. 5.—Court adjourned. Had another talk with Dr. McB. Read, etc.

Saturday, Aug. 6.—Yesterday Hetty took much worse—palpitation of the heart was violent, lasted five or six hours. To-day she is better. This day worked out in the air, harvesting oats.

Monday, Aug. 8.—Worked again in the air a good part of the day, and read some.

Tuesday, Aug. 9.—Same as yesterday.

Wednesday, Aug. 10.—Worked out; six o'clock attended Sunday-school teacher's meeting; and at candle-light prayer-meeting; lasted too long.

Thursday, Aug. 11.—Worked out in the air. Read some.

Friday, Aug. 12.—Attended clerk's office. Read some.

Saturday, Aug. 13.—Attended clerk's office a part of the day.

Monday, Aug. 15.— Read in Cooper's 'Surgery.' Weather rainy. Heard lessons.

Tuesday, Aug. 16.—Forenoon read and exercised. Afternoon tended clerk's office, which I continued to do for Wednesday and Thursday and Friday morning.

Saturday, Aug. 20.—Read and heard lessons in the forenoon. Went to the woods and gathered lobelia.

Sunday, Aug. 21.—Tended Sunday-school. Day fine.

Monday, Aug. 22.—Read some and exercised.

Tuesday, Wednesday, Thursday, and Friday, Aug. 23–26.—Read, heard lessons, and exercised, and neglected filling up my diary.

Saturday, Aug. 27.—This day, the second of the muster, kept store for W. Bingham. In the evening heard our preachers for this year; they were William Knox and Thomas Drummond.

Monday, Aug. 29.—Read, etc. Afternoon went in the country and gathered boneset, and found a plant, square stalk, lanceolate, serrate leaves, close flowers, called by Barton ‘chelone.’

Thursday evening.—Mother took sick with bilious fever.

Monday, Sept. 5.—This day gave Albert G. Osbon twenty dollars for the purpose of purchasing medical books in the cities if they can be procured low.

Tuesday, Sept. 6.—Mother has recovered health in as great a degree as could possibly be expected for the time and the severity with which she was attacked.

Monday, Sept. 12.—This day is general muster. Went to the field at George Moore’s; good order among the people generally, but no attention paid to mustering among the militia. Bought a horse, for the purpose of riding for health, for forty dollars, payable first of April.

Tuesday, Sept. 13.—Went in company with W. C. to Rumley to see the place, muster, etc. Strange habits, outlandish customs; licentiousness, drunkenness, and blasphemy were very prevalent. Fiddling and dancing were going on at almost every wagon of provisions.

Saturday, Sept. 17.—Worked and heard lessons. Afternoon tried to cast zinc plates the size of copper, but could not succeed.

Tuesday, Sept. 20.—Rode three miles. Heard lessons, etc.; exercised and finished reading Cooper’s ‘Surgery.’

Wednesday, Sept. 21.—Heard lessons in the morning; at one started to Freeport; pleasant ride; arrived at half-past five; put up at Holliday’s. Went to McBean’s.

Thursday, Sept. 22.—Got Cooper’s ‘Surgical Dictionary’ of McBean. Started at eight; an agreeable journey; safe home at one. Afternoon heard lessons, etc. Read some in Cooper’s ‘Surgical Dictionary.’

Tuesday, Sept. 27.—Rainy. Read some and wrote in clerk’s office. At night had Dr. McBean with us.

Wednesday, Sept. 28.—My time besides hearing lessons was taken up with hearing election news.

Thursday, Sept. 29.—Same; evening helped open election returns.

Friday and Saturday.—Heard lessons and wrote in clerk’s office.

Monday, Oct. 24.—This day court commenced, and I assisted the clerk. Same all the week.

Monday, Oct. 31.—A. G. Osbon requested me to attend Reuben Allen, who had bilious fever, while he went to Pittsburgh, and I consented. Tuesday, Wednesday, Thursday, Friday, Saturday I attended him three times a day. Saturday evening Albert came home. Reuben had got some better.

Monday, Nov. 7.—This morning court was called on special business. Saw Dr. McBean; assisted clerk some and rode out.

Friday, Dec. 2.—Wrote subscription papers for petition for Bingham as judge.

Monday, Dec. 12.—This day attended clerk's office; in consequence of the indisposition of Uncle Tingley, I went to see him; I found him in bed; upon my entrance he reached his hand to me; I pressed it and inquired how he felt. He replied, 'The Lord has blest my soul. Last night I was very sick, but, thank him for supporting grace, I feel almost willing to say, now let me depart.' I was indeed wonderfully struck; it was such a contrast to the feelings and conversation of others whom I had lately seen afflicted. It caused me to see more and more forcibly the beauty of religion, and made me ready to exclaim, 'O Lord, thou art my God.' Yet it made me feel sorrowful that I had not that clear sense of my standing which I could wish. 'O God! create a clean heart and renew a right spirit within me.'

Saturday, Dec. 17.—This day was extremely severe indeed. Finished reading Cooper's 'Surgical Dictionary.' Began 'Materia Medica' to fill the time till I could see McBean.

Friday, Dec. 23.—Endeavored to abstain.* Oh, that the good Lord would enable me to abstain from all sin, and keep a conscience void of offence! I feel that much I need more religion; much I long after the evidence of my acceptance with the Holy One of Israel. For though I cannot doubt for a moment his goodness and loving-kindness to me, yet clouds seem to hem in my prospects, and prevent me from enjoying that union and communion which my soul so much desires, and without which I am unhappy.

Saturday, Dec. 24.—Wrote in part a New-Year's address for James Meek, Wheeling.

Sunday, Dec. 25.—This morning rose at four o'clock and attended meeting at five, in commemoration of the birth of my Saviour. Pleasant, though not lively. Preaching at eleven, afterwards general class; a very lively and profitable meeting. 'How sweet a Sabbath thus to spend.'

Monday, Dec. 26.—Rose at half-past four. Finished my address for James Meek and sent it by Nathan Summers to Jeremiah Knox, and began to write one for Cadiz.

---

* It was a Methodist custom of that period to fast part of every Friday, especially on the Friday before quarterly meeting.

Tuesday, Dec. 27.—Rose at quarter-past four. Read and wrote. Heard lessons, etc.

Wednesday, Dec. 28.—Rose at four. Read and wrote. Still cold and stormy.

Thursday, Dec. 29.—Address for Cadiz. Read, etc. A little headache in the afternoon.

Friday, Dec. 30.—Rose quarter after five. Cold. This day being the day preceding our quarterly meeting, I fasted till five P.M. and made arrangements for going to the meeting, held at St. Clairsville. Oh, that I may keep myself unspotted from the world and all its pollutions.

Saturday, Dec. 31.—Rose at five. At eight started for St. Clairsville, where I arrived a few minutes after twelve, as the first prayer was pronouncing. Rev. J. Monroe preached. Mr. Drummond exhorted; stayed for the Quarterly Conference, where I was made secretary for the time being. After Conference went to Dr. Wishart's with Rev. Messrs. Drummond, Monroe, and Lambdin, where I lodged. Here I saw a pair of celestial maps, being the first I ever saw.

Sunday, Jan. 1, 1832.—This day is New-Year. Oh, may I lay aside all my old evil ways, and have a heart thoroughly cleansed before the Lord. Attended love-feast at nine; had a pleasant meeting; was particularly struck with the experience of a young man. 'I was,' said he, 'on last Monday a confirmed Deist, but was awakened and convinced on Tuesday evening at a prayer-meeting.' Monroe preached at eleven and Calendar exhorted; a public collection was raised. I was sitting in the gallery, and Mr. Lambdin appointed me to wait on the people in the gallery. I did so, though not without reluctance and confusion. Sacrament was administered, and meeting closed. At night Rev. J. Moore preached, and Calendar and Lambdin exhorted, and meeting closed.

Monday, Jan. 2.—Was invited to Tallman's to breakfast. Left St. Clairsville at half-past ten A.M., and arrived in Cadiz before three. Heard my classes, etc.

Tuesday, Jan. 3.—Read, heard lessons, etc.

Wednesday, Jan. 4.—Read, etc. This day Dr. McBean was in town, but came not to see me; made arrangement for going down to him to-morrow. Finished first volume of 'Materia Medica.'

Monday, Jan. 9.—Cold and snowy in morning; noon thawing. Finished reading second volume of 'Materia Medica.' This evening borrowed Davy's 'Consolation in Travel, or the Last Days of a Philosopher,' from Mr. Christy. So far as I have read, it is well written; ingenious, but rather speculative.

Tuesday, Jan. 10.—Snow and blowing. Commenced reading Dewees.

Wednesday, Jan. 11.—Started at eleven o'clock for Freeport. Cold, blowing ride; arrived at four, where I found Uncle W. Tingley and Mr. McCoy. Spent the evening with Dr. McBean.

Thursday, Jan. 12.—Tarried at Freeport; Dr. McBean commenced examining me on surgery, but had not done much when he was sent for express. Returned to the tavern and read two volumes of Scott's poetical works, in seven volumes.

Friday, Jan. 13.—Got Gibson's 'Surgery,' 2 vols., 8vo, and set out for home at half-past nine. The day was warm and agreeable overhead. The ground in some places slippery, in consequence of a very rapid thaw; arrived home at quarter-past two.

Saturday, Jan. 14.—Heard lessons, etc. Dr. McBean came in town to a special court; had him to dinner; pleasant conversation.

Monday, Jan. 16.—Spent in reading Gibson's 'Surgery,' and taking notes to assist my memory. Still attend to my regular work of hearing lessons, etc.

Tuesday, Jan. 17.—Reading and taking notes of Gibson's 'Surgery.'

Wednesday, Jan. 18.—Rainy. Read and took notes, and commenced a scrap-book. May all my endeavors after wisdom be directed in the right channel, and may I always remember that 'the fear of the Lord is the beginning of wisdom.'

Monday, Feb. 6.—Read and took notes. My classes in school so much increased that I am not able to do much reading.

Saturday, Feb. 18.—Read and took notes. My eyes are so weak that I shall have to desist from taking notes.

Sunday, March 4.—At twenty minutes past two this morning I was roused to join in hunting a lost woman. The circumstances were these: Mrs. C——, wife of James C——, an industrious mechanic, had for some weeks been unwell, but not considered at all dangerous; was able to walk out, and was attended by Dr. Wilson. Mr. C—— had gone to sleep about midnight, and between that and two o'clock she had got up and gone out in her stocking feet. The night was very dark and chilly, and the ground muddy. We searched the places round until towards daylight. At daylight the court-house bell was rung and people gathered. About seven o'clock she was found in Mr. Jamison's house, about half a mile distant; she had made a cut across her throat, and three cuts upon her wrists, but fortunately had done no damage to herself. It appeared she had wandered nearly all that time, and waded a run a considerable distance, and also lain down in it. She seems as well as if nothing had happened.

Wednesday, March 7.—Mrs. C—— seems not much the worse for her exposure, her mind is tolerably composed. I am informed that she had been reading Boston's 'Fourfold State,' and came across the idea that if any were not of the elect, do as they would they could never be saved. She concluded that she was a reprobate, got into despair, and this led her to the state in which she now is.

Monday.—This day court for our county commenced. I attended part of the time, and read some.

Tuesday.—Same.

Wednesday.—Same. This evening had Dr. McBean and Uncle John Simpson with us all night. Dr. McBean commenced examining me on surgery.

Thursday morning.—Continued his examination till court time.

Tuesday, March 18.—Read *Christian Advocate and Journal.* Afternoon, tried with Dr. O—— to cast zinc plates. Weather pleasant. Went in the woods.

Friday, March 21.—Heard my class. Went to Hanover and saw my aunt and grandmother; left aunt some medicine. Went to Mrs. Green's and saw Ruth Graham; left directions, and got home at five o'clock. Heard my class, and attended meeting at candle-light. This day I kept in entire abstinence, praying for the success of our quarterly meeting.

Saturday, March 22.—At twelve o'clock and night attended meeting; had a refreshing time.

Sunday.—At half-past eight was at love-feast; a very refreshing season. At eleven, public preaching; half-past three, prayer-meeting; candle-light, sermon. Altogether we have had a very pleasant meeting, and I hope profitable.

Tuesday.—Pleasant. Attended to accounts. Kept school all day yesterday and part of to-day in consequence of uncle's having a bad cold.

Monday, April 2, 1832.—This day was township election. I was requested by the judges to act as assistant clerk, which I accordingly did, besides attending classes; got done about eleven at night.

Tuesday, April 3.—Heard lessons, read, etc.

Wednesday, April 4.—Same—same. At night attended prayer-meeting.

Thursday, April 5.—Heard lessons, read, etc.

Monday, April 9.—Read, heard lessons, etc. Uncle William offered me twenty-five dollars a month for what time I would write, if I would help him three months out of the ensuing six. This I would prefer to school-keeping. Borrowed his electrical machine to give Betsey a trial of it.

Tuesday, April 10.—Fitted up the machine, but it did not work well.

Wednesday, April 11.—Got the machine in good order. At night attended prayer-meeting.

Friday, April 13.—Usual abstinence. Read, etc. This day quit the school, as I have an offer to write in the clerk's office half my time.

Saturday, April 14.—Uncle William [the county clerk] and Aunt Rachel went to Steubenville. I tended the office.

Monday, April 16.—Tended clerk's office.

Tuesday, April 17.—Read and exercised. Went out some to botanize.

Sunday, April 22.—Was at class, and Sunday - school is doing well. Prayer-meeting at night.

Monday, May 1.—Commenced writing in the clerk's office, and continued at it all the week.

Monday afternoon.—Worked on roads;* rainy, showery.

Tuesday, May 2. — Last night received the draft for our books and sent it on this day to New York. At three o'clock attended meeting to raise a class; a female class was raised and I was appointed leader, much against my wishes and feelings. But if it be the will of the Lord, I pray him to enable me to perform my duties.

Thursday, May 4.—Wrote in clerk's office.

Friday, May 5.—Usual abstinence. Wrote as before.

Saturday, May 6.—Forenoon, worked on roads. Afternoon, wrote in clerk's office. At night, attended young men's prayer-meeting.

Monday, May 8.—Wrote in office.

Tuesday, May 9. — Forenoon, same. Afternoon, at three, attended class. I scarcely know what to write of this; I think that I was given some liberty in speaking to the class; but oh, how lame was the performance!

June 19.—I went down to Freeport, and was minutely examined on surgery. I returned June 21.

June 25 *to July* 2.—Read, preparing myself for examination in chemistry and 'Materia Medica.' Also worked out of doors, securing hay.

July 3.—Went to Freeport; was examined in chemistry and 'Materia Medica.' Returned on July 5. Paid Dr. McBean twenty-five dollars in part of tuition fee.

Monday, July 15.—Wrote; also Tuesday forenoon; afternoon, attended class and read, etc.

Saturday, July 21.—Wrote till ten; then worked at meeting-house, repairing it, till night.

Monday, July 23.—Was attacked with illness, but was relieved on Tuesday. Wrote in office rest of the week. Alarm prevails about cholera.

Monday and Tuesday, July 30 *and* 31.—Had to attend school, except an hour for class; had a good season. Uncle Matthew getting considerably better.

---

* Most likely to pay his road-tax.

Wednesday, Aug. 1.—Sabbath-school books having arrived, I spent part of the day in opening and arranging them. The rest of the day taught school. At night had a good prayer-meeting.

Saturday, Aug. 11.—I went, in company with James Allen and two others, to camp-meeting between Hanover and Rumley. The ground is large, and pleasantly situated; order is excellent. Sunday congregation three or four thousand. Sunday evening and night a powerful stir broke out; suppose one hundred mourners were down. This continued all day and all night.

Monday, Aug. 13.—Sacramental occasion solemn; stir continued all day and all night; many conversions. Eighty joined the church at this meeting.

Tuesday morning, Aug. 14.—At eight o'clock left the ground and came home. At this meeting I obtained, I humbly trust, some fresh spiritual strength. I was enabled in a greater degree to yield my heart to Jesus. I felt an application of these words: 'Come unto me all ye that are weary and heavy laden, and I will give you rest.' And I felt in a good degree that I could come. Peace flowed into my heart, but little joy. Oh, that the Lord would continue to carry on his blessed work unto perfection.

Friday, Sept. 28.—Omitted my diary writing until this time. However, since my last dates, nothing peculiarly striking has occurred. My own religious exercises have been tolerably uniform. I have regularly attended class, and have had to lead every time, as our preachers have not yet arrived.

Dec. 19.—Procrastination is said to be the thief of time, and so I find it. By putting off writing from day to day time has thus far rolled along without any entry. Since the last date there has been much confusion in election matters, much talk and noise. On the 26th of last month I delivered a speech on temperance in the Presbyterian meeting-house, which was published in the *Telegraph* of Dec. 1. With regard to my studies, I have this morning finished Goode's 'Practice of Medicine,' and have lately been engaged in reviewing anatomy. I have regularly attended class, and find it to be much to my spiritual advantage, and I hope the members are all improving. I have also spoken a few times in public; and, though the cross is great, I find action is necessary to my religious life.

Sunday, Dec. 23.—Attended Sunday-school, and preaching by the Rev. Mr. Mills. At night had prayer-meeting. I spoke a little to the people. This I have occasionally done for some time. The Lord was with us, and while speaking I felt much refreshed and raised from my lethargy.

Tuesday, Dec. 25.—This was Christmas. Invited some young people to come and sing hymns before daybreak, to commemorate the birth of the Saviour. Had meeting of Sunday-school teachers and scholars at ten o'clock; prayers, singing, and I delivered an address. At night we had a refreshing prayer-meeting.

Sunday, Dec. 30.—Attended Sunday-school and class. Had Sunday-school prayer-meeting. At night had prayer-meeting; endeavored to speak, but felt as if my words fell to the floor, and did no good. After meeting felt much condemned; thought I had no religion; felt as though I had no power in prayer. Oh, for the awakening energy of the Holy Spirit!

Monday, Dec. 31.—This morning felt as though I could scarcely attend class as a leader on account of fears; yet, while engaged in talking, my fears all vanished, my sorrow was gone. I was able to praise the Lord for his amazing goodness to me. We had an unusually happy season, and several professed great comfort.

New-Year's Day, A.D. 1834.—A whole year omitted in my diary. I will simply record some events which happened the past year. In January we had a revival of religion, and I was transferred from leading the female class to the charge of a class principally formed of the young converts and Sabbath-school teachers and scholars. On April 1st, at a general class-meeting from which I was absent, I received a vote for license to exhort, and was accordingly licensed by the Rev. W. Tipton, who had at that time the temporary charge of the circuit. Shortly afterwards I went to Freeport to finish my study of medicine. While there the Rev. Charles Elliott visited me; and, through an arrangement made by him, the Rev. J. Mills brought my name before my class, and I received a vote of recommendation to Quarterly Conference to preach, the week before its session. I knew nothing of this till Thursday, when I received a letter stating the circumstances, and requesting my attendance next day at Athens. I immediately left Freeport, attended meeting, and received license, and a recommendation to the Annual Conference. Returned to Freeport, and the last of May or first of June returned to Cadiz, having finished the study of medicine. I returned on Friday, and on Sunday preached at Athens and Uniontown my first sermons. And I have continued to preach nearly every Sabbath since. Was invited to deliver an address at Athens to the students Sept. 28, 1833, which I did, and the students had three hundred copies struck off in pamphlet form. It was favorably noticed in the St. Clairsville *Historian.* I practised medicine, and had tolerable success for a young practitioner."

The life outlined in these brief notes is full of interest

when considered in respect to the years beyond for which it was a preparation. Unconsciously, young Simpson draws his own likeness, and the likeness is very attractive. It reveals a youth of unusual mental energy, who makes use of all the helps to culture within his reach and secures from them whatever is possible for him. Teaching, studying medicine, writing in the county clerk's office, working in the fields, or on the road, go on together, harmonized no doubt by an all-compelling will. The day's task begins often in cold December at four and five o'clock, and is carried on with unwearied persistence till night comes again. How he came out of all this with any health whatever is matter of wonder, but the strain kept up so long in this period cost him years of acute suffering. In the church, though extremely modest, his activity touches every point that a layman can touch. A practiced mechanic, he can upon occasion do a little repairing to the building, and then serves the congregation as class-leader, Sunday-school teacher, and leader of prayer-meeting. The simple, beautiful life he is living is intensely religious. He is in dead earnest. No doubt the rustic philosopher and saint, his Uncle Matthew, is near him, giving friendly counsel, and watching the growth of his pupil with a pardonable pride. The reverence of young Simpson for this uncle was mixed with filial affection, and was one of the marked traits of his disposition at this time and at all times.

The young student had the knack of rhyming, and could tag couplets together with great facility. Enough of verse remains to show that he was not loath to express himself in this way, and no doubt the poet's corner of the *Cadiz Register* gave him the satisfaction of seeing himself now and then in print. Poetry it was not, and he seems to have had wit enough to know the fact, but making rhymes was a good literary exercise, and that was enough for his purpose.

Some verses, however, written on his nineteenth birthday,

are of historic value, as showing his sense of obligation to
his uncle :

> " But next, to him who, in my father's stead,
>   Through slippery youth my sliding footsteps led;
>   Who strove to plant within my tender heart
>   The seeds of virtue, knowledge, truth, and art,
>   I should express, as far as words can show,
>   The debt of love, of gratitude I owe.
>
>   My dearest uncle, how shall I recite
>   How frequently you taught me with delight,
>   Commenced with small, then larger things explain'd,
>   That thus, with ease, true knowledge might be gain'd :
>   Still as my mind began to gather strength,
>   And make excursions of a greater length,
>   Your care increased, then double your delight,
>   To lead me still to new and greater light;
>   For minds like eyes, increasing light can bear,
>   Though overpowered with too great a share."

Obviously his models in these effusions were Pope's heroic
couplets and Charles Wesley's hymns. Verses in the metres
of the Methodist Hymn-book occur, and are not badly done.
I find among the papers of the year 1831 an essay on
" Electricity," read, it is stated, before the Philosophical
Society of Cadiz, and another on " Optics," most likely prepared for the same body of rustic investigators. There is
another of the same year entitled, " Description of the Motions of the Earth." While a student of Madison College,
Uniontown, he tried his hand at a Hebrew oration, a desperate undertaking one would think for a scarcely fledged
Hebraist. Diagrams still extant show that he had a passion
for solving hard mathematical problems. Wherever he saw
a new opening to knowledge he rushed in without stopping
to consider whether he should ever be able to possess the
land or not. Possibly he had no hope of becoming possessor of many of these broad fields, but he would see what
was in them at least. Of the acquisitions of this period, he
retained enough of German to serve him in after-life; his

Latin and Greek he utilized in reading, during the time he was professor at Meadville, the Greek and Latin Church Fathers, and his scientific knowledge furnished to his sermons some of their most striking illustrations. One might converse with him often, in after-life, without hearing him mention the fact that he had studied medicine; but he met all the requirements of the law of Ohio as it was then, and the certificate of his medical preceptor, Dr. McBean, states that both in his studies and in his examinations he had acquitted himself with credit.

That a young man of such dispositions should gravitate towards the Christian ministry was perfectly natural. While preparing for another calling, he must have questioned within himself whether he had made the right choice. But no such questioning, no force of impulse towards the ministerial vocation would have sufficed to determine his mind. According to the teaching of the faith in which he had been reared, only a call from heaven could warrant his assuming these sacred functions. An inward monition, which he could refer to a divine source, was waited for. Without the conviction that he was summoned to this service by a higher than a human authority he never would have persisted in it, nor would he have accomplished great results. His distrust of his capabilities as a speaker and his extreme diffidence would have paralyzed him. He tells the story of this conflict of mind most pathetically in his "Yale Lectures on Preaching." Let us hear him:

"Trained religiously, I had come to a young man's years before making a public profession of religion. Occasionally, prior to my conversion, thoughts of the ministry sometimes flashed across my mind, but it was only a flash. After my conversion I was earnest for the welfare of others, and worked in various ways to promote the interests of the Church and humanity. The conviction grew upon me that I must preach. I tried to put the thought away, because I feared I could never succeed. I saw the greatness of the work, and the reproach and poverty, the privation and suffering, connected with the itinerant ministry. Two special difficulties were in my way: First, I had no gift of speech. All through my studies my fellow-students told me I could learn, but I could never be a speaker. In discussing professions, they thought the law was out of the question for me, because I could never successfully plead a cause. My voice was poor. I had always shunned declamation whenever it was possible to avoid it. I had an unconquerable aversion to reciting other men's words, and whenever I attempted to declaim it was pronounced a failure. My associates believed, and I firmly believed, I could never make a speaker. So, when I felt the conviction that I must preach, the thought of the impossibility of preaching successfully made me question the reality of the call. At my work and in my studies—for I spent three years in preparing for the profession of medicine—I was frequently in mental agony.

"I think I should have resolutely rejected the idea, only that it seemed indissolubly connected with my own salvation. I longed for some one who could tell me my duty. I fasted, and prayed for divine direction; but I found no rest until I read in the Bible a passage which seemed written especially for me: "Trust in the Lord with all thine heart; and lean not unto thine own understanding. In all thy ways acknowledge him, and he shall direct thy paths." I accepted it, and resolved to do whatever God, by his providence, should indicate. I never lisped to a friend the slightest intimation of my mental agony, but began to take a more earnest part in church services. One Sabbath I felt a strong impression that I ought to speak to the people at night in prayer-meeting, as we had no preaching. But I said to myself: How shall I? My friends will think me foolish, for they know I cannot speak with interest. Especially I dreaded the opinion of an uncle, who had been to me as a father, and who had superintended my education. While I was discussing this matter with myself, my uncle

4

came into the room, and, after a moment's hesitancy, said
to me: 'Don't you think you could speak to the people to-
night?' I was surprised and startled, and asked him if he
thought I ought to. He said: 'Yes; I think you might do
good.' That night, by some strange coincidence, the house
was crowded, and I made my first religious address to a
public congregation. It was not written; it was not very
well premeditated; it was the simple and earnest outgush-
ing of a sincere heart. I was soon pressed to preach, but
evaded all conversation on the subject as far as possible.

"My second difficulty was that my mother was a widow;
I was her only son, and the only child remaining at home.
It seemed impossible to leave her. I feared it might almost
break her heart to propose it. But as I saw the church
would probably call me, and as I had promised God to follow his openings, I one day, with great embarrassment, introduced the subject to my mother. After I had told her
my mental struggles, and what I believed God required, I
paused. I shall never forget how she turned to me with a
smile on her countenance, and her eyes suffused with tears,
as she said: 'My son, I have been looking for this hour ever
since you were born.' She then told me how she and my
dying father, who left me an infant, consecrated me to God,
and prayed that, if it were his will, I might become a minister. And yet that mother had never dropped a word or
intimation in my hearing that she desired me to be a preacher. She believed so fully in a divine call that she thought
it wrong to bias the youthful mind with even a suggestion.
That conversation settled my mind. What a blessing is a
sainted mother! I can even now feel her hand upon my
head, and I can hear the intonations of her voice in prayer."

And so the loving mother had hid away in her heart this
deepest of her longings for her only son. The years had
come and gone, and still her lips had been sealed; he must
not know, for she would not interfere with God's right to
choose the messengers of his word; but in the silent hours

of prayer, how often must she have opened her heart's secret to him with whom she communed—the Prayer-hearer!
And when this son had been led up to the choice of the
vocation to which, in the fulness of her love, she had consecrated him, she could tell him that she had been waiting
for that hour ever since he was born.

THE OLD COURT-HOUSE AT CADIZ.

III.

HIS TEACHERS.

III.

It is one of Thomas Carlyle's pregnant sayings that, "when a great soul rises up, it is generally in a place where there has been much hidden worth and intelligence for a long time. The vein runs on, as it were, beneath the surface, for a generation or so, then breaks into the light in some man of genius, and oftenest that seems to be the end of it." To quote him again: "Great men are not born among fools," and Bishop Simpson certainly was not. The old uncle, under whose care he grew up, made as distinct an impression upon the circle to which he was known, as the nephew upon the great world that knew him. In outward condition no more than a plain schoolmaster, with no pretensions to classical learning, he was rich in that which is the fruit of all learning—wisdom. To their sense of his worth his fellow-citizens gave expression by sending him for so many years to the Ohio state senate. He also served as associate, or lay, judge in the county court. I have seen a letter from him to his old friend, the Hon. John A. Bingham of Ohio, written in 1865, when he had reached his ninetieth year, which for clear insight of national affairs would do credit to any public man. "Uncle Matthew," says Professor Joseph Tingley, "was well informed in the sciences as then known, and it was his habit to keep up with the new discoveries of more recent times, as far as practicable. His store of information was really remarkable, as was his memory of all scientific terms, dates, magnitudes, etc. He was my instructor and referee in such matters; and always correct and precise in his opinions. He was also an inventor of many ingenious mechanical

contrivances, several of which he put into successful operation. Under his direction I constructed and mounted the
small telescope which gave me the first glimpse of Saturn's
rings and the belts of Jupiter. He laughed loud and long
at my boyish glee, on witnessing this successful result of his
young pupil's scientific experiment. He used to tell how
careful he was to watch the associations of his foster-son.
He had stepped in at an opportune time, when the father-
less child of his brother, James Simpson, needed a father's
care. No one could have performed the duty with more
scrupulous fidelity. He accompanied him in his recrea-
tions and walks, and never allowed him to 'play out of his
sight.' In fact, he discouraged play almost altogether, but
delighted in making the young happy in their duties and
studies. Matthew was an apt pupil, and naturally and
wholly fell in with this mode of life."

Of the standing of Uncle Matthew as a legislator, Professor Tingley gives this report: "In all difficult cases before the House, when his opinion was called for, no matter
how complicated the question, he would proceed to unravel
the knotty points, illuminate the obscure ones, clear away
the fallacies, and in a manner entirely satisfactory to all
parties 'give his sentence.' This generally closed the debate." He was a member of the Ohio senate at the same
time when General William Henry Harrison, afterwards
President of the United States, was also a member, and
used himself to tell this story of their association with
each other: "The General had made a thrillingly eloquent
speech, and was receiving the congratulations of his friends.
I grasped his hand and said, 'General, I wish I had the
eloquence that you have.' 'Ah,' retorted he, 'I wish I
had the logic that you have.'" Mr. Bingham says of him:
"It was a peculiarity of Uncle Matthew's character that
he judged all men by their sincerity and truth, without
regard to their outward circumstances." Such a character is not the best for getting on in the world, as we

phrase it, but is certain to command the respect of all who love sincerity and truth, and this respect Uncle Matthew commanded.

Of Bishop Simpson's mother, her nephew, Professor Tingley (she was his father's sister) says: "She was my ideal saint; always calm, always peaceful and happy, always kind and cheery." Unfortunately no letters from her to her son remain, and I fancy that she did not write to him often, leaving the correspondence, when he was away from home, to the uncle. I infer, too, from a passage in one of the uncle's letters to his nephew, that she was reticent, and in no way given to overmuch expression of her feelings. "Whether you come and see us or not," writes the uncle (the date is Nov. 16, 1834), "I hope you will do me the favor to provide yourself such socks and overclothes as will secure you against injury from the wintry storms, and the more especially, as I am convinced everything that concerns your life, health, and comfort more strongly affects your mother than you might imagine from the fortitude with which she parted with you. However, if her prayers and mine can do you any good, I think we never forget you, probably not one hour in the day."

Dr. James McBean was a Scotchman, had studied in Jefferson College, Canonsburg, Pennsylvania, and was noted in all his active life for his devotion to the Latin and Greek classics. During some years he taught a classical academy in Cadiz, but was best known as a very successful medical practitioner. He had moved to Freeport, about nineteen miles from Cadiz, where Simpson was his student in medicine. There the young man tarried whenever he visited his preceptor, and would spend days together in reading and conversation; whatever of knowledge Dr. McBean had to give he was eager to absorb. Dr. McBean lived to an advanced age, dying in 1875. In a letter to the widow, Bishop Simpson thus expresses his reverence for the doctor's memory:

"Philadelphia, February 10, 1875.

"I received the mournful tidings a short time since of the death of your husband, and of my esteemed friend, Dr. McBean. It seemed to come very near my own heart, as he was for so many years my teacher, both in academic and medical studies.

"I had for his talent and honesty the highest regard. My sympathies are with you in the hour of your bereavement, as well as with the members of your family, and I pray that He who alone can cheer and comfort the sorrowing may be to you unspeakably precious. We are all of us approaching the close of our earthly existence; years roll rapidly away; and as I look back, it seems to me but a little while since I was, for a short time, an inmate of your family when you resided in Freeport, Ohio, and yet when I count the years, they are rapidly approaching towards the half century.

"Our work here is almost accomplished, and the only thing remaining is to act so wisely our parts that, when we are called, we shall be ready to join the good and the wise and the pure in the upper sanctuary. May the blessing of God ever abide upon you and your family."

Next to the uncle, to no one was Bishop Simpson more indebted for his progress in culture than to the Rev. Dr. Charles Elliott. The doctor always came into contact with the young man's life at the opportune moment; urged him to go to college, made him when there an assistant teacher, almost forced him into the Pittsburgh Conference, and recommended him for the Presidency of the Indiana Asbury University. He had evidently made up his mind that this raw but eager Cadiz youth was destined for a great career.

There is a little diary extant, or, as young Simpson called it, "Ephemeris," in which he has jotted down his daily college experiences while under the care of Dr. Elliott. It is yellow with age and the wear of the pocket in which it was carried, here and there illegible, but tells the story of Dr. Elliott's confidence in his pupil. It is prefaced with a few lines, which describe the starting from home; these I will copy as far as they can be read:

"*Monday, Nov.* 3, 1828.—About a quarter of an hour before eight in the morning I bade farewell to friends, and, in company with Uncle Matthew, advanced as far as Craig's plantation, where we parted at half-past

MRS. SARAH SIMPSON, THE BISHOP'S MOTHER.

eight. Arrived at Smithfield at twelve, at Wellsburg at [illegible]. Left Wellsburg in company with two Jacksonites, one of whom was so pleased with my telling him that, as far as I had heard, Jackson was doing well in Ohio, that he alighted and gave me his horse to ride to the next tavern, which was about [illegible] miles. There I put up for the night, and was very agreeably surprised in finding Dr. Hodgens there.

Tuesday, Nov. 4.—At seven in the morning I set out with Dr. Hodgens, who having [several horses gave?] me one to ride to ——.

At eleven left Middletown, and shortly overtook the Rev. Mr. C—— of Harrisville, Dr. Fowler, and Mr. C—— on their journey to the Radical [Methodist] Convention at Baltimore. Kept in company with Dr. Fowler to Washington, where he stopped at quarter of two. Arrived at Hillsborough at dark; stayed all night.

Wednesday, Nov. 5.—Started at six, arrived in Brownsville at eleven, where I purchased stockings and penknife, and arrived in Uniontown at half-past four. Found Mr. Elliott's; college not yet over; in a few minutes he came in and welcomed me to his house."

His expense account for the journey is put down in detail: "Left Cadiz," he writes, "with $11.25, Nov. 25; the balance in hand, after buying one or two books, and paying a trifle on account of tuition, is $3.50." And with this small sum in his pocket, the ingenuous youth bravely faces the world, expecting to pay his way as punctually as if he were the possessor of thousands. In his brief cash footings every penny is accounted for.

In the house of the kindly Mr. (not yet Dr.) Elliott he is perfectly at home, and is put to work the day after his arrival, both as pupil and assistant teacher. He continues the "Ephemeris:"

" *Thursday, Nov.* 6.—Went to the college with Mr. Elliott; entered [he means was enrolled] as No. 46. Was put in a class with Mr. Robert Crawford commencing the Hebrew Grammar. Recited lesson, A.M. ; heard a class recite a lesson in Cæsar, P.M. About forty-six scholars in the classical department, and thirty in the English.

Friday, Nov. 7.—Reviewed the current lessons at home; at the college recited Hebrew Grammar, and Mr. Hamilton [one of the classical teachers] being unwell, I had to take his place excepting in ' Græca Minora.'

Tuesday, Nov. 18.—Recited Latin Prosody and Hebrew Grammar. Had a frolic digging potatoes at the college. Heard 'Græca Majora' and Virgil; continued reading Livy.

Thursday, Nov. 20.—This day being rainy, Mr. Elliott could not attend the school. Therefore I attended to the course, except Prosody, and recited Hebrew to him at home.

Saturday, Nov. 22.—Attended to the whole course for Saturday, Mr. Elliott not attending, except the Prosody. Prepared for the thirteenth proposition of 'Euclid,' but could not recite; continued Livy.

Monday, Dec. 1.—Rose at half-past four. Recited Latin Prosody, also twenty-four propositions, third book of 'Euclid.' Heard Cicero and Greek Testament; continued Livy.

Friday, Dec. 5.—Rose at quarter before five. Mr. Elliott left for Pittsburgh; I had then the management of his part.

Monday, Dec. 8.—Rose at half-past three. Mr. Elliott absent; I attended to his part. Recited from fifteenth to thirtieth proposition, sixth book of 'Euclid.'"

The last entry is dated,

" *Thursday, Dec.* 25.—This day being Christmas, there was no school. At eleven heard Mr. Bascom preach. Received the appointment of tutor in Madison College. Day beautiful; attended prayer-meeting before daylight."

Charles Elliott deserves a fuller record than he has had, as one of the pioneers of Methodist education. Born in County Donegal, Ireland, he was one of that "innumerable company" of Irish schoolmasters who have, through their schools, been the leaders of American culture, and have formed much that is best in American character. Tennent, of the Neshaminy Log College; Samuel Stanhope Smith, the founder of Hampden Sydney, in Virginia; John Blair Smith, the first president of Union College, Schenectady; Wylie, so long the ornament of the University of Pennsylvania, and others, whom it would make too long a catalogue to name, were all of this hardy stock. They were energetic drill-masters in Latin and Greek, and equally strenuous for the pure mathematics. They formed the majority of the public men in the central colonies of the Union, and in those same colonies during the first period of their life as states. Dr. McBean was the product of this Scotch-Irish culture. Bishop Simpson was of the same stock; that he should fall into the hands of Charles Elliott one would think was predestined by both race and church affinities. Dr. Elliott will remain in early American Methodist history as the bright example of the pure and simple scholar, who loved learning for its own sake, and who never ceased, while life lasted, from its eager acquisition. Indifferent to office, and sobered in his judgment of events by the habits of thought which come with culture, he could be unpartisan, and yet true to his sense of right. He has left an enduring monument of his learning in his masterly " Delineation of Roman Catholicism."

Such was the environment in the midst of which young Simpson grew up, and, save for the lack of better opportunities of special training, it left little to be desired. He was in a new world, where the artificial distinctions between man and man which mark old societies as yet were not, where each citizen was valued according to his capability and moral worth, where the necessity of winning bread by honest labor was acknowledged in every household, where moral earnestness was the product, as it always ought to be, of strong religious faith. Cadiz was but an example of hundreds of the villages of Ohio. There had flowed into the state from western Pennsylvania the sturdy Presbyterianism which feared God and feared not man. In company with it had gone the fervid Methodism which, with its omnipresent itinerancy, carried a divine message, when as yet the venturesome settler had barely reared the roof to cover his head. If the Presbyterian drilled with Confession and Catechism, the Methodist roused with exhortation and appeal. Between these two forces a whole population was educated in the sense of responsibility to God and reverence for his law. Effectually, but silently, this training had gone on for nearly a century, and when, in the time of trial, our country called for its best of

heart and brain, and Ohio fairly rained on us heroes and
capable leaders, it needed only a slight knowledge of her
past history to make it clear how she could give so richly
to save the nation's life. The story of Bishop Simpson's
growth in Cadiz, paralleled in thousands of Ohio homes,
solves the mystery.

" From scenes like these " our country's " grandeur springs."

IV.

HIS EARLY MINISTRY

1833–1836.

His Reasons for Hesitating to Enter the Travelling Ministry.—Appointed
to the Circuit on which he Lived.—Remonstrances of his Friends.—
Advantageous Business Offers in Cadiz.—Prefers a Six Weeks' Circuit,
with Thirty-four Appointments.—Good Advice of a Hicksite Quaker.
—Much Work, but Small Pay.—Appointed to Pittsburgh as a Junior
Preacher. — Dr. Sellers.—Appointed to Liberty Street Church, Pitts-
burgh.—Trying Position, but Complete Success.—Marriage.—Wishes
to Graduate A.B., but Receives Unexpectedly the Degree of A.M.—
Stationed at Williamsport.— Begins Housekeeping. — The House.—
Preaching on the Evidences of Christianity.—Rules of Life.

IV.

GUIDED by such leadings of Providence as we have described, the young physician has now entered on another vocation, and has given himself wholly to the service of the Church. We will let him tell the story of his early ministry in his own way:

"Though recommended by the Quarterly Conference for admission to the Annual Conference, I had not fully resolved to enter at once upon the work of a travelling preacher. Circumstances were such that I saw my way might be closed for the time being, and I agreed with my presiding elder, the Rev. Mr. Browning, that if I found I could not travel he was to withhold my recommendation. The week after the quarterly meeting I preached my first sermon in the Methodist church in New Athens, Ohio, on "Walk while ye have the light" (John xii. 35), and in the afternoon my second sermon at Uniontown, Belmont County; and on Monday morning I preached at Styer's meeting-house, filling an appointment for one of the preachers on the circuit. Family circumstances seemed to preclude the possibility of my leaving home. A sister was lying ill with consumption, and her death would probably take place during the year. My mother was a widow and I was an only son, and the only member of the family remaining at home. After reviewing the whole matter I came to the conclusion that my duty was to stay for the time with my mother. As I had finished the study of medicine, I made arrangements to begin its practice, and obtained an office. I had accumulated a handsome medical library, and I entered on the practice in the month of May, 1833. As a young physician, of course,

5

my practice was small; but the field opened much more easily and widely than I had at all anticipated, and indications were not wanting that I should have satisfactory success.

"The Annual Conference sat in Meadville, Pennsylvania, in July; and at this session Dr. Elliott and other ministers who were interested in me claimed that the presiding elder had no right to withhold my recommendation, and that it should be presented. Notwithstanding I had informed him by letter that I could not take any appointment, the recommendation was presented, and at the earnest request of Dr. Elliott and others I was admitted on trial. The difficulties in the way of my removing from home were acknowledged, and I was appointed third preacher on the circuit where I lived, it having been previously a four weeks' circuit filled by two ministers. The appointees for that year were J. P. Kent and Aurora Calender. On the return of the preachers from Conference I was informed of what had been done, and was requested by my presiding elder and preacher in charge to devote my Sundays to preaching in Cadiz, where I lived, and in St. Clairsville, the county seat of Belmont County, some sixteen miles away, and to try during the year to close my business and arrange for taking regular work. This action of the Conference seemed so providential that I resolved to get ready as soon as I could. I filled the pulpit on alternate Sabbaths in Cadiz and St. Clairsville, as there was preaching there on but one Sabbath in two weeks by the other ministers. Late in the summer of that year my sister died. She had suffered much, but was a beautiful example of Christian resignation, and one lovely summer evening, just as the sun was setting, she passed away, leaving a promising little boy in our care. Her husband, who was then a physician, shortly after her decease gave himself to the ministry, and lived and died a member of the Pittsburgh Conference.

"My appointment by the Conference took many of my

friends by surprise, as they had supposed that I was settled for life in the practice of medicine. I found a general remonstrance against my leaving Cadiz. My uncle, William Tingley, who had been clerk of the court for twenty years, and whom I had assisted in the duties of his office, sometimes, in his sickness, attending to his entire work, was very anxious I should remain. The members of the bar, into association with whom I had been brought, showed a deep interest in my welfare, and on their recommendation (as my uncle's term was about to expire, and he did not desire a reappointment) the judges of the court tendered the appointment to me, if I would accept it. The net profits of the office, to one who simply supervised and paid the clerks to do the work, were about a thousand dollars a year. In addition to that, I was offered a partnership in the practice of medicine, and was assured I could at the same time perform the duties of the clerkship, by having skilled assistance, which was already at hand. My friends urged that I could be of service preaching, as I might have strength and disposition, while attending to other duties. These very kind and unsolicited offers, however, I felt were not in the line of duty for me; the local ministry did not seem to be my sphere.

"I felt that God had called me to a more active service, and that it was my duty to relinquish all secular business and to devote myself wholly to preaching. Accordingly, in March, 1834, I closed my office, and the circuit having earnestly requested my entire time to be spent upon it, I took my horse and saddle-bags and began travelling. The circuit was then arranged by my colleagues as a six weeks' circuit, and I found in it twenty-eight appointments, and in the four months we added six others, making in all thirty-four. Three places, owing to the effect of what was termed "the radical controversy," which resulted in the formation of the Methodist Protestant Church, had been abandoned; these were Mount Pleasant, Harrisville, and Georgetown.

In these three places I commenced preaching, though to small congregations. I also introduced Methodist worship into Morristown, some ten miles east of St. Clairsville, though under most discouraging circumstances, the preaching being in a schoolhouse near a hotel. There was but one person who felt any interest in the services, and he lived some two or three miles away. The appointment was on a week-night, with a single tallow candle for light, and my congregation about a dozen persons, one half of whom were from about the hotel; some of them tipsy. At the close of service one of these desired to get into controversy with me on the subject of baptism. With the help of my colleague, however, I had the satisfaction of attending a two-days' meeting before I left the circuit, and witnessed the establishment of a society.

" It was the custom at that day for the single men to give their entire time to travelling on the circuit, and to lodge in the families of the members; nor was there time anywhere to take much rest. I heard of a small place six miles from Morristown where there were two Methodist families that desired preaching, and I sent an appointment for a week-day forenoon. I preached in a small room of a private house to a few hearers, and left an appointment for six weeks from that date. My health then was very delicate, and when I returned at the end of six weeks, and preached, I learned that a physician, a Hicksite Quaker, who was generally represented to be an infidel, had left word that he wished to see me, and that he thought he could be of service to me. After preaching I called upon him and was kindly received. He said he had heard that my health was poor, and, as he had suffered very severely himself and had succeeded in recovering, he thought possibly he might give me some useful suggestions. I had a long and interesting conversation with him. I asked his opinion with regard to my continuing to preach, as I had been advised by physicians that my life was in danger. He said as to the religious question he did not wish to express himself, but as a physician he believed the wisest thing I could do was to travel a circuit that required me to ride from eight to ten miles and to preach once every day. He advised against night services, against my becoming warm in close rooms, urged some care in diet, but said he thought that the exercise and the having of an object which would lead me to be much in the open air would greatly benefit me. I have often wondered at the apparently strange providence which led me to such advice and under such circumstances and from such a man, and I believe the whole was ordered of God for my good. It coincided so fully with my own convictions that I resolved to follow his counsel, though other physicians, with scarcely an exception, urged me to desist altogether from preaching.

"For my services during the year, while engaged in business, I, of course, expected no compensation whatever; for the four months spent on the circuit, to which I devoted my entire time, I had the claim which was allowed then to a young man, at the rate of one hundred dollars a year. While there were four months of the year so spent, there was but one Quarterly Conference held, and consequently the time was counted as but one quarter. My allowance for this would have been twenty-five dollars, but there was a deficiency, and I received eighteen dollars and seventy-five cents, the other preachers on the circuit sharing *pro rata*. This, viewed in the light of the present, would seem to be no compensation at all; and yet I had no expenses. Travelling with my own horse, finding entertainment among my friends on the circuit, riding every day, I was kindly received and freely supported; I had no anxieties, no cares. However defective in my experience, or in my practice, I had fully resolved to leave all for Christ. Friends and home and business had been given up, and I had determined to choose reproach and privation and even suffering if I might be successful in winning souls. I had the happiness of seeing some precious meetings during the year, and while there was no general revival, there were persons converted at many of the appointments.

"At the close of the year I went with my brethren to conference, at that time held in Washington, Pennsylvania. I was the guest of Rev. Dr. McKinney, a Presbyterian minister, who was at that time President of Washington College, having for my associate, Rev. S. E. Babcock, who was some two years my senior in the ministry. In the Pittsburgh conference, at that time, a course of study, not unlike the present course, had been marked out, and the young men were expected to attend the Annual Conference to be examined, and then to return home. After passing my examination, I remained a day or two, and as the custom then was to have preaching in the forenoon and afternoon of Conference, I preached at one morning service on, 'Let us lift up our heart with our hands unto God in the heavens.' (Lamentations iii. 41). I had no care, personally, what appointment I should receive; but my friends, who were very solicitous about my health, had urged me to ask that I might not be sent to a station, of which there were indeed then very few, but that I should be appointed to a healthy region, if possible not far from home. I reluctantly agreed to see the Presiding Elder, told him the wishes of my friends, but said to him, 'I have no thought that you will give me a station. I should like to have a place in a healthy district if it can be easily granted, but I have no desire to be near home; I wish to take my place among my brethren, without any conditions or limitations.' The Elder assured me that he would arrange all satisfactorily, and that he had just such a circuit as would be best for me. I returned home without knowing my appointment, and waited patiently the coming of the ministers from conference. At that day we had no railroads or telegraphs, and the secular papers never troubled themselves with the doings of ecclesiastical bodies. When the ministers came, they brought me back information of my appointment. I was stationed in Pittsburgh, where at that time the cholera was prevailing. My lungs being weak, my health poor, the city smoky and dusty, and an epidemic spreading, my relatives were very unwilling that I should go, and thought it almost equivalent to death to send me under such circumstances to such a place. But I felt the Lord had directed, and as soon as possible I was on my way to the city, travelling by stage, having sold my horse and laid aside my saddle-bags. We had the usual incidents of such travel in those early days over the hills from Cadiz to Steubenville; among them was an upset on the side of a deep precipice; providentially, none of us were hurt. A young lady of my acquaintance, who was going a part of the way under my care, illustrated the force of habit, even in a moment of danger. As the stage had fallen on the very edge of the precipice, I had sprung out of an open window and assisted others in getting out. Among the first to get out was the young lady, and, when freed from the stage, her first exclamation was, ' Oh, my bonnet!' I spent the night in Steubenville, and the next day arrived at Pittsburgh, where, according to directions sent me, I was kindly received by Mr. James Verner, who then lived on Penn Street.

"During my first year of preaching, of which I have given an account, few incidents occurred worthy of note. In my personal experience I became attached to the ministry, and felt that my duty was to continue in it. This, however, had not been without a struggle. Once during the year, at a dedication in St. Clairsville, we had the assistance of the Rev. John Waterman, a minister of unusual mental clearness and force. He had been in delicate health, and at one time had been troubled with doubts, but had emerged from them, and was a very impressive speaker. He preached at the dedication five sermons of unusual intellectual power accompanied by deep pathos. The congregations were large and were greatly moved. As I listened to sermon after sermon, I came to the conclusion that I ought not to occupy a pulpit which might be so much more ably filled, and I resolved at the end of the year to be discontinued by the conference, but to remain a local preacher. I mentioned the matter to one only of my friends, Mr. Thoburn, who lived near St. Clairsville; he seemed utterly astonished, and urged me by no means to entertain the thought. I was relieved from my depression in a rather singular way. At one of my appointments, where I had a very large congregation, I was visited by a brother minister, who was somewhat older than myself in the Pittsburgh Conference. I invited him to preach; but he was unfortunate in the service, was confused in his statements, and incorrect in his language, and I felt mortified. Before he had finished his sermon I resolved to continue in the pulpit until it should be supplied with better men. The Mr. Thoburn to whom I have referred was an Englishman who lived on a farm, was one of the class-leaders and stewards of the circuit, and was a man of deep piety. His son is now in the South India Conference, where he has exercised a commanding influence; a daughter is also engaged in the same missionary work; another daughter was married to B. R. Cowan, who was at one time an Assistant Secretary of the Interior.

"On arriving at Pittsburgh, I found myself in advance of my colleagues. Rev. Thomas Hudson was preacher in charge, and Rev. William Hunter, since editor of the *Pittsburgh Advocate*, and professor of Hebrew in Allegheny College, was associated with me. My first evening was spent in the prayer-meeting at the Smithfield Church, which had then but recently been reopened, having been for a time occupied by the Methodist Protestants. I began making inquiries about the church, its condition, families, etc., of Dr. Sellers, who visited me, and whom I found to be a gentleman of far more than ordinary character and intellect, whose subsequent counsels and advice were of no little service to me. He had been brought up on the eastern shore of Maryland,

and had married a sister of Bishop Emory. On my first Sunday I preached in Smithfield Street Church in the morning, from Ezekiel's vision of the dry bones, and at night in Liberty Street Church from, 'I determined not to know anything among you save Jesus Christ, and him crucified.' The officiary of the church arranged that Mr. Hunter and myself should board in the family of Mr. Hudson. My home associations were to me very pleasant during the whole year.

"Mr. Hudson was a deeply devoted minister, full of hope and joyousness, a fair preacher, and an exhorter of far more than usual power. I frequently thought him, in exhortation, equal to any man I had ever heard. I endeavored to systematize my time, rising early in the morning, usually from four to five o'clock, and spending the hours until ten o'clock in biblical or theological studies. At ten o'clock our practice was to visit the sick, as physicians preferred that their patients should be seen in the forenoon. Returning home in the forenoon from calling upon the sick, I dined, and conversed or read until two, when the afternoon was devoted to pastoral visitation. At my suggestion the city was districted, so that we should each have his field of pastoral duty; and to me was assigned the whole of the northern part of Pittsburgh, from Wayne Street embracing Byrdstown, and also the population on the hill. In these visits I found it the most pleasant for me to select some family or families the most likely to invite me to tea to call on first, and if I received an invitation, to accept and promise to return, excusing myself until through with visiting. This was done because I wished to save time. Very frequently I induced one of the class-leaders, or some lady of influence and general knowledge of the district, to accompany me, and many an interesting call I had upon the poor in cellars and garrets as well as in alleys and back streets, who complained that they had never been visited by a minister before. I found many who had wandered away from church service, but who, under the blessing of God, were subsequently reclaimed.

"Early in the fall arrangements were made to hold a camp-meeting on the land of Mr. Swishelm, near what is now known as East Liberty. Much opposition was expressed, because camp-meetings had fallen into disuse, and it was thought that near the city they could scarcely be held profitably; but the ministers of Pittsburgh were anxious to try the experiment, and to have the meeting closed on Saturday. The meeting was accordingly held, with a much better attendance than had been anticipated. Rules were drawn up for the government of the meeting, prohibiting all conversation of a trifling character in the preachers' tent, and the preachers bound themselves to devote their whole time to earnest efforts for the conversion of the people. From the commencement a deep seriousness rested upon the assembly, and on the third evening a most remarkable scene occurred. The preachers were in the habit of holding morning and evening prayer-meetings; that evening the meeting began about an hour before preaching, and such was the divine influence which came upon the hearts of the ministers that the people gathered around the preachers' tent, and when the time for preaching had arrived it was found impossible to hold regular services. There was exhortation from the desk. The preachers went out into the congregation, and there were vast crowds that filled the altar. So solemn and so deeply affected an audience I think I had never seen, and the number of conversions was very large. The meeting closed on Saturday morning, and revival services immediately began on Sunday in the churches of the city, which continued for about three months, during which time about three hundred members were added to them.

"Visiting the people almost every day, I found myself acquainted with the condition of nearly all who were seeking Christ, and was able to give them such advice as I thought their conditions required. During the progress of the revival I visited a lady who was in feeble health and who

had recently been a subject of strong religious impressions.
I met in her room one of the leading ladies of the city who
was an attendant of the congregation, but not a decided
Christian. The condition of the church led to conversation
of a deeply religious character. I found her to be honest
and earnest, and yet she said she could not bear any excitement; I gave her, however, such hints upon her duty as I
could. The next Monday evening we had a love-feast. I
invited seekers of Christ to make themselves known, and
was much surprised to notice that among the first who
came was this lady. She knelt at one side, but the crowd
was great, the excitement deep and general, and there were
a large number of conversions. I feared lest she should be
not only interrupted, but unhappy in her position, but was
agreeably surprised to learn that, at the close of service,
when some one spoke to her of the unusual noise in the
meeting, 'Why, I did not hear any,' she replied. She became one of the most thorough and earnest members of the
church. Her husband was a merchant and was not a member; she had also a sister, the wife of B. A. Fahnestock, a
druggist of large business and property. A few days after
I was sent for to visit her husband and Mr. and Mrs.
Fahnestock. Mrs. F. was a member of the Presbyterian
Church, but found she had not an experience such as her
sister enjoyed, and on consulting her pastor, he simply told
her, 'she was nervous.' Not satisfied, she desired religious
conversation. Several interviews followed, and Mr. Shea,
the husband of the lady of whom I have spoken, and Mr.
and Mrs. Fahnestock soon enjoyed a happy and satisfactory
experience. Mr. Shea united with the Methodist Church,
but Mr. Fahnestock accompanied his wife to the Presbyterians.

"We had under our joint care two principal churches in
Pittsburgh, Liberty Street and Smithfield, where services
were held three times on Sunday. We had also Sunday
afternoon preaching in what is now the Fifth Ward, then

called Bayardstown, and preaching Sunday morning and evening at Birmingham, in a small church which had recently been built. To keep up these services required of us, generally, three sermons on Sunday; and as it was my second year in the ministry, between ministerial work and my studies preparatory to examination I was closely occupied, but yet found time for some general reading. Conference was held that year in the Liberty Street Church, Pittsburgh. I had expected to leave the city, as it was very unusual for young men, at that time, to remain in a charge a second year; and I had counted the Sundays carefully, fearing lest I should exhaust my whole power of edifying the congregations. I had, however, selected and kept a record of texts which I thought suitable for sermons, and of such topics as pressed upon my mind, and found that the list had rather increased than diminished as the weeks rolled on.

"After my Conference examinations were over, I was ordained by Bishop Andrew, who presided at the Conference, and who preached with great zeal and energy. The morning before Conference closed, I learned from my Presiding Elder that I was appointed to Hudson, not far from Cleveland. I called upon the minister who had filled the appointment to learn something of the character of the work to be done, and was planning how I should reach the place, when the bishop said he desired to see the Presiding Elders a few moments, and they retired. When they returned, I saw that my Presiding Elder looked confused; when the appointments were announced, my name was read out for the city of Pittsburgh in connection with the name of Dr. Charles Cooke. The bishop stated that if the churches remained together, Dr. Cooke was to have charge, and I was to be the assistant, but that if they divided, I was to be placed in charge of the Liberty Street Church. He left the matter to the decision of the official board and the Presiding Elder; these met and by them the division was perfected. The station, to me, was one of considerable perplexity. The Liberty Street

Church had the largest congregation in the city. I had preached, as I thought, nearly all I knew, and had been hailing with delight the thought of being changed to a new place, but found myself so circumstanced that I must preach three times on Sabbath, and once during the week, to the same congregation. The charges being divided under a spirit of rivalry, it seemed to me almost impossible to maintain the pulpit of the church over which I was placed.

" In the separation of the churches, between three and four hundred members chose to belong to the Liberty Street organization. Unfortunately the congregation at Smithfield Street Church declined to permit exchanges between Dr. Cooke and myself, supposing that as a young man I would be unable to maintain the organization effectually if left to myself. The official brethren, however, rallied to my help. The church was thoroughly organized. I endeavored to visit from house to house ; and often found myself on Saturday evening without sermons for the Sabbath, but by some means I had something for each occasion. The congregations grew larger ; the house was crowded and a precious revival commenced. During the revival I procured the assistance of the Rev. F. A. Dighton, one of my Conference classmates, and also once a college classmate in the study of Hebrew. He was I think, without exception, the best specimen of a natural orator I ever saw. Without creating overwhelming excitement, he had the power of holding most closely the attention of his hearers ; was clear in his statements, exceedingly fluent in speech, and succeeded in deeply impressing his congregations. Quite a large number of the young people were brought into the church. A large missionary society of the ladies of the church was organized, and the general influences were of the happiest kind. During the earlier part of our revival, there were some interruptions from disorderly persons who had been in the habit, at such times, of disturbing the congregation by getting upon the seats, conversation, etc. I felt that no church should suffer itself to be imposed upon, and succeeded, after much entreaty, in inducing the officiary of the church to stand by me in an appeal, if necessary, to the civil authority. The rules adopted by them with regard to order were strictly announced in the morning, with the statement that any violation would be reported to the magistrates, and the statement was again made at night. The chief of police of the city was requested to be present in the evening; some young people, not supposing that we would carry out our purpose, began to be disorderly, and their names were immediately taken and handed to the police. Finding we were in earnest, we had no more trouble.

"On November 3, 1835, I was married, by the Rev. Z. H. Costen, to Miss Ellen Holmes, daughter of Mr. James Verner, of Pittsburgh, whose acquaintance I had formed immediately on arriving in Pittsburgh. After a visit of a few days to my friends in Ohio, I returned and prosecuted the regular work of the ministry without losing a Sabbath. The rivalry which had been excited between the Smithfield and Liberty Street churches gradually died away, and before the year was out Dr. Cooke and myself exchanged pulpits. After my marriage I lived in the family of my father-in-law, as they were unwilling to have the daughter leave during the year. Besides pursuing my studies, I read, quite extensively, theological works bearing on the subject of the ministry, occasionally making notes, and wrote also a few articles for the press. One of these was a defence of the course of study against an attack upon it on account of its extent and thoroughness; another suggested a series of questions and items of business which the presiding elder could properly use in Quarterly Conferences, so as to make himself more thoroughly acquainted with the condition of the churches, somewhat similar to those which have since been introduced into the Discipline. I had felt at the close of my first year that the city was not properly supplied with the publications of the Church, and that there ought to be a place where new books could be obtained by our members. On my return, I labored to do what I could in this direction, and having had an interview at the Conference with the New York book agent, Mr. Mason, and having been encouraged by him, I immediately ordered a few hundred dollars' worth of books, resolving, in some way, to secure their circulation. On mentioning the matter to Dr. Elliott, who was then editor of the *Pittsburgh Advocate*, he proposed to me that the order should be enlarged, and that his office should be used as a depository. Accordingly a large list was made out and books were ordered and notice given in the paper. This was the commencement of the book depository at Pittsburgh, which has since that time built up a large business. I had also felt a deep interest in the young men, some of whom, I thought, would probably prepare for the ministry. I had organized an association among them; a few met once a week, and I endeavored to direct them in their course of reading and to inspire them with a thirst for knowledge. Of that little company several subsequently became ministers.

"During my first year in Pittsburgh I resolved to avail myself of the literary opportunities offered at Allegheny College, not only for the purpose of completing the college course, but also of receiving the regular degree, of which I had been deprived by being compelled to leave Madison College. Dr. Ruter, then President of Allegheny College, requested me to attend for a week or two, matriculating as a regular student, and passing an examination on the studies of the senior year. He offered to give me the degree of A.M. without this, but I declined, preferring to enter regularly for the degree, and arrangements were made for me to deliver one of the graduating addresses. As the time drew near I advised with Dr. Sellers, who was one of the stewards of the church, about a leave of absence. He urged that I should not go to Allegheny College, but take my degree at the Western University of Pennsylvania, at

Pittsburgh, at the head of which at that time was Rev. Dr. Bruce. He saw President Bruce, and arranged that I should see him. I had a very pleasant interview; talked over the course of study; he inquired what branches I had pursued, and, after a very full conversation, said to me that I had learned much more than their college required; that if I would attend twice a week for a few weeks his lectures on moral science, so that I might be enrolled as a student, I should receive the degree at the approaching commencement. I immediately wrote to Dr. Ruter that, with the advice of my friends of Pittsburgh, I would embrace the opportunity at the Western University, and arranged to enter the following week. On my way home one morning from the university, which I was about to enter, I called at the post-office, and was surprised to receive from Dr. Ruter a letter saying that their board of trustees had met and had conferred upon me the degree of A.M.

"I was very sorry, because it interfered with the plans which I had formed and designed to carry out, and because it had the appearance rather of an honorary than a real college degree, to which I felt myself entitled; but I was unwilling to seem to undervalue the honor conferred upon me by Allegheny College, and hence felt obliged to decline entering the university. It was intended for kindness on the part of Dr. Ruter, but was to me a very unpleasant occurrence. I availed myself, however, in the city, of opportunities which I found of improving myself in French and German by the help of native teachers. I also felt a very deep interest in the establishment of German services, and gathered together a few Germans, one of whom was a class-leader; German preaching was begun in a private house, which I had the pleasure of attending. This was in advance of the opening of missions among the Germans under Dr. Nast. Hearing of his conversion, I rejoiced exceedingly, and when, some two years after, a proposition was made to start the German paper, I was one among the earliest subscribers of ten dollars each to its funds, and was for many years a regular reader of it.

" The Annual Conference of 1836 was held in Wheeling. The question of the continuance of the *Pittsburgh Christian Advocate* came before it. As Dr. Elliott had been elected editor at Cincinnati, the Conference was strongly advised to discontinue the paper. Some of the older members of the Conference agreed to this proposal; the younger members were opposed. We selected Dr. Hunter as our prospective editor, and when the question came before the Conference, I made my first speech. It was short, but I found I had the majority strongly with me, and when the vote was taken, the Conference resolved, by more than two to one, to continue the *Advocate*, and Dr. Hunter was elected editor.

" At the close of the session I was appointed to Monongahela City, then called Williamsport, twenty miles south of Pittsburgh. Immediately I made arrangements for removal and housekeeping. It was difficult to obtain a suitable house. A one-story building with a sitting-room, off the side of which were two very small bedrooms, and near which was a kitchen, was procured at a rent of fifty dollars a year. It was very much out of repair, but myself and wife fitted it up with our own hands as carefully as we could, painting and improving it within and trying to make it look as neat as possible. The church was a substantial brick edifice without much beauty, but with an embarrassing debt. The leading member and the only gentleman of wealth in the society had just died, and in his will had left directions to his executors to cancel a claim of about five hundred dollars which he held against the property, provided his estate was freed from all liability for the debts of the church, which had been contracted principally in his name. A feeling of discouragement rested upon the people, as he had been their chief financial stay; but having first drawn up a plan which I believed would be successful, I obtained, by personal solicitations, enough sub-

6

scriptions to cancel the debt. The Sunday-school was revived by establishing morning as well as afternoon sessions. I obtained the names of the children of the church, formed them into classes, appointed leaders who met them every Saturday afternoon, and I personally met with them as frequently as possible. I also established prayer-meetings in different parts of the town, appointing leaders to conduct them each night in the week, excepting the night of the general prayer-meeting in the church. In this way a large portion of the members were called into active service, and I had the satisfaction of seeing a largely increased congregation and the addition of a number of persons to the church. I preached morning and evening in the church, had two appointments for Sabbath afternoon about five or six miles each from the village, and filled them on alternate Sabbaths. I found a kind people, plain and earnest, and my association with them was in every way agreeable.

"One or two incidents were especially interesting to me. During my earlier religious experience I was the frequent subject of sceptical doubts, which were never fully removed until I had read carefully the evidences of Christianity, when I felt that, having met all the objections, the position of Christianity was for me wholly impregnable. To my mind the evidences of Christianity were a most interesting study, and I resolved to deliver a series of sermons setting forth the salient points. Three of these sermons had been preached on successive Sundays, and my congregation seemed to me to be deeply interested and, I hoped, somewhat impressed. But I had among my hearers a Lutheran, Mr. Bollman, a brother of the Bollman who assisted in liberating Lafayette from the Olmütz prison. He had been finely educated in Paris, and was at this time engaged in mercantile business. In the lack of a Lutheran church he attended mine, and was one of its regular supporters. As I passed his store one Monday morning he called me in, saying, 'Father Simpson, I want to talk with you.' As I was a very young man, and he was quite advanced in years, this title seemed singular; but it was his European habit of addressing the clergyman as 'father.' He said to me, 'I keep books of account; they are necessary for my business, and I profess to keep them correctly and honorably. Now,' said he, 'if you were passing along the street, and I were to say to you, " Father Simpson, come in and examine my books and see how I keep them; I want your judgment whether they are or are not accurately kept, and whether there is any evidence of dishonesty," you might think it strange that I asked you such a question, but you would consider it a slight peculiarity of mine, and that I had some reason for it, and it would pass from your mind. But, suppose,' said he, 'that I should meet you again and ask you a second time to come in and examine my books, and should say, " I would like you to look over my books and see if they are not accurately and perfectly kept, and every detail correctly carried out," your surprise would be increased, and you would ask yourself, Can there be anything wrong? And,' said he, 'if a third time I would invite you in and insist on your examining my books, you would be sure to go away thinking that there was something wrong in my mode of doing business. Now,' said he, 'I have no doubt that your books are all right, and why is it necessary to preach three sermons to prove what we already believe?' I did not fully acknowledge the force of his criticism, but I confess it had the effect to spoil my series of sermons, and I dropped them, afterwards referring only to such evidences as came in my way in the discussion of other subjects."

I find among the papers of the Williamsport period— 1836—the following scheme of self-discipline. It cannot be told from aught that appears whether it is original or copied from some worthy of the Church; most probably it is his own. Like many other plans of moral regimen, it aims at the unattainable; but of its wholesome, especially its restraining, effect upon his speech there can be no possible doubt. For if ever a man guarded his lips it was Bishop Simpson. Genial, ready to converse with every one, as he always was, he seemed to know by intuition what ought to be spoken and what not. When character was under discussion he said very little, and that little well within the bounds of Christian charity. His anger did not readily find vent in words; this was the more remarkable, for his sensibilities were acute.

He was capable, however, of putting his anger into sarcasm, and yet I never heard sarcasm from him but once. It was during the struggle for lay delegation. One prominent clerical opponent, who held an important financial position, had declared that the purpose was, by means of it, to give a monopoly of power in the Church to the rich. He, therefore, made a stand for the poor, who, he reasoned, could not afford to go as delegates to the general conference. The bishop, in a public address, cited the objection, and then, quoting from the New Testament example of the same objection, added, "This he said, not that he cared for the poor," and went right on. The effect was indescribable.

But to the scheme of moral discipline, those who knew him in after-life will readily perceive how closely he had conformed his conduct to it:

"What I should refrain from:

"1. Never injure the feelings of any person with whom I converse or am associated, unless that injury be the result of the declaration of a truth which it becomes my duty to utter.

"2. Speak evil of no one; never utter disrespectful words, or indulge in a conversation wherein any one is unnecessarily spoken against.

"3. Suffer myself not to give way to a jesting or jocose spirit, or to talk upon unimportant subjects.

"4. Spend no more time at any place than may appear indispensable.

"5. Endeavor to refrain from lengthy conversations with my family and intimates, ever remembering 'Dum loquor, tempus fugit.'

"What I should do:

"1. Rise at four every morning, and if I cannot retire at a corresponding hour, sleep a sufficient time to make up the deficiency during the day.

"2. Dress as expeditiously as possible, and then devote a considerable time to reading the English Scriptures and to private prayer.

"3. If possible, devote some time to studying the Scriptures in their originals.

"4. Fill up all my leisure hours with useful reading, always keeping some book in my hand.

"5. Visit and pray from house to house, and talk pointedly and faithfully.

"6. Reprove sin whenever I may find it, always in the spirit of love and meekness.

"7. Always endeavor to give a religious direction to every conversation.

"8. Ask no questions concerning myself, nor suffer the conversation to turn upon me.

"9. If commended, pray for humility; if insulted, pray for love; if apparently successful, be thankful to God, and pray to feel my own unworthiness.

"10. To preach, exhort, and pray as though in the immediate presence of Jehovah himself.

"Lord, help me to do all these things, and thy name shall have all the glory. Oh, keep me by thy power, or I shall assuredly fall.

"M. SIMPSON.

"WILLIAMSPORT, Jan. 11, 1836."

V.

INCIDENTS OF HIS EARLY MINISTRY.

1834–1837.

Was Bishop Simpson's Pulpit Power of Slow Growth?—Accounts by Relatives of his First Sermons.—Professor Hamnett's Testimony.—His Appointment to Liberty Street Church, Pittsburgh, Proof of his Rapid Success.—Counsels of Dr. Sellers.—His Early Style Impassioned.—His Own Description of his First Attempts to Make Sermons.—His Method Purely Extemporaneous.—Looked for Immediate Results from Every Sermon.—The Itinerant Life of that Period.—The Simple Worship of Rustic Congregations.—His Own Account, from his Diary, of his Circuit Preaching.—Laborious Pastorate in Pittsburgh.—Studies in the Hebrew and in the New Testament.—Pastoral Visitation and Sunday Sermons.—Completes his Twenty-fourth Year.—Dissatisfaction with his Spiritual State.

V.

THE questions of most concern to us who have been contemporary with Bishop Simpson, and who heard his preaching, are: " Was his pulpit power of slow growth ? Or, did he at once apprehend the conditions of successful preaching ?" Most men who have developed power as speakers have gained it at the expense of long-suffering audiences. Time and practice have been required to give them full command of their capabilities. They have had slowly to learn their own limitations; through mortifying failures to find out what they could and what they could not do. Especially is this true of an extemporaneous speaker, and young Simpson would be no other. That he began with fear and trembling has been made plain by his diary. That it was in him to become one of the most eloquent and overwhelming preachers of his generation never, I apprehend, entered his thoughts. I have made careful inquiries of those who heard his first sermons, and the uniform testimony is that he showed ability to command both himself and his audience from the first. Mrs. Amanda Wood, who remembers his earliest sermon in Cadiz, says of it: "I suppose that there were persons in that little, well-filled church who wondered at his self-possession as he rose to speak in the presence of the village wiseacres. But soon the power of his magnetism took hold and fixed the attention of his hearers." Another relative, Mrs. McElroy, now far advanced in years, says of his early success: "I had the pleasure of hearing his second sermon, which was preached at a camp-meeting in Harrison County, Ohio, in the fall of 1833. On that occasion he read as a lesson the second chapter of the Acts of the Apostles, selecting from it as his text the five verses beginning with the fourteenth and ending with the eighteenth. And wonderful indeed were the effects of his words, coming, as it seemed, right from God through his youthful servant. And though more than half a century has passed since then, the scene still remains in my mind as vivid as if it were but yesterday. During his preaching, while dwelling on the pouring out of the Spirit, a young lady, Peggy Simpson by name, a second cousin of the bishop's, was gloriously converted, while on every hand arose shouts of praise to Almighty God."

But this testimony has its abatements; the plan which he adopted precluded uniform success. "He was determined," says Professor Hamnet, one of Simpson's young friends during the Pittsburgh pastorate, "to be an extemporaneous speaker at all hazards, though he knew it would cost him many failures. He persisted in the effort, and some of his early sermons were very moderate. It was his practice to collect texts in a notebook and meditate upon them, and then use one of them quite suddenly for a sermon. He wrote but one discourse during all this period, and after delivering it he asked me if I noticed anything peculiar in the delivery. I said no; he replied it was written and memorized. The experiment satisfied him, for, as far as appears, it was never repeated."

His appointment to the Liberty Street Church in Pittsburgh, under circumstances which made him, unwillingly, the rival of an experienced and highly esteemed minister, is proof of his immediate success as a public speaker. In this position he had the advantage of association with the family of Dr. Henry D. Sellers, the brother-in-law of Bishop John Emory. Dr. Sellers was a man of strong character, clear, penetrating mind, and polished manners. He became for Simpson a friendly and most useful critic. The young preacher, in the impetuous rush of speech, sometimes lost breath, and fell into the habit of catching it again in a gasp, which came to the ears of his congregation as a very audible "ah" at the end of nearly every clause of a sentence. Many will remember how finely this was ridiculed by the eccentric Jacob Gruber in a letter to a young preacher, beginning "When-ah, you-ah, go-ah, to-ah, say-ah," etc. Dr. Sellers characterized it by a strong term, and told Mr. Simpson that he must quit it. The criticism was received in the very best spirit; other criticisms followed, and finally it was agreed that the young preacher should call on Dr. Sellers every Monday morning and discuss with him the delivery of the sermons of the preceding day. In the first year of the Pittsburgh life, when the churches of the city were still organized as a circuit, the two junior preachers—Simpson and Hunter—were constant visitors at Dr. Sellers's house, and must have profited by his conversation, which was of the very highest order.

I take it that his style was then, as in the time of his maturity, strongly impassioned. Mrs. Simpson says that often the foam flew out of his mouth when he was in a high state of excitement. As to structure, his sermons were wholly unartificial; he had never been drilled in homiletics, and had to trust to the instincts of nature to show him the right way. This is his own account of it, given when he had reached the fulness of his fame: "I had listened to good preachers, but the only sermons I had ever read were those of Mr. Wesley. I did not know there was such a thing as a skeleton or a book of skeletons of sermons; and in my youthful innocence I would as soon have stolen money from a bank as appropriate a sermon I had either heard or read. I remember well how, about the close of my first year, an older minister put into my hand and offered to lend me a book of sketches. I happened to have common-sense enough to decline the offer; so, without knowing how a sermon was made, save as mentioned, I began to preach. I did not try to make sermons. I felt I must, at the peril of my soul, persuade men to come to Christ. I must labor to the utmost of my ability to get sinners converted and believers advanced in holiness. For this I thought and studied, and wept and fasted and prayed. My selection of words, my plan of discourse, was only and always to persuade men to be reconciled to God. I never spoke without the deepest feeling, and unless I saw a strong influence on the congregation, I felt sad, and sought retirement, to humble myself before God in prayer. My sermons were not well arranged; they sometimes had divisions, for I had heard ministers say firstly, and secondly, and thirdly. Sometimes I had a line written out here and there, and sometimes a few catchwords on a scrap of paper, but these I seldom if ever carried into the pulpit, and very few of these I have preserved. My ministry was one of exhortation rather than of sermonizing, and I looked for immediate results under every effort, or to me it was a failure. So my early ministry was formed. Whatever my method was, it was purely my own, and was adopted, as I have said, not to make sermons, but to bring men to God. No one could have been more surprised than myself when I began to find not only that souls were awakened and converted, but that friends began to speak kindly of my simple talks as sermons." *

Here, then, we have evidence that young Simpson, warm with deep religious feeling, and prompted by the intuitions of an oratorical temperament, had struck upon a great truth, namely, that the sermon is not an end in itself, but a means to a higher end. Or, as Mr. Beecher has phrased it, a preacher, in making a sermon, should first ask himself what he intends to do with his congregation. Mr. Simpson would have answered this question very simply, by saying that what he wished to do with his congregation was to persuade those therein who did not know God to come to him, and those therein who did know God to cleave to him.

---

* "Yale Lectures on Preaching," pp. 162, 163.

Every one who has read his published discourses is struck with their urgency, and the pressure which he puts upon his hearers to do instantly the thing which just then he wishes them to do.

It was an itinerant life of the old style upon which the future bishop entered, a life which has passed away, but has left delightful memories for all who shared it. He had thirty-three appointments to fill in every term of six weeks. The travel was on horseback; the preaching-places were often private houses—as a rule, the houses of zealous members, who offered their homes for this use. Chairs or rough benches served for seating the congregation; a table, covered with a neat white cloth, made a pulpit. The neighbors gathered in from ten in number to forty or fifty, and, if the season was summer, the men here and there in their shirt sleeves. The tethered horses, the waving grain without, the deep silence of nature, undisturbed save by the song of the rustic worshippers or the voice of the preacher, blended into a scene which no one who has been a participant in such a service can ever forget. The preaching over, the few remain to speak to one another of that hidden, inner life which they prize as the precious jewel of their existence. Here eyes are often suffused with tears, and visages hardened with exposure and toil put on a tenderness of which they would hardly be thought, by the careless observer, to be capable. It is the preacher's golden opportunity to counsel, to reprove, to cheer. The company breaking up, and a simple meal despatched, the itinerant is off to another appointment, to meet another and like company, taking on his way the homes of those who need his presence and his prayers.

There is in this life every feature likely to discourage an ambitious man of worldly temper, especially if he be much superior in culture to the people whom he serves. To the student eager for knowledge it is the breaking up of all opportunities for its acquisition. But to one who has what

Guizot has called "the divine passion for souls" every step in it is taken with joy, moderated only by the ever-present sense of personal unfitness. Simpson, who had put aside for it what were for the times very lucrative offers, threw himself into its labors and privations with unbounded energy. Some brief jottings from his diary will show the feeling with which he regarded his work:

"*April* 5, 1834.—Left home at half-past twelve to start upon St. Clairsville Circuit, now altered to a six weeks' circuit, and containing thirty-three appointments. I passed through Harrisville, thence the creek road to Perrine's, my first appointment, a distance of fifteen miles. This is about half a mile below the road leading from Harrisville to St. Clairsville, and is pleasantly situated on Wheeling Creek, two and a half miles from St. Clairsville. To stand at Perrine's and look around, their farm appears to be surrounded upon three sides with majestic hills, whose sides are skirted with woods, and upon whose summits improvements can be distinctly seen; upon the fourth side you trace the creek wandering down midst smiling meadows. A handsome mill is on the place, running three pairs of stones, also a small stone house in which preaching is held. I was shown in and waited upon by Miss A. A. T. P——, a sprightly young damsel, who, her mother tells me, is just seventeen, neat in her person, handsome-faced, and amiable in her manners. I was very agreeably disappointed in finding some evidences of literary taste—upon her writing-desk, which was very neatly furnished, lay some poetry in her handwriting, while upon her table were the files of the *Western Gem*. After meeting I heard her in another room teaching an orphan girl who lives with them how to spell. The night being dark and the creek high, there were but four men and eleven women gathered, to whom I endeavored to expound Job xv. 11: 'Are the consolations of God small with thee; is there any secret thing with thee?' After preaching met class, and retired about ten o'clock.

Sunday, April 6.—Breakfasted with Perrines—two children and mother members, old man not. In conversation the old man expressed his desire to be religious; I pressed the subject close; he objected that his business of tending mill, etc., was so unfavorable that he could not be religious; I insisted that as his day was so should his strength be, and that every lawful business would leave freedom in religious matters. 'Ah!' said the old man, 'you don't know much about mill-property or you wouldn't think so.' Rode to St. Clairsville with the family, and put up with B. Wilkins. Preached at eleven to a large congregation, from

Hebrews v. 8, 9: 'Though he were a son, yet learned he obedience by the things which he suffered; and being made perfect he became the author of eternal salvation unto all them that obey him.' Before the exercises began, I felt entirely exhausted in spirit, but while giving out, in my first hymn, these words, 'Power unto the strengthless souls he speaks, and life unto the dead,' my soul took courage, and I had considerable liberty. After class I gave an invitation, and two young women who had once been Reformers [*i. e.*, Methodist] offered themselves as probationers. At night I tried to preach from Luke xi. 23, 'He that is not with me is against me, and he that gathereth not with me scattereth,' but I almost entirely failed. The night was rainy and I had few hearers. After meeting went home with Brother Carothers, talked about organizing Sabbath-school, and supped and retired. Oh, how little good am I doing! to how little purpose am I living! my feelings seemed to urge me not to try to speak, because I could do no good.

Monday, April 7.—Breakfasted at Carothers'. Inquired for the sick, and was told that a colored woman called Maria Butler, who enjoyed the confidence of the society, was not expected to live. In going to see her I called at Brother Kent's, and Mrs. Kent was pleased to accompany me. We found the sick woman low in body but of joyful mind; her hopes of salvation through Christ were strong and unwavering. After endeavoring to console her and establish her if possible more strongly in the faith, I prayed with her and retired. Called to see Mrs. Cowen. Left cards of probationship, general rules, and the character of a Methodist, for each of the young women who had joined on Sunday; prayed, and took leave. Rode to Eaton's. Meeting is here held at the house of Mr. James Eaton. It is five miles from St. Clairsville; three miles west of town the road to Eaton's leaves the turnpike. I endeavored to preach from Galatians iii. 22: 'But the Scripture hath concluded all under sin, that the promise by faith of Jesus Christ might be given to them that believe.' After preaching, met class. Society small. Mrs. James Moore invited me to call in the evening and I promised to do so. After dinner I felt so exhausted I fain would have lain down, but I tried to deny myself, and spent a short time in reading and writing.

Tuesday, April 8.—Breakfasted at Moore's and then started for Neff's, where I was to preach at night; but owing to improper directions I travelled thirteen miles instead of seven, and over a very bad road; however, I amused myself in examining the strata of limestone, coal, etc., on McMahon's creek so far as I rode down it. At last I arrived at Mr. Neff's, and preached at night to a small assembly from John iii. 17, 18: 'For God sent,' etc. The family very kind, but only two sons are religious. The people in this neighborhood are generally opposed to temperance societies on account of the influence of a few rich distillers.

Wednesday, April 9.—Rode to Widow Smith's, over the worst piece of road I have yet travelled, and preached at two from Colossians i. 14: 'In whom we have redemption through his blood, even the forgiveness of sins.' Met class and spent evening in reading and writing. The family are very agreeable, and have a large stock of sheep. The boy tells me that a hilly farm is most suitable for sheep, and that in the coldest night in winter they prefer lying on the highest knobs.

Thursday, 10.—Called at Mr. Thoburn's on my way to Farmington where I spent a few moments with this loving family, and prayed and left them. Preached at Farmington from Romans v. 9: 'Being now justified by his blood, we shall be saved from wrath through him.'

Sunday, April 13.—Rode to Bayles's meeting-house near Warren, and preached to a serious congregation from Romans x. 9: 'That if thou shalt confess with thy mouth,' etc. Met class and had a very pleasant meeting. Here I was detained too long to have time to dine. I therefore rode to Mt. Pleasant, but when I arrived I found there was time for dinner, the meeting being an hour later than I supposed. I preached at four from John iii. 17.

Monday, April 14.—After breakfast I rode home to Cadiz, where I remained till Thursday, when I preached at Stier's at eleven o'clock. Returned home at night.

Friday, 18.—Rode to Georgetown to preach at two; but no congregation gathered, but four or five, to whom I gave a word of exhortation and prayed and took leave.

Sunday, April 20.—Had a very good love-feast; the congregation being very large, I preached to them out of doors from Galatians iii. 13: 'Christ hath redeemed us,' etc., and had considerable liberty. When I commenced the sun shone full upon me, but after I had begun speaking I felt no further inconvenience from it, nor from a stitch in the side with which I had been afflicted since morning. Oh, the goodness of God! After dinner I rode to St. Clairsville, stopped at Mr. Hubbard's, and preached from Genesis xxii. 7: 'Behold the fire and the wood, but where is the lamb for the burnt offering?' I know not whether ever my spirits so completely sank within me while attempting to preach. 'Lord, support me or I fall.'

Monday, April 21.—This morning my horse had broken out of the stable, and I did not get him till nearly eleven o'clock, consequently could not reach an appointment five miles from town at that hour.

This week being my rest week, I remained at home engaged in reading and writing, and I also tended clerk's office three days during the absence of Uncle Tingley.

Sunday, April 27.—I preached twice in Cadiz; daytime I felt badly, at night I felt tolerably well.

Monday, April 28.—Met two classes, and visited and prayed with a sick girl who is about leaving the world; she has been a member of the Seceder Church, has been upright in her deportment, and now seems to have a pleasing hope of immortality.

Tuesday, April 29.—Wrote in clerk's office, and prepared for starting from home.

Wednesday, April 30.—Rode to Uniontown and preached.

Monday, May 6.—After preaching in the morning, walked from Day's a mile into the bottom, and preached from Hebrews v. 8, 9: 'Though he were a son,' etc. There was but one candle, and in moving it I unfortunately knocked it down, as it was only set on the top of an inkstand, there being no candlestick there. It was while I was giving out my first hymn, but fortunately I knew the words, and there was fire at which the candle was lighted, so that we proceeded without inconvenience. After preaching walked back to Day's, and as it had rained and the hill was steep I was much exhausted, but I slept very sweetly; it reminded me of the way of duty, steep and arduous, but the effect delightful.

——, *July 26.*—At the conference held at Washington, Pennsylvania, I received an appointment to the city of Pittsburgh. To this I had several objectious; 1st. My little experience in the ministry; 2d. My health might not suit confinement; 3d. I feared that I could not please the people. But as my brethren willed it, I cheerfully acquiesced. Returned to Cadiz from the conference and arranged my business for leaving home. Preached by request of one of the elders in the Presbyterian Church; my text was, 'Besides this, giving all diligence,' etc. On Thursday morning, July 31, left Cadiz in the stage for Steubenville.

Tuesday, Aug. 12.—This morning again commenced my diary, which I purpose, through the help of Providence, faithfully to continue. I have now got regularly settled. I have commenced reading my Hebrew Bible and Greek Testament in regular order, and noting down such texts as I think I may hereafter discuss. I purpose following the plan in the Discipline, and studying every forenoon and employing the afternoon in pastoral duties. I take down skeletons of all the sermons which I preach. When I view myself and the work in which I am engaged, I almost shudder at my insensibility: I am not alive in grace as I ought to be, not dead to the world as I should be, do not feel such continual fervency of spirit as I once felt; yet I try to pray: 'Lord revive me and revive thy work in a glorious manner.'

7

Friday, Aug. 15.—Visited Father Elliott and procured from him an Italian Bible and Lexicon, which I purpose studying.

Friday, Aug. 22.—This day a strange feeling came over me in the midst of danger; the thought passed through my mind that my mother prayed for me, and I felt a confidence that she would be heard. My mind immediately recurred to Jesus as loving more tenderly than a mother, and I believed in a faint manner that he would protect and be with me.

Saturday, Aug. 16.—Visited a sick woman, and prepared for the pulpit on the morrow. This day endeavored to live a more holy life, and I think I feel more in the spirit of my work than at any time since I have been in the city.

Sunday, Aug. 26.—This was a Sabbath day to my soul. I walked to Birmingham and preached at eleven; took dinner at Brother McRee's, and read fifty or sixty pages in the life of Mrs. Judson, the first female missionary from America to Burmah, a woman strong in faith and in love. Addressed the Sabbath scholars at two, and met class at three. Supped with Brother Kramer, and preached in Liberty Street at night. Blessed be the Lord for supporting and consoling grace.

Saturday, Aug. 30.—Read, wrote, and prepared for the pulpit. To facilitate our visiting from house to house we divided our charge into three parts, and agreed to commence next week in order. I had contemplated going to Meadville to graduate the ensuing month, and was preparing the outline of a Hebrew oration, but, on further consideration and the advice of Mr. Elliott, I suspended this until I made inquiry with regard to the university situated in this place.

Monday, Sept. 1.—Read as usual in Hebrew and Greek, Locke's Essay, and *Imperial Magazine.*

Saturday, Sept. 6.—Prepared for the pulpit, read, and wrote. Received a letter from uncle.

Sunday, Sept. 7.—At half-past eight met class; half-past ten preached; after that met class; had unusual liberty in preaching; dined at Brother Stewart's. He gave me a French edition of an English grammar. Took sacrament at three; very solemn time. I tried to covenant afresh with God. Oh, that I might be entirely given up to *him* who hath done so much for *me.* Night preached at Liberty Street, and returned home.

Thursday, Nov. 13.—Spent the forenoon in reading and writing. A plan we have pursued some time is to select a text each day, write skeletons, and compare them. Afternoon spent in visiting families; at eight, preached in Alleghany town, and returned.

Sunday, Nov. 16.—This day was a laborious one. I preached twice, exhorted once, met two classes, addressed a Sabbath school, and visited a sick man. It was a cold wintry day, and the ground was covered with snow for the first time this season. I did not enjoy myself so well as sometimes I do. I fear I have too little personal religion to be useful. I think I will try to live more in the spirit of prayer and self-examination. One fault I notice in my conversation, I converse too freely respecting the imperfections of absent persons.

Jan. 1, 1835.—Last evening we held a watch-meeting in Liberty Street; closed the year with prayer, and commenced the new one on our knees in solemn, silent prayer, and then sang the covenant hymn.

Sabbath, June 21, 1835.—This day I am twenty-four years old. Oh, how rapidly does time pass away! How little have I improved during the past year! God has been very good to me in lengthening my life, in giving me health beyond my hopes; but I have been ungrateful. Oh, help me from this day to dedicate myself anew to thee, to serve thee in newness of life, with all my ransomed powers. Of late I have not visited enough from house to house, nor talked enough upon religious subjects. I would commence anew; I would employ my time better; I would be more serious, more earnest, more persevering. But, of myself, the good that I would do, that do I not. Lord, give me perfect victory the ensuing year, that with all my heart I may glorify thee, and that my life may be spotless. This day I preached twice, and had some degree of liberty. But, oh, how little impression do my words seem to produce!

Friday, 26.—This day spent in visiting the sick and from house to house, and, in the morning, as usual, studied some in the Greek Testament and Watson's 'Institutes.'

Sunday, June 28.—This morning I was so situated that I preached before Bishop Roberts. I made no apology, felt but little embarrassment, and enjoyed my subject very well. At three o'clock I heard him preach from Heb. xii. 1: 'Let us lay aside every weight,' etc. His sermon was a plain, good, practical discourse, which was well suited to produce effect. If, however, it had not been preached by a bishop it would not have been extraordinary. His language is generally chaste and sometimes elegant, but sometimes he errs. Perhaps these are mere tongue-slips."

He was now, for the most part, away from his trusted counsellor, his uncle Matthew, but not so far as to be out of the reach of his uncle's watchful love. The correspondence between them during the first four years of his ministry is very beautiful, but only snatches of it can be given here. They discuss together the exegesis of difficult passages of Scripture, the best treatment of other passages for sermon-making, and the uncle now and then sends his nephew expositions of entire psalms or parables, which he modestly suggests may be useful as material. A close student of the Bible, and a close observer of human nature, the elder Simpson had in him rich veins of thought, which he now disclosed to his foster-child. I think I can see the influence of the uncle's mind upon the bishop's preaching, especially in its intensely Scriptural character, and its habit of tracing the connection between prophecies and their fulfilment. Some one — perhaps President Garfield — is reported to have said that with a student sitting on one end of a pine log and President Mark Hopkins on the other there would be a college. In the same sense it may be said that, given this watchful uncle on the one hand and a docile nephew upon the other, there are brought together the rudiments of an effective theological discipline. The pupil soon rises beyond the reach of the homely-wise instructions of his preceptor, but during the years of his inexperience one cannot see how he could have been better guided. The cautions as to personal conduct are most admirable; and the firm trust in God's providential care, which the uncle continually expresses, seems to have been wrought into the nephew's habits of thought, for it is one of the characteristics of his entire life. "All things work together for good to them that love God," is the repeated lesson given to him by the teacher of his early years, and by this tie the bishop held always to the unseen, but all-seeing One. The correspondence was long and various. A letter was a letter in those days of dear postage; no little snip of a note sufficed for the purpose. We can only cull here and there a few passages to show the deep affection on both sides.

The first letter from the uncle indicates that the talkers had begun to talk, and that the nephew was annoyed:

"Wellsville, June 14, 1834.

"The best way is, if you should meet with any difficulties or any finding fault or any whispering about you, as is often the case with preachers

16878

towards the close of the year, to remember that no prudence of yours nor the advice of your best and wisest friends will, of themselves, be sufficient. You must cast your burden upon the Lord and he will sustain you. See that instead of housing yourself up in retirement, you stir about as heretofore in the discharge of duty; for if you do not you will be liable to imagine that everybody is talking about you and even despising you, but if you do as I have advised, though some few may talk, the great majority will esteem you as they ought. And remember Satan desires to have you, that he may sift you as wheat. The best way of getting out of his power is fearlessly to do your duty in all things. Let God and man have it to say, as you began so you continued until the end. And while there may be outward puzzlements, see that the peace, love, and presence of God are within, and all will be well.

"Remember you are in the critical time of life, and in the critical time of your ministry, and, of course, will need all the grace, patience, and humility you can have. If your health should fail, come home until it mends, but come away in such a manner as will show that it is only on account of your health you leave for a time. Watch diligently and pray much, and the Saviour will make your way plain before you, and he will shine upon your path. May the God of grace and wisdom guide you in all things."

The second letter is about the proposed Hebrew oration:

"Cadiz, Aug. 20, 1834.

"If you conclude to speak the Hebrew oration, recollect the hearers will generally judge of your performance merely by their hearing. You must therefore consider it a main point to be able to pronounce each word according to the best directions you have on that subject, and you must string them together in such a manner as will appear to be natural. This will require you to speak slowly and impressively, and not to emphasize too many words, and as we do not know the manner of emphasizing used by the ancients, we should in an oration in any dead language place the emphasis on the same words and in the same manner as we would in our own tongue; otherwise it will not fall agreeably on the ear. So I think; perhaps a scholar would think differently. The subject selected for a Hebrew oration ought to be of the most solemn kind; such as describes the attributes of God, his wonderful works of nature, or Providence, such as marvellous deliverances, and an exhortation to serve him, backed with suitable examples. And perhaps the Scriptural account of the Messiah's kingdom ought to be a part. It should be first composed in English in the best manner and then translated into Hebrew; and if you conclude to do it, you ought to commence immediately; for it will be the hardest task you ever performed to compose even the English, so as to be worthy of that language in which wonderful things of God are revealed, and in which are found the most sublime accounts of him and of nature, and narratives the most simple, affecting, and interesting in the world. Let us, if you do make it, have your English draught, for it ought not to exceed what you can put in a sheet."

Sending him an exposition of the parable of the householder who went out to hire laborers for his vineyard, he adds this caution upon the use of proof texts:

"Cadiz, Aug. 24, 1834.

"I want you to profit by this hint: never quote a text to prove what it does not say, without showing by proper argument that the text so quoted must mean the very thing you bring it to prove. Remember how Euclid would argue, and try to make an argument equally conclusive in divinity. You, by a little attention, can easily do it.

"And perhaps there may be an impropriety in my sending anything explanatory of Scripture to you, because it may fall into other hands, which I think would not be for your credit or mine. I want, for some time, to hear from you at least once a week, and am willing to send you a sheet such as this just as often, if you would rather have it."

In another letter he advises him against attempting to find in the Bible the discoveries of geology and the kindred natural sciences:

"Cadiz, Sept. 7, 1834.

"And, now that I think of it, let me put in a caution, to myself and you, not to find allusions where they are not natural, for by overdoing we may spoil any hypothesis; as the proving too much proves nothing. And another caution is needed: to guard against the opposite extreme, which the philosophical theologians of the present day are running into; that is, they find the sacred writings to establish every principle of geology and natural philosophy. The sacred writings were intended principally to inculcate every moral and religious principle connected with the love of God and man; and that this may be the more effectually done, there are interspersed among the instructions given two chains or systems intimately connected. One of history, showing what man has done through a succession of ages, and how God has dealt with him, granting him prosperity and success when faithful, and punishing or chastising him when unfaithful, to bring him to repentance. The other of prophecy, which shows what God will bring about in the history of redemption and of providence until the end of the world. But though the Scriptures were intended principally to teach morality and religion, as above stated, yet the study of them greatly improves the natural powers of the mind by continually bringing into requisition all the knowledge the mind possesses, whether of language, history, or nature, so that, even in a natural sense, it may be said of them 'they make wise the simple.' But be you content with doing good, that will shine in eternity, when they will be dim who study to gain the adulation of their hearers more than their profit."

As his pupil has asked for an exposition of the phrase "idle word" in Matt. xii. 36, an elaborate essay is sent. He had probably heard that his nephew was becoming popular, and admonishes him that it is far better to be useful than to be eloquent. This to the growing orator was timely:

"Cadiz, Oct. 30, 1834.

"I rejoice much that God is carrying on his work in your station, and to hear of your being useful; that you are instrumental in doing good is much more pleasing to me than to hear of your being called a popular orator. I somehow suspect that very few of those popular pulpit orators will rate high in God's account when the day of reckoning comes; for the question will not then be how many they pleased, but how many they saved. At that day, when all things will be seen as they are, many a doctor of divinity will rate lower than some reputed to be ignorant and unlearned, but whose hearts have burned with love to God and man, and whose zeal carried them successfully over almost every obstacle.

"You know I do not like to write much, but now that I cannot talk to you face to face, I so love to talk to you by paper and ink that, would my eyes stand it, and were it not for making you pay too much postage, you should have one epistle every mail. And, now that I have used the word, I will just add I hope you do not say, 'Paul's letter,' instead of 'Paul's epistle.' It is a very poor way of showing one's learning. I wonder if any learned man does so. As I missed the right word, idle, in a former communication, I have written my thoughts on the 'idle words' in Matt. xii. 36, but I shall not probably send them to you, but keep them until you come."

Another letter outlines a Christmas sermon for "his boy:"

"Cadiz, Dec. 19, 1834.

"Thus I have given an imperfect outline, which you may transpose, enlarge, and back with references and quotations and instances. If you do this correctly you will make the most interesting Christmas sermon I have ever heard. It ought to be made out in some degree that Jesus was the person prophesied of, that his lineage, the time and place of his birth, his works, his death and the circumstances attending it, showed him to be the very person; but this supposes a good deal of time for preparation."

In the next letter he grapples with a most abstruse subject—the difficulty of making exact definitions in theology:

"Cadiz, Dec. 21, 1834.

"On the subject of Adam being our representative, I admitted in a former communication that there might be some senses in which he could be so called; but on the principles of representation, as understood and practised in the affairs of this world, Adam's children could not justly be answerable for their father's sin. And here let me observe, that in some subjects it is very hard to find a term which will fairly express the meaning wanted; and perhaps there is no science in which it is more difficult to find suitable terms than in that of theology. This, I suppose, has been a fruitful source of vexation to the Church in all ages. And this was almost an unavoidable evil; for we cannot well discuss any subject without the use of technical terms, even when we know that they do not fully and fairly express the things for which they are used, and no more. The nearest we could come to avoiding this difficulty would be, on using a term, to show at the beginning that in no other sense is it to be understood by the hearers or readers on that occasion, or in that treatise."

His transfer to Pittsburgh, and the probability that he would never more live in Cadiz, led to the breaking up of the old home. His sister Hetty had married Mr. George McCullough, and Mr. McCullough had purchased a farm at Wellsville, on the Ohio River, whither he purposed moving; uncle and mother decided to accompany him. It was while the family were in Wellsville that the son married Miss Ellen H. Verner, of Pittsburgh. The uncle tells of this in the letter following:

"Cadiz, Jan. 19, 1835.

"George McCullough has articled for a farm on the Ohio, seven miles above the mouth of Yellow Creek, and between the towns of Wellsville and Fawcetstown, three miles from the former and one from the latter.

UNCLE MATTHEW SIMPSON.

The hill, viewed from the river, is a perpendicular precipice of rocks, or nearly so, but on the hill it is a level and beautiful farm. George expects to be on it about the first of April, and he wants us to go along, and it is likely we shall go then or not very long after. If we do, the steamboat would conduct one from Pittsburgh to the place in a few hours almost any day."

There follows a description of the way to the new home, and then a reminder to the growing orator that if he does well, and *because* he does well, he will meet with detraction, even from Christians.

"Liverpool, April 12, 1835.

"At about a mile below the little town of Liverpool, in Columbiana County, a little run, on which is a saw-mill, empties into the river; below the mouth of the run there is a small field, said to contain five acres of bottom; you would guess two acres instead of five. Below the field is a little cabin, where there is always wood piled up for the steamboats. If you put out at the cabin and turn up towards the run, taking the left-hand road, at a little distance from the cabin it will wind you up the steep hill and bring you to a log house, where you will see us if we live so long."

"Liverpool, April 28, 1835.

" We are all in our usual health, and I spend my time in weaving foundations for stocks and in setting and keeping things to rights. The solitude is not disagreeable. I know nobody and nobody, or but few, seem to know me. If it goes on so it will not be hard to cover the defects of age. God is good to me in giving me almost uninterrupted tranquillity, and as much indifference to earthly things as perhaps comports with the condition of one dwelling in a mortal body. Your own health and welfare are the greatest drawback to this indifference. When you were young I taught you some things which you would do well to remember. One was that whosoever will excel others in anything, even in learning or piety, and, what is still more strange, if you exceed others in the diligent discharge of ministerial duties, you will become an object of envy. Others will industriously find and impute to you sinister motives for all you do more than the common drones, and even some, who may be above detracting anything from your character themselves, will have no great objection to others doing it, for the young man will need 'a taking down.' You are to expect all this from preachers of the gospel of your own order, and that, too, from men who really do love you. Every man pays for his wealth in land, cattle, or money; and this detraction is the

tax which men of superior attainments or qualifications have to pay.   I
mention these things to stir up your mind by way of remembrance."

Already the young preacher was named for a college professorship; the call was sufficiently strong to warrant asking the uncle's advice.   The wise answer comes: " Do not
reach forward for preferment; let God choose.   Think only
of your work.   Remember that you are the child of Providence."

"Liverpool, May 11, 1835.

"The promise is, ' If thine eye be single thy whole body shall be full
of light;' so, if you lay down your own will and study only the will of
your Lord, as he has heretofore directed you, opened your way, and prospered you, so he will now.   Your mother's prayers and mine will, as
heretofore, be joined to yours that God may direct you in all things.

"With regard to the French and German languages, you ought not to
hesitate about the expense, as I hope your design would be to use such
knowledge to the glory of God; the gold and silver are his, and he can
supply you.   He has heretofore supplied you with tuition-fees and books
in such sort as few would have expected at the time you were left an
orphan.   Remember, therefore, you are the child of Providence, and,
whether you are to preach or teach in a seminary, you could make these
languages worth more than all the trouble and expense.   But if you will
think the expense too much, then take the French by all means, for you
may never again have so good an opportunity; the German you could
acquire from the Germans themselves, and it is not so much sought after
as an accomplishment.   I would not, for fear of your health, insist on
this were it not that I suppose the pronunciation is nearly all you have
to learn."

"Remember you are the child of Providence."   I doubt
if any one of the old uncle's lessons took a deeper root in
the heart of his foster-child than this.   His faith in the divine watch-care over him never wavered for an instant, and
with this there was growing in his mind the conviction that
he was preparing for a large and important life in the world.
He writes at this period to his uncle : " When I reflect upon
the course which has been marked out for me by Providence these few years, I think that he either designs me for
a very short life, or else one marked with peculiar incidents

of an arduous and responsible character. In the meantime write often, write long, and pray a great deal that the God of all consolation may be my support and sure defence."

Here is a picture of the simple yet thrifty way of life at the old home in its new place:

"Wellsville, July 3, 1835.

"Your mother and Hetty, on yesterday evening, went half a mile to visit our very kind neighbors, the Blackburns; on returning and crossing a fence she twisted a leg and caused a sprain, which was very painful all night; so she slept none, and this day she cannot walk about; but she sews at stocks, for she helps a good deal at that business, and since coming here they have made above one hundred of them; the greater part were disposed of at Cadiz.

"Recollect, a young man just entering the ministry, by undertaking too much may render himself incapable of doing anything at all.

"Write to me every week until Conference, and I expect to do the same to you; I will suffer considerable anxiety about you till after Conference, but I would much more did I not know that God, your Father, possesses all you need; you are his and he cares for you. My daily prayer is, that he would give you health, grace, wisdom, and fortitude to do his will in all things. Your mother's anxiety is no doubt more, and her prayers more frequent and fervent for you than mine; we often talk together about you. Oh, remember what I wrote you on meekness."

I fancy that the young preacher was sensitive to unjust criticism; and in this fashion the old uncle braces him up:

"Wellsville, July 11, 1835.

"Was ever a brave soldier the least downcast by any opinion which subalterns or others might form of him; when he knew that all his actions, sufferings, sacrifices, and the motives which governed him, were perfectly known to his commander-in-chief, because done under his eye, and that he would most certainly see to the bestowment of the proper honors and rewards? Would not a soldier in such circumstances, conscious that all was safe, laugh at the unworthy opinions formed of him, or at the mean attempts of any to lessen his reputation? Jesus is your commander-in-chief; he knows what you have left, so follow him. He knows all that you are, and all you have; for he made you what you are, and gave you what you have. And oh, my son, let this consideration keep your heart at ease; nay, let it make you joyful, independent of other men's opinions.   Be meek and patient under opposition, avoid throwing out any hints which could be construed unfavorably to your present colleagues.   Take care to leave every member, if possible, of your charge in peace, and let every one see that you are steady to your purpose."

When reappointed to Pittsburgh his colleague was the amiable and gentle Doctor Cooke.   But the relations of the two churches, Liberty Street and Smithfield, were strained, and the sagacious uncle sees reason for the utmost prudence:

"Wellsville, Aug. 8, 1835.

"We were a good deal surprised at your being continued in Pittsburgh, but it is no doubt for the best, or may be made so, 'for all things shall work for good,' etc.   We were not made to do our own will, but the will of our Heavenly Father.   To do his will is our greatest interest and should be our greatest delight, or, at least, we should try to make it as much so as possible.   Your continuance there is no doubt providential, and will work for your good, and that of others; if not immediately, it will by and by.   So endeavor cheerfully to set about your work as though you were in the very place you wanted to be.   Your colleague in charge is a scholar and a business man, and that will make your burden somewhat lighter than that of last year; but then scholars and business men are apt to be absolute, and you don't bow to great men; so if you do not both keep your hearts with diligence you may quarrel."

Here is a letter full of sweet counsel.   It repeats the old lessons, old as the ages: "Empty your heart of selfishness; cast all your care upon God:"

"Aug. 23, 1835.

"If you will leave self out of the question, and make the honor and cause of God all your concern, then he will in his own time and manner vindicate your character and cause.   And when it shall be best he will raise you up friends, perhaps out of enemies, who will not see you suffer wrong.   The elect person spoken of by Isaiah was, though perfect, to be blind and deaf.   He openeth the eyes but he seeth not, he openeth the ears but he heareth not.   O Jesus, how wonderful thy conduct and character, but how unlike to thee are many of thy followers!   I rejoice to find so much conformity to your divine Saviour in you; that you may be preserved from evil and have heavenly wisdom and divine aid is my daily prayer.   The Lord has marvellously preserved you, and directed your path from your infancy, and now will you not cheerfully and in faith commit yourself to his care and protection? In this respect take no thought for the morrow; be content with what he gives in every sense, and do not suffer anxiety to prey upon your spirits."

The old folks at home had been living, as we have seen, in a log cabin on the Ohio bluff near Wellsville. They were getting, however, a frame house ready, and this is the uncle's account of it to his nephew in Pittsburgh:

"Wellsville, Oct. 24, 1835.

"The house is shingled, and about a day's work after this would finish the weather-boarding; the chimneys are to be built, and floors to be made, together with doors, washboards, surbase, and cupboards. The sash is made; no lime can be got near this, and I think it probable the plastering may not be done this winter, but it will be barely filled in and lathed. The carpenter thinks he will have it done by the first of December; then there will be nothing but the filling in and lathing to finish the lower story, for that is all we aim at now. And as the weather-boarding is remarkably close, we could lodge comfortably in it, if the weather should not be very cold, even if it were not filled in. I have a partition of rough boards across the loft of the old house, which makes me a comfortable though unsightly chamber to work and sleep in. I have my vise-bench in it, and I also weave foundations [for stocks] in it. But if you should come before we have a room in the new house, then you must try to forget that you are city people and think yourselves travellers or missionaries, and you know they often fare much worse than to spend a few days among friends in a rough old house."

"Cadiz, Feb. 15, 1836.

"It is likely that a day has not passed since you were born in which I have not prayed for you or in some way tried so to do. So now I pray the Lord to give you understanding in all things."

Let it not be supposed for a moment that these instructions of his wise but unpretentious foster-father were lightly esteemed by the rising young preacher. They were not received by him as the superfluous expressions of an over-anxious love. He had sense enough to value them at their true worth. If the correspondence is not so active on his part, it is full of reverence. Questions are asked on points of exegesis, advice is sought for upon matters of practical import, and much of his inner feeling in relation to his public life is confidentially disclosed. A more beautiful example of unreserved intercourse between youth and age one rarely meets with. In the first letter we cite, the nephew is quite astray on the question of the essence of the Christian Church, and shows how much he needs guidance in theology:

"Pittsburgh, Oct. 20, 1834.

"I thank you very much for your several interesting letters. I was indeed highly gratified with your remarks upon the drawing of the heart by the Holy Spirit, and also your remarks on seeing Him as he is. You, however, misunderstood me respecting the word 'idle.' The passage to which I referred is, 'For every idle word that men shall speak,' etc., and not, 'Why stand ye here all the day idle.' What was the primary design of the Christian Church? To do good to the world at large, or to its members? My mind inclines to the first, and consequently I think no person ought to be received into the church until qualified to do some good. Hence children while in infancy ought never to be spoken of as belonging to the Church, or making part of the body of Christ. And the argument that children make a part of the Church here, because they constitute a part of the one above, is fallacious, because that state is one of enjoyment, this of action; and a child may enjoy though it cannot act. Your thoughts upon this if you please.

"My health is good, but my studies progress very slowly. I am here, there, and almost every place it seems to me, with the well and with the sick; present at almost every kind of scene except marrying, and I have so far received more invitations for that than any of my brethren, but I have to turn them all over to Brother Hudson.

"What do you think of my going home? Dr. Ruter asked me if I would come to Meadville as professor of chemistry, etc., receive a partial salary, and depend for the rest upon my lancet, and added that I could have plenty of business, as there was no Methodist physician."

"Pittsburgh, Nov. 10, 1834.

"I get to read or study but little. Yet I can say, I have learned more of religious experience than I ever knew before, and I think this is one of the best places for acquiring information of that kind which I ever knew; for we are bound to converse with so many different persons in such different circumstances.

"Still write to me as often and as much as you can, for there is no person here who can in any degree supply your place. I am obliged to act altogether upon my own judgment in all I say or do here, and it may be that oftentimes I blunder very much. However, I try to act right and simply trust to God for direction. Your letters you may rest assured are all carefully preserved and I think shall be.

"What do you think was the original meaning of, 'Thou shalt surely die?' Did it mean anything more than what has been taking place from that time to this?

"I have just commenced, with my brethren here, a plan which will be useful I trust. We select a text every day and each writes a skeleton, and then we compare and discourse upon the subjects. Tell mother I still feel I am her son and that she is my mother, and as soon as business here will justify I intend to see her."

"Pittsburgh, July 31, 1835.

" Conference closed about one o'clock to-day, and we have all received our appointments; mine is in this city. C. Cooke is in charge, if the station is not divided. The bishop advised to this, but if it is desirable to the people, he authorized them to divide, and in that case I have charge of Liberty Street. The state of feeling for the last few weeks has been very gloomy, and many apprehend a squall only inferior to the radical separation. God can and will direct to his glory; I shall need your prayers more than ever; I am truly in a difficult place. He alone who is the author of wisdom can bring me safely through. The stationing for this city was very difficult; more so, perhaps, than it ever has been. At first I was set at Williamsport; then the Liberty Street people petitioned, and sent a delegation for me to the bishop, at the head of which were Father Cooper and Dr. Sellers. The presiding elders opposed, and succeeded in getting K. for Pittsburgh, and last night sent me to Hudson, a little place one hundred and nine miles from this, near the lake, where nearly all are Presbyterians. This morning the people got word of it, and just as the bishop was nearly ready to commence reading out the appointments he received a letter from Liberty Street, which had the effect of placing me where I am. I cannot now see you for some weeks until we get things started; as soon as that, I will go on a visit of some days."

"Pittsburgh, Aug. 21, 1835.

" You may think my last was gloomy, yet all was and is true. However, prospects appear to be brightening in several respects. First, in the division of members I have received more than I anticipated. Second, although they have refused an exchange, my congregations are as large as ever, and the impression is decidedly in my favor. Third, I have many warm and attached friends, and indeed my whole congregation appears unusually affectionate. Fourth, my officiary is said to be superior to any ever in the city, and I know it to be much preferable to that before the division. Fifth, our class and prayer meetings are lively and profitable. And, sixth, my own liberty in preaching is very good. I feel that I am in an opening sphere, and have been enabled thus far to speak strong words, and on last Sabbath night the feeling in the congregation was unusual."

After a six-months' experience in his new and difficult position, the young preacher was in better spirits. He writes of great success, but modestly:

"Jan. 28, 1836.

"Everything has advanced harmoniously; our society is at peace with me and at peace with one another. The spirit of prayer went up from many hearts, and the Spirit of the Lord came down. Our congregations increased in number and seriousness, and occasional accessions and conversions took place, until the beginning of the month, when I sent for Brother Dighton to come and help me hold a protracted meeting. This was done because I thought he would please the people, and because I feared I would get no old men to help me vigorously. He came and preached plainly and pointedly and faithfully. The altar was crowded with mourners, many were converted, and fifty-four have joined the church, making a few over a hundred since Conference. To God be all the glory. I still need your prayers and advice, for only six months of the year are past, and I know that much prudence and wisdom will be necessary to keep along still, although I fondly hope the worst of the storm is over."

It remained to be seen whether his marriage would seriously withdraw his care from those who remained in the old home. He had taken another life into his life, and some change in his relations to mother and uncle was inevitable. His uncle had, it seems, expressed an apprehension of this, perhaps had chided him for an apparent forgetfulness. He replies in this way:

"Jan. 28, 1836.

". . . Surely you cannot think I could forget, while this heart beats or this mind acts, one who has been so long the object of my warmest regard, one who 'raised the tender mind,' who gave me what little intellectual culture I may possess, and to whose precepts and example, under the blessing of Providence, I am indebted for those traits of character which have placed me where I am. Can I forget that uncle who nursed me frequently in his arms, sang to me in gleeful mood, turned my infant mind to science, supplied me with books, introduced me to public life, filled my mind with moral and religious sentiments, and followed me from home with prayers and his fondest wishes, and, to use his own expression, felt that 'his life was bound up in the lad's life?' Can I forget that uncle? No, never, 'while life or thought or being lasts, or immortality endures.'

* * * * * *

"The Sabbath I returned I preached twice, I believe to universal satisfaction. Dr. Sellers and many others were pleased to say, as I have since heard, that I preached better than ever I had before; and some said that if marrying had that effect on the preachers they wished they would all get married."

Uncle and mother were cherished with the tenderest affection, and spent most of their latest years with him, the mother dying at his house.

The diary of his life in Pittsburgh in 1835 and 1836 shows some facts very plainly. First, his sensitiveness of conscience, and the strictness with which he watches over himself. Occasionally there are passages which show an almost morbid state of mind; in these he is unlike himself, for his habit is of healthful, forward-moving energy. His anxiety to be a faithful pastor is likewise apparent, but with this appears too an inability to settle down to methodical study, which is the chief defect of his Pittsburgh life. However, he is growing on the practical side, and winning golden opinions from the people:

"*August* 27, 1835.—I received my appointment from the Conference to the city of Pittsburgh another year with mingled and various emotions. Many of the people I tenderly loved, and with them I knew that I could enjoy sweet converse; again I knew that there was an open door to much work, shown by there being a large population not attendant upon any ministry, and by our having a large house to accommodate them. Further, I had every reason to believe that I enjoyed the full confidence of my entire congregation. These views were pleasant.

But upon the opposite side there was, first, my youth—never having had charge of any congregation, and now receiving the hardest in the Conference. Second, my want of experience, and consequently of variety.

8

Third, my having spent one year with the charge, and that one of labor, but blessed with the outpouring of the Holy Spirit; and, fourth, that I expected the opposition of the Smithfield Church, and also the jaundiced views and expressions of my brethren in the ministry. These reflections were far from being agreeable. The Conference rose the last day of July, and on the same evening I had an interview with the bishop in presence of Brother Cooke, who is stationed at Smithfield, in which the bishop strongly recommended a frequent interchange of pulpits, and that if three or four of the Smithfield people remained waspish, not to pay any attention to them. In the ensuing week we proceeded to the division of the station. On Wednesday night, August 5, the officiary divided themselves; on Thursday evening I held my leaders' meeting, and they passed a resolution requesting an interchange. Friday night his leaders met and he laid the subject before them, when after considerable discussion, in which the interchange was warmly opposed, the subject was postponed, and so it remains until the present time. The division has thus far proceeded in an amicable spirit in the main, although the utmost effort has been used to draw the members and congregation to the Smithfield house. However, with all this I am receiving a very fair proportion of members, and the congregation is large and attentive, if not increasing. My official meeting is harmonious, and the officials seem determined to sustain my hands, and the members generally live in love.

September 4.—Since my last entry, by the pressure of engagements, and the natural slothfulness of my habits, I have let the time pass away without any entries. I will now, however, note the principal events. On Saturday I read, wrote, and visited. Sabbath I preached twice. Monday I read some, and visited some. At night had a very harmonious and pleasant leaders' meeting. In the evening received and opened a box of books from New York. Tuesday made arrangement of books, wrote love-feast tickets, and met my class. Commenced 'Watson's Life;' find it written in a solid, agreeable style. See in it very forcibly the effects which discouragements may have upon a young preacher, and the almost irreparable injury which one misstep may occasion. Thursday, sent for a large supply of Sabbath school and other books in conjunction with Brother Elliott, for the purpose of opening a small depository. This day (Friday) I recommenced my weekly fasts, which I had suspended for a few weeks. I desire a full conformity to the mind which was in Jesus. And oh, if God will only make me useful this year I think my whole soul will swell with gratitude to him.

October 19.—Since camp-meeting our meetings have been generally pretty good, although nothing special. My own experience is not so satisfactory as I could wish. Sometimes I have been much drawn out in prayer to God, and have promised to give myself to him in newness of life, but I as often break my vows, forget my purposes, and live dead and cold before God. I often wonder that he at all blesses my labors. Yesterday I was more troubled with hardness and unbelief than I have been on any Sabbath for a long time. This morning I think I feel determined, *Deo juvante*, to live more methodically, to fill up my time better, to spend less in conversation, to visit more from house to house, and to study my sermons more. I think I will write two hours every day, partly notes of sermons, partly original thoughts, essays, diary, etc. Oh, that I might be a faithful steward of the grace of God.

October 21.—Yesterday I attended to some perplexing business, in which I became involved by marrying a couple improperly. Have not yet got it settled. Have not written two hours per day, but think that I am becoming more systematic. Had a very good class yesterday afternoon. Oh, that I might grow in both grace and knowledge.

Tuesday, *Oct.* 27.—On Wednesday evening Brother Hunter arrived from Williamsport, where he is stationed this year, and preached for me at night. On Saturday I rode to Williamsport to preach for him, while he remained in the city and preached for me. On Sabbath heard the celebrated T. H. Stockton, of the Reformed Methodist Church, preach a beautiful sermon on the Resurrection. At night preached to an attentive congregation. Returned on Monday. And on Saturday finally settled my marriage suit by paying one hundred and forty dollars and twenty-five cents. A pretty considerable sum for one marriage scrape.

Tuesday, *Nov.* 3.—This day rode about twelve miles into the country, and married a young man of my acquaintance, returned the same afternoon, and at six o'clock was united in matrimony to Miss Ellen H. Verner, daughter of Mr. James Verner, of this city. Mr. Coston performed the ceremony. We had been engaged since the nineteenth of September, and I trust that this union may be beneficial in a high degree to ourselves and to others. On Wednesday morning started to see my people, in the *Beaver*, and arrived about four o'clock. Remained with them until Friday, and arrived amid a shower of rain in the city. Saturday morning at five o'clock held Quarterly Conference. Brother Hopkins, the presiding elder, would not attend because it was so early. It being quarterly meeting, I preached Saturday night and twice on Sunday. I seldom have enjoyed more liberty in preaching than I did on the Sabbath before and after my marriage. For this I was truly thankful, as it would prevent any idea of my being less useful and devoted than formerly. The whole arrangement appears to be peculiarly providential, for although people are so apt to be dissatisfied with their ministers marrying, yet in my congregation up to this time (Nov. 26) I have heard nothing but approbation."

Preachers in those days were almost invariably disciplined if they married before they had "travelled" four full years. This was only the third year of Simpson's itinerant life.

"*November* 27.—I am trying to improve my time some better than formerly. I board at Mr. Verner's, where we have a very comfortable room. I have the use of Mr. Coston's library, and since my marriage have read a number of books. My prayer is to see my heart more fully, know all my imperfections, repent of all my sins, have the love of God shed abroad in my heart, and be enabled in all things to discharge my duty both to God and man.

November 30.—Yesterday I preached three times, once in the Smithfield church, and enjoyed myself very well, but yet, owing to my living so far from God, I see very little fruit of all my labors. My principal hinderances are, first, indolence—I do not fill up my time as carefully as I ought; secondly, timidity—I suffer myself, for fear of offending people, to have my time run away with, I pray too little, and visit too little, and when I do visit do not converse as closely as I ought. This day makes up four months since Conference; one third of the year has passed away, and I have spent my time more pleasantly than I had at all anticipated. The church has prospered more than I thought it would, but much less than it would had I been more faithful. Oh, for a closer walk with God, and more burning zeal for souls.

December 7.—Since my last entry, the weather having been unusually severe, I have visited less than usual. I purpose, however, to commence afresh. Last Friday, being Conference fast, I preached morning and night, and yesterday once on infant baptism, besides administering the Sacrament and preaching again at night. I have not zeal as I should have. Oh, that I may acquire a proper spirit before God in the discharge of all my duties!

Monday morning, Dec. 14.—Yesterday preached three times. I think it would be more profitable for the congregation were the same person not to address them more than twice. This, however, cannot be the case at present, owing to the sentiments of some who stand at the head of affairs in the congregations. In the afternoon had President Morgan to hear me. I invited him into the pulpit, and he closed meeting after me. I think Providence is showing me my evil heart in an unusually clear light. Selfishness is so mingled with all I say and do I sometimes fear it is all abomination in the sight of God. Oh, for the spirit of constant watchfulness."

February 2, 1836. — Well was it said 'procrastination is the thief of time.' A month and a half have passed since my last entry, and nearly all the time I have been thinking that I would write. I am, indeed, a strange compound: now, full of good wishes and desires; again, lost to all feelings of spiritual ambition. Now I resolve to abound in every good work, and again yield to slothfulness; now I promise how much I will do this very day, and then night finds me with nothing done. Mr. Dighton assisted me in holding a protracted meeting the middle of last month, which resulted in much apparent good—fifty-two joined society, and many professed conversion. Since then the work has been going gradually forward. Last night we closed our quarterly meeting with a love-feast, which was rather dull, but a few joined society.

March 1.—Another month has passed away, or nearly so, since an entry. It does absolutely seem to me that I cannot conquer this evil heart. I *know* that God has the power and that he is willing to exercise it in my behalf, but I do not SEE it and FEEL it. I think that I would fain give myself anew to God, but my 'heart is deceitful and desperately wicked.' I know that I have time and that I ought to write a little every day, yet, so slothful am I, that week after week finds me still delaying. Sometimes I have seemed to lie on the edge of the pool, but now I cannot say that I am so near. 'Now far from thee I lie; oh, Jesus, raise me higher.' This day I have seen my own unfaithfulness in a very reprehensible light indeed. I have not visited the sick; I have not sought the weak; I have not prayed, nor preached, nor anything else as I ought to have done. Oh, Lord, without thy graces and thyself, I am a wretch undone.

March 8.—Intermitted diary a few days. I am more than ever convinced that that which is not done for the glory of God will in the end produce confusion; that pain and sorrow are the only rewards for flying from duty. Oh, my treacherous heart, what will become of thee! I feel that I am far from God; almost dead and buried in sin and hardness of heart. I know there is still hope through Jesus; but whether I shall ever reach my 'Father's house and in his bosom rest' seems very uncertain. My prayers, my sermons, my all, are, I fear, abomination in the sight of God. Oh, my soul, when wilt thou know, feel, and do better?

March 9.—Still I am under deep confusion before God for my neglects of duty, my wanderings of mind, and my sinful propensities. Can I be truly converted and yet be thus? O God, take some means to bring me right."

It may, and very naturally will, be asked " What are we

to think of this frequent bemoaning of his spiritual state?" One answer is quickly suggested: it shows a constant watchfulness over himself, and a careful sifting of the motives of his public life. To get rid of self-seeking, self-gratulation, and to lose sight of himself in the service of the Master whom he followed, are worth the honest struggle which he made. His after-life proved that these endeavors had not been in vain; for from the vice of self-seeking he was wholly free; he rose from place to place because he was sought for and compelled to ascend. His indisposition to write, unless under pressure of necessity, was never overcome; he had not trained himself to do his thinking, pen in hand, but meditated, more satisfactorily to himself, without the pen.

With the appointment to Williamsport his pastoral life closed. In reviewing it several facts are clear: one is that it was a laborious life. He literally went about doing good in every possible way to all. He was a much-visiting pastor, and especially attentive to the poor. Remembering his own early experience, he was ever on the outlook for promising young men, and urged them forward in the pursuit of knowledge. One whom he thus aided was Professor Hamnett, long one of the faculty of Allegheny College, and now the college librarian. "I was," says the professor, "a boy in Pittsburgh at the time Bishop Simpson was in Liberty Street Church. My father was a tanner and currier, and I learned that trade. Mr. Simpson encouraged me and two others to try to be educated, assuring us that God would take care of us. Before the party of three started for Meadville on foot he had us to call at his study and prayed with us. This was early in the morning of a summer day. I went to college with ten dollars only in the world."

He was equally watchful to do good to young men who had no such stirrings of ambition as Hamnett. At one time, while in Pittsburgh, probably during the first year of his ministry there, he boarded with Mr. Joseph Woodwell. Mr.

W. had a number of apprentices, who had an early break-fast before the rest of the family. Mr. Simpson would at times take breakfast with them, in order to gain an influ-ence, by this personal intercourse, over their minds.

His interest in those whose welfare he had at heart did not soon abate. He wrote to Hamnett after the latter had gone to Meadville; one of his letters from Williamsport, in 1837, is remarkable both for its wise counsels and its vigor-ous expression. This young friend was disposed to rush through his college studies, and is dissuaded from attempt-ing to do so:

"Williamsport, Jan. 16, 1837.

"But you know that the old proverb runs, 'the more haste the less speed,' and this is especially true in reference to excessive haste in lit-erature. My opinion is that you may accomplish the work in the time specified, but I fear that if you apply yourself from 6 A.M. to 11 P.M. without taking considerable recreation, you will produce a latent disease, and this in time will exhibit itself in languor of spirits, dejection of mind, pain in the head, fulness of stomach, capricious appetite, cold feet, and a host of symptoms which, though generally disregarded, ad-monish that the system is near prostration. You should also bear this truth in mind, that when the body is thus enfeebled, the powers of the mind are weakened, if not in the same proportion, yet to a great extent. And although you may finish your collegiate course without any 'spell of sickness,' yet if you enfeeble your system, you will bring with you into the grand work of saving the human family a body and mind *partially paralyzed*. And yet what work requires such perfect powers as that upon which you design to enter! Let me then advise you strongly, 'Take care of your health at all hazards,' and let my admoni-tion have the more weight, as I have felt some of the evils of a contrary course.

"With your arrangement of studies, so far as you informed me, I am well pleased, and I hope you will persevere in studying, especially the Septuagint, not merely as a task or lesson, but that you may be fur-nished thoroughly for Bible criticism. Let others regard it as they may, for us nothing is so useful as to be expert in wielding 'the sword of the spirit, the word of God.' And while I urge you on the one hand against excessive study, let me guard you on the other against yielding to hypochondriacal fears, which would make you believe that you are continually trembling over a premature grave, and consequently that you are unfit for serious study. In these matters it would be well to take frequent counsel with your instructors."

Another fact which becomes clear in the review of his pastoral life, is that it gave unquestioned intimations of his power as a speaker. He found his way at once to the hearts of men. Dr. Sellers, his friend and critic, predicted a great career for him, and in his own house would often call this young pastor bishop. When put in charge of the Liberty Street Church, he had nothing to rely upon but his character and his attractiveness as a speaker. Any failure to meet the demands of the position would have been followed by a transfer of the bulk of his congregation to a rival church. No ties woven by long habit attracted the people to Liberty Street as a separate organization. He met the test fully and closed the year triumphantly. It may be said here as well as elsewhere that throughout his public life Bishop Simpson was most reticent in relation to his successes in the pulpit. One might read all his confidential letters to his family, and never find out that he was one of the most brilliant orators of his time. His most frequent account of himself in these is that he "had a moderate time only." Occasionally there is mention of "a great crowd," and especially of a great crowd at an open-air service, but nothing more.

I think it may be said, too, that in this pastoral period of four years he had settled upon the mode of pulpit preparation to which he adhered to the end of his life. It is a hazardous method for any one who has not the resources of genius to draw upon. He preached from skeletons, and, as has been seen, came to his Saturday nights with no other preparation than his note-book of texts, his meditations, and the rich material supplied by daily contact with his people. His visiting of his congregation was not social, but strictly pastoral, and it lay largely among the poor, the tried, and the suffering. His sympathetic nature must have been deeply stirred by much that he saw during the week. He was also a close student of the Bible, and had the most profound conviction of its absolute truth and authority. Even with these resources, and his own heart-felt experience added, he needed to be a rapid workman to get himself ready for the requirements of each Sunday in so short a space of time. But he was a rapid workman and had unusual constructive power. His methods underwent no change in after-life. In his later years he would walk his room for a couple of hours before going to the pulpit, meditating his theme; when on the point of starting for church, he would sit down and draw off a skeleton, which would be left lying on the table where it was written.

VI.

PROFESSOR IN ALLEGHENY COLLEGE AND VICE-PRESIDENT.

1837–1839.

The Beginnings of Higher Education in the Methodist Episcopal Church.
—Asbury's Notice of the School in Uniontown.—Dr. Alden, the Founder
of Madison College.—The Madison Merged in the Allegheny School.
—Young Simpson Elected to the Chair of Natural Science.—Success
as a Teacher.—A Close Reader of the Books of a Choice Library.—
Elected President of the Indiana Asbury University in 1838-9.—Rough
Journey to Indiana.—His own Review of his Life in Meadville.—The
Course of Natural Science in Allegheny College.—Repairs the Appa-
ratus with his own Hands.—His Various Reading in these Years.

VI.

It was not possible that a man of such vigor as Matthew Simpson should remain long in obscurity. The church whose service he had entered was beginning anew the task of educating the people. Its early efforts to this end had not been successful; but the founder of American Methodism, Bishop Asbury, bravely persevered, in the face of repeated failures of his plans. Before the beginning of our century the Methodists had founded the school in which Simpson, the youth, had received his very brief college training. The good Bishop Asbury, May 31, 1792, makes this entry in his journal. He was crossing the country northward from Tennessee and Kentucky, then almost a wilderness. It was the practice of travellers over this route, as a protection against Indian attacks, to move in large parties: "Pennsylvania — Both men and horses travelled sore and weary to Uniontown. Oh, how good are clean houses, plentiful tables, and populous villages, when compared with the rough world we came through. Here I turned out our poor horses to pasture and rest, after riding them nearly three hundred miles in eight days." At Uniontown the tired wayfarer tarried nearly two weeks, and adds to the above entry : * "We have founded a Union School; Brother C. Conaway is manager, who also has charge of the district. This establishment is designed for instruction in grammar, languages, and the sciences."

"Grammar, languages, and the sciences;" this was the foundation, and no other was thought of in the last century.

---

* See "Early Schools of Methodism," by A. W. Cummings, pp. 59-62.

One cannot but admire the ambition of our church fathers to build up culture solidly on the Latin and Greek classics. What the most of them did not know they were resolved their sons should know, and wrought in faith till their struggles were crowned with victory. By 1826 Union School had expanded into Madison College, where, as we have seen, Simpson spent two months, under the care, among others, of Bascom and Elliott. In the year 1833 the Presbyterians of Pennsylvania transferred their college in Meadville to the Methodists; Madison College was thereupon closed as a Methodist school and merged in the new organization. This magnificent gift of Presbyterianism, like that other gift to us of Dickinson, in Central Pennsylvania, deserves to be gratefully recorded. It enabled a young and growing religious body to enter upon its educational career with better equipments than could then have been furnished from its own slender resources. The Presbyterians had still remaining in Western Pennsylvania colleges at Pittsburgh, Canonsburg, and Washington, and felt, no doubt, that they could well afford to spare what they gave. The spirit of the founders of Allegheny was very Catholic. One of the articles of organization required that the institution should be conducted "on liberal principles, no person having any advantage, or being subjected to any disadvantage, on account of his religious views."

This college was the product of the zeal and energy of the Rev. Timothy Alden, of New York. Removing from that city to Meadville in 1815, he resolved on founding a school of learning, enlisted the co-operation of the people of Meadville, and procured a charter. At this time the village contained only seven hundred persons, and the County of Crawford, of which it was the county-seat, not more than nine thousand. At the first commencement, held in the court-house, July 25, 1817, the audience were treated to a Latin address to the president by one of the citizens, a reply in Latin by the president, Mr. Alden, a prayer in Latin, a Latin oration, a Hebrew oration, a Latin dialogue, and an English dialogue. It is said by the historian of the occasion that in the basement of the court-house where the commencement was held was the county jail, and that "the prisoners must have had the benefit of this intellectual treat." * The ambitious purpose of young Simpson to graduate with the delivery of a Hebrew oration was not without precedent; it was in harmony with the old order of Allegheny College. Best of all, Mr. Alden had the sagacity to perceive that the one thing needful for his college was a store of good books : he had the thought which Carlyle expressed afterwards, that the true modern university is a great library. He succeeded in securing, by bequest, the collection of the Rev. William Bentley, of Salem, Mass., considered at the time one of the best belonging to a private person in the United States. It was especially rich in the Latin and Greek church fathers, and was the means of doing more for the intellectual growth of Professor Matthew Simpson than all the advantages, excellent as they were, which he had before enjoyed. The call to the chair of natural sciences in Allegheny College was made in 1837, while he was pastor at Williamsport; in the same year he was elected vice-president of the faculty. His autobiography narrates this change, and his entrance on his new mode of life :

"A little after the middle of my Conference year I received notice of my election as professor of natural science in Allegheny College. Dr. Ruter, its president, had felt himself called to undertake a mission to Texas, then just

---

* The dominance of the classic spirit in Mr. Alden, mingled, it is true, with reverence for Puritanism, is nowhere better seen than in the account of the laying of the corner-stone of the college. In the cavity of the stone, besides a fragment of Plymouth Rock, were placed " a piece of marble broken from a pillar which tradition states to have belonged to Queen Dido's temple in ancient Carthage; a specimen of plaster from the tomb of Virgil," with more of a like kind.

opened to American population and Protestantism. Being about to resign the presidency, Dr. Clark, who had been professor of mathematics and natural science, was elected president, and I was elected to the chair of natural science, he remaining professor of mathematics. The appointment was not to go into effect until the first of May. After consultation with my friends I agreed to accept. Before that time Dr. Ruter had advised with me about accepting a professorship in La Grange College, Alabama, the presidency of which was then offered to him. He desired to go if I would take a position under him, but I had declined at that time, telling him I would not accept any professorship until I had completed my four years' course in the ministry. As this would close at the coming Conference, and as he and other friends strongly urged my going to Allegheny, in the latter part of April my pulpit was supplied, and I left for Meadville, where I entered upon the duties of my office.

"I found, upon my arrival, that I was expected to teach not only the elements of natural science, for which there was a handsome apparatus, but that I was also expected to teach some classes in mathematics—one of these was in surveying and navigation. After a few weeks I returned to Pittsburgh, where my wife had remained with her parents for the time being, and where she was confined by a protracted illness after the birth of our first son. I also attended the session of the Pittsburgh Conference, which was held at Steubenville, Ohio, in July, 1837, and there I was ordained elder by Bishop Roberts. Dr. Ruter, the president of the college, left very shortly after my arrival, taking the Pittsburgh Conference in his way on his route to Texas. He was a very pleasant gentleman, amiable and yet decided; a man of great industry, and fair, rather than brilliant, talent. He had edited an abridged work on church history, had been professor in Augusta College at a very early period, and had been in charge of the Book Concern at

Cincinnati. One among his earliest undertakings in Texas was the founding of a literary institution; but, partly from overwork and partly from the influence of the climate, he was prostrated by sickness, and died before he was able to accomplish much. His successor in the presidency, Homer J. Clark, was a graduate of the Ohio University at Athens, had been a member of the Pittsburgh Conference for several years, was very popular as a preacher in the city of Pittsburgh, and had served as professor in Madison and Allegheny colleges. He was a chaste and eloquent speaker, a man of clear thought and beautiful expression, and was a successful teacher. He was, however, more successful in teaching than in administration. Professor G. W. Clark had charge of the department of Latin and Greek when I took my place in the institution, and Calvin Kingsley, an active and devoted young man, was tutor of a few classes. He afterwards graduated with honor, held a professorship for a number of years, became editor of *The Western Christian Advocate*, and in 1864 was elected bishop.

"The college department was not very largely attended. The institution had been originally founded in 1816, principally through the influence of Dr. Alden, a Presbyterian minister, and, while its charter was general, it was under the control of the Presbyterian Church. But as the population of Western Pennsylvania was small, and as that church had in Pennsylvania Jefferson College at Canonsburg and Washington College at Washington, they had not patronage for more, and the students were very few. It became financially embarrassed, and a proposition was made by the trustees to place it under the care of the Methodist Episcopal Church. The school at Uniontown, called Madison College, had but poor buildings, no endowment, and the transfer to Allegheny was easily made. The main building was good, and there was a large library and a fair laboratory for that era. The students in attendance were chiefly in preparatory classes, though there were also small

9

college classes. Of the students, some were very bright—young men who have since made their mark on their country's history. As the buildings were on the hill, at least half a mile from the town, the college held but one session a day. I had charge of six classes, embracing those in natural science, sometimes one or two in mathematics, and occasionally one in languages. As the professors were few in number, such distribution was made as enabled us to give proper supervision to all. The students were generally young men making their own way in life, and were industrious and orderly; occasionally there were cases of discipline, involving some difficulty, but these were comparatively rare.

" In the autumn of 1837 I removed from the house which Dr. Ruter had occupied, and which was on the edge of the town, to one on the public square, that my family might have more society, and there we remained until I left Meadville in the spring of 1839. Very shortly after taking charge of my department I was also elected vice-president of the institution, and was thus associated more or less with Dr. Clark in administrative duties. Professor Allen, a West Point graduate, was made, shortly after my election, the professor of mathematics. He was an able professor, diligent and attentive, but quick in his conceptions, so that he was sometimes impatient with the students. His sister, then living with him, was subsequently married to Jay Cooke, so widely known as a financier. Towards the close of my connection with the institution he was offered a professorship in Kentucky, and Dr. Barker was elected to succeed him, and subsequently became president. The library of the college was large for those days, and, among other books, had a collection of the church fathers in Greek and Latin, which I prized highly and carefully read. Little of moment occurred in my college life. I took, however, a deep interest in the work of the ministry, visiting the charges within from six to twenty miles of

Meadville, and assisting also in quarterly and protracted meetings, and in the founding and dedication of churches. I also had a class of young men, who met me on Sunday afternoons at my house and read the Greek Testament. Among the members of this class were Gordon Battelle, who became a distinguished minister, and Frank H. Pierpont, afterwards governor of Western Virginia. To these two men, who were members of the convention called to frame the Constitution of West Virginia, were its freedom from slavery and its school system largely due. Battelle accepted a chaplaincy during the war, and died of typhoid fever. Pierpont became governor, and is a distinguished member of the bar. About the time of my accepting the professorship I received from Dr. Elliot, who had removed to Cincinnati, a most earnest letter urging me to prepare for wider Christian work, assuring me that my services would be needed in some larger sphere, and advising me to read the history of the Christian Church and the writings of the fathers, and to make myself acquainted with all the great questions of controversy. I received it as a friendly suggestion from a partial friend, but did not change my course, as I had from youth an insatiable thirst for knowledge for its own sake, and was anxious, to the full measure of my strength, to improve every opportunity.

"I assisted in introducing Methodism into Seagerstown, where, at a protracted meeting we held, the leaders of the Lutheran Church, who had controlled the village, came forward and read a paper protesting against 'the errors of Methodism,' as they styled them. After they had finished reading their protest, we went on without making any allusion whatever to them, and were gratified to witness a precious revival of religion. Methodism had encountered great difficulties in its establishment in Meadville, as the public opinion of the country was very unfavorable to it. A union church had been built by the citizens, but the Presbyterians, being the strongest body, had taken possession of it; gradually the other denominations, one by one, had secured lots and built churches for themselves. Methodism was introduced into Meadville by Bishop Roberts, then a young man, who preached in a bar-room. No society was, however, formed, and years afterwards, when a society was organized, services were held in the upper story of a blacksmith-shop. At the time when Allegheny College came under our control, the number of members was very small. A plain brick church, however, had been erected, but it was very far from inviting; it was somewhat improved during the time I remained in Meadville, and quite a number of young persons were added to the congregation.

"Meadville was the seat of the operations of the Holland Company in that part of Pennsylvania; the leading man of the company, Mr. Huidekoper, a Unitarian, and a man of wealth, gathered around him a respectable society, which built a neat church; subsequently a Unitarian theological seminary was established. A most humorous story is told of the dedication of this church. One of the distinguished Unitarians of New England came to officiate on the occasion, preached an eloquent sermon to a full house, setting forth in forcible manner the views of his people. A well-read man of the Presbyterian Church had become insane, and yet was quiet and inoffensive. He wandered about among friends, and was fond of talking of religion. By some means he was present in the congregation that day, and listened attentively to the discourse. At its close, rising from his seat and stepping out into the aisle, he reached out his hand and said in a tone of sadness, 'They have taken away my Lord, and I know not where they have laid him,' and left the house. The utterance of those simple words, it is said, produced a profound impression on the congregation.

"In the spring of 1838, I received notice of my election as a professor in the Indiana Asbury University, an institution then opening in Greencastle, Indiana, with the intimation of the Rev. Allen Wiley, who wrote to me that the probabilities were, that if I accepted the professorship, I would be in a year or so elected president. As my health was poor, and I was suffering from trouble with my chest and a cough, I thought well of a change of climate. But on submitting the matter to my ministerial brethren of the Pittsburgh Conference, they advised me not to go, saying, had the presidency been offered directly, they would approve of my accepting, but this change of one professorship for another they thought was not desirable. Accordingly, I declined the offer; but in the winter of 1838–39, I received notice of my election to the presidency, and, submitting the matter again to my brethren, they advised my acceptance, subject to the decision of the bishop who would next preside at the Pittsburgh Conference. Receiving the assent of my presiding elder and my colleagues—though reluctantly given—and of the board of trustees, I communicated with the bishop, and, being authorized to do so, agreed to accept the presidency to begin with the spring term.

" I accordingly left Meadville the latter part of March, sent my goods to Franklin and down the Allegheny River. My goods were shipped from Pittsburgh for Terre Haute, according to directions given me, but, unfortunately, the Wabash River was low that spring, and they were detained at Vincennes until the next fall. Taking boat on the Ohio River, the only means then of travel, we tarried with friends in Cincinnati; then through Indianapolis to Putnamville, on the National Road. The roads were execrably bad; much of the way they were what was termed 'corduroy'—that is, in marshy places made of sticks laid crosswise, over which the stage jolted. Sometimes the sticks were misplaced or broken, and then the wheels went down deep into the mud; once we were upset, but without any serious harm. Reaching Putnam, we secured a private conveyance six miles across to Greencastle, where we arrived on Saturday afternoon in the latter part of April, 1839.

"During my college life in Meadville, which was about

two years, there were general quiet and good discipline. On one occasion there was a difference between the Faculty and the young men, and for a time it seemed as though the majority of the students would revolt; the exercises were deranged for several days, but in the end order was restored, and the authority of the college fully vindicated. Of the students, a number besides those already mentioned have occupied distinguished positions. Dr. Cyrus Nutt had graduated before my connection with the college, but was still in Meadville. He had been employed a few months as tutor, and left shortly after my arrival to take charge of the preparatory department of Indiana Asbury University; he was, after some years, professor of mathematics in that institution, and then president of the Indiana State University at Bloomington. Dr. Alexander Martin graduated at Allegheny College, and was afterwards president of the University of Western Virginia, and is now president of Indiana Asbury University. Dr. John Wheeler was a student at Allegheny, and was subsequently president of Baldwin University at Berea, Ohio, and afterwards president of the Iowa Wesleyan University, at Mount Pleasant, Iowa.

" A large number of active ministers, attorneys, physicians, and teachers, alumni of the college, are scattered over Western New York and Pennsylvania and throughout Eastern Ohio. Professor Hamnett, who has long been in the faculty of the college, was a student whom I had induced to attend while I was pastor in Pittsburgh. Dr. Marvin, once president of Kansas University, graduated after I left. My associations with President Clark and the other members of the faculty were pleasant, and I presume I should have remained with them for some years, had it not been that the severity of the climate unfavorably affected my health. A severe cough, pain in the side and chest, and other symptoms of pulmonary disease, led me and my friends to think that I needed a warmer climate. But the access to the large library, and the experience I had gained in college management, were of good service to me."

What was the length and what the breadth of the course of natural science in Allegheny College we have no means of knowing; we do know, however, that Professor Simpson met the requirements of the position with complete success. No manuscript lectures on natural science are found among his papers; the presumption, therefore, is, that he taught by text-book and experiment, although this is not certain. Professor Joseph Tingley says of him: "I spent two years in Allegheny College, after the resignation of Professor Simpson, when he had been called to the presidency of Asbury University. There I was shown the large electrical machine which he had reconstructed and used in teaching. I was told that he found all the apparatus in bad condition and almost useless, but had repaired, remodelled, or replaced it to such an extent as to establish his reputation as a remarkably ingenious and practical scientist. His name even then was held in reverence, and it was felt that in parting with him the college had suffered a great loss." The Rev. George W. Clark, one of the senior members of the Allegheny faculty of that day, says of him: "His years in the professorship here advanced him more than any of the students." This is most likely the exact truth. I find in his commonplace books of this period copious notes on Origen, taken from the reply to Celsus, and the treatise "De Principiis," on Sale's Koran, "American Antiquities;" notes also on chemistry and mineralogy, showing considerable reading of the older authorities; lists of experiments, instruments, etc. I find also careful abstracts of Calvin's "Institutes," with citations from his commentaries and sermons, as well as readings from Jonathan Edwards and Lyman Beecher. The references are to old editions of old authors, such as would not have been, under ordinary circumstances, accessible to him. The truth is that in the library of Allegheny College he had a rich storehouse to draw from such as he had, in all probability, never seen before. To the valuable collection of Dr. Bentley, to which the college had fallen heir, had been added, also by bequest, that of the Hon. James Winthrop, of Cambridge, Massachusetts. By the industry of President Alden, eight thousand volumes—many of them rare—had been gathered together and placed upon the shelves of the college library; so that the county historian says of it, with evident pride: "It was mentioned by ex-presidents Thomas Jefferson and James Madison as a most valuable collection of books."

Here were "green pastures" and "still waters" for the hungry and thirsty professor of natural science. He gave "attention to reading," read in many directions, and, as we may infer from the carefulness of his notes, digested his reading. Had he enjoyed these opportunities for a series of years, he would have become, in the strict sense of the term, a learned man; for his mind was exact in its habits, and its apprehension of subjects clear as sunlight. Yet the commonplace books he has left do not show him as one who had made study the business of his life. They are wanting in method, and are not arranged in such a way as to be readily available for use. Blank-books are taken up, notes on one or more subjects or authors are jotted down in them, and then they are thrown aside. And so it happens that there are a good many beginnings which are not carried forward to completeness. All the facts show an eager mind, which only needs leisure for the attainment of the highest scholarship. But there were other instincts, each craving for adequate expression. He was a born orator, and his oratorical power was developing with unusual swiftness. The pleasurable exercise of this power was accompanied by the joy of its use for the highest spiritual welfare of men. He was equally a born administrator, and the circumstances of his position were constraining him to be, in a large degree, a man of affairs. A Church but a half-century old was laying foundations everywhere; and its two imperative needs were leaders with the gift of eloquent speech and capacity to guide the ever-growing hosts of adherents.

VII.

LIFE IN INDIANA.

1839–1848.

VII.

When Matthew Simpson removed to Indiana to take charge of the Asbury University at Greencastle, the state contained not quite seven hundred thousand inhabitants. As there had been established in the colonial period a " New England " on the eastern coast of North America, so there had been established in the interior a " New France." The two leading powers of Europe struggled during the seventeenth and eighteenth centuries for supremacy in the western world. Until the transfer of Canada to the British crown in 1763, Indiana had been a French possession. By the lakes, the Maumee, which flows into Lake Erie, and the Wabash, the French held communication with their inland posts, and, following the Ohio from the mouth of the Wabash to the Mississippi, and the Mississippi to the Gulf, linked together Montreal and New Orleans. As early as 1732 Vincennes (originally Vinsenne) was an established post, with its outfit of soldiers and priests, fort and church; for the broad scheme of French ambition comprehended both temporal and spiritual dominion. These lands were to be conquered not only for "his most Christian majesty," but also for *his* lord, the pope. Jesuit father and knightly commander worked together for a common end. But the fruition of this scheme was not to be, and the cession of Canada to England in 1763, preceded by the cession of Louisiana to Spain in 1762, put an end to French ambition in North America. Another and speedy change impended; for although the colonies, during the war of the Revolution, failed to conquer Canada, they did wrest from the mother country the Northwest Territory. In February, 1779, General George Rogers Clark, with a little band of one hundred and seventy soldiers, who had marched four miles through freezing water breast high, compelled the surrender of Vincennes by the British commandant. Clark had the year before captured Kaskaskia, the first capital of Illinois, then also in possession of the British. "This was," says Judge Law, "as regards its ultimate effects to the Union, decidedly the most brilliant and useful of any undertakings of the Revolutionary War. Clark, by that campaign, added a territory embracing now three of the finest states of the Union to the confederacy, to wit: Indiana, Illinois, and Michigan —a territory which, but for this very conquest, must now have been subject to British dominion, unless, like Louisiana, it had since been purchased." *

Once opened for settlement, and secure from the blight of slavery, the people poured into the fertile and attractive state of Indiana. From Kentucky, Tennessee, West Virginia, Pennsylvania, and Ohio they came, and the Methodist itinerant came with them. Wherever the pioneer settlers were, there he was sure to be. To Peter Cartwright is traditionally ascribed the honor of delivering one of the first, if not the first, Protestant sermon in the state. The time was 1804, the place the border of the Ohio River. The same sturdy pioneer has also the distinction of forming the first Methodist society in Indiana, crossing the Ohio River for the purpose from his own native Kentucky. The itinerants who travelled this wilderness, and made it blossom as the rose, were men who have left imperishable names. William Winans, often called, when he became, in after-years, a leader in Mississippi, "the forest Demosthenes," James Havens, Russell Bigelow, Edwin Ray, and John Strange were the leaders of the hosts of men through whose labors the foundations—civil and religious—of society in Indiana were laid.

---

* Address delivered before the Vincennes Historical and Antiquarian Society, Feb. 22, 1839.

It is difficult for us, in our easy-going days, when the study of all the world is to have "a good time," to conceive the intensity of these godly men. In the first place, they believed with all their souls the truths which they preached. Whatever doubts they had known they had conquered by prayer; the evidence of the truth of Christianity, on which they staked their destiny, was Christ's power felt within them. Christianity as a divine and renewing energy was the master thought with which they subdued the people. The invisible world was so real to them that they lightly esteemed the world to which they visibly belonged. Life was short, and they looked to be compensated for its privations in that better life which, as they said, "was hid with Christ in God." Of the logic of the schools they knew little and cared less, yet had a manly and forcible logic of their own. They were aware that there was culture, and that there were cultured men in those communities which had endured for ages, but they valued as above all price the culture which they drew fresh from nature's founts. Speaking of this school of nature, said one of them, in a strain of genuine eloquence: "Her Academic groves are the boundless forests and prairies of these Western wilds; her Pierian springs are the gushing fountains from rocks and mountain fastnesses; her Arcadian groves and Orphic songs are the wild woods, and the birds of every color and every note, relieved now and then by the bass hootings of the night-owl and the weird treble of the whippoorwill; her curriculum is the philosophy of nature and the mysteries of redemption; her library is the Word of God; the Discipline and Hymn-book, supplemented by trees and brooks and stones, all of which are full of wisdom and sermons and speeches; and her parchments of literary honors are the horse and saddle-bags." *

The author of this strain of eloquence—John Strange—

---

* "Early Methodism in Indiana," by the Rev. J. C. Smith, pp. 38, 39.

was a person of extraordinary character. His power of speech was such that strong men would at times fall under his preaching as if shot, and his power of song so attractive that he would with apparent ease lift his listeners up above the disquiet and unrest of our common lot. Wherever he went he sang, sang like an old Celtic bard, without accompaniment of harp; sang little of earth, but much of heaven. And his chief song, that by which he is most remembered, was from John Wesley's Pilgrim hymn, in which are the lines:

> " No foot of land do I possess,
> No cottage in the wilderness,
> A poor wayfaring man."

And for him it was literally true: no land, no house had he, or would he have. Friends offered him the title-deeds of a home. " No," he replied, " I would rather sing my song." And with mellow voice he preached and sang in cabin and forest, the people listening, and melted by the pathos of the strains:

> " No foot of land do I possess,
> No cottage in the wilderness,
> A poor wayfaring man."

Of James Havens, a soldier both of the church militant and church triumphant, even on this earth, for he was fearless and all-conquering, Mr. Beecher gives, in his " Yale Lectures on Preaching," this testimony: " I knew good ' Old Sorrel,' * as we used to call him, of Indiana; now a sound, well-educated, cultivated man, a man of great influence and power. But when he went on the circuit in the Whitewater valley he didn't know enough to tell the number of the verse of the text. He had to count off from the beginning ' one, two, three, four,' in order to announce ' the fourth chapter and sixteenth verse.' They take just such

---

* A playful nickname given to Havens by the people of Indiana from the color of his hair.

men in the West and put them into a field and set them at work, and they grow all the time. They are reading as they ride; their library is in their saddle-bags; they are reading in the cabins. They unfold slowly, but the beauty of it is that they are all the time bringing what knowledge they have to bear upon their fellow-men."

These were the men, many of them living, among whom the lot of Matthew Simpson was now cast, and in association with whom he was to live for nine years. Out of their poverty, and with the help of laymen not much richer than themselves, they had founded a university. Heroic as preachers, they were equally heroic as founders of schools. In this new sphere for the application of their energy they walked, as they had walked in subduing the wilderness, by faith. Indeed, they were compelled to do something as educators for themselves. The state university at Bloomington had fallen under the control of a single church, and all applications to the legislature to right the wrong, and to give Methodists a representation in the governing board, had been repelled with scorn. Even good men are warranted in resenting such an indignity; and the Methodists, already the most numerous religious body in the state, resolved on securing a charter for a university of their own. Here, too, they met the expression of a half-concealed contempt. An unlucky member of the state senate was heard to declare that "there was not a Methodist in the whole United States competent to fill a professor's chair." This was remembered when, afterwards, he became a candidate for the governorship of the state, and defeated. Finally, after a conflict with an opposition which was felt rather than publicly avowed, an ample charter was secured in the year 1837.

I would not mention these latter facts, which are not particularly pleasant, but for the reason that they make a part of the truth of history, and also for the reason that they occupy a considerable space in the correspondence of Bishop

Simpson in the first years of his living in Indiana. That the Methodists of Indiana were stung by the spirit in which their early efforts to educate their people were received by the more wealthy churches is very clear. I am inclined to believe that the Calvinistic churches, working in union with each other, had marked the Western States for their own. With a sagacity which speaks well for their large-mindedness, they had planted schools for the higher learning at the most eligible points; they had reinforced these schools with men and money from the richer East. But they had failed to reckon with another body, still struggling with poverty, yet growing prodigiously, and filled with lofty aspirations for all knowledge, as well as for all virtue. They made a mistake, and paid the penalty of their mistake. Let us be thankful that those days are past; that we have done with the bitterness of theological strife; that Ephraim has no more occasion to vex Judah, nor Judah Ephraim.

I have said that the Methodist preachers of Indiana had, out of their poverty, begun the building of a university, and so it was throughout the West. I well remember a visit made by me, in 1840, to Lebanon, the seat of McKendree College, then newly formed. Its sole real-estate basis was a section of government land, purchased, it was said, for this purpose, by the bishop whose name it bore. How accurate this account was could not then be determined by me, but it was the popular account. In a wood near the village was a frame building without pretensions, the faint tinkling sounds of whose bell could scarce be heard as they sought for egress into open space. It was a time of discouragement, almost of despair: professors were unpaid, president was unpaid, means of subsistence for those who had stood faithfully to their teaching work were scarce to be had. Still the work had gone on, as appeared from the examinations, solidly and well. I was privileged to be present at the meeting of the college trustees. The preachers and members of the board had the hard, weather-beaten look of men who were accustomed to the exposure incident to frontier life; the well-worn clothes of some of them told as plainly as words could of penury. When Cartwright, to whom all looked for counsel, stood up to speak, it was astonishing how quickly his sanguine spirit reassured his colleagues. Unfortunately, I took no notes of his words, but their purport was: " Let us hope on; we shall see better days; we are doing a work for the future and cannot fail." It has always seemed to me a pity that Peter Cartwright has been caricatured as a mere humorist, when both his chief qualities were sterling good sense and unflinching courage. On that day he appeared at his best, brave, buoyant, and capable of inspiring with his own unconquerable temper the men who were gathered about him. I shall have no accounts to give of the meetings of President Simpson with his board of trustees, but the reader may be assured that the same elements of trial entered into them.

We will now hear his own story of his arrival in Greencastle, and of the unpromising aspect of both his college and his personal affairs for a brief time:

" During the winter I received notice of my election as president of the institution, and an earnest letter from Dr. Elliott urging me to accept. Taking the advice of friends again, I accepted and left Meadville in March, 1839, at the close of the winter term of college. We went by stage to Franklin, and took boat down the Allegheny River, staying for some time in Pittsburgh, with Mrs. Simpson's parents, who lived then near the city. I shipped our goods down the Ohio, to be carried by the Wabash River to Terre Haute, and we ourselves took steamer for Cincinnati, where my mother and sister then lived, and thence by stage and private conveyance to Greencastle, the seat of the university. We reached Greencastle on Saturday about two o'clock; it was then a village of about five hundred inhabitants; the houses were generally one-story frames, and small. I asked to be driven

10

to the best hotel, and was taken to a two-story log building, weather-boarded; but it was court week, and the house was full. We were sent to the next best hotel, a small frame building on the public square. It boasted a small bell, but as that was cracked, its tones grated harshly on the ear, and I felt despondent. That hotel was full also, but some of the guests were to leave in the evening, and they agreed we might stay. They were scrubbing the floors, and we were shown to the back porch, where I was compelled for a time to sit with my wife and little boy. I asked in vain for a room, but finally learning that one of the best was occupied by an attorney from a neighboring county seat attending court, I took the responsibility of entering it, and getting a place where my wife could rest until his return from court.

"When he came he was exceedingly polite, and proved to be Judge Hester, then of Bloomington, and afterwards of California. His kindness I shall never forget. In the evening we were invited to the house of one of the trustees, Mr. Hardesty, where we were most kindly entertained until we made other arrangements. Mr. Hardesty's daughter was afterwards married to D. W. Voorhees, then a student in the institution, since United States Senator from Indiana. We had difficulty, however, in securing a boarding place, and on the advice of his relatives and friends we took possession of a tenement house belonging to Dr. Cowgill, a trustee of the university, who was absent with his family in Kentucky. Before his return, I succeeded in renting a house for a few months.

"A college campus of about three acres had been purchased for the university, but was unfenced; the foundation of a college building had been laid and the walls were partially raised; the school exercises were conducted in a small academy building, a two-story brick, containing two rooms below and one above. Two teachers were employed in instructing some forty or fifty boys. The outlook was not very promising, and yet in a new country and in a state

THE OLD SCHOOL-HOUSE FIRST USED BY THE ASBURY UNIVERSITY.

which had a large and fertile territory and a growing population there was room for work and hope. The university had been projected by the Indiana Conference, which contained a number of wise and active men, because there was no other where the sons of Methodist parents could be properly educated without detriment to their faith or morals.

"The board of trustees was composed of members of the Conference and of citizens of Greencastle, with a few from other places who had been selected by the Conference; the preparatory school had been begun the year before I arrived. At the opening of the summer session our number enrolled amounted to between seventy and eighty. I took possession of the upper room of the academy with some of the higher classes, and we endeavored to lay a foundation for the future. As we had then no Sabbath services in the academy building, I visited, as far as I could, the churches in the vicinity, preaching and endeavoring to create an interest in the university. I was most kindly greeted by the brethren in the ministry everywhere, and endeavored to cooperate with them in their work. An educational convention was called to meet in Indianapolis the summer after my arrival, and I attended; it was my first meeting with any of the preachers in Indiana except a few in the vicinity of Greencastle. I was then young, very young for a college president, being only about twenty-eight. I was somewhat amused when Dr. Allen Wiley, an aged member of the Conference, who had corresponded with me and urged me to come, said frankly, though rather bluntly, that he felt rather disappointed in seeing me, I looked so much younger than he expected to find me. I simply replied that that was a difficulty which time would help to cure.

"As to the village of Greencastle, it was then small. The houses were primitive, and the people largely from Kentucky, Tennessee, and North Carolina. There were three church edifices, a Baptist, a Presbyterian, and a Methodist, all of them very plain. The Methodist society was the most numerous, but its building was unfinished. It had a single aisle with movable benches; the men and women sat apart, the men on one side, the women on the other of the aisle. It was not uncommon for the women to come to church in their sun-bonnets, which they took off during the service. While the people were both respectable and pious, society was in almost every sense in a very primitive condition. The outlook was not promising, though it had some elements of hopefulness. As the state was only thinly settled, it was believed that with its growth we might be able to plant an institution which should ultimately become a power for good, and in this spirit I began my labors. The school remained confined to the academy building until the spring of 1840, when some rooms were finished in the new edifice in which recitations were held. The college session closed that year in September; in the vacation I visited Cincinnati, and, returning, attended for a few days the Annual Conference at Lawrenceburg. As this was the first session of the

THE ACADEMY BUILDING USED TILL 1840.

Conference which I had seen, I took a deep interest in be-coming acquainted with its members, and in noticing its mode of doing business.   A sermon was to be preached on the centenary of Wesleyan Methodism, which had its rise in 1739.   Bishop Roberts and Bishop Morris, who were pres-ent, were both unable to deliver such a sermon, and so the invitation came to me.

"The services were held in the forenoon, Conference hav-ing adjourned; the sermon was founded on the 'Vision of waters,' in Ezekiel, and its chief part was a review of the spirit and principles of Methodism.   The effect was some-what peculiar, and was marked by a most singular incident. When I had finished the introduction to my subject, a lady arose in the middle aisle, and, waving her hand, exclaimed, so as to be heard by all, 'Sun, stand thou still and let the moon pass by.'   I was surprised and annoyed, and paused for a moment.   Dr. Goode, who was in the pulpit, began singing a verse or two, and while the congregation joined in the singing some friends led the lady out of church. She was a person of considerable culture and distinction, and her husband was one of the wealthiest men in the community; her mind had been for some time impaired.

"The ministers spoke very kindly of the services, and I was at once taken into the hearts of the preachers of Indiana, who ever after remained my warm friends. At that time the Indiana Conference embraced the whole state, and also a part of Michigan; but in the following General Conference a portion of Michigan was separated from it.

"I did not remain until the Conference adjourned, but learned of a peculiar incident which occurred at its close. During the session I had become acquainted with a young preacher, tall and slender, whose friends lived in the neighborhood. He had been expecting an appointment in that part of the country; when the appointments were read for Indiana he listened patiently for his name, but it did not occur. Last of all, the Michigan appointments were read, and his name was announced for 'White Pigeon.' He had never so much as heard of it, and when Conference closed he sprang upon a bench, and in a peculiarly shrill voice called out aloud, 'Who can tell me where my pigeon is?' He, however, found his 'Pigeon' in due time, and did grand work, establishing the Michigan *Christian Advocate*, and in 1852 was elected editor of the Northwestern *Christian Advocate* in Chicago. He was James V. Watson, whose early death was lamented throughout the Church. I returned to Greencastle in due time and organized the classes for the year.

"We had a small senior class consisting of Thomas A. Goodwin, afterwards a member of the Conference, and long a resident of Indianapolis, and John Wheeler; to these was added, from the state university at Bloomington, Joseph E. McDonald, since United States Senator. Goodwin and Wheeler graduated at the end of the year. McDonald had not finished all his previous studies, but not desiring to spend more than a year, had taken the senior course; subsequently the university gave him the degree of A.M. At the end of the college term, which occurred in September, the new building was finished; indeed, we had occupied some of its rooms during the summer. At the commencement an immense throng filled its chapel. In addition to the graduating services, Governor Wallace delivered the charge, and handed me the keys, and I followed with an inaugural address. Several short impromptu addresses were added. At night Henry Ward Beecher, then a Presbyterian minister settled in Indianapolis, delivered an address before the literary society. Conference sat that year in Indianapolis, Bishop Soule presiding; great interest in the college was shown, and the ministers resolved to found a library. The bishop was impatient to finish the Conference business, but our catalogue was in press and about ready for distribution. As a leading member of Conference wished the distribution to be made before Conference adjourned, he used a stratagem to detain the bishop. The bishop had been appointed by the General Conference to visit the Wesleyan Conferences in Ireland and England the next year; a resolution was introduced requesting him during his visit to act as a friend in purchasing suitable books for our library, should the money be raised on that resolution. Speeches were made showing the importance of this action, and how much the bishop could do for the interests of the university. He listened with comparative patience until the catalogues were brought in; then the resolution was adopted, and the bishop closed the Conference.

"When I removed to Indiana, a railroad extending a few miles from Madison towards Indianapolis was the only public improvement of that period in the state. A canal had been constructed, for which the state had incurred much debt, but which was not a success. A few Indians lived on a reservation near the Wabash, and a few colored people had migrated from the adjacent slave states, but the people being largely of Southern origin, there was but little anti-slavery feeling, though a large percentage of the population had left the slave states to get away from slavery. There were very few manufactures at that time attempted. There being no outlet by railroad for provisions, and the soil being rich, provisions were abundant and cheap. The subsequent opening of railroads and the establishment of manufactories tended to raise the price of food. The state had a fair common-school law, but owing to the scattered condition of the population, and the lack of the early education of many parents the system was not worked efficiently. There were a few academies in the larger towns, and the state had built and endowed the state university at Bloomington. The Presbyterians, then divided into old and new schools, had established a new college at Hanover, near Madison; the new-school branch had established a college at Crawfordsville; the Catholics had a college at Vincennes, and the Baptists were about founding a college at Franklin. "

VIII.

THE COLLEGE PRESIDENT AND HIS TRIALS.

1839–1848.

Disappointment on Both Sides.—The Bare Beginnings of a University.—
President Simpson Enlists the Aid of the Methodist Preachers.—En-
couragement Given to Plain but Promising Boys.—Cynthiana Circuit.—A Stirring Appeal.—The First Faculty.—Descriptions of the
President by Former Students.—Colonel John Ray's Account.—" He
is My President."—Dr. Simpson's Versatility.—His Methods in the
Lecture-Room.—Ex-Governor Porter's Narrative.—Dr. T. A. Good-
win's Story of his Journey to Greencastle.—Rough Riding with
Two on One Horse.—" Not Much of a University, I Reckon."—The
President's Rules for the Direction of His Own Life.—The Inaugura-
tion.—Governor Wallace's Address of Welcome.—The President's
Address.—The Charge of Sectarianism Answered.—The University
and State Politics.—Incessant Labors.—The Heroisms of Methodist
Education.

VIII.

The reception of Matthew Simpson in Greencastle was decidedly chilling; indeed, it may be said that there was, for a time, a feeling of discontent on both sides. To begin with, the appearance of the new president was wholly disappointing. He was a younger man than the friends of the university had expected to find him, being barely twenty-seven. A leading trustee said that he had supposed he would see in the new president a man, but found only a stripling. Tradition, which delights to exaggerate personal peculiarities, declares that in his outward bearing he was, at this time of his life, altogether unprepossessing; with a stooping gait, and awkward, almost bashful manners. The president, on the other side, must have been sick at heart to find that he could, with difficulty, secure a resting-place for his feet, or a shelter for his head. Among the people of the village there was a general shaking of heads, accompanied with the ominous foreboding, "He won't do!" "He won't do!" Sunday came; the villagers flocked to the church to hear the stranger preach. Of what was the theme, and what its treatment, there is no report. In the pulpit he was on his throne, and he laid on his hearers the spell of his eloquence. They were charmed, melted, conquered. And as they separated, after the close of service, the changing opinion expressed itself on the vital question. "He will do!" "He will do!" was whispered or murmured by every Methodist of the outgoing crowd to his neighbor; and the place he won in the hearts of the people of Indiana that day was never lost.

It makes one smile when one pauses to consider what a

contradiction it was of the fact, to read that a school so elementary was called a university. But the title drew upon the future, and expressed the hopes and ambitions of the founders rather than their achievement. They outlined boldly, and, in this country at least, the man of large conceptions, if he have a good cause and common-sense, usually proves to be right. Yet the facts of the condition of the school were discouraging enough. Of endowment there was not so much as a beginning; the means for the payment of teachers had to be derived from tuition fees—of necessity, small—the sale of scholarships (and these sold at low rates), and collections from the churches. Money was scarce ; the financial disasters of 1837, which almost wrecked the business of the country, were still felt in 1839. The university paid its professors in its own scrip, and the scrip was turned into money on the best terms that could be made.

In this condition of affairs President Simpson judged that the vital matter for him was to secure the university a warm place in the affections of the Methodist preachers of Indiana, and through the preachers to reach the churches. To this end he associated himself with them as closely as he could consistently with a right performance of his college duties. His Sundays were given to preaching throughout the state ; long tours were taken on horseback, with a preaching appointment for nearly every day; at the great gatherings, the camp-meetings, he was always a conspicuous figure. In these tours he rapidly developed his extraordinary preaching power ; his name became a household word in all the state, and his eloquence was so prized that he was called for from all quarters. The effect of his exertions was that a genuine enthusiasm for the university was created among plain people. Promising boys, who had known nothing all their lives but farm labor and the little knowledge which the common schools could give, were drawn from their secluded homes and set upon careers of usefulness and honor. But the struggle for life was very real and very serious. Professor Larrabee writes in 1844 to President Simpson, during one of the absences of the latter from Greencastle:

" Owen ——, the university's agent, has been here. He arrived after dark one Saturday night, and left at three o'clock the next morning. He brought scarcely any money. They scraped together enough to pay the bank instalment, but had nothing left for us. He has obtained subscriptions for the endowment of your chair amounting to $1010 in notes and $400 in produce. The $1010 was collected from the 24th of February to the 9th of March, on Evansville and Cynthiana circuits, but he did not get over all parts even of these. The conclusion to which he has come is, that he can raise $1.50 to every member on the poorest circuit in the state. The junior preacher in Cynthiana circuit received only $7.50 at the last quarterly meeting. The circuit members are more willing to subscribe for the university than for paying their preachers or building parsonages."

We of our time may be disposed to pity that junior preacher of Cynthiana Circuit, but his was the common lot of the junior preachers of the day. Besides, had he not the privilege of preaching the everlasting gospel? Had he not, too, a home in every Methodist house within the boundaries of his circuit? And were not the motherly dames who attended his ministrations knitting for him woollen socks and mittens by the dozen, to keep fingers and toes warm in the rough winter weather? What need of money for him? But a circuit subscribing more for a university—partly in Greencastle, but mostly in cloudland—than for its own wants, presents a spectacle worth dwelling upon. We suspect, too, that the like was true of other circuits; all such cases go to show the force of the feeling aroused in the Methodists of the state by the whirlwind of President Simpson's eloquence.

There is among the papers of Bishop Simpson a draft of an address to the Methodist preachers of the state, which tells clearly the story of the difficulties environing him and the school placed under his charge. In it he appeals for money wherewith to procure a library and philosophical apparatus; for both these the necessary Conference resolutions had been obtained. We quote some passages which let in light upon the situation:

"At least from five to eight thousand dollars will be necessary for philosophical apparatus, and from twelve to fifteen thousand for a library. Brethren, furnish these to the institution, and its course must be onward and upward.

"You owe it to the Church of which you are members to do this. You know that as a community we have patiently borne more than ordinary reproach. In our commencement the pulpit, press, and mob were all against us. But arguments held in check the denunciations of the one, and Christian meekness calmed the violence of the other. But when more direct attacks ceased, then the indirect commenced. The united voices of the literary class were against us. We had no college, and, though we increased in numbers, we were allowed no representation in the management of those institutions in which, as a part of the people, we had equal interest. If our sons were sent to college the religion of their fathers was made a subject of derision, and many were drawn into the bosom of other churches, or ruined with the licentiousness of infidelity. We were branded as ignorant, as fanatics, as enthusiasts. What should we do? Just what you have done; quietly leave others in possession of the public funds, patiently be refused any representation in the Faculty of state institutions, and in answer to the charge of ignorance, incapacity, etc., found institutions that should shun comparison with none around them. This, brethren, has been your course, and as a church we are prospering greatly, but we must not stop until we possess every advantage essential to prosperity.

"You owe it to yourselves. You have begun in this enterprise; your character is staked upon it. Friends are wishing you success, and enemies are hoping for your failure. Predictions were made some time since that the institution would never go into successful operation, but now that more students are found in its halls than in those of any other college in the state, the predictions are now that it will not be permanent. It has been stigmatized as the "Poor Man's College" by those who desire to claim for themselves all the wealth and honor of the community. By others it is denounced publicly as "sectarian." Yes, there be some that even in this matter appear to glory in their shame. They have denounced you as ignorant, monopolized the public funds among themselves, pronounced you as unable to manage the institution, and when, in the spirit of meekness, you have resigned your money into their hands rather than engage in angry contention, and turned aside to found one of your own where you were willing to send your sons, then the cry has been raised—"You are sectarian." Yes, brethren, you are sectarian for daring to educate your own children according to the dictates of your judgments. Ah, brethren, I have misjudged both your intelligence and piety if such a course will have any other effect than to awaken pity for your enemies, and to show them by your acts that you are both able and willing to rally unitedly around your own university. If you do this, the venom of our adversaries shall be their own poison, and posterity will applaud both your Christian meekness and your liberality."

It is plain that the relations between the State University at Bloomington and the Methodists of Indiana were not, in this period, at all comfortable. This subject occupies, for several years, a large part of the correspondence of President Simpson and his friends. The letters speak of covert and open attacks of enemies of Methodism in such terms as to show that the antagonism was felt to be very real. More than this need not be said; this much needed to be said to show the feeling with which the president wrought at his tasks from 1839 to 1848. The first distribution of duty among the members of the faculty was wholly provisional. All the professors were ministers: Matthew Simpson is professor of mathematics and natural science, Cyrus Nutt, professor of Latin and Greek, and John B. Weakley is principal of the preparatory department; the total number of students is eleven. In 1840 there are twenty-two regular and forty-three irregular students, fifty-eight in the preparatory school, and the large college building is announced as finished. As it is not the purpose of this book to follow the history of the university, it will suffice to say that from these feeble beginnings it has grown to an attendance of nearly nine hundred students, a faculty of forty-three members, and an endowment of nearly a million and a half of dollars from the estate of Washington C. De Pauw, in addition to the endowment previously accumulated, with schools of liberal arts, law, theology, music, and art. The confidence of President Simpson that through the Methodist preachers enthusiasm for culture might be made a passion of the every-day people of the state has been justified by the event. De Pauw University—to give the new name—is one of the best evidences the country can furnish of the thoughtful liberality of a homely but self-respecting democracy.

The university students of the Simpson period speak of their president with unbounded enthusiasm. Their terms of eulogy seem to the cool and unbiassed hearer excessive, but all concur in the testimony given. Those who have risen to the highest positions of honor, as they look back upon their college days with the eyes of men thoroughly versed in the world, abate nothing of their early admiration of Dr. Simpson. The qualities on which they dwell are his unfailing tact, great versatility, and absolute devotion to the young men placed under his care. It will best show this part of the bishop's life to hear from some of them. We will take first Colonel John Ray, now of Indianapolis, a son of one of the pioneer preachers of Indiana:

"The first year the institution was manned by Professor Cyrus W. Nutt, who constituted the entire faculty, and did not get money enough for that year's service to pay his postage. Two years passed before Dr. Simpson took charge as president. There was no endowment fund nor money in the treasury; in fine, not a very encouraging outlook. All the faculty, save Tutor Wheeler, however, were Methodist preachers, and therefore the work must be wrought, sacrifices endured, faith must end in fruition.

"Dr. Simpson early grasped the situation. He knew that if Methodist hearts were warmed, Methodist wills set in action, the university would prove equal to the plans of its projectors. Therefore he spent the greater part of the Sabbaths in the pulpits of the state. Indiana then had no railroads, save as rails were taken off the fences and laid crosswise to prevent the miring of horses and wagons. The trusty horse, saddle, and saddle-bags were the travelling conveniences of the Methodist preachers, and a swimming horse was both bridge and ferry over the creeks and rivers. Many of the roads were indicated only by the felling of trees along the line. From town to town Dr. Simpson went, conquering opposition to higher education, overcoming the many objections which were raised, and everywhere stimulating Methodists to put forth their noblest efforts in behalf of Asbury.

"The writer first saw Dr. Simpson when thus engaged. He was to preach in our village. One student had ventured, and several were thinking of entering the university. Of course all the boys whose heads had been turned towards Asbury went to hear him preach. Mother's rule required, when she did not go to church, that two hymns and the text must be reported, as evidence of attendance. Until the day Dr. Simpson preached, hymns and text were about all of the service appropriated. When he went into the pulpit, clothed in a blue cassinette suit,* with his low brow, stoop shoulders, and ungainly appearance, boyish disappointment filled my mind, and the thought was, 'Not much of a president.'

"He took the hymn-book; a bright gleam shot over his face, his voice was so musical that melody was not needed, and then, as he lined the verses, inspiration seemed to fall on the people. Never had such reading charmed my ear. And then the prayer. So importunate, so full of loving trust, so like a child pleading with the Father; surely this man is talking face to face with God. By the time the prayer closed all disappointment vanished. The Scripture was read in that same sweet, flutelike tone; again the hymn, and then the sermon—such a sermon as Matthew Simpson only could preach. Enraptured, completely satisfied, flying steps took me to my mother, who could not go to church that day, and the greeting was, 'Mother, I tell you he is my president.'

"All over Indiana he went, like a hero, winning, with their parents' sympathy, scores of boys, who in like manner, though compelled to sacrifice and economy, entered themselves as students.

"He was not only the preacher who went through the state arousing hearts to new ambitions, but when the boys reached Greencastle he was their best friend. Easy of approach, with an ear ever ready to listen, wise in counsel, willing to aid in every way possible, he endeared the students, who appreciated their opportunity, to him. Of course his rule was firm; but his hand of steel was always cased in velvet. Though comparatively a young man, the boys soon dubbed him 'Old Doc.' He measured the young men critically. They were all known to him by name. Carefully did he look after them from the hour of entering the university, and long after he became bishop would he recall the names of the old students and manifest intense anxiety concerning them. He

---

* When President Simpson came to Indiana, he was clad in the clerical black; but before long he dressed in the home-made blue-gray cloth much used throughout the state.

11

was a rigid disciplinarian. Laws were to be obeyed, and we all understood that so well that discipline was but seldom required.

"He knew just how to treat each so that lasting impressions would be made. Even in rebukes he was kind. An incident will illustrate. A student, of a leading family, unfortunately loved his cups. There were no crossings between the few sidewalks in the village, and one dark night, with the mud several inches deep, this student wanted to cross the street to reach his room. Just then Dr. Simpson came along and was gruffly accosted, 'Buck up here and carry me across this street.' The request was complied with, and when the other pavement was reached the doctor said, calling him by name, 'I think you have ridden far enough.' That voice was recognized instantly, and the young man reached his room, hearing nothing further from his president. The occurrence would not have been known had it been left to the president to tell it. The student told it himself, and he never again tampered with liquor while in the university.

"He was a most excellent judge of human nature. In an adjoining county a family lived, poor in this world, but rich in brain, grace, and industry. Their son, a boy whose pocket-money was the result of his gatherings of nuts and wild fruits, heard of the university, and tying up a change of homespun clothing, started to obtain an education. Board in Greencastle ranged from fifty cents to one dollar and a half a week. But so slender was the chance for this boy to pay, that he could not get board. So, true to his manhood, he went to Dr. Simpson's room and asked 'if he was the man who kept school there?' Being answered, he said 'he had come to get an education, but he failed to find a boarding-place, and if he could have the use of an empty room in the building he would make fires and sweep rooms for pay, and try to get his board some way.' Of course he was accommodated. When he graduated, his best dress while receiving the highest honors of his class was a calico morning-gown. Within sixty days of the commencement a committee visited Dr. Simpson, looking for a president for a Western college, and were told the man was then within thirty miles of Greencastle. They had started for the east of the Alleghanies, and were surprised to hear Dr. Simpson so speak. But they sent for the Indiana boy, and took him home as their college president. The legislature the same year made him superintendent of public instruction, and since then he has served the state of his adoption as United States senator, and has also been a cabinet officer. When a student, Dr. Simpson had measured him, and therefore could sincerely commend him as suited for the presidency of a college.

"He loved to help the ambitious. At the opening of the second term of a student who was freshman in Latin and mathematics, but preparatory in Greek, Dr. Simpson was surprised to see him present himself for admission to the freshman Greek, just one year in advance of the class he should be in. 'Why are you here?' was the query; the answer, 'I want to go into this class.' A shake of the head and another query, 'Where were you last year?' 'In the preparatory.' 'But you cannot maintain yourself in this class.' 'Try me.' At once the cloud went off from Dr. Simpson's face, and smiling he turned to Prof. Tefft, who had charge of Greek, and said, 'Professor, what do you say?' Tefft questioned the lad, and finally said, 'Dr. Simpson, I'll vouch for the boy.' He went in the class, and Dr. Simpson helped him from that day on to graduation.

"Thoroughness in study was required of every one who sat in the classes taught by Dr. Simpson. He said to one of the boys, 'There are three things that make history a difficult study — names, dates, and events.' Being answered 'if he would excuse the names and dates, he should have the events,' at once he pointed out the need of thorough mastery of every study. His teaching was eminently practical. Theories that did not work well in practice found no favor with him. In teaching mental and moral science he was constantly illustrating the text from occurrences of every-day life. He taught us the advantage of woman suffrage, as opening wider fields of usefulness for women, employing all their faculties; and demonstrated that neighborhood gossip and scandals were largely the result of unoccupied heads and tongues. He was at his best when, the regular recitation past and the hour not yet spent, he would engage with his classes in conversation. With a mind filled with knowledge, varied as the walks of life itself, he sought to turn our thoughts to the duties of the future which we were fitting ourselves for. Our talks were as free as though he were our comrade instead of being our president. Never once was there a trespass on the proprieties of the relation he held to us, but his great loving nature expanded so that there was no hedge between us.

"In conversation he was brilliant, magnetic. It mattered not what the theme was—abstract science, mathematics, logic, rhetoric, languages, history, politics—he was equally versed in all, and his classes were always delighted when he would lead them outside the routine of the hour. Many a plan was arranged to have part of the recitation hour given to these delightful talks in which all were free to participate, he leading.

"He had great faith in putting the students on their honor. A rule forbade a student going beyond the limits of the town during college hours, unless by special permission of one of the faculty. Of course acquaintances were made with many of the families near the village, and an application to Dr. Simpson for suspension of this rule as to individuals was always granted, if the student would promise good behavior while absent from the town. By every means he sought to build up the manhood of those who were placed under his charge. At times during the temporary absence of other professors he taught their classes, and it was a matter of amazement to all of us how admirably he taught Greek, Latin, physical science, equally as well as the studies of his special chair.

"Eminent as Dr. Simpson was in his position of president, teacher, friend, all his greatness was magnified when he sought to teach the religion of the Lord Jesus Christ. He was more zealous to make Christians out of the students than to impart secular instruction. Never, in the three years the writer was a student, did Dr. Simpson lead in prayer in the chapel that he failed to use substantially this sentence, ' O Lord, we pray thee that while these young men are seeking knowledge which will fit them for this life, they may obtain that higher knowledge the beginning of which is the fear of the Lord.' He loved to meet the students in class-meeting, the prayer circle. Rarely did he let a chance pass when he did not talk of religion. He never spoke in the chapel about the doctrines and polity of the Methodist Episcopal Church, but he so thoroughly illustrated the results of an unwavering devotion to his Church that no words were needed to turn large numbers of the students into the Methodist fold. In the revival meetings he was almost always present. Actively engaged as he might be, neglecting no duty connected with his chair, his place in the revival meetings was rarely vacant. During a most wonderful season in 1847, recitations were practically suspended for ten days or two weeks. Classes met on bell-ringing in their respective rooms, and religious services filled the hour. During this meeting none were so active and so constantly employed as Dr. Simpson. He seemed like a father, weeping with the penitent, and utilizing the matchless power of his eloquence to win souls for Christ; and with such success that the entire town was for days more like a camp-meeting than anything else. There were three public services daily, and for a time the stores and places of business were closed during service hours.

"More than forty years have passed since the writer first saw Dr. Simpson, heard his voice, listened to his expositions of secular and spiritual knowledge; and while enlarged acquaintance has afforded opportunity to compare others with him, the brief sentence of a college friend expresses the thought now uppermost—'He was the greatest man I ever knew.' Of course boyhood's ideas are of the superlative degree; but the speech above quoted was made since Bishop Simpson's death, by an active business man past sixty years, and is now repeated by one who is not far from the same age."

Ex-Governor A. G. Porter, of Indiana, who has had large experience in public life, speaks in the same affectionate terms of President Simpson. We draw from an address upon the life and character of Bishop Simpson, delivered by him shortly after the bishop's death:

"I remember, as if it were but yesterday, the occasion when I first saw him. I was a bashful boy of sixteen, who had come to enter the preparatory department of the college, and I called at his house. He looked to me like a plain, warm-hearted, and hospitable farmer, and in after-life he always looked to me so. He greeted me with overflowing kindness; he talked to me of the studies that I was about to pursue; he called in his wife and introduced me to her; and they both invited me to visit them often, and assured me I should always be gladly received. And they meant what they said; as they welcomed me, so they welcomed other students. He was in like manner social and kind with the townspeople of Greencastle. They have always been warm-hearted and generous, and they repaid his kindness with boundless affection. I do not believe there was ever a day, after he became known to the people of Putnam County, until he quit the college, that he was not the most popular and best-loved man in the county.

"He took a personal interest in every student, and watched over the education and morals of them all. He appealed to their honor and manliness when they were inclined to go astray. He seemed always to know what was going on among them, and wanted no spies. On one occasion, I remember, after there had been some rude disorder at night on the streets, which he disapproved, he called attention to the matter in chapel. He expressed mortification at the occurrence, and uttered strong words of reproof. He said that he should not institute investigation to learn the names of the guilty. He knew the parties. He had been with them. He had affected to take part with them. He knew the names as well as the deeds. He would not repeat these names. He would trust to the honor of these young men that there would be no repetition of disgraceful occurrences. The reproof and appeal were the most effectual of punishments. And there grew up a feeling afterwards that he was ubiquitous, and that if doors were barred to conceal any forbidden thing that was going on, Bishop Simpson was more likely to be locked in than to be locked out.

"He had a keen appreciation of whatever was humorous. I recollect that at a time when the third story of the college was unfinished, students were told that they must not go into that part of the building, as their noise disturbed the professors who were conducting recitations below them. One day a mischievous and frolicksome boy, now a banker of this city, conducted a number of his companions to the prohibited third story. Dr. Simpson came upon them, and, picking up a lath, applied it to the embryo banker; not so much to hurt as to frighten him. A day or two after, this boy was one of a considerable number at a dinner, when, speaking up, he addressed the doctor with, 'Dr. Simpson, you lathed me the other day; I'd like to know when you are going to plaster me.' The bishop became very red in the face, and, unable to restrain his mirth, broke into a hearty laugh. He made himself familiar with the students, and enjoyed them and was enjoyed by them.

" He was a great teacher, for he encouraged pupils to think. No book was authority. Whatever statement would not stand the test of argument was to be condemned. He encouraged students to challenge every statement which their judgment did not approve; and, when challenged, the soundness of the statement was debated in the class-room. It was the custom in his day for ambitious young men to have mottoes as an incentive to endeavor. These mottoes were written in their books. His was, I remember, " Read and know. Think and be wise." He did not read idly for amusement, but to store his mind with knowledge. Nor was knowledge enough. Thought must be applied to it; it must be assimilated; it must make wiser, and thus make the man more useful. He did not usually read a book line for line, but had that faculty for rapid reading which Macaulay had of taking in nearly a page at a time —like those mathematical prodigies who can add up columns of figures by seeming to grasp the sum of a whole column at once instead of adding up the figures separately."

The first graduate of the university, the Rev. Doctor T. A. Goodwin, has described his journey in 1837 from his home in Indiana to Greencastle, the seat of the university, a distance of one hundred and ten miles. It cost the student, in those days, no small exertion to reach the place where he would be educated :

" At last November came. The fall term was to open on the first Monday. There was but one way to get to Greencastle, that was by stage to Putnamville, and from that place to Greencastle as best I could. I left Brookville Wednesday at noon, expecting to reach Greencastle by Friday night. The first seventeen miles were travelled in a two-horse coach. It had been raining for two weeks. There were no turnpikes then in Indiana. We were six hours in reaching Bulltown. From that to Indianapolis the coach that had been running three times a week had been taken off on account of bad roads, and a two-horse wagon, without cover or springs, had been substituted. In this, before daylight, we started, hoping to make Indianapolis, fifty-three miles distant, before the stage west should leave at ten that night. But we failed. It rained all day, and Rush County roads were at their worst. The corduroy was afloat in many places, and the creeks and rivers, unbridged, were bank full. Night overtook us about ten miles from Indianapolis, and it was dark as pitch. About eight o'clock our wagon broke down six miles from Indianapolis, in the middle of a mud hole. We were half a mile from any house and without a particle of light. We soon discovered that the wagon could go no farther. There were three of us, the driver, an agent of the stage line, and myself. The only baggage was my trunk and the mail pouch. After considering the situation, it was determined that the driver should ride one horse, without a saddle, of course, and carry my trunk before him; the stage agent should ride the other, and carry the mail pouch before him and me behind him. By this conveyance I made my first entrance into Indianapolis about eleven o'clock, the first Thursday night of November, 1837. The town was fast asleep, and hence our procession down Washington Street, single file, the driver in the lead, with my trunk before him, created no marked sensation, and no mention was made of it in the city papers next morning. As the stage for St. Louis had been gone an hour or more, nothing could be done but to wait a day."

His troubles were not at an end; another stage ride of like kind had to be encountered, and in four days the journey was accomplished. This is what he saw upon his arrival:

" Notwithstanding I had been informed before leaving home that the necessary buildings were not yet finished, and Mr. T. had told me they were not even begun, and probably never would be, I had not been able to fully realize the situation. Visions of stately buildings like those at Oxford, and a corps of learned professors, would stand before me; hence, after reaching the town I had strained my eyes to catch a glimpse of things that were not. Gladly dismissing Mr. T. with his two dollars, I turned for comfort to Mr. Lynch, my new landlord, still unwilling to topple my air castle and dismiss my dreams. In answer to my question where the university was, he said, 'I don't know for certain. It was, last summer, at the deestrict schoolhouse, but I have hearn that they have moved it to the county siminary. Be you come to go to it? You will not find it much of a university, I reckon.' "

The following passage shows the primitive condition of society in the state, and, as a rule, the character of the homes, rich in all Christian graces, from which the young men came:

" Surveying the field from this semi-centennial elevation, one who was a part of its earliest struggles and triumphs would emphasize a feature of this university which has characterized it from the beginning. Its first students all came from homes of comparative poverty, from that class whose daily bread is dependent on daily toil and constant frugality. They were led to these halls in most cases by the faithful agents whose duty was to at once obtain pecuniary aid and create a hunger and thirst for knowledge. It is not extravagant to say that of the first thousand who attended this institution seven hundred would never have attended any schools higher than the very poor country schools of the period but for the influence of the college agents, seconded by the faithful preachers of that day. To this must be added the wonderful magnetism of our first president. Wherever he went to preach he awakened an interest in the university.

Reticent as President Simpson was in relation to his personal feelings, we find notices here and there of the sense which he carried with him of the serious responsibility of his undertaking. He knew that the source of all his strength was a real spiritual life. I find, under date of August 1, 1840, this memorandum :

" 1. I purpose, God being my helper, to rest at nine and rise at four invariably.

" 2. Always to read a chapter in the Bible with notes or three without.

" 3. To write every duty down which occurs to my mind.

" 4. To allot it its proper time, and suffer nothing but what is uncontrollable to prevent me from doing it at that time.

" 5. Converse no more on politics, unless in answer to a question propounded.

" 6. Avoid foolish jesting, and try to turn all conversation to profit.

" 7. Have seasons of prayer each day : 1. Rising. 2. After reading. 3. After breakfast. 4. After morning college. 5. After dinner. 6. After evening college. 7. After supper or walk. 8. Before retiring.

" 8. Resolved to leave all company resolutely at half-past eight, and spend fifteen minutes in writing diary and reading Greek Testament, and fifteen in prayer and retiring.

"9. This I purpose if Christ strengthen so poor a sinner as I. Here I covenant, sign with my hand, solemnly and irrevocably to give myself to God. But I must watch incessantly. O for power to prevail with God! These rules are especially designed for August, 1840. May God in mercy for Christ's sake enable a poor sinner to keep them. M. SIMPSON.

"P. S.—Read these rules once every day."

It is customary, nowadays, to speak slightingly of such plans for methodizing spiritual exercises. They are thought to imply a morbid condition of mind; but the mind of President Simpson was eminently healthy; no one could be more cheery, more buoyant, more practical; no one could enjoy more gratefully the blessings which life brought him; but he knew himself, feared for himself, and fled to the strong One for refuge. Thomas Carlyle has sneered at the introspective habit of Methodism, by describing it as "always looking at its own navel." It would be easy to retort upon Thomas Carlyle always looking at his own stomach, and finding in its miseries the centre of his mortal life. This would be unjust and unreasonable, but no more unjust and no more unreasonable than his own contemptuous phrase. The symptom-watching style of Christian life is in some measure passing away; but it had in it a sober sense of human weakness, and a constant fear of the approaches of wrong. It was satisfied with nothing less than a conscious communion with God through prayer.

By September, 1840, the university was sufficiently organized to admit of an imposing demonstration. The people were called together from all parts of the state, and the president delivered his inaugural address. Governor David Wallace, after a suitable speech of welcome, handed over to him the keys of the newly completed university building. His speech of welcome recognizes the fact that Indiana had just passed the log-cabin stage of growth, and that the pioneers who had carried through the wilderness the message of divine truth were, with their immediate successors, the founders of this rising school of learning. The style is flowery, but the thought is good:

"But to whom, it may be asked, are we and the country indebted for this noble manifestation in behalf of such a cause? Whose minds conceived, whose benevolence prompted, whose energies achieved the erection of this edifice, and on a spot, too, where the sound of the woodman's axe, as he felled the forest around him, has scarcely died away upon our ears? Nay, whose imaginations so vivid—so pregnant, as it were, with creative power—as to give birth to so wild and novel a conception as that of planting the garden of the Muses on the yet unredeemed bosom of the wilderness? Be not surprised, and revere them none the less for it, when I tell you that they are old and familiar acquaintances—endeared to us by some of the sweetest, purest, and holiest recollections of the heart. They have been the companions of our pioneer fathers; they have been our moral and religious instructors. Spurning the luxuries of life—the refinements of taste and elegance, the comforts of ease and affluence, the allurements of the world—with the spirit of a Wesley only to nerve them they laughed the dangers of flood and field to scorn, looked the terrors of the wilderness in the face with cheeks unblanched, endured cold and hunger without a murmur, encountered privation and peril without shrinking, and died by the wayside even, leaving no memorial of their burial place—and for what? That the voice of supplication and prayer might rise from the deepest solitudes of our valleys; that the lamp of eternal life might be lit up in the recesses of our lone cabins; that the departing spirits of their rude but noble tenants might be cheered and sustained and reconciled in that awful hour by the glorious promises of another and a better world. And now—even now—that all these stirring scenes are with the past; that the dreaded solitudes are no more; that fen and forest and river have been shorn of their terrors; that hungry want and chilling privation have been banished from our hearths; these men—so fearless, so self-sacrificing, so persevering, whose approach to our solitary abodes has so often brought childhood's sunniest smile to our cheeks—are still with us; but, unlike everything else about them, they have not changed. The same sternness of purpose, the same unflagging zeal, the same untiring effort as in the beginning still stamp their conduct and action. They have suffered no pause in their labors, and follow the steps of improvement now, only to gather materials and to seize occasions the better to scatter the choicest of Heaven's blessings along their pathway."

ORIGINAL COLLEGE BUILDING, GREENCASTLE.

BENTLEY HALL, ALLEGHENY COLLEGE.

The inaugural address was admirably suited to its purpose, namely, to awaken a sense of the value of education
in the minds of a frontier people. It has, what many addresses of the kind lack, a beginning, middle, and end. It
starts out with the assertion that man is the creature of education; that he is perpetually receiving an education; that
our only power is to *choose in what* youth shall be educated.
The thought of an election of studies by students fresh from
farm and forest was not in his mind or in his plan. He
proceeds to argue that individual character depends on the
kind of education received, and that national character depends upon the same cause, and so gathers up a cumulative
argument which must have made a great impression upon
the assembly. His plea for the ancient classic languages is
manly, and is the plea of one who has tasted their sweetness.

But still better is his plea for Christianity in culture,
and his repulse of the charge of sectarianism if culture
be made Christian: "If by sectarianism be meant that any
privilege shall be extended to youth of one denomination
more than another, or that the faculty shall endeavor to
proselyte those placed under their instruction, or dwell upon
the minor points controverted between the great branches
of the Christian family, then there is not, and we hope
there never will be, sectarianism here. But if by sectarianism be meant that the professors are religious men, and
that they have settled views upon Christian character and
duty, then we ever hope to be sectarian. And what institution is not? Where can the line be drawn? If it be
sectarian to differ from one man's religion, then it is equally
sectarian to differ from that of another. Where shall we
pause? We must not believe in a future state of rewards
and punishments, for that is sectarian. We must not teach
that the Messiah has appeared, or the Jew cries out "sectarian." We must not claim the Bible as inspired, or the
Deist is shocked at our illiberality. We must not deny the
existence of pagan gods, or Nero's torch is the brilliant

argument against sectarianism. Nay, we must not admit
the existence of a God, or the Atheist will rail at our want
of liberal feeling. What then shall we do? Whether Pagans or Atheists, Mohammedans or Jews, Deists or Christians, still they are sectarian. The only persons who are
properly free from sectarianism are those who either believe
all things or who believe *nothing.*"

The inaugural address, both while in preparation and
after its delivery, deeply interested the watchful uncle, who
was still the mentor of his beloved boy. He advises the
president that he must not undertake too much, or expect too much from himself in the circumstances of his
position:

" Your having to attend to all the duties of the college, together with
the anxiety about your absent family, and other incidental labors, must
make much against you in preparing the inaugural; for that would need
your undivided attention, and I have no doubt that those who have made
such luminous addresses had leisure to attend to the subjects of them
and were free from other embarrassments. But you, in all your attempts
to do anything important, have been clogged with other cares; yet, the
Lord being with you, you have acquitted yourself with as much credit
as you ought to desire; and I hope so it will be in this case. And, indeed, if the prayers of one so unworthy as I am can avail in your behalf, you will always excel, both in knowledge and usefulness; reputation
would follow as a matter of course. There are few men, if any, who
have had greater facility in acquiring a knowledge of literature, languages, and science than yourself. And why should you be mortified if
some others should be rated higher than you in speech-making? Yours
will be good and fully equal to what the best of them at your age and
experience could have made; therefore endeavor to avoid anxiety about
it; commit yourself and your work to God, and be content to pass for
what you are worth."

Upon the assured success of the address, the uncle writes
again, mingling with the reports of the approbation of distinguished men sober counsels:

" I had a conversation with Charles Elliott on your inaugural, and he
said it was great, but had some faults; no, not faults either, but in some

places it might have been improved, but it was such as he could not make. Some two or three weeks since I was at Hamline's house, and he said he had been looking over President Simpson's address; and I said, 'What do you think of it?' He answered, 'It is great.' I said, 'He has never had time to cultivate a fine style.' He answered, 'The language of that address is fine indeed; upon the whole it was the best inaugural made by any Methodist preacher at the head of a college. President Olin's might be written in a smoother style, but was much inferior.' I said, 'You do not think it above criticism?' He said, 'No; he had never yet seen anything so perfect as not to leave some room for the critic. You were so perfectly unassuming you must command an unbounded respect.' When such men as L. L. Hamline praise your work it amounts to something. But while I am exceeding joyful at the success of your performance, I would admonish thee to remember whence cometh thy strength, and in deep humility adore that fountain of light from whence a ray has enlightened thee. And remember, too, that popularity of any kind is very uncertain; it is a variable breeze on which you may now float to the clouds, and then sink to the bottom of the ocean, and mere trifles may be the occasion of the rise and fall."

His manner of roughing it in Indiana, when trying to serve the university, is described in a letter to Mrs. Simpson, then in Pittsburgh visiting her father's family:

"The evening after you left I spent in Cincinnati, and the next day I expected to leave in the mail boat, but just as I got through my business and reached the wharf the boat shoved off and I was left. I engaged my passage on one to leave at four o'clock, but it did not leave till eleven at night. We ran slowly all night, and did not arrive in Madison until after the cars had started. There I was detained a day. Next day took the cars at Madison and arrived at Vernon, where I had left my horse, expecting to go on immediately, as the waters were rising and it was supposed would soon be impassable. The gentleman with whom I had left my horse had loaned him to a young man to go into the country. The young man had not returned, and so there I was detained. An appointment was circulated for me to preach, and I endeavored to fill it; but it commenced raining, and rained so incessantly I had a small congregation. The next day it continued to rain and the waters were much swollen, and the young man did not return with my horse. I found myself obliged either to remain there, or to procure some other conveyance; a man who had seen my horse offered to trade for him another horse by giving some boot. This I concluded to do, and so left in the afternoon.

The streams were all high, and over three of them my horse swam, while I went over in a canoe. With much difficulty I reached Indianapolis Saturday night, after Mr. Wilkins's family had nearly all gone to bed. I stayed with them and preached twice on Sabbath. I also spent Monday and Tuesday morning there. Tuesday noon I left for Belleville, where I arrived in the evening, and, according to previous appointment, preached a sermon. And on Wednesday noon found myself once more in Greencastle in as good health as I usually enjoy. Our college commenced at the usual time in our new building, and thus far things move pleasantly."

With the university it was a question of life or death. All depended on the energy of the young president; by a vote of the trustees he was requested to travel through the state, and to preach and lecture to the people on education. As between himself and the university, we may be sure that President Simpson had his mind made up that he would die before it should fail. Here is another brief account to his wife, then in Pittsburgh, of one of his tours.* The date is June, 1843:

"I suppose I need hardly say that I most cordially join you in wishing to be at home. You know me well enough to be perfectly assured that there is 'no place like *home*.' But duty, at least duty to fill my engagements, demands that I shall spend another week before I turn my steps homeward, and then, when I do start, I shall be a week on the way. Take good care of the children, keep up your spirits, and Providence may yet intend to give us a happy life.

"My health has been better than I expected, considering my labors. I think that I am over the severest work, and though my voice is much broken, I was able to speak twice yesterday with considerable ease. Since I left you I have delivered *thirty sermons*, and *twenty-three lectures*, and have travelled upwards of *four hundred miles* in *twenty-three days*. So you see I have not been quite idle. Yet in all my labors I have thought much of you, and perhaps have sent some thoughts thither that I should have directed to a higher source. . . . Before you receive this I presume I shall have passed my thirty-second year, and entered on my thirty-third. Oh, how time flies! Four years longer have I lived than I expected to, and yet how little have I done!

---

* Much of his travelling was on horseback.

"Before I see you I have yet to travel two hundred and twenty miles, to preach twelve or thirteen times, and to deliver some ten lectures. Pray that I may be sustained, and that God may give me such favor in the eyes of the people that his own cause may be advanced.

"Take care of our pretty flowers; let me see how pretty a garden you will have when I get back. I must close, as I presume, by the sound, breakfast must be nearly ready, and I have snatched the first moments of the morning for conversing with you."

His diary of travel through Indiana, in the service of the university, shows both the primitive condition of the country and the energy with which he prosecuted his work. We give a few passages only:

"In obedience to a resolution of the Annual Conference, and the request of the trustees of the university, I left Greencastle to take a tour through the state:

Monday, May 23.—Half-past nine started with the Rev. S. C. Cooper, agent of the university, on horseback. . . .

Thursday, June 2.—Started for Valparaiso. On the way collected a number of flowers and plants. The principal ones among them are beautiful. On the way, saw in the road a very large gray wolf, which showed little disposition to run from us. Arrived at Brother Wallace's just as it began to rain, and at three preached to a small audience that had assembled, notwithstanding the weather, in the temporary court-house.

Friday, June 10.—Rode to Elkhart, and stopped with Squire Beardsley, and preached at night to a large congregation.

Saturday, June 11.—Arrived at half-past nine on the Goshen campground, where we spent our time till Tuesday morning. Had a very pleasant meeting; preached Saturday and Sabbath, lectured Monday, and exhorted Monday night. Here I became acquainted with a number of persons, and several will send us students."

And so it went on week by week, travelling, lecturing, and preaching every day, with all the ardor which a politician would throw into a well-contested campaign. It is not surprising that under these conditions the university prospered.

His friend, E. R. Ames, afterwards his colleague in the episcopal office, but then a presiding elder in one of the

Indiana Conference districts, co-operated with him most vigorously. Ames thus writes to Simpson:

"I received a letter from Wiley last week; he says in his district the preachers will raise the whole amount pledged for the current expenses of the university, but adds he is convinced we must at least have a partial endowment, as the preachers will not long consent to beg for it, as they now do. The 'grasshopper' seems to have become a 'burden' to the good brother. Eddy was at my Quarterly Meeting, at Jeffersonville, two weeks ago, and told me his district would raise their amount. On the whole, I think we shall get $1200 for you, if you do not all starve to death before we collect it."

The first thought of the Methodists of that time, in relation to the ministers who were drafted for service as educators, was that these lucky favorites were assigned to places of comfort and ease. Invidious comparisons were made, much to their disadvantage, between them and the toil-worn itinerants. If the appointees to college chairs were Conference probationers, it was in some sense felt that they had not entered into the ministerial fold through the door of self-sacrifice, but had climbed over some other way. The feeling, if not reasonable, was natural; from the unrest of the itinerancy, from the sense of homelessness which the travelling preacher carried with him, till he had learned to regard his Conference as his home, the educators of the Church were happily free. But, on the other hand, what a story of privation, of struggles with narrow means, of consuming anxieties, of hopes deferred, is crowded into their lives! The heroisms of Methodist evangelism are fully paralleled by the heroisms which give splendor to the lives of the men who founded and built up our Methodist schools. And when we remember that much of this work is missionary; that wherever Methodist churches are planted, whether in our own South, in Africa, or in Asia, the Methodist school rises up in the midst of them, we cannot rate at too high a value the men and women who have consecrated themselves to teaching. The preacher has an instant triumph, the triumph of his persuasive power, visibly appearing in the changed dispositions of the people; the teacher must wait years for the ripening of his harvest. Never was Bishop Simpson so truly a seed-sower as in the days when he planted the love of learning in the hearts of the Methodists of Indiana. Never before was the care of the highest cul-ture, usually confined to the rich, so bravely committed to the love and support of the common people.

12

IX.

LIFE IN INDIANA.—THE MATURED ORATOR.

1839–1848.

Bishop Simpson in the Maturity of his Oratorical Power.—Deep Interest
of the People of Indiana in Preaching.—Religion and Politics.—His
Unquestioning Faith in Christian Truth.—Sympathetic Quality of his
Voice.—The Great Preachers of Indiana, Simpson, Ames, and Beecher.
—The Influence of Methodism on Henry Ward Beecher's Preaching.—
Rev. James Hill's Account of the Centennial Sermon, 1839.—Pounding
an Excited Hearer on the Back.—Description by Rev. O. S. Munsell of a
Sermon Delivered at a Camp-meeting near Greencastle.—Hurrying of
the Crowds to the Meeting-ground.—An Extraordinary Climax.—
Some Incidents of that Day.—The Lawyer at the Church Door.—The
Rev. John L. Smith's Narrative.—The Rev. Aaron Gurney's Reminis-
cence.—Contrast Between President Simpson's Appearance and the
Exhibitions of his Power.—A Comical Mistake.—The Rev. B. F. Raw-
lins's travel with President Simpson on Preaching Tours.—Marvel-
lous Effects of Simpson's Descriptions.—The First Redeemed Sinner.
—A Break-down in the Midst of a Quagmire.—Bishop Simpson at the
Tremont Temple in 1866.—The Rev. R. H. Howard's Narrative.—The
Old Vigor Still Alive in 1870.

IX.

HITHERTO we have traced the growth of Matthew Simpson in character and in the confidence of his fellow-churchmen; little has been said of that which gave him his chief distinction—his power of speech. In Indiana he matured as a preacher, and displayed perhaps there, as nowhere else, his overwhelming energy in the presentation of Christian truth. The times were auspicious. Public speakers did not then, so much as now, carry in their minds the consciousness that they were addressing two audiences, the audience immediately before them, and the greater multitude who heard through the eye. Sermons and speeches did not then reappear within a few hours in cold type. Nor were speakers hampered in those days by the thought that their invisible and innumerable audience was for them the most important. They addressed only their actual hearers, and summoned all their powers to the task of swaying them. They reckoned on instant effects which their language, as afterwards reported, would not wholly explain. The times were propitious, too, in the condition of the population of the state. It was a new world, and the people were quickly receptive of fresh, if also strong, impressions. Traditions counted for little, save only the elementary traditions of Anglo-Saxon and Protestant society. Religion and politics were the two interests which took the deepest hold upon all hearts. This is indeed true of mankind the world over, but in the stage of society of which we now speak there were no interests rivalling these two. Art, literature, the study of the merely agreeable in life, the devotion to enjoyment for its own sake, were as yet wholly unknown or, at best, barely visible. The citizens of the state had in a high degree the quality of moral thoughtfulness, and in dealing with the problems of politics and religion were wholly in earnest. A merely acquiescent faith in republicanism or in Christianity did not suit their temper.

Bishop Simpson was in the strongest sense the pupil of the fathers of Methodism, the inheritor of their methods of address. His conviction of the reality of the truths which he preached was all-controlling. The invisible world, as outlined in Scripture was—we beg to repeat it—as immediately near to his apprehension as that in which he lived and moved. If he ever philosophized, which was seldom, it was in showing that the controlling forces of the universe are the unseen forces. "He literally illustrated Paul's language: "While we look not at the things which are seen, but at the things which are not seen; for the things which are seen are temporal, but the things which are not seen are eternal." He did not need, therefore, to fall back on his artistic imagination in order to give a quasi-reality in his own mind to the truths which he handled. They had already become real to him by the power of a sincere faith; and he used his imaginative power in presenting them vividly, and at times dramatically, to his hearers. But above all he had a sweet, sympathetic nature. He could have said to Abou Ben Adhem's angel,

> "then
> Write me as one who loves his fellow-man."

He had learned from the New Testament that there are infinite possibilities in every man, and that Christ can make those possibilities actual. He longed to persuade men to come under Christ's sway, that so his transforming power might be wrought in them. This is the characteristic of his preaching. Behind all his speech there lay a deep, outwelling tenderness, which began to stir and move as soon as he saw the people before him ready to receive his message.

Yet it was not a feminine tenderness which spent itself in tears; it was wholly masculine, and plied argument upon argument, convincing, persuading, mastering, while it melted the hardest hearts. And then he had for the execution of his instinctive impulse, which had shaped itself into a purpose, a marvellous instrument in his voice. Some have called it harsh; but that was scarcely the proper term. His voice was not so much harsh as thin when its first pulsations fell upon the ear. It was not deep, but it was penetrating; it had not a single bass undertone, but it went out from him surcharged with feeling. I have seen hearers in tears before he had finished the exposition of his text, and while he was speaking in the plainest and most didactic style. It was not that he had spoken an emotional sentence, but the voice, with entire unconsciousness on his part, blended with feeling, was knocking at every heart's door and making an entrance for itself. No one listening to him could at any time say, " Now he is summoning his utmost energy to take me by storm." All was spontaneous, as if the sympathetic nature could only thus find expression, as if it instinctively sought to make its own habitual feeling the feeling of all who heard.

There were then in Indiana three preachers of mark, Matthew Simpson, Edward R. Ames, and Henry Ward Beecher. Simpson and Ames were associates and close personal friends. Of the preaching of Ames during that period tradition reports that in the great out-door meetings its effects were beyond description. Often in the torrent-height of appeal he would drop on his knees, and in that posture continue pleading with the people. Mr. Beecher was trained in the schools after the New England method. The traditions of his education were New England traditions modified by the personal influence of his father as a revivalist. It may be said without hesitation that the pulpit style by which he was known was acquired through his contact with Western life, and perhaps Western Methodist life. He says himself of his entrance upon his Indianapolis parish, in 1839, the year that Matthew Simpson went to Greencastle, near by: "At that period, after having preached about four years, I began to know how to preach a little, and how to gather souls into the kingdom. I began to know what a revival was and how to conduct one." * With the Methodist churches of Indianapolis all about him, he could not fail to learn that much. He broke through the traditions, and was free, energetic, dramatic. When he was transferred to Brooklyn he was known as a Western orator, and his modes were recognized as Western. He shocked severely the staid sense of propriety which till then had reigned in the Brooklyn pulpit; the people turned from the scholarly Bethune, whose written discourses, delivered in a voice of flute-like melody, were models of purest English, to this wonder from Indiana, who spoke with subduing energy to the hearts of the people.† Indiana's gift to the country of Simpson, Ames, and Beecher was one of rich fruitage, not all of it perhaps yet gathered in.

There may be some doubt felt of the accuracy of our statement concerning the manner in which Mr. Beecher learned the art of preaching. On such a point he is himself the most competent witness. The year before his death, when in England, he gave much of his personal history to a meeting of the Board of London Congregational Ministers. Speaking of the time when he first knew Christ as a personal Saviour he thus describes himself: "I will not repeat the scene of that morning when light broke fairly on my mind; how one might have thought that I was a lunatic escaped from confinement; how I ran up and down through

---

* "Henry Ward Beecher: a Sketch of his Career, by Lyman Abbott and S. B. Halliday," pp. 43, 44.

† I have heard it said that Bethune was in early manhood a hearer of Summerfield, and had modelled his manner upon Summerfield's. But what feasts for the soul Bethune's sermons were, and on the platform how few could compare with him!

BISHOP EDWARD R. AMES.

the primeval forest of Ohio, shouting ' Glory, Glory !' sometimes in loud tones and at other times whispered in an ec-
stasy of joy and surprise; all the old troubles gone, and,
light breaking in on my mind, I cried, ' I have found my
God, I have found my God.'

" From that hour I consecrated myself to the work of the
ministry. I had been studying theology. You would not
suspect it, but I know a good deal of theology. [Much
laughter]. Well, I was called to work in Ohio and Indiana, and very soon I found that my work was very largely
missionary, for the states were then young—it was fifty
years ago — and they were very largely peopled by emi-
grants, men that had come without fortune to make fortune. I went through the woods and through camp-meetings and over prairies. Everywhere my vacations were all
missionary tours, preaching Christ for the hope of salvation. I am not saying this to show you how I came to the
knowledge of Christ, but to show you how I came to the
habit and forms of my ministry. I tried everything on to
folks." *   Thus, when nearing the close of life, Mr. Beecher
dwelt with evident fondness on those influences which had
formed him as a preacher, and they were the same as the
influences which had formed Simpson and Ames. On a
New England stock had been engrafted a Methodist life
for experience, and Methodist energy for the preaching of
Christianity.

For any account of the effects of Bishop Simpson's preaching, we must of course depend upon the recollections of
those who heard him. The sermons as secured for us by
shorthand reports do, however, show much. They reveal
a body of scriptural thought, good arrangement, striking
and often beautiful illustrations, direct vision of the scene
described, for both speaker and hearer, and tremendous
intensity. What they cannot reveal is the power of the

---

* Abbott and Halliday, p. 607.

preacher's personality; for this we must have recourse to the testimony of eye and ear witnesses:

One of the best remembered of his Indiana sermons is that preached before the Conference at Lawrenceburgh, in 1839, the centennial of British Methodism. The Rev. James Hill thus describes it:

"In the fall of 1839 the Indiana Conference held its annual session for that year in the court-house at Lawrenceburgh. Bishop Morris was in the chair. The services for the Sabbath were held in the Methodist Episcopal Church, a small brick building of one story, with two aisles, and a narrow, high pulpit. The morning sermon was by Dr. Simpson, recently elected president of Indiana Asbury University. As this was his introduction to the Conference, great interest was felt in the success of the occasion. His text was Ezekiel, forty-seventh chapter, first nine verses, the vision of the healing waters. Their increase and life-giving properties were to indicate the spread and saving influence of Christianity. No one knew what to expect. He had the appearance of a mere youth—beardless, a little stooped. I thought, as he was being conducted to the pulpit, that he was the most pure and beautiful young man I had ever looked upon. Wonderful expression as he proceeded to wade into the waters to the ankles, knees, and loins. His great soul came into his face, with a naturalness indescribable. Light seemed to flash from side to side. The packed audience was thrilled and swayed at the will of the orator. With every fresh unfolding of the subject there came a fresh gust of tears and shouting. On went the stream until we from the mountain-top could see a mighty torrent sweeping everything before it, cutting for itself a deep and wide channel, carrying huge rocks and giant trees in its course. We could see the waters spreading over all the plains. To give some faint idea of the eloquence of the speaker: Brother W. sat by me—a good preacher, and intelligent. I could not keep him quiet: he stamped the floor with his feet; shouted aloud, 'Did you ever hear the like?' and kept on at this, so that I would lose a word now and then. I tried to hold his feet still by pressing on his knees. Finally, I forced his head down between the seats and pounded him on the back; one loving blow on the back of his head brought him to his senses. When the preacher came to the 'multitude of fishes,' the sermon was almost overpowering."

From the Rev. Dr. O. S. Munsell, formerly of Illinois, now of Kansas, we have an account of a sermon preached during the period of his student-life at Greencastle:

"In the summer of 1842 I was a student in the Indiana Asbury University. One Monday, this summer, at 11 o'clock A.M., I was reciting with my class to Professor Larrabee, when we heard some one running hastily up the stairway; the door was thrown open, and the messenger called out to us, 'President Simpson preaches at the camp-ground at one o'clock.' At once all was confusion; the students, without dismissal or leave, gathered up their books, and hastened away. On my way to the camp-ground, with a comrade, we noticed the fact that roads, fields, and by-paths were alive with people hurrying to the place of meeting, and my companion quoted the Master's words: 'Say ye not there be four months, and then cometh the harvest? The fields are already white to the harvest.' The audience was very large, much larger, indeed, than it had been on the Sabbath, and I noticed that the great altar-rail, enclosing a space that would seat five hundred persons, was filled with the earnest Christians of the town and surrounding country.

"Dr. Simpson took his text from the Prophet Joel, iii. 14: 'Multitudes, multitudes, in the valley of decision: for the day of the Lord is near in the valley of decision.' In the outset he pointed out what he understood to be the literal meaning and application of the text; but said that, in a proper sense, and without violence to the spirit of the divine message, it might be applied directly to the great multitude gathered there that day; and that he could truthfully address them personally and say, as a messenger from God, ' Multitudes, multitudes in the valley of decision.' He then proceeded to consider the people before him, in groups, in the light of their personal characters, as God saw them: the scorner, the hardened sinner, the hypocrite, the backslider, the penitent, and the child of God; and he portrayed each type of character with such clearness, vividness, and power that its personality seemed to stand before us a living thing.

He brought the congregation one by one to ' the valley of decision,' warning them that to some of them it was, probably, the valley of final decision which should determine for them, severally, the weal or woe of eternity. His personal appeals to each were almost terrible in their simple directness, pathos, and energy. Then, swiftly changing the scene, he called up before us that other, more trying, because final, valley of decision, the judgment-bar of God, and marshalled before it the mighty hosts of kindreds, tongues, and peoples who should be gathered there; and with terrible power, in the person of the Judge, one by one, he pronounced the doom of the several classes he had previously portrayed, bringing out a thought which I had never before realized, if, indeed, I had ever conceived it at all—that the several peculiarities of our individual characters will be the chief and determining elements in our several awards. He then, in words of marvellous force, dismissed them to their dooms or rewards, closing with the blessing on the humble, faithful Christian. The picture he drew was thrilling beyond all description as he portrayed the glorified Christ leading the hosts of God's elect children from the judgment-bar to the gates of heaven, while the angels cried, ' Lift up your heads, O ye gates, and be ye lifted up, ye everlasting doors; and the King of glory shall come in.' It seemed that in this triumphant entrance into heaven thought and language alike must be exhausted, but not so; the almost inspired orator, grasping in his vision the individual soul of an humble but glorified saint, whose life he had previously described to us, placed him before the throne, and face to face with the King; and then, in language almost indescribable, he pictured that same soul gazing, gazing, ever gazing upon the unveiled face of its Redeemer, and, as he looked, being evermore changed into the same likeness, and yet evermore hungering more and more as the soul expanded in its attempts to grasp the infinite beauty, the infinite perfections, and the infinite glory of God.

"At this point the preacher seemed wholly to lose all consciousness of the presence of the vast, excited multitude hanging upon his words, and, with lifted eyes he soared upward, and still upward, till human souls could endure no more; and, as with a voice of many waters, the multitude of the people in the great altar sprang to their feet, with shouts and cries and tears and laughter. There, in that mighty mass of surging humanity, were the young and the old, the black and the white, the polished student and the ignorant day-laborer, the earnest Christian and the apostate —all shouting, laughing, crying, as their emotions moved them. The speaker was silenced at once, and sat down exhausted; but the spiritual influences which he had called into being moved on, and on; for not only were wicked deniers of Christ there reclaimed, but men who never before had sought God were converted and saved. For more than an hour the excitement was so intense that all efforts to control it, even by singing, were unavailing.

"I noted some strange facts. It was well known that while Dr. Simpson had no antipathy to the shouting quite common in that day, yet he could not make head against it when preaching, and was compelled to stop when it began, so that it was no uncommon thing to see persons under his preaching sitting with clenched teeth and struggling with excitement. On this occasion there sat nearly in front of me two good women in the Church, noted equally for their earnest piety, who long sat with compressed lips and trembling with excitement as the discourse went on.   One of them started to her feet, unable to restrain herself longer; but instantly a good brother sitting behind her laid his strong hand over her lips and pulled her down into her seat.

"The intensity of the excitement upon some nervous organizations in the audience was so great as to produce prostration amounting to illness for days afterwards.   Among those thus affected was Professor Larrabee, who, in speaking of this sermon, said it was the most eloquent and powerful to which he had ever listened, and declared that, if Simpson had been permitted to speak fifteen minutes longer, the excitement, which in him (Larrabee) could find no vent in outward demonstration, must have killed him. The scenes of that wonderful day are as fresh in memory now as if they had occurred but yesterday."

Whether his hearers were cultivated or not, the effect was the same.   A lawyer of Greencastle was, on a dark night, passing a church in which President Simpson was preaching.   It was crowded; aisles were full down to the door.   It was raining, and the lawyer squeezed himself partly into the doorway.   He could see little, but he could hear; he remained standing and listening till the sermon was over, and did not observe till then that the drip of the rain had wet him through and through.

The Rev. John L. Smith, the old and close friend of the bishop, tells a like story:

"In 1844 I was stationed at Indianapolis, and from that time on we were much together.   In the spring of 1845 we attended the dedication of the first Methodist Episcopal church erected in Cambridge city.   It was in the month of April, and the national road was in its spring dress of mud, corduroy, and floating bridges.   The university president arrived at Indianapolis from Greencastle on Friday evening, and early on Saturday morning we started for the place of the dedication, fifty-two miles distant, both on horseback, with leggings, saddle-bags, etc., in primitive Methodist preachers' style.

"Among other distinguished persons who heard the sermon was the Rev. Dr. S. K. Hoshour, formerly minister of the Lutheran Church at Gettysburg, Pa. Dr. H. was a man of broad scholarship, and was, after the time here mentioned, professor of German in the Indiana Asbury University. About midway of his discourse Dr. Simpson drew a vivid picture of Luther at Worms, who, when he had finished his defence in German, was required by the Diet to give it in Latin; and when Dr. Simpson, in his own impassioned manner, quoted in German Luther's final reply, Dr. Hoshour broke down and wept like a child.

"We had at that time in Indianapolis a witty and very eccentric shoemaker by the name of Joshua Cooper, who invariably used the language of his craft. During a revival a stranger from Illinois preached, and seemed confused and utterly failed. Some one asked Brother Cooper what he thought of the sermon? His laconic answer was, 'Well, I think the brother got the bristle off.' The next night Dr. Simpson preached that grand and glorious sermon of his on the text, 'I beseech Thee, show me Thy glory.' Cooper, a long, lean Vermont Yankee, as he was, became greatly moved, as were many others on that memorable occasion. On returning home a friend said to him, 'Well, Brother Cooper, what do you think of the sermon to-night?' He quickly replied, 'A good job; that work won't rip.'" *

Before he became well known to the people of Indiana the contrast between his unpromising appearance and his overpowering eloquence heightened the effect of his preaching. The Rev. Dr. Aaron Gurney shows this in the account of a sermon which, in the days of his boyhood, he

---

* We need not, surely, make apology for the homely dialect in which this and some other incidents are narrated.

heard President Simpson preach. The place is a camp-meeting grove:

" As that song rolls a stream of melody out through the forest, through the open door there enter upon the plat-form John L. Smith, Samuel H. Brenton, Aaron Wood, Richard Hargrave, and several other well-known circuit-preachers. Along with them enters a very young-looking man, smooth shaven, ruddy in face, with low forehead, a shock of brown hair, almost red, growing very near to his eyebrows, dressed in a suit of blue jeans such as farmers of that day made and wore. He does not look to be over twenty-five, but is past thirty. This plain young man attracts no attention; all eyes are fastened on the great preachers so well known, so much loved, who come with him. They bow in prayer, rise, take their seats, and the presiding elder hands to this stranger the Bible and hymn-book. Listen! a little hum of a whisper goes like a ripple through the throng. ' Who is he?' ' Do you know him?' We turn to our friend, a class-leader, saying, ' Who is that?' ' I don't know him. He hain't a travelling preacher. I know all the preachers of the Conference. He is a local, I reckon.' ' Will they put him up to preach?' ' Certainly not; the elder has more sense. I think Brother Hargrave will preach. They are going to let this local preacher open the service, I think, to save Brother Hargrave's strength." Now the stranger rises, reads the hymn, and they sing again; then he prays, and John L. Smith reads the Scriptures; again they sing; and now the stranger, looking like a farmer in his Sunday suit, rises, and the hope, that had become general, that Mr. Hargrave would preach, is dashed away as he announces as his text Hebrews xiii. 12 : ' Wherefore Jesus also, that he might sanctify the people with his own blood, suffered without the gate.'

" He began with a simple, plain description of the Jewish sacrifice of atonement. As he warmed with his theme he seemed to have a mental vision of the whole scene. In realistic terms he described the beauty of the Temple, the smoking and blood-stained altar, the slain lamb upon it, the golden altar of incense, the sprinkling priest within the veil, the white-robed Levites intoning the silvery psalms, until the congregation seemed to see the imposing rites of the Jewish service in action before their very eyes. Then he changed the scene, and took them to Golgotha, and contrasted the Christian sacrifice without the gate, the true 'Lamb of God' offered on Calvary's altar, the offering of the body prepared by the divine High-priest of our confession. So real was his description that we seemed to be gathered about the cross, and to hear reviling Jews and insulting mobs; we saw the gambling soldiers and parted raiment; then the awful horror of darkness; the earthquake, the bursting rocks; the convicted centurion's confession.

"Then, at the cry from the sufferer, 'It is finished,' he turned, and, pointing to the spot where he had placed the Temple, he said, 'See! See! Its veil is rent, its holy of holies is uncovered. The Jewish priests we need no more, for our great High-priest has entered through death into the unseen holy, having obtained eternal redemption for us.' This is but a dim outline of the sermon, remembered from my boyhood. Its effect on the audience I can never forget. The surprise and power of the contrast between what the people expected from the boyish stranger, and what they received from that prince of preachers, heightened the effect. Again I seem to see their eyes kindle, their faces brighten, as the eye of the preacher burns with the light from heaven, and his glowing periods roll like a river of fire in an unbroken tide of pathos and power on their hearts. They swayed to and fro in sympathy with his movements, they rose and fell to the rhythm of his gestures; they sobbed, they wept; they shouted as the theme opened before them the agony of the sacrifice and transformed the vision of the cross into the vision of the throne. Amid a chorus of shouts, as the King of Calvary was depict-

13

ed as ' bringing many sons into glory,' the preacher sat down
and the service ended. 'Who is he? What preacher is
that?' flew from lip to lip as they broke up. The answer
was, 'That is Matthew Simpson, the new president of Indiana Asbury University.' "

Sermons usually enjoy an immortality of scarce a week,
many of them of scarce a day. These last two narratives
are descriptions of preaching heard in youth, sermons which
burned themselves into the memory, and whose impression
is as distinct, after forty years, as though it were made only
yesterday. The Rev. Dr. Thomas M. Eddy was a younger
contemporary of President Simpson and a member of the
same Conference. He describes a remarkable scene—a Conference sermon by the president, and its effect upon preachers and people :

"We have often witnessed manifestations of his marvellous power over his audiences. We reproduce here one
scene. It was in the fall of 1846, at the Conference held in
Connersville. He was announced for Sabbath evening, at
seven o'clock; but long before six there was a dense crowd
of eager men, women, and children gathered for a whole
square around the church, waiting the opening of the doors.
When they were at last opened, what a scramble! I had
climbed up by the aid of a plank, entered a side window,
and had a comfortable position where I could see the struggle for seats. When so many of the congregation as could
gain admission were seated, he entered and pressed his way
through the aisles to the pulpit. His appearance during
the opening services indicated something of embarrassment.
He selected for his text the memorable words of Jesus,
'Behold, I send you forth as sheep in the midst of wolves :
be ye therefore wise as serpents, and harmless as doves.'

"His theme was, the 'Call and qualifications of the Christian minister.' The arguments employed on the call were
most masterly. And although he did not treat the modest claims of 'the succession' with all the deference its

votaries might desire, he did honor the truth of God, and clearly demonstrate that the Great Head of the Church had never surrendered his right to send forth his own laborers; and that without this divine call no talents, no education, no human ordination could authorize any man to enter upon the work of the ministry. The qualifications for this vocation he presented as twofold. The wisdom of the serpent, the harmlessness of the dove; that is, great knowledge and deep personal piety. Having exhibited clearly the essentials of ministerial qualification, he drew a vivid picture of ministerial toil and reward. We saw the devoted itinerant obeying the command of Jesus, ' Go.' Go in the face of poverty, danger, death, disgrace! We saw his family afflicted, his own frame wasted and worn. We followed him with anxious contemplation until we heard the same voice speak again. But it no longer said ' Go.' In sweetest accents it said ' Come, come, come up higher!' At this point there was an irrepressible burst of feeling among the preachers in the congregation, which was so overwhelming and prolonged as to render it impossible for him to proceed for several minutes. As for me, I would, at the close of that sermon, have willingly received an appointment to Central Africa."

The contrast between the outer and inner man still led, in this period, to some comical mistakes. Perhaps he took a pleasure, by the use of a plain and farmer-like dress, in mystifying those who did not know him, and therefore judged from appearances. One of his old friends tells the following:

" When Dr. Simpson was president of Asbury University he was invited to dedicate a church built by the Rev. John S. Inskip, at Dayton, Ohio. He was to be the guest of Mr. Thomas Parrott, a wealthy citizen of that city, who had invited a number of friends to take supper with Dr. Simpson on his arrival Saturday evening. The stage was a little late, and Dr. Simpson walked from the hotel to Mr. Par-

rott's, with his valise in hand. When he rang the bell the
oldest daughter opened the door and invited him in, supposing him to be a local preacher. She told her father a plain-
looking man was in the parlor, and he said, ' Prepare him a
place at the corner of the table, and I will come down and
see him.' In a few moments, while the doctor was taking
his supper, Mr. Parrott came in, and said to the stranger,
' We are expecting Dr. Simpson to arrive from Greencastle to
dedicate our church to-morrow, and we have delayed supper,
waiting for him. The doctor looked up in a quiet way, with
a twinkle in his eye, and said, ' That is the name they call
me by at home.' The company was quickly invited in, and
a pleasant evening followed. The next morning at the dedication he began his sermon in his quiet manner, and as he
proceeded great interest was manifested, and he drew all
hearts. Mr. Parrott told him afterwards, ' There was no
judging from people's looks what they could do, or who they
were.' "

The Rev. Dr. B. F. Rawlins, now of Texas, but a native
and for many years a resident of Indiana, heard President
Simpson first in his own boyhood. One of the early Asbur-
ians, he shows how easily Simpson swayed the minds of
young and old:

" My first acquaintance with Bishop Simpson began in
Bedford, Indiana, in the summer of 1842. It was in the
month of July or August, in the hottest season of that year.
He was then canvassing the state as the president of Indiana Asbury University. He was comparatively unknown,
except to the preachers; but he was never afterwards unknown to the community he now visited, and to which he
preached one of his great sermons. At that time he was
called Simpson, Mr. Simpson, Doctor Simpson, and President Simpson. An old woman, in shaking hands with him
after services were over, called him Brother Simpson, using
the old Methodist language, and then apologized for it, saying, ' Excuse me, I ought to say doctor; but I am so used

to saying brother, I forget.' ' Oh,' said he, 'never mind, my sister; it is far sweeter to say brother. Call me Brother Simpson, and I will like it better.' At the time I am writing of, I was myself quite a lad, but partook of the common excitement which pervaded the community on the occasion of the visit of such a celebrity. His visit was in the interest of education, and the boys were stirred up by that fact.

" His coadjutor in the work was the Rev. Samuel Cooper, the college agent. Mr. Cooper was venerable in appearance, a much older and a much better-looking man than Dr. Simpson, and, being also a stranger, he was taken for the president. He generally conducted the opening service, and always made a very fervent prayer; and when, after this, the ungainly Simpson rose to preach there was a perceptible feeling of disappointment; but before he was through it was felt no mistake had been made. On this occasion the text Doctor Simpson preached from was the forty-fourth verse of the second chapter of Daniel. ' And in the days of these kings shall the God of heaven set up a kingdom, which shall never be destroyed : and the kingdom shall not be left to other people, but it shall break in pieces and consume all these kingdoms, and it shall stand forever.' I have never forgotten that text, and the place where it was to be found. The sermon I have borne with me all through life ; Simpson as he then appeared, his manner, his intonation, his suffused fiery eye, his gesticulation, have all ever since stood out impressively before me. There are not many of that audience now living; but I never return to Bedford without finding a few who recall it all as vividly as myself, and I am led to believe that this is an instance of a sermon producing a lasting impression upon a whole congregation.

" I think I heard him when he preached for the first time on a text that afterwards became memorable, and on which grew one of his greatest sermons. ' But none of these things move me, neither count I my life dear unto myself, so that I might finish my course with joy, and the ministry, which

I have received of the Lord Jesus, to testify the gospel of the grace of God.' It was in California, in 1853, before a conference of ministers who were confronted with great discouragements. In fact as an army corps, at that time, they were in a demoralized state, and needed almost a revelation from Heaven, as did Israel at the sea. The holding up of so conspicuous an example as St. Paul, the picturing of his life, with its deprivations, and the secret of its power in consecration to Jesus, was well chosen; and the picture he showed was one such as only a fertile mind could have created, and in such lines as drew forth the admiration of Paul's successors, the preachers, and wrought up their courage to its greatest height. Its effect, indeed, was wonderful upon all, and seemed to save the day and the cause, and sent it bounding onwards.

"My next reminiscence shall be of a Conference scene in Indiana. It was at Rockport. Many people there had never met the man, and they came long distances to *see* Bishop Simpson. Our church at this place was small, and built in the days of the fathers. It was scarcely large enough to hold the Conference and the visitors who gather at one' of these annual feasts of Methodism. Arrangements were, therefore, made for services in an adjoining grove on the Sabbath day, so that all who came should have the privilege of both seeing and hearing. Though the preparations, as was supposed, had been ample, it was found that many had to stand, as they did, or they sat in wagons and buggies drawn up so closely that they could hear. The morning was pleasant, the air fresh and inspiring, and the song of the multitude, as it floated out, seemed to roll up towards the Source of all song — towards heaven. The scene was inspiring. The platform was large and high, and on it many of the leading men of the Conference—among them the Rev. C. D. Batelle, a man of large frame and stentorian voice. The bishop at length announced his text, and himself gathered inspiration from an evidently expectant audience. 'By faith Enoch was translated that he should not see death, and was not found, because God had translated him; for before his translation he had this testimony, that he pleased God.' The text was read as if the inspiration that was upon the writer who penned it was now upon the preacher in the nineteenth century who was to expound it. Without hesitation, and smoothly, he went on unfolding its treasures. Among the notable passages of the sermon was a description of the first redeemed sinner's arrival in heaven. The scene was dramatic and overpowering. The gates stood ajar, and the ranks of shining ones parted that *this* one, washed in the blood of Christ, might pass on up to the throne, the wonder of heaven! Simpson was calm, but his whole audience were moved and in tears as they saw the sinner going up! Just then Batelle shouted, out of his full and overflowing soul, 'Amen. Let him go!' That outburst was a relief to the rapt congregation, and enabled them to take breath again."

Dr. Rawlins furnishes also a reminiscence of a sermon, preached after a day's travel over a corduroy road, in a broken-down hack, and its wondrous effect, in spite of the preacher's weariness:

"Once I was in company with him on a church-dedication occasion. It was at Corydon, Ind. There were three of us: Rev. C. B. Davidson, the Presiding Elder of the New Albany District, myself, and the bishop. We were in a two-horse livery hack, and had a wornout corduroy road to go over in the month of March. The distance was about twenty-five miles. We did tolerably well in going, but on returning our hack became disabled when we were yet some five miles out. It was so disabled that we were compelled, by fence-rails and poles, to raise the bed from the front axle. We unloosed the horses, and, as the bishop was our guest, we must needs assign him the least difficult part of the work to be performed. We, therefore, gave him the horses to hold, which he did with grace, leaning up against a rail-fence! We had only our Sunday suits, and how to keep from soiling ourselves with the abundant and cold mud was a question. We divested ourselves of coats and vests and went to work, and yet were a sight to behold before the job was done! The sun was shining in a clear sky, and, as the bishop looked at us in our bedaubed state, he seized upon the fact for a moral for the occasion, and said, ' Ah, brethren, it is a great deal better than if it were raining right hard!' But we mended the hack and drove on. Among the familiar questions put to the bishop as we rode along was this: ' Now, bishop, we know you can outpreach us all, but did you never, in your younger days, get into the brush?' 'Oh, yes, very often.' ' Well, bishop, when you got into the brush, what did you do?' 'Oh, I would rub my hands, and say, Oh, my brethren, till I would see a way out or make one!' We reached New Albany, and found there was an appointment out for the bishop to preach in the Centenary Church that night. It was the largest audience-room in the city, and when we entered we found every available spot occupied, and with the *élite* of the city. Despite his weariness—he never seemed weary—he gave us a wonderful discourse on the text, ' The steps of a good man are ordered of the Lord, and he delighteth in his way.' The next day the most eminent jurist of the city was asked how he liked the bishop. ' Like him! Why, he takes possession of your soul, and gives a man no chance.' ' Well, but isn't he logical?' ' Yes; but his logic is all on fire. My! wouldn't he take a jury?' " *

This power over men by simple speech remained with him to the close of his life. If not always exhibited in its fulness so frequently as the years went on, it was still visi-

---

* The same thing was said years afterwards when he was engaged in a lawsuit growing out of a will in which he had been named as one of the executors. During the trial Sunday intervened, and the bishop preached. A leading lawyer, a judge, said to his brethren of the bar: " If that man were of our profession he would leave us all out of sight."

ble. Probably it was at its height during the years of the civil war—from 1861 to 1865. It burst out again with all its old energy during the centennial year of Methodism—1866. The Rev. R. H. Howard, of New England, gives some reminiscences of his preaching during the latter period :

"Not all his pulpit efforts were attended by marked oratorical results. The writer has often heard him preach when he hardly seemed to get on the wing. Though always able, eloquent, and grand, a stranger would have hardly been led from these discourses to infer that the preacher was a man of phenomenal eloquence and power. Yet the results following some of his sermons and platform efforts have been simply overwhelming. No such scene of wild enthusiasm probably ever attended the delivery of any lecture as attended Bishop Simpson's lecture at Boston Music Hall, during the war, on ' Our Country,' when the entire auditory sprang literally to their feet, swung their hats, and shouted until they cried.

"On the occasion of a Methodist Convention in Boston in 1866, Bishop Simpson delivered his lecture on Methodism, one evening at Tremont Temple, to a crowded and enthusiastic audience. The peroration, which, of course, was eloquent, was not unnaturally attended with fervent Methodist responses. This seemed to stir the blood of the orator, and he launched out on a few extemporaneous utterances, surcharged with magnetic power. The whole audience sustained a simultaneous shock, and there went up from that vast multitude one instantaneous and volcanic eruption of hallelujahs. I have never seen the like on any other occasion. I had a vague recollection, at the time, of screaming myself, at the top of my voice, ' Hallelujah!' and yet my own voice was utterly lost amid the grand chorus of shouts that on that occasion made the welkin ring as it will never, probably, again.

"There is reason to believe that no sermon ever delivered in this country was attended by such results as one preached by Bishop Simpson at the session of the Vermont Conference at St. Albans in 1863. I have often heard of congregations being stirred by the voice of a speaker as by the blast of a trumpet. On this occasion we seemed to be trampled down as beneath the resistless onset of a tempestuous cavalry charge. Strong men wept like children, and the more hardened worldlings yielded to the preacher's power the tribute of a tear. This sermon was delivered in the Congregational Church. The next morning an Episcopalian good-naturedly rallied the Congregational deacon as follows: 'Well, deacon, I hear you had a bishop to preach for you yesterday.' 'Yes,' replied the deacon, with great energy and manifest satisfaction; 'yes, and a bishop that was a bishop, too.'" Thus, as we see, the staid, self-contained New-Englander yielded as readily to the spell of his eloquence as the more demonstrative native of Indiana.

Sometimes, too, the critic, who attended his ministrations resolved to observe and coolly analyze, was compelled to surrender to his power. The Rev. Dr. H. B. Ridgaway tells this story of his own failure to maintain, while Bishop Simpson was preaching, his critical attitude: "It was our good-fortune to hear the bishop when he preached as our representative before the British Wesleyan Conference at Burslem in 1870. Bishop Foster, then Dr. Foster, his co-delegate, said to me, 'Let us go up into the gallery and take seats where we can see the effect of the sermon on the Conference.' And so we took seats in one end of the deep gallery of the old chapel, whence we could overlook the platform on which sat the 'one hundred,' and have a general view of the audience. The preacher's text was: 'But none of these things move me' (Acts xx. 24). I do not remember the order of the sermon. He discussed the call to the ministry, gave a graphic picture of Paul's career—his trials and successes—pausing as the apostle was confronted by each successive conflict, and hearing him cry, 'But none of these things move me.' We followed with the rest, and were glad to see that our great bishop was carrying the British with him. When his explanations were well through, the antitheses and climaxes made, suddenly he adverted to his own call to preach. He depicted his youth, his orphanage, his long struggles. Finally the Spirit of God fastened the conviction upon him, and now the difficulty was to break it to his mother. How would she be affected by it? Could she give him up? Could he ever leave her? He was her only son. Approaching her one day, he said, 'Mother, I think I shall have to preach.' Without hesitation she said, 'Why, Matthew, I have been expecting this since you were a child. Your father and I dedicated you to God when you were born.' * At this recital my heart went to my throat; my eyes overflowed. I tried to hide my emotion from Dr. Foster, but, as I did so, I glanced at him; and he, if possible, was more overcome than I was. We both wept, forgetful of others. We also had fallen under the spell of the great preacher; this, too, when we had meant to study in cold blood the secret of his power over an audience."†

It has been my privilege, in recent years, to visit England several times, and during each visit to see more or less of Wesleyan ministers and laymen; and I have never failed to hear something said by them of the wonderful sermon preached by Bishop Simpson at the Burslem Conference. He had been in England in 1857, and was there again in 1881, but this sermon made such an impression that he is remembered as the orator who so mightily stirred the hearts of English Methodists in the year 1870.

---

* This incident has already been given in the bishop's own language, p. 50.

† From the *Methodist Review*, No. 325, p. 26.

X.

BISHOP SIMPSON'S THEORY OF PREACHING.

Methodist Preaching the Style Adopted by Laymen.—Ridicule by Society of the Early Methodist Preachers. — Goldsmith on the State-Church Sermons of his Time.—Bishop Simpson's Theory of Preaching Contained in his " Yale Lectures."—Preaching is for the Common People. —The Minister a Connecting Link between the Rich and the Poor.— A Beautiful Illustration.—The Sympathetic Voice.—The Exhortation at Lock Haven.—Persuasion rather than Instruction the End of Preaching.—The Minister a Witness.—Extemporaneous Preaching the Most Effective.—His own Mode of Acquiring the Power of Extemporaneous Address.—Bascom, Summerfield, Olin, Durbin, and Simpson.—Durbin and Simpson Contrasted.—Examples of Durbin's Electric Power.— Account of the Sermon on " The Victory of Faith," by an Editor of the *Andover Review.*

X.

WHAT was the secret of the extraordinary power in preaching of which we have given a scant account? To answer this question we must go back to quite another: "What is Methodist preaching?" Shortly answered, it may be said that Methodist preaching is the style of public speech unconsciously adopted by laymen, who addressed the people, not professionally, but from the impulse of overmastering conviction. They fought the schools, which had gone astray, and overthrew them. Summoned by Wesley to the field, they doubtless fell into many blunders, but they had the capital qualities of directness, energy, and intensity. Fortunately for them and the truth they served, they were incapable of writing sermons. Their earnestness roused the anger of cultivated society; poets and essayists ridiculed them; Cowper retorted by ridiculing the fashionable preachers of his day. Goldsmith, holding, as he did, enthusiasm in religion to be vulgar, and denying to the Methodist preachers common-sense, notes how often and justly they affected their hearers. He asks, "What might not be the consequences did our bishops testify the same fervor and entreat their hearers as well as argue?" This same keen-sighted essayist describes the common people of England as being "the most barbarous and most unknowing of any in Europe," and charges their ignorance chiefly to their teachers, "who, with the most pretty gentlemanlike serenity, deliver their discourses and address the reason of men who never reasoned in all their lives. They are told of cause and effect, of beings self-existent, and the universal scale of being. They are informed of the excellence of the Bangorian Controversy and the absurdity of an intermediate state. The spruce preacher reads his lucubration without lifting his nose from the text and never ventures to earn the name of enthusiast." * The war with formalism raged for a century, until the perfunctory style of pulpit address disappeared. In the nature of the case, preaching, as taught in the schools, will, unless carefully guarded, tend to become professional. This tendency is best checked by the appearance of men from the ranks of the laity, who speak from intense conviction and bring the churches back to nature again.

That these laymen were led in England by trained clergymen does not impair the truth of our contention, for their clerical leaders had themselves been driven from the churches, and were compelled to deal in the fields and streets with miscellaneous crowds. Audiences on foot, with neither roof above them nor walls to shut them in, will not tarry to hear a dull sermon. How far this direct method of address was carried into other than the Methodist churches of the United States can never be told. We do know that one of its representatives, John Summerfield, was much sought for by those churches, and was regarded by their young and rising ministers as a model of pulpit excellence. James W. Alexander calls him the most enchanting preacher he ever heard.† And yet Summerfield was, as to training for his vocation, merely a layman, and rendered scarcely any service to the churches as a pastor.

To this school, if we may so call it, Bishop Simpson belonged, both by inheritance and by the manner of his entering upon the ministry. To tell the secret of his power was beyond even his ability; neither poet nor orator can unfold the mystery which comes the nearest of all we know to a preternatural endowment. But he has left us in his " Yale Lectures on Preaching " an account of the

---

* *The Bee*, No. 7. † " Thoughts on Preaching," p. 147.

conditions of mind under which he worked. He has set forth, with much modesty, a theory of preaching—and, as he draws from his own experience, the theory of his own preaching.

And in the forefront of his lessons is this one, that preaching is pre-eminently for the common people, and should be on the level of their understandings. To illustrate this he refers over and over again to the example of Christ and his apostles: " When I take the New Testament in my hands, I find the Saviour and his apostles teaching the people, visiting the sick, healing the wretched, comforting the sorrowing, and being much in prayer; but I find not a single direction how to write a sermon or to read it, or how to manage the voice and the gestures so as to be accounted an eloquent orator. They had the truth by direct inspiration; we must study to attain it. But, with that truth given, they seem to have thought of nothing but going forth, burning, shining, blazing in all the glory of a gospel of glad tidings, and, without one thought of appearance or manner, swiftly presenting the truth so as to touch the hearts and consciences of the people. As Christ and his apostles did not dwell at all upon what occupies the minds of so many young ministers, so I fear that many think but little of what burned in the hearts of Christ and his apostles. . . .

" . . . In the time of our Saviour the question was asked, 'Have any of the rulers believed on him?' and under the labors of his disciples it is said, 'Not many wise, not many noble are called,' yet the common people heard them gladly. In the Reformation the masses rallied around the standard of Luther and his coadjutors. . . . If ministers expect success they must tread in the footsteps of the great masters and throw themselves fearlessly upon the sympathies of the people. . . . It is well not to keep in mind the distinguished men who may chance to be present, but to speak for the benefit of the masses. Luther said that he did not think of the doctors and professors, of whom he had some forty,

14

but he addressed his sermons to the masses of the working
people, of whom there were some two thousand." *

In harmony with these convictions was his sense of the
importance of the position of the minister as a connecting
link between the rich and the poor. He looked with dread
upon the fact, daily becoming clearer, that a wall of separation is rising "between the capitalist and the laborer, between the higher classes and the lower." He reminded the
young minister that the "masses generally identify the minister with the higher classes of society," † and warns him
never to give the common people reason to doubt for a moment his sympathy with them. He believed with all his
soul that the ministers of the country, by winning the confidence of the poor, will control the solution of our coming
social problems. This he was confident they will do not by
elaborating theories, but by the force of a genuine sympathy
with men as men. Lamartine said that he had conspired
with the communists of Paris as the lightning-rod conspires
with the thunder-cloud, by drawing down innocuously its
threatening fires. So Bishop Simpson held that the minister is a bond between the extremes of society, and that
his office is to keep them in peaceful touch with each other.
The question, "how to reach the masses," never was a question for him; he sought them, loved them, and found his
way without effort to the inmost recesses of their hearts.

He completes his discussion of the question, "Who are
the special objects of the preacher's address?" with one of
the most beautiful illustrations he has anywhere used. He
appears to be solicitous to place his view of the spirit which
should animate Christian ministers in such clear light that
it cannot be misunderstood: "On the ministers of our country, now and for years to come, rests, and will rest, a fearful responsibility. No other class, I repeat, can stand between the rich and the poor, the learned and the ignorant,

---

* "Yale Lectures," pp. 260, 175, 191.   † Ibid., p. 302.

the virtuous and the vicious, but men divinely sent and commissioned of the Lord Jesus to stoop to the lowest depths of degradation, and yet to keep themselves unspotted from the world. The minister must ever give a helping hand to his brother; while he looks with affection on the wretched outcast struggling in the mire of the pit of degradation, he also looks heavenward, whither he draws his erring brother; and there he beholds a Saviour's face wreathed with a smile of approbation. While he struggles to draw his brother from destruction the Saviour's hand holds him and draws him nearer to himself. It is safe to reach out one hand to rescue the sinner from the verge of hell, if with the other we can grasp the hand of Omnipotent love. The office of the true minister is to stand between God and sinful man, listening to the whispers of love and repeating them in the ears of the fallen. How deep he may go who can tell?

" I shall never forget an exhibition I once attended. Shortly after schools for the imbecile were commenced in Europe a young man, moved by benevolence, crossed the ocean to examine their mode of operation and success. Assured of their utility, he returned and commenced a similar institution. He advertised for the most idiotic and helpless child that could be found. Among those brought to him was a little boy of five years of age. He had never spoken or walked, had never chewed any hard substance, or given a look of recognition to a friend. He lay on the floor, a mass of flesh, without even ability to turn himself over. Such was the student brought to this school. The teacher fruitlessly made effort after effort to get the slightest recognition from his eye, or to produce the slightest intentional act. Unwilling, however, to yield, at the hour of noon he had the little boy brought to his room, and he lay down beside him every day for half an hour, hoping that some favorable indication might occur. To improve the time of his rest, he read aloud from some author. One day, at the end of six months, he was unusually weary, and did not read.

He soon discovered that the child was uneasy and was trying to move itself a little, as if to turn towards him. The thought flashed upon his mind, 'It misses the sound of my voice.' He turned himself closely to it, brought his mouth near the child's hand, and after repeated efforts the little fellow succeeded in placing his finger on the teacher's lips, as if to say, 'Make that sound again.' The teacher said that moment he felt he had the control of the boy. He gained his attention, and by careful manipulation of his muscles succeeded in teaching him to walk, and then to read; and when I saw him, at the end of five years, he stood on a platform, read correctly, recited the names of the presidents of the United States, and answered accurately a number of questions on our national history. I looked with astonishment, and said to myself, 'Was there ever such patience and such devotion?' I said, 'Was there ever an instance of one stooping so low and waiting so long?' Then I said, 'Yes, there was one instance—the Son of God came down from heaven, laid himself down beside me, his great heart by my heart, watched me with perpetual care, infused into me of his own life, and waited for nearly twenty years before I reached my finger to his lips, and said, 'Speak, Lord, for thy servant heareth.' What condescension! what love to fallen man! Christ stooped so low— it authorizes us to stoop and wait on and wait ever. Some of these wretched ones have been suffering for more than eight-and-thirty years, and have been lying at the edge of the pool, waiting for us to come and help them into the troubled waters."

I have spoken of his sympathetic voice, whose tones, without apparent effort, opened a way to the heart and took full possession there for his thought. He never captured his hearers by bursts of energy; least of all was he ever for an instant declamatory. What seemed most visible to the hearer was that the speaker was wholly possessed of his theme, and yet he, it was equally visible, was wholly possessed of himself. Not a movement of hand or arm, not a tone, exceeded the due limits which Nature prescribes for the highest effects. A sort of rhythmic harmony was kept up between the subject, the feeling which it awakened in himself, and the expression of thought and feeling which he was giving to his audience. His account of this quality of preaching is too brief for our entire satisfaction, and yet it runs in the direction of explanation.

"The voice," is his account of it, "should always be in harmony with the subject, and should indicate the earnest love, the deep solemnity, and the ardent zeal of the preacher. It is sometimes called the sympathetic voice, and seems to blend the speaker both with his subject and with the feelings of his audience. He stands as if forgetting himself, and tries to bring about a perfect union of the subject and the hearers." * This appears again in his definition of unction : "What is usually termed unction comes from a heart filled with love to God and man, and a voice and manner brought into perfect harmony with that mental and spiritual state. It is impossible to convey in words what this harmony is. It is a perceptible, but indescribable, concord between the subject and language employed and the tone of voice and sympathy of spirit manifested in the entire movement of the speaker. As this mental state is kindled very largely by prayer, so it harmonizes with a prayerful utterance and a prayerful spirit." † This is as near to a disclosure of the secret of his power as the great master could probably come.

The harmony between subject and voice he, of course, attained without conscious effort. It was remarkable, too, that he who drew tears so freely from others scarce ever dropped a tear himself. His eyes became suffused with moisture, and glistened with that peculiar brightness which the moistened eye wears, but seldom overflowed. Once

---

* "Lectures on Preaching," p. 183.   † Ibid., p. 109.

only I saw him reach for his handkerchief to relieve his eyes, and, *horribile dictu*, it could not be found. He was at the time in a conference, addressing the candidates for ordination. With the utmost composure he leaned over to the secretary, at his right hand, and whispered a few words in his ear. A handkerchief was reached to him without the movement being observed save by the few who sat behind him, and the address went on. All this time his hearers were in a tremor of tearful excitement.

The most extraordinary exhibition of this peculiar sympathy which I ever witnessed in him was at our church in Lock Haven, Pennsylvania, in the spring of 1872. The Central Pennsylvania Conference was in session; it was Sunday afternoon, and the ministers of the Conference were present in full force. He had been ill for months, and was wholly unable to preach. Indeed, at that time, but a handful of bishops were left us. Death had been busy among them, and the strain of administration coming upon the four remaining was too much for their strength. The sermon of the occasion was preached by another, and the people sat at its close, half hoping (yet doubting) that Bishop Simpson would say a few words to them before the service broke up. He rose from his seat with evident effort, and repeated from the Revelation of St. John the words: "I saw seven golden candlesticks; and in the midst of the seven candlesticks, one like unto the Son of Man; . . . his head and his hairs were white like wool, as white as snow; and his eyes were as a flame of fire; . . . and his voice as the sound of many waters. And he had in his hand seven stars. . . . Write . . . the mystery of the seven stars which thou sawest in my right hand; . . . The seven stars are the angels of the seven churches." His theme was: "Christ holds his ministers in his right hand." Briefly explaining that he was unable to say much, but wished to address a few words to his brethren, he proceeded to unfold Christ's supporting power as imaged in St. John's vision. I can only describe from recollection, but

I well remember being impressed by the extreme beauty of the exhortation. As he proceeded he seemed to me to be taking in his survey all the trying experiences of the minister's life; but, barely suggesting these, he led his hearers up to the thought that Christ holds the angels of the churches in his right hand, and that, held there, they shine as stars. As he proceeded, the languor of illness fell away from him; the sunken chest and bent shoulders passed from sight; the pallid face was lit up by the glow of his feeling. But the eyes, who can describe them? Moistened, as usual with him in the high states of feeling, they appeared to be looking into infinite distances, as though, beyond congregation and church, John's vision was palpably before him. As he saw, he reported to the expectant people gathered about him, and by instinct his theme came forward at times as a refrain: "The stars in his right hand are the angels of the churches."

While thus apparently rapt in vision, he was evidently conscious of the presence of his hearers and of their sympathy. Their tears, their sobs, their ejaculations, must have reminded him that he was in the midst of a throng whose hearts were wholly subject to the cadences of his voice. They saw as he saw, felt as he felt, and were lifted up as far as it was his wish to carry them. As I listened I wondered how the address would come to an end; it did not end in any sense of artistic closing. The voice ceased, and the people still sat, sobbing and ejaculating, till, by slow degrees, they came to themselves again. He had spoken about three quarters of an hour, and in that time had wholly carried his hearers out of their ordinary consciousness of themselves.

His method was also largely determined by his opinion of the end to be kept in view. By one brief distinction, namely, that the end of preaching is persuasion, he separated himself from a large school of sermonizers. To use his own words, " Persuasion, rather than instruction, is the great end of preaching. Instruction is essential, but without persuasion the sinner is never moved or saved." * In order to persuasion, he insisted that the preacher should be a witness, and that, as a witness, should be capable of giving his personal testimony. He dwells much upon this thought in his sermons: "A man," to cite a single passage, "might have argued with the Jews until his head was gray, but when one stood up and said, 'One thing I know, that whereas I was blind, now I see,' that was an argument which they could not resist. And so it is. We may preach delightfully, but can we testify? Paul testified. When he stood before the Roman governors, he told his experience. He knew that what had touched his own heart would touch the hearts of others. My brethren, let us go in like manner and testify to the great truths of the gospel." † He proceeds still further; he makes this the chief element in the personality of the preacher, which, in his opinion, should be exhibited in every sermon. "He [the preacher] stands as a witness and an illustration of the influence of divine power. As he knows the truth of the gospel, others may know it; as he has felt the power of the gospel, others may feel it also. He tells them how he was moved; out of how deep a pit he was drawn; how his feet have been placed on the Rock of Ages; how he repented and believed; how he was delivered from tribulations, and how he is now filled with power to resist the allurements which once took him captive; how that once he was influenced only by the visible and earthly, but that now he is under a sweet attraction of the unseen and heavenly." ‡ The personality which he would have the preacher throw into every discourse is a spiritual personality, and this he regards as essential to the highest success.

It follows from these principles that he regards extempo-

---

* "Yale Lectures on Preaching," p. 174.
† "The Christian Ministry: Sermons," p. 76.
‡ "Lectures," pp. 167, 168.

raneous preaching as the most effective. For this will best express whatever unction the preacher has; will best create the harmony between the theme, the feeling which it inspires, and the preacher's tones and action. He is careful, however, to insist that this direct mode of address, as he prefers to call it, is compatible with the most careful preparation. "It may be abused by ignorant and indolent men, but it is not designed to diminish the necessity for extensive reading and careful thought. The order and parts of the discourse should be clearly fixed in the mind; illustrations may be selected and arranged; suitable language for certain portions may be well studied, or the whole sermon may be written; yet, at the time of delivery, with the heart full of the subject, and with the outline clearly perceived, let the speaker rely on his general knowledge of language and his habit of speaking for the precise words he may need. If he be deeply in earnest he will, as he proceeds, feel a glow of enthusiasm which will give warmth and vigor to his expression." *

As to himself, his power of expression was very unusual. No matter how suddenly summoned to speak, he had apt words at command. The human interest of every occasion was instantly perceived by him, and out of that he readily drew the materials of discourse. In framing his thought into speech, he was aided by the fact that his thought was never recondite. His meaning was instantly obvious; he remembered that the public speaker deals with the ordinary experiences of mankind, and to these, as they are known in the home, the school, the church, and the state, he addressed himself. If ever abstract, it was in pursuing some analogy between the visible and the invisible world; in this he was aided by his unusual facility of illustration. I do not remember a single nice distinction in the whole range of his sermons; he took the leading truths of Christianity

---

* "Lectures on Preaching," p. 173.

and exhibited them in large outlines. Thus he was distinguished for breadth rather than depth of thought. Before the people he was not a miner tracing out hidden veins of truth; rather he lifted them up to his own lofty position and pointed them to the scenes beyond. And in nothing did this broadening of the people's thinking show itself more than in his habit of reminding them of the thinness of the veil which separates the seen from the unseen; one world where, apparently, there are two; one consistent movement of Providence towards a definite goal; one life for the believer, though called here and in the hereafter by diverse names; one kingdom, whose duration is eternal—these are the truths which were most present to him. These are not small, not superficial thoughts; they are the greatest with which the human mind is occupied. He treats them not speculatively, but biblically; not as matters of purely intellectual apprehension, but of trusting faith. On these truths he had staked his destiny, temporal and eternal, and he called on men to do the same.

But how did he acquire his extraordinary facility of extemporaneous address? On this point, also, he has in his usual modest way, but satisfactorily, given us light : " Without any expectation of its influence on my future life, I acquired the habit when a youth of reading aloud to my friends, from books in any language I studied, whatever I found to be either very beautiful or very interesting. Especially was this the case with the writings of Xenophon and the orations of Demosthenes, Virgil's 'Æneid,' and Fénélon's 'Telemachus.' It was also my practice for a number of years to read in family worship from the original languages, thus accustoming myself to instantaneous choice of words to express the ideas of the writers. This practice, however, while giving me greater command of language, may not have made me quite so familiar with the idiomatic structure of other languages; at least I never advanced as far as the sophomore who, descanting on the study of Latin, said that he could think best in Latin. I confess that all my life my thinking has been in English. Another method is to hold personal religious conversation with individuals. The process of explaining to one attentive mind some doctrine of the gospel, or urging motives for immediate personal action, imparts a directness of address and readiness of language which will be of great service in the pulpit. There is philosophy as well as piety in visiting those who are sick and in prison, in going out into the highways and hedges, and compelling men to come in to the feast of love. To acquire clearness and beauty of language, some have recommended the reading of Cowper or Milton, or some poet who has written on religious topics, a half-hour before entering the pulpit, that the mind may be carried in this elevated strain to its pulpit work. I would greatly prefer, however, spending that time in reading the words of Jesus or of inspired penmen."*

Doctor James W. Alexander, in his "Thoughts on Preaching," speaks of ministers who "preach twenty years, and yet never preach on Judgment, Hell, the Crucifixion, the essence of saving faith, nor on those great themes which in all ages affect children and the common mind, such as the Deluge, the sacrifice intended of Isaac, the death of Absalom, the parable of Lazarus. The Methodists constantly pick out these striking themes, and herein gain a great advantage over us." This peculiarity of the old Methodist preachers was eminently the peculiarity of Bishop Simpson. Running over the list of his published sermons, such titles as these meet the eye: "The Gospel the Power of God;" "The Resurrection of Christ;" "The Great Commission;" "What Think Ye of Christ?" "The Effect on the Human Mind of the Manifestation of God's Glory;" "The Victory of Faith;" "The Contest for Eternal Life." He valued the privilege of addressing the people too highly to waste his

---

* "Lectures on Preaching," pp. 190, 191.

opportunity. There is not one in the many topics of his discourses which does not touch some vital part of Christianity. The suggestion that he was to preach merely to entertain he would have repelled with scorn.

Among the chief Methodist preachers of this century, whose power was proved by immense followings of the people, the most conspicuous were Bascom, Summerfield, Olin, Durbin, and Simpson. The first three were born in the latter part of the last century, and, in the period of their highest influence, preceded Bishop Simpson. Bascom was one of his teachers in Madison College; Summerfield had died when Simpson was quite a lad. Olin, too, was more his predecessor than his contemporary. We more naturally compare him with Durbin, who was eleven years his senior, and with whom he was, during the public life of both, in frequent association. They were alike in one particular; their oratory was wholly natural, and in no sense the product of formal training. They were alike in choosing, by preference, the great themes of Christianity; alike in simplicity and clearness of statement, and alike in the frequent exhibition of dramatic power. And yet, though each was genuinely eloquent, they differed. In the delivery of Durbin's sermon there were two men, wholly contrasted with each other, the one didactic and almost dryly expository, the other brilliant, explosive, and at times overwhelming. In Bishop Simpson's expression of himself there was more unity. If his sympathy kindled, and it almost invariably did, it kindled simultaneously with the development of his theme. When in its greatest force it glowed as a penetrating warmth, and left the people subdued and weeping. If he went beyond this he led them to rapturous expressions of Christian joy. Durbin's great passages were surprises, lightning flashes, and in their suddenness would almost lift his hearers from their seats. When inspired by high-wrought feeling, some of his strokes of oratory were so daring that the critic would be amazed at the perilousness of the venture. There was, however, no peril, for the power given him when thus inspired was irresistible. As he said of himself, in these moments, it seemed as if the earth were too small for him. I recall an instance of this power exhibited by him in one of the years of my student life, and in a sermon on the Judgment. He had been dwelling in his argument on the point that penalty is proportioned to the degree of light vouchsafed. He quoted, in tones which feeling always gave him, the words of Christ: "Woe unto thee, Chorazin! woe unto thee, Bethsaida! for if the mighty works which were done in you had been done in Tyre and Sidon, they would have repented long ago in sackcloth and ashes. But I say unto you, it shall be more tolerable for Tyre and Sidon at the day of judgment than for you. And thou, Capernaum, which art exalted unto heaven, shalt be brought down to hell." With a rapid suggestion that we shall be judged by the same principles, and that, if we fall, we shall fall lower still, he leaned over the pulpit, bent his eyes earthward, and, with tones, look, and gesture which are difficult to describe, called out: "Ye inhabitants of Chorazin and Bethsaida, rise up and let us come down." It was done in an instant, but the picture of the falling mass, calling as they went down for their lower places, was before every eye and shook mind and heart with a perceptible quiver.

Let no one imagine that this was a piece of art; it was the sudden prompting of high-wrought excitement in a speaker capable of exhibiting his thought and feeling dramatically. Doctor Durbin once said to me that in these exalted moods which expressed his greatest power, he seemed to himself to be in a picture-gallery, and to be taking down one picture after another and showing them to the people. This was only saying that in such states of mind all his thoughts became images. Another example of this sudden expression of power, belonging to my college life, is ineffaceably impressed upon my memory. He was describing the displeasure of God with sinful men, and then, with a quick transition, turned his discourse into a direct appeal. " Sinner," he broke out, "the wrath of God smites you; it not only smites you, but it abides on you; it not only abides on you, but it grinds you." When he struck the word "grinds," it was in such tone and such dwelling on each of its separate letters that we instantly saw the mills of God crushing the doomed criminal. The difference between these two eloquent men may be summed up in saying that Durbin gave his hearers sudden flashes of that light which "never was on sea or land," to be followed, after a brief interval, by others just as sudden; while Simpson fixed the thoughts on one object and poured light on it until it not only stood out in perfect clearness, but was invested with the halo which we ascribe to whatever belongs to the supernatural sphere.

To the student of oratory, the memorials which these two preachers have left of their pulpit preparations are of the profoundest interest. I have in my possession a collection of Durbin's skeletons of sermons, comprising the bulk, probably, of his remains in this kind. They are in the most precise sense skeletons, mere bones, but the bones are all articulated, and the skeleton has feet to walk with, when the orator, by the magic power of his genius, shall have created a soul under the ribs of death. I have before me, at this moment of writing, the outline of the sermon from which I have cited the striking passage on the wrath of God. Its date is Carlisle, 1836; the text, Matthew xvi. 26: " For what is a man profited if he shall gain the whole world and lose his own soul?" Under the second general head, the loss of the soul, comes as one of the points: " *The actual infliction of misery by the visitations of God. Enlarge.*" That is all. He had, doubtless, the vision in his mind, more or less distinct, of all that this reminder suggested. And he did enlarge; he himself was enlarged, and his audience with him; walls, roof, and all that pertained to the structure we were in, were swept away, and we had the vision of the things which no mortal eye can discern. This hint of purpose occurs almost habitually, sometimes varied by such forms as " enlarge—enforce earnestly." The outlines prepared by Bishop Simpson for his preaching are of the briefest. A narrow slip of paper, as long as one's hand, is the average size. Take the famous sermon on the " Vision of the Waters," founded on the first part of Ezekiel xlvii. It is on a sheet of ordinary note paper, and is written in pencil. The line of thought is traced and no more. In preaching, Bishop Simpson never used his skeleton; it was left in his study. Doctor Durbin's habit was to keep his outline very closely under his eye.

I know it is usually said that Methodists are quickly susceptible to the awakening of emotion, and that their standard of pulpit eloquence would not be accepted by the world at large. We doubt if this be a correct judgment, for we shall show more fully than we have already that the power of Bishop Simpson was confessed by all conditions of men, in whatever country he preached. It will appear too, as we proceed, that he was equally effective in handling other classes of subjects. Meanwhile we will close this chapter by presenting an estimate of the bishop's preaching by one of the editors of the *Andover Review*. It is a critical judgment, and therefore comes within the scope of our present discussion:

" Some years ago, at a Conference over which he was presiding in a New England city, it was our privilege to hear him, and to hear him at his best. His sermon happened to be what is generally conceded to be pre-eminently his ' great ' sermon on ' The Victory of Faith.' Such an opportunity rarely occurs twice in a lifetime. The preaching service had been preceded by a ' love-feast,' and the mental condition of most of the vast audience was both that of eager expectancy and deep spiritual preparation. When the sermon was reached, the bishop slowly rose from his seat and advanced to the side of the pulpit upon the open platform. He had, as is said to have been often the case, the languid and exhausted look of a hard-worked man. His height and gently stooping figure suggested a kind of scholar-like awkwardness. His features, pale, strongly and sharply cut, but by no means classic in their mould, intimated a certain strength of character, but nothing more, unless we except the large, firm mouth and sensitive lips that betokened the orator. The eyelids drooped slightly over the sad, almost expressionless, leaden-blue eyes, deeply sunken under his broad, low brow, which was surmounted by thin, straight, light-brown hair, slightly tinged with gray. The voice began in a thin, husky, nasal, high-pitched, and an almost feeble tone, uncertain in its fibre, and unimpressive in its general effect. The words were slowly but clearly enunciated, and yet called for an effort of attention on the part of the audience. There was little in the appearance of the man to indicate the treasure within. For the first fifteen minutes a stranger would be likely to experience a sense of disappointment. But the eagle was only reserving his strength for an upward flight. As he gradually worked himself into the heart of his subject, as feeling gathered, and he became increasingly sensitive to the subtle, sympathetic influence proceeding from the audience, his quavering tenor voice grew penetrating, resonant, sympathetic, and impassioned; the stooping figure became erect; expressive gesture was no longer restrained; the dull eyes were kindled into a blaze by the long pent-up fire within; his thoughts seemed to play over his face like a luminously radiating atmosphere, and, unconsciously, one felt the force of the shrewd description of a famous preacher, 'the ugly man who becomes beautiful when he speaks;' the sentences grew short and pithy, and were uttered with an incisiveness and a rapidity of enunciation and a peculiar stress of voice upon the final words.

"Whenever he touched the finer chords of feeling there

was a thrilling melody in his tones, like the native music of the land of his Irish ancestors, full of plaintiveness, with now and then a kind of wailing tenderness of pathos. Soon rising on his theme's broad wing, he struck into a most daring allegory. The Genius of Atheistic Science was conducted over the vast realm of things visible and material in earth and air and sea, far up and out into the stellar worlds, and all were given to him for a possession, even to the most distant star on the outermost rim of the universe. Then, in boldest contrast, he graphically pictured the Genius of Christian Faith as he surveyed his sublime inheritance. These riches of the material realm—' all are yours.' He bore him aloft and lifted the veil that hides the gleaming splendor of his inheritance in the world unseen and eternal, prepared for the conquering sons of God. The effect was electric. Hundreds shouted, clapped their hands; some rose to their feet; strong men and women wept and laughed at once, as they gazed upon the vision of their ' inheritance with the saints in light.' It was preaching to a full orchestra with the Hallelujah Chorus. The flight was a lofty one, but the pinions were strong enough to bear the combined weight of the theme, the speaker's emotions, and the throbbing hearts of the audience. Gradually and skilfully he brought us back to earth, and traced the way in which our sorrows, failures, and secret wrestlings of soul were preparing the crowns, and already giving us the earnest of the glorious future, and clothing us even now with the garments of the children of light.

" In order to estimate the great preacher's power and art of public address, it is not necessary to describe the character and effect of other specimens of his oratory. In the one effort we have referred to may be found the salient characteristics and principal elements of influence in his eloquence; it was a perfect type of his best manner. But to gauge him while he was speaking was next to impossible. The critic was insensibly compelled to yield himself to the orator; he

15

had neither time nor inclination to think of more than one word—genius. But in the cooler moments of recollection the student of the bishop's eloquence would find that its distinction was due more to the peculiar combination of a profundity of evangelical earnestness, and the power so to communicate his earnestness as to arouse popular enthusiasm in evangelical truth, than to any one distinguishing excellence that separated his power from that of other eminent Christian orators."

It is sometimes said despondingly that these great preachers have left no successors. We doubt if that be true. They will always have successors so long as there are inheritors of their deep conviction of the truth of Christianity. They did not live in the dim border-land between faith and doubt. They believed, and therefore they spoke, and they believed with a faith so intense that it gave them no rest. What else could have borne Durbin along, through years of ever-accumulating labor, from 1820 to 1872, or Simpson from 1833 to 1884? Yes, they will have successors so long as they have successors to their faith. Modes of address may change, and natural endowments may vary, but that subtle, indescribable power which leads men captive will never fail a ministry speaking with the consciousness of a vocation from God. To this consciousness co-working with native gifts, and helped by self-culture, Durbin and Simpson owed all that they were.

XI.

DELEGATE TO THE GENERAL CONFERENCE, 1844, 1848, 1852.

General Conference of 1844.—Diary of President Simpson's Trip to New York.—His Weariness of the Conference Proceedings.—The Case of Bishop Andrew.—He is Asked to Resign.—Dread of the Effect upon the Country of a Division of the Church.—Position of Olin.—George F. Pierce: "Let New England go."—Brilliant Reply of Jesse T. Peck. —Constitutional Argument of Hamline.—Address of Bishop Andrew. —Bishop Soule Threatens to Secede.—Durbin's Reply to Soule.— Southern Tact.—The Protest of the South Read by Bascom.—The Reply of the Majority.—A Contingent Plan of Separation.—The Louisville Convention of 1845.—John C. Calhoun's Reference to the Division of the Methodist Episcopal Church.—The General Conference of 1848. —The Plan of Separation Repudiated.—Conference of 1852.—Simpson's Report on Lay Delegation.

XI.

PRESIDENT SIMPSON represented his ministerial brethren of Indiana in three successive General Conferences, those of 1844, 1848, 1852. The first of these authorized the division of the Church, the second rescinded the "Plan of Separation," and the third pronounced lay delegation to be inexpedient. In the first of these he took little part; in the second his influence upon its most important measure was decided; in the last he was a recognized leader. In the General Conference of 1852 he was chairman of the Committee on Lay Delegation, and presented the report which postponed the consideration of the subject to some future time. We would naturally expect to find a man so well fitted for leadership a conspicuous member of the General Conference of 1844; on the contrary, he does not appear at all in its memorable debates. He writes to his wife while there: "I am in delightful obscurity." One reason of this probably was, his temper was more that of a diplomatist than of a debater. Moreover, he was one of the younger delegates, being at that time only thirty-three years of age. The controversy, which largely turned upon the questions of the usage of the General Conference in the election of bishops, and its authority over them when elected, naturally fell into the hands of the elder preachers. Bangs, Olin, Griffith, Collins, Durbin, Finley, Cartwright, Hamline, George Peck, Jesse T. Peck, Bascom, Crowder, W. A. Smith, Longstreet, Lovick Pierce, George F. Pierce, Winans, Capers, Green, were the champions on the two sides. Whatever may be thought of the measures advocated or opposed by these men, there cannot be two opinions of their extraordinary ability.

Bishop Simpson has left a diary of his trip to New York, the seat of the General Conference. Part of it was rough, and in some of its aspects amusing:

"I left Greencastle March 20th, 1844, in company with Mrs. Simpson and children, about twelve o'clock. We travelled in a three-horse wagon, accompanied also by the Rev. E. R. Ames, Rev. E. G. Wood, Mrs. Barns, and Miss Wheeler. The air was cold, occasionally filled with falling snow, and the roads were excessively muddy. Notwithstanding these unfavorable circumstances, the company were in fine spirits, and we had lively conversation, interrupted occasionally by the fears of the ladies, as we plunged into deep holes or slid upon sidling spots.

March 22.—At seven o'clock we were upon the way. A great part of it was cross-road (*i. e.,* corduroy) and very bad. A snow-storm came on, and the ground was, in a few minutes, covered. It, however, entirely disappeared before middle of the afternoon. Without stopping, except to warm, we forded Sugar Creek and Blue River, and reached Irvin's about dark, having travelled twenty-nine miles—the day before twenty-six. Here we lodged very comfortably, and were joined by friends from Greencastle on their way to Cincinnati.

March 23.—We started about eight. After having travelled two miles Mr. Ames missed his carpet bag, which the jolting had torn loose. The wagoner was sent back to find it, while, to save time, lest we should be too late for the train, Mr. Ames turned teamster. He mounted the saddle-horse, which, by the way, had no saddle on him, and whose back was as sharp as a nor'wester; his feet were rested on the trace-chains, for want of stirrups, and a large beech stick held erect over his shoulder served for a whip—and then the wagon, a red bed with a white muslin cover, in road-wagon style, well filled with live-stock and lumber—all together not a bad subject for a Cruikshank. At Columbus we took the train to Madison, and at that point a steamer to Cincinnati."

This was his first crossing of the Alleghany mountains. Arriving at New York the day before the opening of the Conference, he was welcomed to the house of Mr. James Harper, then mayor of the city. "To me," he writes in his narrative, "the scenes of the Conference were new. It was my first session. It had pleased the members of the Indiana Conference to elect me at the head of a delegation composed of Ames, Wiley, Havens, Ruter, Miller, and Wood

—all good and able men. Ames had been one of the missionary secretaries for the four years preceding. It had long been the custom for the delegates to select the general committees on which they would serve, and usually the first on the list was a member of the Committee on Episcopacy. As, however, my colleagues were all older men than myself, and had longer been members of Conference, I gave to them their choice of places—Ames selecting for himself the Book Committee, Wiley Episcopacy, and I the Committee on Education. Owing, however, to the excitement which subsequently followed, the Committee on Education met only a few times and did very little business. Dr. Bascom, an active leader of the Southern party and author of the protest of the Southern delegates, was its chairman. I formed a very pleasant acquaintance with Doctors Paine and Pierce, both of them afterwards bishops in the Church, South. There were two subjects in which I took interest and on which I offered resolutions. One of them was on the exercising of more care in the examination of titles to church property, the other the appointment of a committee to look after the preparation of historical records in each Conference."

In his letters to his wife, then at Pittsburgh, he repeatedly confesses to a weariness of the Conference proceedings. With regard to the debates upon the case of Bishop Andrew, he is reticent, except barely to mention the facts. Under date of May 18, 1844, he writes: " Ames is talked of for bishop, but as yet there is no telling the result." In the third week of the Conference he writes thus to Mrs. Simpson :

" We are in the midst of such a storm on the subject of slavery that everything else is forgotten. I think it possible that we shall split.; if so, we shall only need one bishop. . . ."

On May 25 he writes again :

" Another week has passed since I last wrote, and it is difficult to say how many more will pass before I shall be able to see you. Conference has been engaged nearly the whole week on Bishop Andrew's case, and in all human probability will be engaged a large part of next week. I am staying with Mr. Harper, the mayor of the city—a very pleasant family. My acquaintance is small with the ladies of the city, whom you mentioned in your last. Some of them are handsome, some ugly; many are very amiable and accomplished, but, taking all in all, '*I wad'na gie my ain wife for ony wife I see.*' Perhaps after I get away I shall be glad that I came, but at present I have no pleasure here, worried with the excitement and fatigue. I believe a month more would destroy my health. . . ."

" New York, May 30, 1844.

" . . . We have now been upwards of four weeks in session, and have done about nothing. When we shall get through Heaven alone can tell —probably not under from ten days to two weeks. So you must be patient, and well you may be when you remember that it is for me much more disagreeable to be absent than it is for you to have me absent."

The events of this historic General Conference deserve to be dwelt upon from their connection with the event succeeding them—the struggle for the preservation of the national union. They had an important bearing, too, upon the life of Bishop Simpson; they formed a part of the preparatory training by which he was fitted for the service rendered by him to the country from 1861 to 1865. He was a witness of the first breaking of the bonds of the national union; for the claim of the inherent right of slavery to go anywhere in the Church, in the person of a slaveholding bishop, was followed by the claim of the right of slavery to go anywhere within the limits of the nation.* Mr. Calhoun trod in the footsteps of the Southern Methodist leaders; what they demanded for slaveholding as Methodists, he demanded for slaveholding as an American. The schism in the Church not only preceded in time, but led on to the greater schism — the attempt to create two nations out of one. What wearied President Simpson to witness was

---

* As to the free states, it was asserted that slavery had the right of protection, when it was there in the persons of slaves in transit; and as to the national territories, that it had there the right of undisturbed occupation.

the preliminary rehearsal of the struggle of 1861 to 1865. The Northern delegates to the General Conference who engaged in the debates of 1844 knew that another debate, with far other weapons, was impending if they failed to save the unity of the Methodist Episcopal Church. The Southern delegates were generally prepared to accept the ultimate consequences of their action.

The issue before the General Conference of 1844 is thus stated in Bishop Simpson's personal narrative: "The main interest gathered around the question of slavery. A preacher of the Baltimore Conference had married a wife who inherited slaves. As he did not emancipate them while the laws of Maryland, with some restrictions, admitted of emancipation, he was arraigned, tried, and excluded from the ministry by his Conference. He appealed to the General Conference ; the Southern delegates were excited by a disciplinary act which they thought might reflect upon some of them. More interest was occasioned by a rumor that Bishop Andrew had married a slaveholding wife. The laws of Georgia did not admit of emancipation, but as his episcopal duties carried him through the entire Church, and he could choose for himself his place of residence, his remaining in Georgia and his slaveholding were believed to be a revolution of the policy of Methodism. In the first case the decision of the Baltimore Conference was confirmed by a vote which was almost sectional. The Committee on Episcopacy addressed a note to Bishop Andrew, asking him the facts in relation to the report of his slaveholding. He replied in writing, and his case came before the Conference."

The flood-gates of debate were now opened, and never, in the history of our country at least, has there been a debate more memorable. The participants were wrought up by the sense of the magnitude of the interests at stake to the highest tension of their faculties, and in their faculties they were richly endowed. The possible consequences of the division of the Church—the division of the nation and civil war—

were clearly before the minds of the speakers. Between the contestants on either side stood Olin, in stature and bearing a king of men, his head Northern, his heart Southern, appealing for moderation, for delay, for whatever this side of compromise could avert the catastrophe of division. Davis and Griffith, from a Southern Conference— the Baltimore—offer a resolution asking Bishop Andrew to resign. From the episcopal board comes the voice of Soule counselling the delegates to be calm and to avoid loudness of speech. He is ready to be "immolated" on the altar of Union, but in what precise way he does not explain. Winans, of Mississippi—an orator with the air of a backwoodsman—retorts that he cannot help loud speaking, and is going to speak loudly. He is calm, he tells his brother delegates, but it is the calmness of despair. He is the first of the speakers to suggest secession, but shrinks from pronouncing the word. Bowen, of Oneida, is bolder, and predicts the disunion of the states as the probable result of the division of the Church. Crowder, of Virginia, draws a vivid picture of the dreaded civil war : "The division of our Church may follow, a civil division of this great Confederacy may follow that, and then hearts will be torn apart ; master and slave arrayed against each other, brother in the Church against brother, and the North against the South ; and when thus angered, with the fiercest passions and energies of our nature brought into action against each other, civil war and far-reaching desolation must be the final results."

This array of the probable consequences of the decision of the General Conference must have made a strong impression upon the delegates. None could declare that Crowder's forecasting of the future was extravagant. Bangs made the point that Andrew was elected bishop in preference to Capers, of South Carolina, because he was supposed not to be a slaveholder. Davis followed this up by saying that he had himself, in 1832, asked Capers if he could not in some way rid himself of slaveholding, in the event of a nomination to the episcopacy. The resistance of the South to the Griffith and Davis resolution had, however, had some effect. A substitute was proposed by Finley and Trimble, merely expressing it as the sense of the General Conference that Bishop Andrew should desist from exercising the functions of his office till he had freed himself from all connection with slavery.

Around this substitute the final contest was waged; the South fought as if for life, the North with the conviction that nothing less than this would satisfy the churches of the free states. At the outset one misapprehension had to be removed from the minds of the Southern delegates, namely, that the pressure put upon them was prompted by abolitionism, so called. The delegates on the other side took pains to show that they were acting on established Methodist usage, and were only expressing the ancient anti-slavery feeling of the Church. Olin especially labored to make this point clear to his Southern friends. Yet he at the same time declared that any one who doubted the compatibility of the Methodist ministerial office with slaveholding might be a very good man, but was a very bad Methodist. He did not consider that slaveholding necessarily worked a forfeiture of the right to hold the office of bishop; avowed that he himself had been a slaveholder, and had never dreamed that thereby he had become unfitted for the functions of the Methodist ministry. Yet, cherishing these convictions, he was in favor of the Finley resolution, and advised the Southern delegates to accept it. He spoke to the Southern Methodists as one of their number, but with a knowledge of Northern opinion which they had not and could not have. Still the Southerners were unconvinced; even this passionate pleading failed to move them. George F. Pierce followed him and charged all the trouble on New England. "Let New England go," he said, with vehemence. "She has been a thorn in our flesh, a messenger of Satan to buffet us. Let her go, and joy go with her." These last words became memorable, and provoked Jesse T. Peck's defence of New England, for happiness of retort perhaps the most brilliant speech of the Conference: "Let New England go, no, sir, never! And here I beg to say that our Southern brethren cannot induce us to use such language with reference to them. Let the South go, no, sir! We cannot part with our brethren whom we love so well. True, we cannot compromise principle to save them, nor to save the East. We shall live and die with them; we will not let them go, unless they tear themselves from us bedewed with the tears of affection. Never, no, never!"

By this time the Southern delegates, being hard pressed, had resolved on two points: (1) To claim that any censure passed upon Bishop Andrew was also a censure upon them as slaveholding ministers; (2) To deny the administrative authority of the General Conference over Bishop Andrew, while fully admitting its judicial authority over him. The last stand was made on the constitutional right of the Conference to deal with a bishop in the manner of a principal with his agent. Longstreet, of Georgia, admitted that Bishop Andrew had offered to resign, but the Southern delegates had refused their consent to his resignation. "If it has come to this," he said, addressing Bishop Andrew, "that being connected with slavery disqualifies you, we too are disqualified." Green, of Tennessee, added to this, that if Andrew were deposed the preachers of the South could not serve their people.

It must now have been obvious that a clear, dispassionate statement of the constitutional powers of the General Conference was needed, and it was furnished by Hamline. He chose a propitious hour. A Sabbath had intervened; the surging feeling of the preceding week had had time to subside. The overflowing emotion — not anger — which had accompanied the first opening of the question had spent itself. Conviction was hardening into purpose. To yield a particle seemed impossible to the delegates on either side.

In view of its constituencies the North declared it could not but act, the South that it could not but resist. There was in both the ingrained Anglo-Saxon reverence for law. What was precisely the law in the case? And who will show it to us? Hamline's speech was like a cool stream of north wind poured into a sultry summer atmosphere. That he felt intensely was unquestionable, but his argument was wholly dispassionate. With the ease of conscious mastery he touched the vital point of the controversy—the administrative authority of the General Conference. After showing what all agreed to, that the Conference has legislative and judicial powers, he argued that it is the fountain of executive power in the Church, and as such has in possession what it bestows. The argument of Hamline must have puzzled the Southern delegates. Smith, of Virginia, the first important man who followed him, scarcely touched it, if at all. He argued that the adoption of either the original resolution or the substitute would be proscriptive; would be a most humiliating degradation of the whole Southern ministry.

On Thursday, May 23d, Bishop Andrew rose and addressed the Conference. He revealed the fact that, prior to his election in 1832, Winans had refused to vote for him, on the ground that he was nominated as a non-slaveholder. As to his own connection with slavery he justified it, and called himself a slaveholder for conscience sake. He had no apology to make, and would make none. "But," he added, "if I have sinned against the Discipline, I refuse not to die." His address, while very positive, was free from any exhibition of dogmatism; indeed, it accorded with the amiable temper which has been universally ascribed to him. Winans, always aggressive, denied the administrative authority of the General Conference over a bishop. The Kentuckian, Cartwright, whose strong common-sense always shone through his oddities of speech, replied vigorously to Winans. "If," he said, "we have, in the economy of our

Church, rules and regulations by which we can manage all the officers of the Church until we come up to the bishops, and then have no law, as was argued to-day, but the act of expulsion, we are in a deplorable fix."

But the end of surprises had not come. Bishop Soule, the senior bishop, had prepared one of his own for the Conference. Rising in his place, he repudiated the claim of an administrative authority over himself and his colleagues. It was clear that he, New England born, was going over to the Southern side. He gave notice that their decision would affect others besides Bishop Andrew. He was even then ready to separate himself from the Church. "I am about," he said, "to take my leave of you, brethren. You must know, you cannot but know, that, with the principles I have stated to you, with the avowal of my sentiments in regard to this subject, it will not be Bishop Andrew alone that your word will affect. No, sir! I implicate neither my colleagues on my right hand nor on my left; but I say the decision of the question cannot affect Bishop Andrew alone. I wish it to be understood: *it cannot affect him alone.*" The Conference had thus brought before them the prospect of a schism in the episcopate.

Here was a situation to try the nerve and courage of the majority. The certainty of the secession of the Southern Conferences, the cleaving of the episcopate in two, the possibility, in case the Church divided, of the secession of the Southern States from the Union, had all to be taken into their thoughts. But they did not shrink from these or any consequences, however appalling. A duty to God and the Church was laid upon them, and they did their duty. Durbin replied to Soule, on the afternoon of that same day, in a speech of most telling eloquence. Rarely are points more skilfully taken or more powerfully enforced. He showed that the Church had left the South to contend with slavery as it could, but that the North would not have a slaveholding bishop forced on it. He denied that the Finley substitute deposed Bishop Andrew. " If I am pressed to a decision in this case, I shall vote for that substitute, and so will many others; but if, after we have voted for it, any man should come and tell us personally that we have voted to depose Bishop Andrew, we should consider it a personal—shall I say insult, sir? The substitute proposes only to express the sense of the Conference in regard to a matter which it cannot, in duty and conscience, pass by without suitable expression, and, having made the solemn expression, it leaves Bishop Andrew to act as *his* sense of duty shall dictate. And now," addressing himself personally to Bishop Soule, who sat in the chair that afternoon, he continued, " I will take the excellent advice which you gave us this morning, sir, and not appeal to the passions of the Conference, nor to the audience in the gallery, but if an appeal must be made to any tribunal out of this body, we are willing to abide by the verdict of the world and by the decision of a far higher tribunal. There we shall fear no reversal of our action in this case. Oh, sir! when we were left to infer this morning, from the remarks of the chair, that the passage of this substitute would affect not only Bishop Andrew, but perhaps others of our bishops, I could not but feel a momentary cloud gathering before my eyes to dim the clearness of my vision. The feelings which that remark excited were not likely to give greater freedom to the action of my reason, or greater precision to my judgment. But strong as were and are those feelings, they cannot stifle my conscience or darken my understanding." Soule was effectually answered. With the high-bred courtesy which never forsook him, Durbin had made it plain to Soule's mind that the majority would not flinch from the performance of their duty, even if there should be a divided board of bishops, or even if the Church were to be left wholly without bishops. To show his pacific spirit, however, he offered a substitute for the Finley resolution, which postponed the determination of the Andrew case till the next General Conference.

At this juncture Bishops Soule, Hedding, Waugh, and Morris presented a paper proposing the postponement of the subject until 1848, their colleague, Andrew, limiting his superintendence during the intervening four years to the Southern States. It was seen at once that the latter part of the proposal, inasmuch as it localized the episcopate, was of doubtful constitutionality. Moreover, it was felt that such distribution of episcopal service would only help to consolidate the South and make it more perfectly ready for separation. The paper, Bishop Hedding having withdrawn his name, was laid on the table by the close vote of 95 to 83. The subject had now been viewed in every possible light, time was passing, and on June 1st the Finley resolution was adopted by 111 yeas to 69 nays.

"We thought," says President Simpson, "that this would be the end of it;" but the end was not yet. He affirms in his narrative that during the progress of the debate correspondence was had by the Southern delegates with Southern politicians. "The attention of the nation was turned towards the proceedings, but more in the South than in the North, as Methodism at that time had more friends among the public men of the South than among those of the North. Doctor Capers was in correspondence with John C. Calhoun and other Southern leaders who were watching this phase of the slavery question and the threatened division of the Union. The delegates of the South in the General Conference were more shrewd and diplomatic than those of the North. The latter felt themselves strong, both in the rightfulness of their cause and the strength of their numbers; the others knew that they were in the minority, and resorted to the use of tact."

As a specimen of Southern tact, President Simpson furnishes a bit of his personal experience. "Doctor ——, afterwards a bishop of the Methodist Church, South, frequently visited at Mayor Harper's and talked very freely upon the questions at issue. Near the time of taking the vote, he came to me to consult upon terms of educating some of his near relatives, and spoke of the friendship of the South for the North, and of the necessity of maintaining full intercourse. As he had not spoken to me before of sending his friends to Indiana, I feared at once that it was an effort to conciliate me. I told him I did not expect him to send his friends to the university. He colored, and asked why not. I simply replied that it was far from their homes; other institutions were nearer and easier of access. The conversation at once ceased, and I heard no more of the students."

The decisive vote was taken on Saturday, June 1st. How much did it mean? Was it advice or command? That it implied a censure no one could doubt, for it said that Bishop Andrew had made himself, for the time being, an unacceptable bishop. Should this bishop any more perform episcopal functions? Should he be provided with the usual support? Should his name appear on those documents, such as the preface to the hymn-book, which the bishops then signed and still sign jointly? The Conference answered these questions explicitly. He was still a bishop; his support was still to be provided for; he was still to be a joint signer of episcopal documents. Whether he performed episcopal duty or not was to be left to his own judgment. A gentler sentence of disapproval could hardly be expressed in words. Every concession but one was made; that, however, was the vital one—the admission of slaveholding to the episcopate.

On Monday, June 3, Capers offered a series of resolutions proposing two General Conferences, one Northern the other Southern, with power granted to each to elect its own bishops, the book-publishing property to remain apart for the benefit of both. Those who remember John C. Calhoun's proposal of a dual executive of the United States, one for the North and one for the South, will see the resemblance between the two schemes. To consider the resolutions of Capers the famous committee of nine was created. Two days later the Southern delegates made a declaration

16

in form that the proceedings against Bishop Andrew, which they considered a virtual suspension of him from office, made it impracticable for them to continue their ministry and at the same time remain under the jurisdiction of the General Conference.

Events now hurried forward. Bascom, in behalf of his Southern co-delegates, read a protest against the proceedings in the case of the bishop, insisting again that these were extra-judicial, and mandatory in fact if not in form. A committee, of which Durbin was the head, replied to the protest, rehearsing the facts and law of the case, as understood by the majority, with great vigor. But what a situation! The New-Yorker, Bascom, Northern born and bred, a son of the Pittsburgh Conference, leads the Southern wing of the Church; the Kentuckian, Durbin, whose boyhood and early manhood had been spent in the midst of slavery, voices the "Thus far and no farther" of the General Conference. Both were among the foremost orators of their generation; both were gifted with extraordinary powers of persuasion. What a mockery of men! Surely destiny is sporting with and laughing at them! Rather what an example of the power of our associations over our opinions, and what a lesson in charity for all of us!

As Durbin proceeded in the reading of the reply of the majority to the protest of the Southern delegates, the slant rays of the sun shone through the western windows of the Old Greene Street Church, in which the sessions were held. Just as he closed the sun went down, leaving the room where the delegates were sitting in deep shadow. The moment the last words were pronounced, Capers rose from his seat and advanced rapidly towards Durbin, exclaiming, "Then there is no hope!" No hope, no hope! The fabric built by the toils of the fathers and the equal toils of their sons was about to be riven asunder, and a still greater catastrophe was to come. A plan of separation, if the contingency of separation should occur, was provided, and the delegates

AT THE SOUTHERN METHODIST CONVENTION. 243

went to their homes, saddened by the thought of what was
yet to be.

"Before the close of the Conference," says Bishop Simpson's narrative, "a number of the delegates who had voted
for the plan of separation deeply regretted their action when
they saw the leaders of the South were determined to produce the separation at all hazards." They regretted their
action still more when they conferred with their people and
found that while their resistance to the bringing of slaveholding into the episcopate was approved, their sanction of
a plan of separation was condemned.

The firm position taken by President Simpson and the
Indiana delegation in this General Conference led to a correspondence between him and the Church leaders of the
Eastern States. Dr. Thomas E. Bond writes, soon after its
adjournment, to inquire about the attitude of the West. His
letter shows a clear prevision of coming events: "Slavery
will die hard wherever it has foothold, and will not be content to act on the defensive. It will contend, both in Church
and State, not only for perpetuation, but for extension. Over
its perpetuation the Church has no control; but against its
propagation into other Conferences than those where it has
already fastened itself, we must contend in the fear, and with
the assurance of the favor, of God." Durbin writes: "I am
now satisfied that the South will separate, unless the question take a political turn and alarm them—provided they
object to the division of the Union. . . . I fear most of all
the effect of this movement on the Union. I see it has already been the subject of resolutions at political meetings."

In the spring of 1845 President Simpson visited the Convention of Southern Methodist Ministers, held in Louisville,
which organized the Methodist Episcopal Church, South, and
writes thus of it to Mrs. Simpson: "I learn that seventeen
brethren of the Kentucky Conference have declared themselves openly Northern men, and a number are undecided;
that an effort will be made to postpone action until the next

General Conference, and that Northern men may make terms of compromise, etc. If any effort should be made to get Northern men to pledge themselves, my stay at Louisville will be very short, as I shall compromise nothing by any act or word of mine."

He writes again on May 7th: "Division is inevitable. Bishop Soule presides in the convention and leads the South. Warm speeches are made from day to day to convert the people of Louisville, who are yet halting between two opinions. On the whole the South will go pretty much *en masse*, and slavery will be the cause of ultimately severing the Union as well as the Church. Winans avows that if voting for dividing the Church should divide the Union, he would still do it."

How far the report of a correspondence between John C. Calhoun and the Southern leaders in the General Conference was true, we have now no means of knowing. In his speech to the Senate, March 4, 1850, he notices the division of the Methodist Episcopal Church and the probable effect of it on the integrity of the national union. He was closely watching the rupture of ecclesiastical bonds, both Methodist and others; but he had the sagacity to perceive that the dissolution of the Union would be a gradual process. Dwelling on this thought, he said: "It is a great mistake to suppose that disunion can be effected by a single blow. The cords which bind these states together are too numerous and powerful for that. Disunion must be the work of time. It is only through a long process and successively that the cords can be snapped, until the whole fabric falls asunder. Already the agitation of the slavery question has snapped some of the most important, as I shall proceed to show. . . . The strong ties which held each denomination together formed a strong cord to hold the whole Union together; but, powerful as they are, they have not been able to resist the explosive effect of the slavery agitation. The first of these cords which snapped was that of the powerful

Methodist Episcopal Church. The numerous and strong ties which held it together are all broke and its unity gone. They now form separate churches, and instead of the feeling of attachment and devotion to the interests of the whole Church which was formerly felt, they are now arrayed into two hostile bodies, engaged in litigation about what was formerly their common property." *

This declaration is in harmony with Mr. Calhoun's well-known opinions. In 1847, two years after the holding of the Louisville Convention, which, as we have said, organized the Methodist Episcopal Church, South, he introduced into the Senate his well-known resolution denying the right of Congress to prohibit slavery in the territories. He claimed that the equality of the states with each other included in it the right of the Southerner to carry slavery into any part of the national domain : " I say for one, I would rather meet any extremity upon earth than give up one inch of our equality ; one inch of what belongs to us as members of this great republic." †

Thus the Southern Methodist leaders and the Southern statesmen were moving on parallel lines ; the first demanding the sanction of slaveholding by its introduction into a national (as distinguished from a diocesan) episcopate ; the other the sanction of the system of slavery by extending to all the national territories Southern municipal law.

In the General Conference of 1848 President Simpson proved himself to be a most influential delegate. He was no longer " in delightful obscurity." The great debates were over, and he found himself more congenially occupied as a man of affairs. There was something to be done, as well as something to be said. The South had separated, carrying off with it Bishops Soule and Andrew. Its first General Conference had been held in 1846. Its fraternal

---

* See Benton's "Thirty Years' View," vol. ii., pp. 745, 746.

† See ibid., vol. ii., p. 696.

delegate was at the door of the General Conference of the old Church waiting for admission. Meanwhile a great revulsion of feeling had swept over the Methodist churches of the Northern and Middle States. They looked with alarm upon the prospect of a division of American Methodism, and had refused all sanction of the plan of separation. The plan itself was voted down almost unanimously in the Annual Conferences, then, as now, composed of ministers only. The authority of the General Conference to enact such a plan was denied. It was said, very truly, that no Church provided, or could, in its organic law, provide, for its own dissolution.

In addition to all this, the purport of the plan itself was a subject of controversy. Some contended that it was never designed to be a scheme of separation, in any sense whatever, and pointed to the fact that it was not so named in the General Conference of 1844.* They quoted, with telling effect, the words of the Rev. Doctor, afterwards Bishop, Paine, the chairman of the committee of nine from whom the plan came. He had said in 1844: "If on arriving home, in order to keep down faction and prosecute the great end of the Methodist ministry, the Southern delegates find it necessary to act upon this measure, they should feel bound to do it; and out of love to Methodist doctrines and institutions, to the souls of men, and the honor of their common Master, carry out the provisions of the enactment. But they would not thus act unless driven to it. The separation would not be effected by the passage of these resolutions through the General Conference. They must pass the Annual Conferences, beginning at New York, and when they came round to the South the preachers there would think and deliberate and feel the pulse of public sentiment and of

---

* The report of the committee of nine was called "A Report on the Declaration of the Delegates from the Conferences in the Slaveholding States."

the members of the Church, and act in the fear of God and with a single eye for his glory."

Under these circumstances the General Conference of 1848 met in a state of mind which might be very moderately described as bordering on exasperation. The forms of courtesy were, however, carefully observed. Immediately upon its assembling, Dr. Simpson, with Dr. Durbin, offered a resolution appointing a committee of two from each Conference, to be known as the committee on the State of the Church. He was not, however, made a member of this committee.* In due time its report was ready. Its declarations of a want of power in the General Conference to divide the Church were quickly passed, but when the statement of the reasons for discarding the " Plan of Separation " was reached, the Conference faltered, and, after some contention, another statement prepared by President Simpson was accepted and carried almost unanimously. To him, therefore, with Dr. Durbin, belongs the distinction of framing the declaration on which the Church planted itself in its long conflict with Southern Methodism.†

" At this General Conference," says the bishop's record of it, " an important step was taken to organize a Pacific Con-

---

* The two members from each Annual Conference were elected by the delegates of that Conference.

† The points of this declaration were : (1) The report of the committee of nine, adopted in 1844, was intended to meet a necessity which might arise; (2) It was made dependent on the concurrence of three fourths of the members of the Annual Conferences; (3) It was made dependent, also, upon the observance of the provisions for a boundary line between the two churches, should a new Church be formed; (4) Action was taken in the premises by the Southern delegates, without waiting for the anticipated necessity; (5) The Annual Conferences have refused to concur in that part of the plan which was submitted to them; (6) The provisions respecting a boundary have been violated by the separating body; (7) There is, therefore, no obligation resting upon the Methodist Episcopal Church to observe the plan; (8) And the plan is hereby declared null and void.

ference.   The war with Mexico was closed, California had
been annexed, and population was beginning to flow towards the Pacific.   The resolution was drawn by myself and
was signed by Dr. Curry and myself.   The measure met
with considerable opposition; the board of bishops did not
see its propriety, and used their influence, to some extent,
against it.   It was adopted by the General Conference, after
a brief but animated debate, in which I took the leading
part in supporting the resolution.   Upon the discovery of
gold in the ensuing summer, the stream of population rushed
to the coast, and none too soon was a Conference organized."   Among his first episcopal acts, after his election in
1852, was a long, and, at times, a perilous tour through California and Oregon.

The General Conference of 1852 was the last attended by
President Simpson as a delegate.   He obviously appreciated
this mark of distinction at its full worth.   He says of his
last election: "At the Conference preceding the General
Conference of 1852 I was again chosen to represent the
Conference, at the head of the delegation, lacking on the
ballot only four of the entire vote.   One of the four votes
was my own, another that of a decided friend, who was so
anxious for the success of another friend that he left my
name off his ticket, because, as he said, he was assured of
my success; who the other two were I never knew nor
cared to know.   I was surprised at so thorough a vote of
confidence on the part of my brethren, especially as I had
been assured by one of the elder ministers that, after accepting the editorship of the *Western Advocate*, and going out
of the bounds of my Conference, I need not in future expect
the marks of confidence from my brethren which I had previously enjoyed."

Lay delegation and pewed churches were the chief topics
of debate in the General Conference of 1852, and here again
President Simpson was among the foremost.   The notice of
the lay-delegation movement belongs to another part of this

volume. The Conference found itself compelled to act upon numerous memorials, both for and against this change in its polity, and appointed a committee of twenty-nine, at the head of which was President Simpson, to formulate the judgment of the body. The committee unanimously reported: (1) that lay delegation was inexpedient; (2) that the laity had already ample opportunities in the Church for wholesome activity; (3) that the mass of the laity were opposed to the change. Twenty years later, in 1872, lay delegates took their seats in the General Conference, but before that could be effected many things had to be said and many things to be done. Among the delegates who voted for the report were four who afterwards earnestly promoted the lay movement—Matthew Simpson, Abel Stevens, John P. Durbin, and John McClintock.

XII.

EDITOR OF THE "WESTERN CHRISTIAN ADVOCATE."

1848–1852.

The Life of a College President Forty Years ago.—The Failing Health of President Simpson.—Advised to Change his Mode of Life.—Elected Editor of the *Western Christian Advocate.*—Invited to be President of Several Colleges—Power of a Methodist Official Editor.—Doctor Elliott, President Simpson's Editorial Predecessor.—The New Editor's Idea of the Administration of his Paper.—No Controversy to be Tolerated.—Doctor Foster Replies in the *Advocate* to Doctor Rice, notwithstanding.—The Make-up of the *Advocate.*—Is Drawn into Controversy on the Great Political Question of the Time.—The Situation North and South. — Threats of Disunion. — Henry Clay's Omnibus Bill.—Positions of Clay, Calhoun, and Webster.—The Famous Editorial on "The Union."—Its Reception.—Attacks the Fugitive-Slave Bill.—Controversy with the *Indiana State Sentinel.*—Ridicules Compromising Politicians.—Rapid Growth as an Editor.—Mr. S. P. Chase's Letters to him.

XII.

By the year 1848 President Simpson's fame as the successful head of a university (really a college of liberal arts) had spread throughout the entire country. Positions were offered him more than he could accept. Between 1848 and 1852 he was invited to take charge of Woodward College in Cincinnati, of the newly organized Northwestern University at Evanston, to become president of Dickinson College, and also of the Wesleyan University at Middletown, Connecticut. To all of these offers he gave a decided refusal. Nay more, he was preparing to resign college work altogether. Perhaps he was weary of the stress of privation and toil under which he was compelled, as a college president, to live. Such positions have never been sinecures in the Methodist Episcopal Church, and he who entered upon them in that day might well begin by bidding farewell to peace. No learned ease for him; no roaming for him with boundless content through the shapely walks and among the seed and flower plots of an ample library; no plucking of the rich fruits of thought mellowed by age. For him money was the one thing needful. Grace he was supposed to have in abundance, especially the grace of patience. If he lacked that, Heaven might pity him. To keep the wolf from the college door; to provide the ways and means of subsistence for himself and his colleagues; to gather together the equipments of a high-class school; to arouse interest in a constituency slow to apprehend the value of his work; to meet prejudice and opposition with unfailing suavity; these were only some of the tasks put upon the heart and brain of a Methodist college president forty years ago. A

Methodist college president, as his work was then understood, must teach and preach; must know how to make a telling address to a conference of ministers; must be a scholar and yet not a recluse, a popular leader and yet be scholarly; must be such a financier as can make twice two come to eight; must have a good eye for real estate; must build; must know how to judge of the sharpness of mortar, the hardness of brick, and the availability of stone; must have a smattering of law and comprehend the important points of contracts; and, while meeting the demands of a very practical age, must keep abreast of it in learning, and breathe enthusiasm for knowledge into the souls of young men. And all of these perfections for —— dollars a year; and for many of them this blank sum was very blank indeed. And while carrying on his hard-fought battle in the world his wife is probably struggling with the harder problems of housekeeping, as those problems are known in a raw, unformed country. And it would not be an exaggeration of fancy to surmise that the careworn president has had often, at close of day, to do as Melanchthon did before him —hold his book in one hand and rock his baby's cradle with the other.

Some such life as this President Simpson had to live in Indiana for nine years, and it wore out his health. But he so lived it as to win the affections of the people of the state. The students loved him, and the common people heard him gladly. It was not his fault that the people were poor; out of their poverty they gave him freely for his infant university, and, more than all, they gave their precious jewels— their sons. His name was a household word in the humblest Methodist log cabin, and no Methodist boy in the state, following the plough, but knew that at Greencastle there was a great-hearted man who would help him if he aspired to a higher education than could be found at home. But the strain upon President Simpson was too much for him. He gives this account of the reasons which induced him to change: "The summer before the General Conference I had a severe attack of typhoid fever, which had been preceded by chills and fever. The opinions of my physicians were that I must either change my habits of life or my residence. I consulted doctors in whom I had great confidence and who knew me in Pittsburgh, and, such being their judgment, I felt it my duty to say to the delegates from Indiana that they must look for a new president.

"My purpose was to return to the Pittsburgh Conference, of which I had formerly been a member; but when it was rumored that I was to retire from the presidency, I was nominated, by a number of friends, as editor of the *Western Christian Advocate*. The delegates from the West learning this, proffered me that position, and claimed that I should remain in the West. Attending a preparatory meeting to nominate officers for the West, I protested, when named for the *Advocate*, against accepting. I urged that Dr. Elliott, who was my friend, and who had been editor, should remain, and that, if desired, I would accept the place of assistant. The General Conference, however, refused to appoint more than one editor, and, without my consent, I was elected. I returned from the General Conference to Greencastle, where I remained until the college year closed.

"I had scarcely become settled in my office as editor, in 1848, when I received a letter from the faculty of Dickinson College, saying that the trustees had authorized them to nominate a president, and that they would officially elect him. Though thankful for the courtesy, and esteeming the position an honorable one, I felt obliged to decline, as I had determined to obey the voice of the Church, and, as far as I could, to discharge the duty committed to me. The following year I was urged to accept the presidency of the Northwestern University, then about to be founded. This I was also obliged to decline; but I conferred freely with Doctor, afterwards Governor, Evans, and made suggestions which resulted in the purchase of the splendid site at

Evanston.　On my way to the General Conference in Boston, in 1852, I was also approached by members of the faculty and trustees of the Wesleyan University at Middletown, and asked to accept the presidency of it, then vacant. All invitations of this character I declined, believing that my health required more exercise and a change of air.　I preferred the regular pastorate."

He was now in a position of enormous power, for to the plain Methodist his *Advocate* is the fifth gospel.　Its editor, whoever he may be, is the Church's champion, who is expected to do valiant battle for him with the enemy at the gate. The champion is not of his own choosing, but is sent by the higher powers.　To him he looks for cheer, for warning, for the quickening of zeal.　To admire, even to revere, and to follow this man of war, is to the plain Methodist just as obvious a duty as it is to obey his Discipline or to express his religious feeling in the language of Charles Wesley's hymns. This enormous power of the official editor over the Methodist mind has been wielded sometimes wisely, sometimes despotically, at all times vigorously.　Through its penetrating force, the Church has well maintained the conception of a militant body.　President Simpson had been preceded in the editorial care of the *Western Advocate* by Dr. Charles Elliott, his former preceptor at Madison College and his steadfast friend.　Whether the old hero was surprised to find himself superseded by his pupil we have not the means of knowing.　At all events he took the displacement in good part, and retired cheerfully to the pastoral work.　He thanks God, he says, that young, gifted men are raised up "to fill the places of the aged when their voices and their pens shall no longer instruct or encourage the armies of Israel." In the review of his editorial life the good doctor confesses that he had lost ground in solid study.　"We can scarcely suppose," he writes pathetically, "a more unfavorable position for systematic study or severe preparation for the press than the miscellaneous gatherings and vagrant researches of the weekly editor." And now that he is free from these "vagrant researches," he promises a solid work on the "sinfulness of American slavery;" this he lived to execute. Judge Longstreet, of the Methodist Church, South, had challenged the proof of this thesis, and the veteran Elliott took him up.

At first, Dr. Simpson's conception of the scope of a Church paper was the old and, as we all now think, the narrow and exclusive one of the defence of Methodism. All assaults of foes without were to be beaten off; all uprisings of disloyalty within were to be firmly repressed. In the nature of the case, the free and healthful criticism of the Church's methods could scarcely be borne, and was not. The times were, indeed, not propitious to criticism from within. The Church had been rent in twain, and the dissevered portions stood in an attitude of ill-suppressed hostility towards each other. The slavery question had come into our national politics, and had come to stay. The old disputes, which had formed political parties, about a national bank or state banks, currency, and tariff, were fading from sight. The new editor had no taste for doctrinal or ecclesiastical controversy, and he says, in his memoir of himself, that he did his utmost to exclude both. "When I took charge of the *Advocate*," he writes, "I found it in the midst of a discussion both with the editor of the *Methodist*, a paper published by Dr. Latta, in behalf of the South, and also with Dr. Rice, on the doctrines and polity of Methodism as compared with the doctrines and polity of Presbyterianism. I resolved that no controversy should be begun by me, nor would I take up one already begun. I consequently excluded from the paper all communications of this kind, announced in my salutatory my determination to avoid personalities and to make the paper strictly a Church paper for the defence of the doctrines and polity of Methodism. For several weeks I permitted no reply to any strictures. Dr. Latta began and kept up for months a constant attack,

17

but I never so much as noticed the existence of his paper or of any of his assailing articles. Dr. Rice soon commenced again his assaults on Methodism. I wrote a brief article or two deprecating controversy, but he became still more belligerent; after writing a defensive article, I allowed Doctor Foster, since bishop, to present his objections to Calvinism, which were afterwards published in book form. The articles were very able, and the friends of Dr. Rice were the first to discover that controversy was not profitable. The paper edited by Dr. Latta finally died, he himself became my warm personal friend, and then told me that he had wished to discontinue his articles very soon after my accession to the editorship, but his friends had urged him to go on with them."

The means placed in the hands of a Church editor then seem to us in our time to be ludicrously inadequate. In his opening article Dr. Simpson calls for help: "We have but little original matter in this week's paper, and we have no supply for our next issue except obituary notices. Send us short articles written in a plain hand." The editorial cupboard was empty; nothing was laid up in store for the proverbial rainy day. Of money for the payment of contributions, carefully prepared, there was none; the thought of such an outlay had not yet been entertained.

In default of original matter, much reliance was placed upon selections which were skilfully chosen. Kirwan's letters to Bishop Hughes were copied from the *New York Observer;* the *Wesleyan Methodist Magazine* of London was freely drawn upon for supplies; and much attention was given to scientific discovery and travel. Soon signs were visible of increasing breadth; a regular New England and New York correspondence was maintained—no doubt paid for. Dr. Curry was the New York correspondent, and sent invariably a good miscellany of news. The leaders were for a time practical and hortatory; having determined to avoid controversy with the Church South, other course was not open to the editor. Soon, however, he found a subject which kindled him and set him aflame. Next to his strong determination towards men for their conversion to Christianity, his strongest impulse was towards politics in the highest sense of the term. He knew that the right administration of the State demands the best faculties of the best citizens and should be the serious concern of all citizens. His old uncle was one of the early abolitionists, and, although he had never been able to convert his nephew to the opinions of that small but resolute party, he had not failed to discuss with him the issues which the abolitionists had forced upon the attention of the country. The correspondence had not been without warmth on both sides, nor had it failed to arouse the nephew's conscience. Though guarded in his speech, Simpson, the preacher, president, and editor was an active anti-slavery man.

We will let him give the account of this part of his editorial career himself : "The anti-slavery spirit was strong in some parts of Ohio ; in some places there may have been, in the height of excitement, mistakes committed on one side or the other. While the paper was, in tone and spirit, thoroughly anti-slavery, and unwavering in its devotion to temperance, still I would not allow the personal mistakes of the friends or officers of the Church in any place to be made the subject of unfriendly or severe comment. On public measures the paper was outspoken. For a very decided editorial on the fugitive-slave law it received the commendation of the Indiana Conference by a rising vote. It defended against political assailants the position of the Church ; it advocated public improvements, looking to the development of the West. For its interest in California, it received commendatory letters from Thomas H. Benton ; for its course on slavery and its editorials on the measures of Congress, it received friendly letters from Judge Chase and others."

The political situation was very grave ; the territory acquired in the war with Mexico was about to be brought into the Union as free. The citizens of California had framed a constitution by which slavery was forever excluded from the state, and had adopted it by an overwhelming majority of votes. The soil of New Mexico was already free by the laws of the Mexican republic; slavery could be now established there only by the positive law of Congress. The South threatened immediate disunion if the carefully maintained equilibrium of slave and free states, then existing, were seriously disturbed. On this subject Mr. Calhoun made his last speech in the Senate, March 4, 1850. He insisted that the balancing of free with slave states once lost, the South could not remain in the Union. He claimed, too, that the admission of California was for the South a test case, and that if this state came in without slavery, the only remedy left for the South was either an amendment of the Constitution giving it a veto on the action of the Northern States, or disunion.* He was at this time in a dying condition. The speech containing this declaration was read to the Senate by a brother senator, and in four weeks thereafter Calhoun passed away, leaving followers who had adopted his theories and were ready to carry them out to the last results. Mr. Clay, to whom the country had so often looked for measures of peace, was now an old man, so infirm that he could with difficulty climb the steps of the Capitol. He had passed his threescore years and ten, yet his eye was not dim, nor was his persuasive power seriously impaired. He was alarmed by the temper of the South; he knew that there were bold leaders of the Southern people who were bent on secession if they could not secure for slavery a controlling influence over the Union. At heart and in his spoken utterances, he was an advocate of a peaceful ending of the slave system. He had urged the people of Kentucky to enter upon a gradual emancipation of their slaves. Man-hunting he detested,

---

* See Schurz's "Life of Henry Clay," vol. ii., p. 338.

and had but once in his life given his services as a lawyer for the reclamation of a slave, and then only to oblige a personal friend. In the course of his long political life he had conceived of but one remedy for the evils of the times ; that remedy was a mutuality of concession by North and South. This remedy he sought to apply once more. Summoning all the energy of his failing body, he spent the entire winter of 1849–1850 in urging the adoption of a series of measures for composing the excitement which now pervaded the country.*

He did not perceive that his scheme for making peace would be of no avail, and that the day for compromise was past. Nor did he know how thoroughly the Northern conscience had been aroused to the enormity of the system of slavery, and how inevitably, before the action of its aroused conscience, the system must go down. But he did know that the followers of Calhoun were terribly in earnest and meant every word they spoke. So during that long winter and the following spring, often scarcely able to stand in his place in the Senate, he appealed for the Union. Dissolution, he said, meant civil war, and civil war he would not, he could not face. To pacify the North his series of bills provided for the prompt admission of free California, and to pacify the South New Mexico was made a territory with or without slavery as its people might choose, and a stringent fugitive-slave law

---

* Nothing in the entire debate is finer than Clay's outburst of feeling against Mr. Rhett of South Carolina. Rhett had avowed strong disunion opinions, and one of his friends had said that his opinions might prove to be the opinions of his state. " Mr. President," replied Mr. Clay, " I said nothing with regard to the character of Mr. Rhett. I know him personally and have some respect for him. But if he pronounced the sentiment attributed to him, of raising the standard of disunion and of resistance to the common government, whatever he has been, if he follows up that declaration by corresponding overt acts "—the old man's eye flashed, and his voice rang out in a thunder peal—" he will be a traitor, and I hope he will meet the fate of a traitor."—Schurz, " Life of Clay," vol. ii., p. 357.

was passed. It ought to be said, in justice to the humanity of Mr. Clay, that the original draft of his fugitive-slave bill provided for the trial of every case of the reclamation of a slave by a jury, but this, its only humane feature, was struck out. Mr. Webster, three days after Calhoun's speech had been read to the Senate, astonished the country by turning his back upon the convictions and declarations of a lifetime. Thus the old statesmen who had led the country for years failed to comprehend the situation. Perhaps, in mercy to them, the things to come were hid from their eyes. In that memorable winter of 1849–50 Mr. Seward was in the Senate, and had amazed Southern senators by declaring that the public domain was already devoted to justice and liberty by a higher law than the Constitution. Chase was there, and told the senators that the people would unsettle their settlement, even if it should prevail in Congress.

The country was aglow with excitement, and Simpson the editor was in touch with the country. While the compromise bills were pending, he addressed his readers, on May 1, 1850, in the strong editorial of which he speaks with such evident satisfaction. It will be seen that he judged the South superficially, just as many in the South underrated the earnestness of the people of the North.

" THE UNION.

"Is there any danger of disunion? At present we see not the slightest indication of it. Why, then, all this outcry, and why all these flaming speeches at Washington? At the risk, gentle reader, of offending aspiring politicians, we will tell you.

"The pro-slavery party in this nation desire to introduce slavery into New Mexico, and they wish more stringent laws to recapture fugitive slaves—laws which will enable any petty postmaster to call out every good citizen and turn him into a police officer, to assist him in this degrading work—laws, too, which will greatly facilitate the process of kidnapping the free colored population. But these laws cannot be passed without Northern votes. The problem is then presented, how can Northern votes be obtained? The desire for office and emoluments they know is very strong, and hence they whisper their purpose to make a certain

Whig or Democrat the next president, if they can give him the votes of the South. Others they wish to see in the Cabinet, or in important foreign embassies. But how can these Northern men manage to vote with the South without calling down upon them the indignation and curses of the North? Only by the South getting up the cry of disunion. Then when they get the country excited, these Northern champions magnanimously step forward to save the Union. They compromise the rights of humanity, pretendedly to save the Union, but really to get into the Presidency, Cabinet, or some important station. In Washington these things are well understood; but both political parties are involved, and the press is expected to keep silent. Among themselves they laugh at the scheme, but they expect to gull the 'dear people.' Nay, these very men will claim the honor and gratitude of the North for their efforts to save the Union; that is, to get offices for themselves by betraying their constituents.

"This, dear reader, is, so far as we can learn—and we have conversed with many gentlemen from Washington—the true history and position of affairs at present. What the issue will be we cannot say; but we will venture the prediction, that every Northern man who votes with the South will soon be nominated for some important office.

"In this surrender of rights, a stupendous fraud is attempted by our senators and representatives. By admitting California along with the territories, the Wilmot Proviso must be abandoned.* Some of the senators and representatives will vote for it from the lips, expecting to deceive the people by parliamentary tactics. Already all the schemes are laid, and Northern men are known to be parties to the plan to sacrifice the territories; and yet, by a vote cunningly given, they expect to divert the attention of their constituents from their real position. Such men will learn that the eyes of the people are upon them, and that the people are not quite so ignorant and stupid as they imagine them to be. They will learn that it is dangerous to expose the freemen of the North for sale in the shambles at Washington, even for the sake of the Presidency or Cabinet; and office, however desirable, may be too dearly bought.

"Again: if the proviso is deemed wholly unnecessary, who cannot see that this union of California with the territories† is an admonition to the

---

* A resolution offered in Congress by a representative of that name, forbidding the extension of slavery to our territories.

† Mr. Clay's bill—known as the Omnibus Bill—included California, New Mexico, Deseret, and the reclamation of fugitive slaves in one legislative measure. In this form it was defeated; subsequently, the several parts of his bill passed Congress as separate measures.

territories not to adopt the same kind of a constitution? California has now been kept knocking for admission for nearly five months. As yet she knocks in vain. And if she comes in only by compromise, is it not virtually saying to New Mexico and Deseret: 'Dare not to insert the odious principle of freedom in your constitution; if so, you may not be admitted at all, for California was only saved by compromise'? Such a compromise is a premium upon slavery.

"But, says a sensitive politician who dreads free speech, I thought the *Advocate* was a religious paper—how dare you discuss political questions? We answer, the *Advocate* is a religious paper, and that is the reason we dare to pursue an independent course. We are not sold to the Whigs or Democrats or Free-soil men.

"We ask no support from any or all of them as parties; and we dread not the frowns or censures of any man among them, however distinguished, though some of them we most highly respect. We meddle with no merely political questions. We seek not the triumph of any party. They may arrange at pleasure the questions of banks, and tariffs, and sub-treasuries, and spoils of office. We care not what may be their peculiar party machinery. We stand upon higher ground. We are Christians—we are Christian freemen—and this question deeply affects us. It is a moral as well as a political question. It affects churches as well as states.

"Who does not know that the churches of the North are, in a great measure, excluded from slaveholding territory? Some of the ministers of the Methodist Episcopal Church have been mobbed, and some have been compelled to escape to save their lives, simply for preaching the gospel among slaveholders. One of our brethren was driven by an officer of the United States government, through the influence of slaveholders, out of the Indian Territory. That missionary was sent out by the bishop; he was then, and is now, an energetic and laborious member of the Ohio Conference, but he was sacrificed to slavery. That, *too, was in a free territory*—free by law, but not in fact; for in it church members and ministers traffic in the souls and bodies of men. And yet, when Daniel Webster and Lewis Cass, the great leaders of the Whig and Democratic parties, dwelt upon the injuries the South had sustained, they could never stoop to notice the insults and injuries committed against ministers and churches, contrary to all law and all propriety. Now let New Mexico be made slave territory, and it will be, to a great extent, closed against the churches and ministers of the North; and yet we are commanded not to utter a word of warning, or a voice of remonstrance. It is a political, not a religious question! Men of state! politicians of every hue and party! we tell you we will not bow down and worship the image which you have set up. You may heat your oven as you have threatened, but we are persuaded that its flames shall not injure us.

"Besides all this, the plan now before the Senate is an artful attempt to make a treaty law. We have heard that the solemnity of a treaty is now claimed, even by Northern politicians, for a joint resolution admitting Texas.* The men who would not vote for a new slave state say they are bound by treaty! What is this committee of compromise? An attempt to make a treaty between the North and the South in the United States Senate. Let it carry, and for all time to come we shall hear of the solemn compact, the compromise that saved the Union; and men will be invoked to beware of breaking a treaty. Were we a member of the Senate or House of Representatives, we would vote for no bill of any kind brought in by such a committee, because we believe it to be an attempted fraud. And when such a measure is adopted to bind suffering humanity upon the altar, and offer it up as a sacrifice to appease the dark spirit of slavery, we beg leave to be neither priest nor party in the dreadful orgies.

" We have now spoken freely and fully, both because we believed it to be our duty, and because the threatening note from aspiring politicians has warned us to let these objects alone. To all such threats we can only reply: 'Gentlemen of the political school, you may muzzle the political press if you can, *but the religious press shall be free, and for its support we shall throw ourselves upon the country.*' In using the word 'South' in these remarks, we wish explicitly to state that we mean the pro-slavery party. The majority of the citizens of the South, we believe, are firm friends of freedom, but their voice and feelings are suppressed by the tyranny of the slaveholders."

The responses to this editorial were immediate. One friend writes: "How glad I am to see a man at the head of our Church paper who has the nerve to do right." Another: "That editorial on the Union makes everything tingle; politicians hear of it, inquire for it, read it, and some commend and a few condemn. I believe it is the most popular editorial you have written, short as it is." Mr. Chase had already written from the Senate chamber: "I do not

---

* Texas was admitted, as an independent state, to the Union by a joint resolution of the two houses of Congress, approved by acting-President Tyler, March 1, 1845. All of New Mexico, east of the river Rio Grande, was claimed by Texas at the time of its annexation to the United States.

choose to resist the inclination which impels me to offer you my sincere thanks for your manly and more than manly, your Christian article on the late scene in the Senate "— the assault by Senator Foote of Mississippi on Senator Benton. He was now fully committed to the political struggle, which he regarded as a battle for the maintenance of the fundamental principles of Christian morals. Already, on April 3, 1850, he had asserted the right of the religious press to take part in the discussion which had now spread over the entire country : " When moral principles are the ground of controversy, and when the discussion turns upon the great questions of human rights, then no tongue should be dumb, no press should be silent." Having entered this field, he remained in it, a champion in complete armor. He had already begun to despair of the support of freedom by public men, and he appeals to the people : " Yes, Christian freemen, these Washington politicians are negotiating for your votes, as coolly and deliberately as their twin brothers are for flesh and blood in the shambles, over which wave the stars and stripes of our national banner. How forcible are these expressions of Holy Writ : ' Cease ye from man whose breath is in his nostrils.' ' Put not your trust in princes, nor in the sons of men, in whom there is no help.' Truth shall yet triumph, the right shall yet prevail. The omnipotence of God is pledged to bring to naught the counsels of wicked men. On that we rely, and though, for a season, oppression and iniquity may exalt themselves, yet their triumph will be short-lived."

When the fugitive-slave bill was passed, he reviewed it with great keenness. He was not of the number of men who would deny the legal right of slaveholders to reclaim fugitive slaves ; he would submit to all that was nominated in the bond, but he would have the bond strictly construed. He insisted that, until the title of a master was fully proved, the claimed negro should have every right which the law secures to a freeman, especially the benefit of a trial by jury and of the writ of habeas corpus, both of which the fugitive-slave law denied. He poured unending satire upon " the ten-dollar commissioners " whom the law made judges of the freedom or slavery of colored men. By the terms of the law the commissioner was allowed five dollars if he adjudged the negro brought before him to be free, and ten dollars if he adjudged him to be a slave. " The law," he wrote, "authorizes the employment of deputy marshals to any extent, who may call into requisition the services of every good citizen. The minister may be on his way, on the holy Sabbath, to address an assembled congregation, but, at the requisition of a deputy marshal, the creature of *these ten-dollar commissioners*, he must let his congregation wait, for the law commands him to aid in the more glorious enterprise of capturing a runaway slave, or more likely of *aiding in kidnapping a freeman*."

His criticisms of the law were felt, especially in Indiana, and the *State Sentinel*, then edited by a member of Congress, attempted a reply in a style once common to the political press when noticing the intrusion of a religious paper into the domain of politics. Its editorial said : " We have always admired Dr. Simpson for his eloquence in the pulpit and the simplicity and beauty of his style. But divinity, not law, has been his study. We shall review his article in the spirit of Christian forbearance." Very admirable, indeed, but the unlucky editor found that Dr. Simpson knew something of law as well as of divinity ; for he showed, from the highest authorities, that a law enacting a crime is, by the force of natural reason, null and void. The *Sentinel* was left in a pitiful plight. The correspondence of Dr. Simpson, of this period, shows the instant effect of his rejoinder. One friend writes " that the members of Congress and others had been censuring his course, but that since the appearance of the editorial they all seemed to have the lock-jaw." Another, after speaking of its effect, adds : " Politicians took it upon them to exercise a censorship over clergymen and religious journals altogether unwarrantable. I wonder if they will never learn to reply respectfully to an article in a religious paper without closing with an exhortation or a long string of advice."

It is clear that a change was going on in his mind, and that having begun his editorial life with a deprecation of all controversy, he was becoming, in mid career, a vigorous controversialist. His foes were not such as he had at first looked for; they were without, not within, the Church. There grew up in him, too, a purpose to free the Church, or, at least, the Church press, from political dictation in matters not purely ecclesiastical. His eyes had been opened to the meanness of much American political conduct, and he grew more and more determined to hold public men to their accountability before God's law. They had assumed a patronizing tone towards him; he retaliated by exposing their ignorance of things they ought to know. A Texas governor, rejoicing over the grant of ten millions by Congress, in settlement of the boundary claim of that state, had said, in a thanksgiving proclamation, "In the beautiful and expressive language of the Bible, *the winter of our discontent is gone;* the rain is over and past; the time of the springing of the flowers is come, and the voice of the turtle is heard in the land." Dr. Simpson, in satirizing this jumbling together of Scripture and Shakespeare, says he suspects that there is a politician's Bible, and conjectures that "it may contain the code of ethics followed by our leading politicians, and which the divines, who have only the light of the old dispensation, are at a loss to comprehend. How shall we obtain a copy? Cannot some of our friends in Congress, who take a deep interest in theological subjects, procure and furnish us one?" The issue between the churches and the politicians having now been drawn, he returned to the attack upon these foes of righteousness, as he believed them to be, again and again. In an editorial of April 16, 1851, he outlines the plan of a temperance campaign in Ohio. He speaks thus to the preachers of the state : " Ministers of the gospel, fear not the charge of meddling in politics. The demagogue may assault you, but you have nothing to fear. Sobriety will prepare the way for the gospel. We have a special promise to plead in behalf of the Church, as if written in view of such men and such opposition : *The gates of hell shall not prevail against it.*"

His interest in politics had always been strong; during the years of his early manhood he had been a follower of Mr. Clay and a zealous supporter of Mr. Clay's protective policy. From this time he threw off all political yokes. The truth had dawned upon him that the country was to be saved by an appeal to its conscience, and he knew that its conscience would be found most highly developed within the churches. As the questions in debate were both moral and political, he felt himself bound to take part in the debate; he was accumulating an influence very unusual for a minister or bishop to wield. He was making ready for the memorable years of his life, from 1861 to 1865. The editor of 1848 was not the editor of 1852. There had been rapid growth in the four years. A keen controversialist had been developed : capable of sarcasm ; capable, upon occasion, of being severely personal. Henceforth his constitutional caution was to be useful as a saving common-sense which deterred him from rash enterprises; but his equally constitutional energy, his ambition for the utmost possible development of his Church and his country, carried him forward to the front rank of the public men of his time.

Two letters from Mr. S. P. Chase, then in the United States Senate, will show the estimate which he placed upon Dr. Simpson's efforts to arouse and guide public opinion :

" Washington City, April 26, 1850.

" MY DEAR SIR,—I do not choose to resist the inclination which impels me to offer to you my sincere thanks for your manly, and more than manly, your Christian article on the late scene in the Senate.

" You are right in the opinion that, had a Northern Senator been guilty of bringing arms into the chamber, of using provoking and insulting language towards the Senator oldest in service and among the most distinguished, and then, when that language led to a demonstration of intended chastisement on the part of the Senator assailed, had drawn a pistol for a bloody affray, that Northern Senator would have hardly escaped expulsion. I fear you are right in the opinion also that the Slave Power is predominant in the Senate, as it has long been in the country.

"Never were truer words uttered than yours: 'The hour of trial is upon us, and though, in the end, humanity will triumph, yet personal duty demands free and full utterance now for every lover of liberty.' Hardly any subject can now more worthily engage 'the action and the prayers of all true Christians.'

"I have endeavored to do a *part* of my duty in the premises; not, I trust, without some proper sense of my responsibility to God, and not without looking to him for guidance and direction. I have sent you what I have spoken, and hope it may meet your approval.

"I wish Colonel Benton were a Christian indeed, that he could regard with composure, and even with forgiveness, the reckless assaults made upon him. But while I so wish, and while I cannot approve all he does and says, neither can I be insensible to the great moral courage he displays, or the strong sense of justice and right which marks his course in the present struggle between the Slave Power and Freedom in relation to California. He is, indeed, a great and heroic man, and the country will yet appreciate as they merit his efforts in this crisis.

"I think the probability strong that the unnatural and forced union of the admission of California with governments for the territories will be defeated. I am astonished at the favor which it has found. It has always seemed to me that the bare statement of the proposition would satisfy any one that it was morally wrong. Mr. Benton exposed its true nature last Monday in a forcible speech. I wish I had a copy to send you, but probably you have seen it in the *Union* or the *Intelligencer*. This letter, of course, is not designed for publication, but only as a friendly note to yourself.

"With sincerest respect, yours truly,   S. P. CHASE."
"Rev. M. Simpson."

"Washington, July 17, 1850.

"MY DEAR SIR,—Your suggestion in relation to the Missouri Compromise line fell in with the views of some of our friends here; but, after reflection, it was thought best to meet each question as it arose distinctly, and vote in accordance with our best judgment as to the fitness or unfitness of the amendments proposed. I am now satisfied that, so far as the Missouri Compromise was concerned, this was the wisest course.

" The prospect at present is that the Omnibus Bill will be defeated in the Senate. The test question will be taken on a motion to lay the bill on the table within a day or two—perhaps to-day. It ought, in my judgment, to have been taken yesterday. The motion would have prevailed yesterday, and so divided is the Senate that it is impossible to foresee what a day may bring forth. Should I be disappointed in the expectation that the bill will be defeated on that motion, I shall still hope for its defeat in the House, but with less confidence. The death of General Taylor and Mr. Fillmore's understood favor to Messrs. Webster, Clay, and that side, change aspects much.

" Yours truly,   S. P. Chase."

XIII.

FIRST EPISCOPAL TOURS.

1852, 1853.

XIII.

In May, 1852, Matthew Simpson was elected a bishop of the Methodist Episcopal Church by the General Conference then sitting in the city of Boston. The political situation was gloomy. Mr. Clay, who had captured Simpson's heart in the time of his early manhood, and who had been for years his ideal of an American statesman, was dying, and in the following month passed away. The two political parties, assembled in convention this same year, agreed in resolving that the so-called compromise measures were a legislative finality. Both called for peace, but there was no peace; the country was ill at ease; among the people there was everywhere unrest. Honest citizens of the free states were exasperated by notorious instances of slave hunting in their own neighborhoods. The principle of non-interference, which was embodied in that part of Mr. Clay's measures relating to New Mexico and Utah, was quickly applied to Kansas and Nebraska, and thus " Slavery and Free Labor were brought face to face, musket in hand, for a deadly conflict on the plains of the West." * In the Church the excitement produced by the division of 1844 had somewhat subsided, and each of the two bodies was pushing its enterprises forward with the old-time Methodist vigor. The discovery of gold deposits in California was drawing to the Pacific coast thousands of enterprising men, mostly young men, and the Church was following in the footsteps of these hardy adventurers. William Taylor, with his Bethel

---

* I quote here from Mr. Carl Shurz's admirable life of Henry Clay, to which I have been elsewhere under obligations.

ship and open-air services, was already there, and, as we understand it, founded the first Methodist Episcopal Church in that state. The new bishops, Baker, Scott, Ames, and Simpson, who were to be associated with Waugh, Morris, and Janes, were men of energy. Scott volunteered at once to go to Liberia; Ames and Simpson contended with each other in friendly rivalry for the honor of making the first episcopal visitation to the Pacific slope.

Of his election, its incidents, and of his first self-distrustful administration of his office, Bishop Simpson has left us a full account in his diary; and we shall draw upon this freely. Of diary writing there is very little to be found among his papers; that little, however, will enable us, better than any other testimony can, to perceive the spirit in which he lived and the manner in which he looked at himself and his work.

" *May* 25, 1852.—At nine o'clock this morning the General Conference proceeded to ballot for four bishops, and on the first ballot 173 votes were cast. L. Scott had 113, M. Simpson 110, O. C. Baker 90, and E. R. Ames 89, and were elected. The next highest were E. Thomson, G. Webber, C. Kingsley, G. Gary.

" I had the active and uncompromising opposition of nearly all the Ohio delegation and of most of the North Ohio. The grounds of hostility were that I was tolerant on the pew question,* and that I had not travelled sufficiently as an itinerant preacher. Yet the same persons supported Ames, who was with me on the pew question, and the most of them supported Thomson, who had travelled little, if any, more than myself. Perhaps a few in New England declined to vote for me, as I had been unanimously nominated by the faculty of the Wesleyan University for the presidency of that institution; they desired to retain me for that position. Under these circumstances the vote I received was wholly unexpected, and deeply impressed me with the kind feelings of my brethren. May I have wisdom and grace to fit me for the high responsibilities which

---

* This question came before the General Conference, on the appeal of John S. Inskip, of the Ohio Conference. He had permitted mixed sittings in the church at Dayton, Ohio, of which he was pastor. The General Conference decided that the old rule, " Let the men and women sit apart," was advisory only, not mandatory.

may devolve upon me, and especially may I be led to a more thorough consecration to God and his cause."

In an autobiographic sketch, without date, which he appears to have dictated to some one, he states more in detail the circumstances of his election, and modestly mentions his refusal to as much as try, by word or act, to influence votes—an example to be commended in these days of ecclesiastical office-seeking.

" The few of the brethren of the West, and especially of the Cincinnati Conference, who were opposed to my liberal views as to pewed churches, and as to the erection of neater and more beautiful church edifices, were so anxious to prevent my election that they combined to vote for Bishop Ames, and by that means defeated their special favorite, Dr. Thomson. With that exception there was no party question whatever involved in the choice. A few of the delegates on the border thought me to be too anti-slavery, and sent a committee to question me upon my position. I simply referred them to my course as editor, and to the views I had publicly expressed, and declined to make any further expression of opinion whatever. I had resolutely and conscientiously refrained from any arrangement with any person looking towards securing a vote, and declined to make any expression which might be interpreted as wishing to gain any favor. In the earlier part of the Conference I had offended a few of the New England delegates by expressing a preference for free churches; while advocating the erection of a Metropolitan Church in Washington, I said I should like to have it as commodious as the church in which we were then sitting, and would be pleased to have it in all respects like that church, ' save,' as I pointed to the pew-doors, ' these bonds.' Father Taylor, who afterwards became one of my warmest friends, and a few others, complained bitterly of this expression, and felt for a time unpleasantly towards me. It was suggested to me that it would be better to leave the expression out of the report of my speech, but I declined to have it done.

"The choice of my brethren led me to very serious reflection. My health was delicate; my life had been largely sedentary, and many friends doubted whether I could bear the fatigue and the exposure then connected with the work of a bishop. I had greatly enjoyed the society of my family, and had several children in whose education I was deeply interested. But, as I had resolved to accept the voice of the Church as the will of God, and as I had never solicited in any manner a vote as a delegate to the General Conference or for any office connected with it, I felt that the arrangement was wholly providential."

He had reached the episcopate with clean hands and spotless fame. Contrary to the practice of our times, he was an active and speaking member of the Conference that elected him. He did not consider himself to be doomed to silence because he was a possible or probable candidate for high place.

We return to the diary :

"*May* 26.—I was relieved from being chairman of the Committee on Education. Received many congratulations from my brethren, and assurances of hearty welcome at their Conferences. Am very sensible of many defects and infirmities.

May 27.—This morning the Lay Delegation Committee made a report by M. Raymond, secretary. I had drawn it up by the direction of the committee, but the secretary presented it.* The vote was taken by ayes and noes, and lest I might be thought unwilling to express an opinion I voted aye, though they were willing to excuse the bishops elect, if they desired it. Brothers Scott, Baker, Ames, and myself, at the suggestion of Ames, retired to a committee-room, conversed in reference to the ordination ceremony, and spent a season in prayer, each engaging in turn. We were presented to the bishops at eleven. Father Haven, of Indiana, and Brother Hudson, of Pittsburgh, presented me, and in presence of an immense crowd we were ordained, and invited to seats by the bishops.

May 28.—This day it came my turn to preside in Conference, and I was very kindly received and treated by my brethren. But few difficult questions arose, and I felt but little embarrassment.

May 29.— Conference sat only in the afternoon. Met with bishops in the afternoon and also at night. It was arranged for me to take the Western Virginia, Pittsburgh, Erie, and North Ohio Conferences, and to accompany Bishop Janes to Ohio and Cincinnati, and if convenient to Missouri, and to go out in the fall of 1853 to California.

May 30.—Being Sabbath, I preached to a large congregation in Bromfield Street Church with some liberty. Heard Dr. McClintock preach an excellent sermon at three in the afternoon.

---

* The report said: "Having examined the probable effect the introduction of Lay Delegates into the General and Annual Conferences would have upon the interests of the Church, your committee are unanimously of opinion that such a change is inexpedient."

May 31.—Conference sat both forenoon and afternoon. Anticipating a speedy adjournment, I took some time to look for various articles which I needed. At night bishops Morris, Janes, and Scott, as committee, retired to make the Episcopal plan, and I was called on to preside. We had a trying time, and Conference sat until about ten. The session was pleasant, but the brethren hurried exceedingly. Bishop Waugh gave a very beautiful and appropriate address, urging to coolness and deliberation.

June 1. — Our session was prolonged, and we adjourned about two o'clock P.M. After purchasing several articles, I met with the bishops both afternoon and evening copying Episcopal decisions and advising in arranging plans.

June 2.—Presented revised plan of study and plan for local preachers. We finished our consultation about one P.M. At five we bade farewell to our friends in Boston and took cars to Stonington.

June 3.—We went to Mayor Harper's and took breakfast. Went to Book Room and ordered portfolio, Journals of Conference, etc., with parchment, to be sent by express to Morgantown. At two left for Philadelphia by Amboy route. Stopped at McKibben's for supper, and at quarter-before eleven left in cars for Pittsburgh.

June 4.—Crossed the mountains from noon to five; had a very pleasant trip. At night our stage ride was unpleasant.

June 6.—On Sabbath heard Mr. Burkitt preach a missionary sermon in the morning. At two visited German Sabbath-school and addressed scholars, and at half-past two addressed the Smithfield School. At three assisted in administering the sacrament at Liberty Street, consecrating the elements. And at night preached in Smithfield to a large audience from Rom. xiv. 12.

June 8. — At eight o'clock started on Brownsville boat *Atlanta* for Morgantown, having first had an interview with Dr. Cooke as to the work in Pittsburgh, etc. At Brownsville took stage for Uniontown."

Uniontown reminds him of his early struggles for knowledge, and he writes thus to his wife, under date of June 10th :

"Uniontown to me has some pleasant reminiscences. Nearly twenty-four years ago I entered it one afternoon, as a poor student, having walked from Cadiz, Ohio, carrying my clothes and books in a budget on my back. I left home with a few clothes, a few books, and eleven dollars in money to enter upon a college course among strangers. I could not afford a stage passage, nor could I well afford to pay for regular meals, and hence I got but one meal a day, and lived on cakes for the other two till I reached the town. Then I called on Dr. Elliott, entered on my studies, was needed as a teacher, and in a few weeks was elected tutor. Change after change has since occurred, until this evening I entered it again by the same road on which I travelled then."

HIS FIRST CONFERENCE.

" *June* 10.—This morning Conference commenced at nine o'clock. After prayer and singing twice I addressed the preachers a few minutes, and after the election of a secretary, adoption of rules, appointment of committees, at half-past ten o'clock Conference adjourned, as by previous order a sermon was to be delivered at eleven. Mr. Martin gave us an excellent discourse from ' Whosoever shall confess,' etc.

June 17.—Conference continued in session until Wednesday evening. It was a very pleasant session. I was very kindly received by the presiding elders, and we had comparatively little trouble in making our arrangements. We sat one night till near one; other nights we adjourned about ten. Saturday evening a missionary anniversary was held; the speakers were Mr. Hunter and myself. On Sabbath I preached at eleven, and after sermon ordained fifteen deacons. After three-o'clock sermon I ordained eight elders. On Monday afternoon spoke at Sunday-school anniversary, and at night, holding first a short cabinet session, we attended sacramental meeting.

June 18.—On yesterday afternoon I left Morgantown at half-past three, having to wait for the stage from nine in the morning until that time. When it came it was but a miserable hack. We had five passengers; among them was Mr. King, of the Cincinnati Conference. After riding and walking alternately, we arrived at Uniontown—twenty-five miles—at half-past three in the morning, having made the journey in twelve hours! At half-past four took stage for Brownsville, and after breakfast went aboard the steamer *Atlanta* for Pittsburgh, where I arrived about four.

June 22.—Started in a stage at six for Washington, Penn., and arrived at twelve. Found my lodging at Bro. Hazlett's. At three invited in the elders and commenced preparing our circuits and districts."

In holding the Pittsburgh Conference he is among the friends of his youth, and opens it with characteristic modesty. We follow the diary:

" *June* 23. — At half-past eight commenced Conference. After two prayers gave an address, referring to my inexperience, my early ministry, the duties of the Conference, etc., etc. During the session I gave a

Sabbath-school address and also spoke at the Missionary Anniversary. Preached on Sunday at eleven. A number of gentlemen sent me a note on Monday requesting me to preach again, and in the Presbyterian church; the pastor called upon me to join in the invitation, but I was so hurried I was compelled to decline. Sat up very late at night on Tuesday and Wednesday, and on Thursday night until three o'clock in the morning. Conference met at five in the morning to receive the appointments. Generally they were satisfactory, but a few were greatly disappointed.

August 23.—Started for North Ohio Conference, stopped at Mr. Gill's at Cleveland. Left Cleveland next noon and arrived in Delaware about five.

August 25.—Conference commenced with several prayers, and I gave an address. I applied myself closely to appointments, and had the satisfaction of seeing the work progress without as much loss of sleep as at some previous conferences. On Sabbath preached with much liberty and ordained deacons; in the afternoon ordained elders.

Monday afternoon I was greatly gratified by the arrival of Bishop Janes, who came to Delaware to see the Conference, though it was out of his route to the Ohio Conference. He sat with us in council in the evening, and we conversed until a late hour. He had a severe chill and suffered much pain during the night. In the morning he attended Conference, and tried to get volunteers for California. He also gave a short address to the Conference, and left for Zanesville.

Sept. 1.—Conference closed its session at eleven on Wednesday, and I left for Zanesville—but on reaching the station found the cars were detained; they did not arrive for an hour and a half after their time. The result was that they failed to make the connection at Shelby, and I was compelled to stay at Shelby until next afternoon. This was unpleasant, as I wished to join Bishop Janes at the Ohio Conference."

This, the Ohio, was one of Bishop Janes's Conferences, and the young bishop is anxious to profit by the experience of his senior colleague. He writes thus to Mrs. Simpson, Sept. 3 :

"I feel somewhat relieved from the pressure of Conference duties, though I have considerable trouble with the work in Cleveland, and will probably have a storm in Mansfield. Otherwise, I should have a breathing-spell, as far as deep mental anxiety is concerned. I shall go through this Conference, Xenia, and St. Louis, with Bishop Janes, and shall probably learn something which will be of service to me."

We resume the diary:

"*Sept.* 3.—Conference proceeded pleasantly. I was welcomed cordially. I addressed the Sabbath-school Anniversary in Seventh Street church, as also, along with Bishop Janes, the Missionary Society, and preached by request on the same subject as at the North Ohio Conference. The session closed on Monday night about eleven o'clock.

Sept. 20.— Left for Cincinnati Conference at Xenia. General Scott was on the train, and at every station large crowds were collected to see and hear the veteran soldier and presidential aspirant. He is evidently not a man of the people as was General Taylor. He is rather cold, and the effort to be bland and familiar sits rather awkwardly upon him. At Cleveland he was received with firing of cannon, and stopped for the night. I passed on for Columbus by a night train just started and poorly arranged. But the engine gave out, and we were detained several hours, failing to make a junction next morning at Columbus.

Sept. 21.—When about starting out the Cleveland train arrived, bearing General Scott. Cannon were fired amid the huzzas of the crowd, but one poor fellow, loading too quickly, was blown almost to pieces. His eyes were put out, his limbs broken, and the flesh torn from part of his chest. Even the semblance of war has its horrors. That weeping wife must ever hate the cannon's roar.

Sept. 22.—Conference [the Cincinnati] commenced, Bishop Morris attending from Thursday with Bishop Janes. They sat in council all the time. I spoke at the anniversaries and attended Conference during the sessions when the council could be spared. I preached on Sabbath at three, ordaining deacons, after Bishop Morris, at eleven. Conference closed on Thursday night."

After the close of the Cincinnati Conference he went to St. Louis, in company with Bishop Janes, to attend Conference there. Bishop Janes presided; Bishop Morris was also present. The junior bishop was still anxious to secure from his colleagues points of information, and used his opportunity to the best possible advantage. From St. Louis he writes to his wife:

"Oct. 8, 1852.

"You say in your second letter, forwarded to me yesterday from Cincinnati, that you wish me to write every day, as it comforts you in affliction. If I can add, by any act of mine, to your comfort I will gladly do it, and hence, while sitting in Conference, I steal a few moments to write. But let me say that I should enjoy a letter *occasionally* as well as yourself.

"Conference is progressing pretty briskly, and I presume that, by the time this reaches you, it will be drawing to a close. Bishop Ames arrived last evening in excellent health and spirits. He is enjoying his visit to the Western Conferences very much, and is, I learn, very popular. He would be very glad to have me go with him, but I have begged off, as you are not in very good health and just commencing housekeeping. Yet I really sympathized with him, and if my visiting his Conference had allowed him to go home I should have felt half inclined to it, as he has not seen his family since the 28th of July. How would you like to have that kind of absence?

"Be careful of your health. Be cheerful. Look aloft. The stars display their beauty to us only when we look at them; and if we look down at the earth our hearts are never charmed. Be resolved to be happy to-day—to be joyful now—and out of every fleeting moment draw all possible pure and lasting pleasure."

Being greatly interested in the condition of our Church in the western part of Virginia, he made a tour of inspection and preaching up the Great Kanawha River, starting from Parkersburg, and thence down the Ohio to Point Pleasant. As between the two Methodist churches—North and South —this was contested ground. Many of the people had adhered to us, and Bishop Simpson wished to strengthen all such and to make plans for the future. During this tour he was much in company with the Rev. Gordon D. Battelle, who afterwards did much in forming the Constitution of West Virginia as a free state.*

---

* In his autobiographic sketch Bishop Simpson speaks thus of Mr. Battelle: "To no two men was Western Virginia so much indebted for its separate state form, its freedom from slavery, and its common-school system as to Gordon D. Battelle and F. H. Pierpont, its first governor. They were fellow-students, room-mates in Allegheny College, and were closely identified both in sympathy and in judgment. Governor Pierpont became a member of the Methodist Protestant Church, but retained his life-long attachment to Mr. Battelle." This modest Methodist preacher was a statesman of the highest order.

"*Parkersburg, Dec.* 25.—This morning wrote in my diary. Preached at eleven from the angelic song, 'Glory to God in the highest,' etc., to a small congregation, and went with Mr. Logan to dinner; after which I finished writing up this diary to the present time. This will account for many imperfections, and especially for the lack of an account of my religious experience. As I did not record from day to day, so I could not speak of my position and enjoyments. Now, however, I have brought it up to the present afternoon, and hope to be more punctual in noting events as they occur. May the great Head of the Church endow me with wisdom and grace, that I may serve him acceptably and finish my course with joy. I fear that my conversation is not sufficiently seasoned with grace to the use of edifying. May my every act be as in the presence of him who searcheth the heart. At night I preached from 1 John v. 4, to a very full house; there was considerable feeling, but I preached too long, and I feared my voice might be impaired for to-morrow's services. Oh, how little good follows my pulpit labors in comparison with what would follow were I in the full spirit of my mission, and could preach with the Holy Ghost sent down from heaven. May my Heavenly Father lead me into the full knowledge of the truth, and may I serve him with sincerity all the days of my life.

Dec. 26.—This morning I awoke early, but, having had a sleepless night, I rested for a while. The habits of the people in Virginia are not of as early rising as in the free states, and here, late as I was, I was still in advance of the family. I feel somewhat the hoarseness of last evening. The continued rains for some days past until yesterday have swollen the waters, and this morning the Ohio is nearly level with its banks. Attended love-feast at nine, preached at eleven from John xvii. 22, assisted in the administration of the sacrament at three, and preached at night from Romans xiv. 12. It has been a busy day, and I have borne my labors better than in the morning I thought was probable.

Dec. 28.—At night preached from Job xiv. 14, and after service went to the wharf boat to sleep, but, between high water, and storms of wind and rain, and taking passengers, I got but little sleep. Took passage on the *Buckeye* at three. While sleeping, about half-past five, there was a crash succeeded by another and still another, and, hearing persons running, I sprang from my berth, but found that the boat, in trying to land, had encountered some brush. Sleep, however, left me, and I did not lie down again. About eleven arrived at Point Pleasant, Ohio, and stopped at Colonel Sly's Hotel. Mrs. Sly is a member of our Church, and from her I learned that no appointment had been received, but she immediately put one in circulation for evening preaching. I also learned that no boat goes up the Kanawha until Wednesday night, and perhaps not until Thursday night.

For various reasons I am much depressed. My heart greatly needs a deeper work of grace. I labor in some respects sufficiently—indeed, I feel sometimes that I cannot bear the physical efforts I make, together with the mental excitement under which I suffer, but must soon wear down to the grave—and yet my heart is not right. It requires a something not yet possessed to make me victorious over all my infirmities and temptations, and give me triumph in the Lord Jesus Christ. A pure heart, a simplicity of purpose, thorough self-denial, and all-conquering faith and love, I greatly need. Oh, that I did even now cast myself fully upon the atoning merit of Christ, who forgiveth all sin and cleanseth from all iniquity. I need to be *created anew* in Christ Jesus.

Point Pleasant, Dec. 29.—Preached to a small audience last night, assembled in the Methodist church. It is a neat building as to walls, and is very delightfully situated as to the population, but is on ground subject to overflow. It is unfinished, being seated but not plastered. I gave out an appointment for to-night, conditioned upon my inability to get a boat up the Kanawha. The church is held by us and also the Southern Methodists, each occupying it alternately. The Southern Methodists have been very bitter, and much bad feeling has existed, and yet we number only twenty-five or thirty, with but *two* men; they number about as many, but they come from a greater distance and have *two* or *three* men. Presbyterians are weak and have *one* man, and I learn that the Episcopalians are very few. The women generally belong to some church.

This morning rose tolerably early. It is a clear, cold, beautiful morning, and the river is beginning to fall. I feel less fatigued, but I greatly need a purified heart; one washed and quickened by redeeming blood.

Dec. 31.—My rest last night was considerably broken, as I supposed a boat might arrive, and I was anxious to secure my passage. Hence I rose frequently, but it did not come until half-past eight in the morning. At that hour, after taking my baggage to the boat, I called for Miss Thomas, who accompanied me to Charleston, and we left Point Pleasant in the *Salem* at half-past nine. The land along the Kanawha is poorly cultivated, but there is a rich and fertile soil in the bottoms which skirt the stream. Seams of coal are seen occasionally cropping out, and there must be much mineral wealth along the river. The mouth of the Pocotaligo must furnish a town yet of some note. Enterprise is greatly needed in every department.

This is the last day of the year. Alas, how poorly I have spent its fleeting moments! How many missteps I have made—how many errors have I committed—how little spirituality have I cultivated! When I reflect on my life, I can but wonder and adore. Oh, the depth of that mercy which may save even me! My time has gone to waste—my sands of life are ebbing out.   Shall I ever live more to God's glory?   I trust I shall. And yet so often have I formed good resolutions, and so fearfully have I broken them, that I distrust myself.   I can confide alone in the redeeming fulness of my Lord Jesus Christ.   May *he*, at the close of this year, even now while I write, wash away all my past offenses, forgive all my iniquities, and make me a *new creature*.   Nothing but creating power is sufficient to reinstate me in God's image and to purify and invigorate all my faculties.

We are now running at a moderate rate up the Kanawha, and bid fair to reach Charleston a little after dark.   The day is chilly, and the atmosphere and clouds indicate a fall of snow.   A pleasant company is on the boat, but there are a few gamblers constantly engaged in betting on cards.   I arrived at Charleston about seven P.M., and was met cordially by Mr. Battelle and taken to his house.   He informs me that appointments had been made for me at eleven to-day and to-night at Malden, as the boat was expected up at the latest this morning.   I regret the disappointment, but it could not be avoided.   To-night, 1852 is passing away.   Its record is almost finished, and while I write these lines between ten and eleven at night its minutes are rapidly diminishing.   How stands the record of my life as written by Omniscience?   I solemnly ask myself how am I closing this year?   How mixed are human motives when closely scanned!   How shall man be pure in the sight of his Maker? Happy would I be, could I feel that singleness of purpose which makes the whole body full of light, that purity of heart which sees God in everything—and that full consecration which devotes every moment to the divine service.   May He who has protected me this far protect me still, and may I be washed from every stain, and be prepared for glorifying God in my body and my spirit which are his.

Jan. 1, 1853.—The new year has opened upon me in Charleston, Virginia, and is wintry in its aspects—a cold rain has been falling during the night and still continues.

This morning as the clock in an adjoining room struck two I awoke and knelt down by my bedside, to ask for wisdom and grace to guide me through this New Year, or through such part of it as I may live.   I think I felt truly grateful, that I had been spared to witness the beginning of another year, and that Death had not been commissioned to cut me down.   Oh, that my life may be free from the defects of the past, and that I may truly do the will of my great Creator.   For this I need forgiveness of the past, purifying grace for the present, and animating and quickening power from on high.

I should on entering on the New Year aim at a higher life than ever heretofore—I should seek to cultivate and guard my physical powers so that I may be able to labor most successfully—I should redeem time, conversing less with friends, and especially on topics other than the Church and its institutions and personal holiness. I should deny myself every pleasure that my judgment does not approve as being in accordance with growth in grace. And I should study to do in every possible manner God's holy will.

I rose at six this morning, and, after bathing, read *three* chapters in the beginning of the Old Testament and two in the New. I purpose a regular reading after this general method.

Jan. 2.—This morning rose about five, and read my lessons in the Old and New Testaments. I was also forcibly impressed with a passage in the Apocrypha—Ecclesiasticus—touching the tendency of God's Word to impart elevated views. After breakfast rode into Charleston about nine. The morning was pleasantly cool, and a heavy fog rested upon the river's bank. At eleven I preached from Luke xxiv. 46, 47, to a good congregation. Yet in no place have I seen those large congregations which indicate any general interest in the public mind.

Jan. 5.—Rested tolerably well last night. Rose rather late also, but finished my usual lessons. I am told that on Sunday night some three negroes ran away, crossing the Ohio, taking some of their effects with them—two men and one woman—and that they have not since been heard from. I am also told that it is comparatively seldom that a fugitive negro is retaken. If this is the case it seems probable that the uncertainty of holding negroes as slaves will cause owners to sell them farther South, and that the land along the river will be settled by free laborers, and if so a spirit of enterprise will be awakened and lands must rise in value. From having visited the Kanawha valley I am more and more satisfied that with any enterprise Point Pleasant must become a place of considerable note."

After his return home from Western Virginia, he occupied himself with abundant labors in and near Pittsburgh. The entries in the diary are chiefly noteworthy, as showing his restless activity :

"*Jan.* 9.—This day preached in the morning at Beaver Street, Alleghanytown, from Psalms cxxxvii. 5, 6, to a well-filled house, their ordinary congregation. At night preached in South Pittsburgh to a good house from Ephesians i. 13, 14. Prospects seem to be brightening. My labors in the pulpit I fear are beginning to affect my eyes—too much blood I think flows to my head. But I dislike the thought of ceasing to set an example of earnestness in the Christian ministry—either in manner or in quantity of labor. Were I sure it is an injury, duty would require me to cease.

March 13.—Pittsburgh: This has been a Sabbath of toil. Last night Matilda received a severe fall from our front steps, occasioning concussion of the brain to some extent, and I felt fearful of cerebral excitement following. Hence I had but little sleep. This morning she was better, but has been confined to her bed all day. At half-past ten I preached in Liberty Street to a very full house from 2 Peter i. 19: 'We have a more sure word,' etc. After dinner Dr. Sellers called, and we had a long conversation on Christian experience, embracing particularly the witness of the Spirit, and the relation of the subjective to the objective in religion. At night preached in Wesley Chapel to a full house from 2 Corinthians iii, 18. The house was excessively hot, and I did not enjoy myself in my labors. My personal condition in religion is far from satisfactory to myself. I have not that clear, abiding, and constant sense of the presence and communion of the Holy Spirit which I believe is the Christian's privilege, nor have I the full experience that the blood of Christ cleanseth from all unrighteousness that the Scriptural warrant authorizes the believer to expect. May that experience in all its blessed fulness speedily be mine.

April 29.—This morning had made my arrangements to leave for New York Conference, via Philadelphia, but Mrs. S. had been so sick through the night that she was unwilling for me to leave, so I remained until evening. At nine o'clock took cars. I felt rather depressed leaving Mrs. S. so ill, and to be absent from home so many weeks. Slept but little through the night, and at daybreak reached the summit of the mountain. At the foot of the long descending plane a freight car was off the track and detained us near an hour. I walked over two of the levels and down two of the planes before the train came up. It was a beautiful, clear morning. The atmosphere was pure and bracing, and the wild mountain scenery was inspiring. The dark foliage of the pines, interspersed now and then with the buds and blossoms and leaves of light green, the tall peaks of the mountains, and the deep precipices, amid which here and there could be seen the silvery, winding Juniata, yet but a little stream, whose waters gently reflected the morning light, all impressed me with a love of nature. I desire above all to feel an increasing love for its great Creator, my glorious Redeemer.

April 30.—The delay of the train consumed our time so that when we arrived at the Mountain House the Eastern train had just started. The passengers generally were much out of humor, as we had seen the train or the smoke of the engine as it moved off. The presumption was that it was perhaps designed to keep us at the Mountain House during the

day; and hence a large portion of the company started for Hollidays-
burgh, about one and a half miles distant. Thinking I could find as
much, if not more, retirement there, and could also see the village, I accompanied them, and stopped at the hotel. After breakfast Mr. Bell, a
broker, who learned I was a minister but did not know who, asked me
over to his office, where I wrote letters and also a sketch for the *Western
Christian Advocate*. After dinner wrote this entry in my diary. Thus
delayed upon my journey, I am closing the last day of April. Time flies
away. Alas, how poorly improved!"

He reached Lancaster, on his way to Philadelphia, after
midnight Saturday. As he would not travel on Sunday, he
tarried in that city till Monday morning. While there occurred the amusing incident, so often quoted. He thus tells
the story in a letter to his wife:

"Lancaster, May 1, 1853.

"A bright and beautiful day is this, but my mind anxiously reverts to
Pittsburgh and inquires for your health. After spending the day in Hol-
lidaysburgh and surveying the various churches, etc., I returned to the
Mountain House and took the train. At Lancaster I stopped, as it was
after midnight, and I could not reach Philadelphia until six or seven in
the morning. Brother —— and wife kept on. How ministers can recon-
cile Sabbath travelling with a sense of duty I cannot tell.

"I preached to-day for Mr. Bishop, who is the stationed minister. I
introduced myself to him, telling him that my name was Simpson, and
that I was from Pittsburgh. Finding that I was a minister, he asked me
to preach, and introduced me to the congregation as Brother Simpson,
from Pittsburgh. Going into the pulpit, he asked me if I belonged to
the Pittsburgh Conference. I told him not now; that I had belonged to
it. After I had preached he took my hand and apologized; said he had
not thought of my being bishop till I was preaching, and told the congregation that they had been listening to Bishop Simpson, etc. Whether
they thought any more of the sermon for the name I cannot tell. Mr.
Bishop, notwithstanding this little blunder, is a very fine man, an excel-
ent preacher, and is greatly beloved."

A sharper-sighted man than the Lancaster pastor might
readily have failed to recognize a bishop under the plain outward appearance of the Rev. Matthew Simpson. Episcopal
manner, if there be such, he never had and heartily de-

19

spised. To move among his countrymen as an unpretending, equal fellow-citizen was the study of his life. His dress was wholly unclerical, not even the customary white necktie indicating his vocation. Besides, there was ascribed to him by his friends at this period of his life an ungainliness of manner which gave him the air of a good, wholesome lay preacher from a rural district. A certain lack of grace must have been visible, for it is a point of frequent mention in the newspaper notices of the period. It must be admitted that in hats he was always weak: this important article of clothing, as he wore it, usually looked as if it had been tumbled about in a crowded mass-meeting. Bishop Hurst tells me that once, when visiting the Germany and Switzerland Conference, Bishop Simpson appeared before the astonished brethren in a steamer cap which was neither beautiful nor graceful. Immediately after the first session of the body he was taken by them to a hatter's and properly habited. In later life this indifference to the details of dress was not noticeable. His manners, however, were always engaging; no one could be more scrupulously, and at the same time quietly, attentive to every point of courtesy.

He reached Kingston, the place of the meeting of the New York Conference, in good season, with a day to spare. He thus notes one or two items:

"*May 5.*—This evening Bishop Janes arrived, and I find his aid in the council-room very valuable. Yesterday I had a very severe attack of pain in the region of the heart, which compelled me for some hours to suspend my duties and dismiss the elders. It was a strong admonition to be always ready. Oh, for a closer walk with God!"

He writes from Kingston a letter to his wife, and in it mentions his recovery:

"Kingston, Saturday morning.

"I was interrupted in writing on yesterday; this morning I feel moderately well. Bishop Janes arrived last night and will stay till Monday evening, when he leaves for the New Hampshire Conference. Bishop Waugh will pass within two or three miles of this place either to-day or on Monday, and it is possible he may turn aside to see us.   Thus far I have heard nothing from home.   I hope, however, that you are in good health and spirits.   It is matter of consolation to know that we are in the hands of a merciful and all-wise Providence, who numbers the very hairs of our heads, and without whose permission a sparrow cannot fall to the ground.   It is pleasant to me, while I cannot hear the voices of those I love on earth, to turn to the Book of God and hear him speaking in his word and uttering his admonitions and counsels to guide my wandering feet.   And while I cannot see the forms of wife and children around me, yet I can recognize the handiwork of him who is my best friend, the father and guide of my youth, whenever I cast my eyes on the heavens above or on the elements around me.   Would that I could feel that whenever I lay me down the arms of Omnipotence surround me, and that I am in the immediate presence of him who is my Redeemer, my Saviour, my all.   And well would it be for me if I could recognize when I awake, in the beamings of the morning, the sweet smiles of that countenance which watched me ceaselessly through the shadows of the night.

"Commit yourself, with all your cares and anxieties, into the hands of your Heavenly Father, and I trust you may experience and enjoy the peace that passeth all knowledge."

With an account of a visit to Miss Garrettson at Rhinebeck and of a trip to West Point the diary abruptly closes. His papers contain numerous diaries begun in as many blank books, but there is no instance of a book filled.   Journalizing was, no doubt, irksome to him; his letters, too, are usually very brief and contain little more than abstracts of the events of a day or week.   Sentiment, except in occasional and these beautiful expressions of domestic affection, is wanting; with regard to individual men he is absolutely reticent.   Nor does he often in his correspondence indulge himself in reflections upon society or the course of events. A busy man, always in motion, he is continually absorbing information and forming estimates of men as he meets them, but reserves expression for the public occasions which call for the exercise of his highest faculties.

XIV.

AN EPISCOPAL TOUR
THROUGH CALIFORNIA AND OREGON.

1853, 1854.

New Conditions of Life for Bishop Simpson.—Incessant Travel Required of him.—His Mental Activity.—His Secretary's Account of his Mode of Preparing for Preaching and Lecturing.—Skeleton of the Sermon on 2 Corinthians iv. 18.—Too Busy to Write.—A Compensation for the Loss of Opportunities of Study.—The Many Applications for his Services.—Readiness to Help the Churches.—Sails for California, December, 1853.—Crossing the Isthmus of Panama.—Hotel Experiences in the " Gem."—The Chagres River.—Cruces.—Spoiling of Romantic Expectations. — The " St. Charles " or the " American," Which ? — The " Refuse of Creation " Brought Together.—Riding on Mules through the Gorges.—A Native Forest.—Panama.—Another Crowded Hotel.— A Little Prayer-meeting on the Last Evening of the Year.—A Broken Cot, and a Night's Sleep on the Floor.—The *Golden Gate* Breaks her Shaft.—Drifting on the Pacific Ocean.—A Glorious Sunset.—Arrival at San Diego. — The *Golden Gate* nearly Wrecked. — Failure of Attempts to Rescue the Ship.—Subsidence of the Storm.—Arrival at San Francisco.—Meets William Taylor.—Preaching nearly Every Day.— Delay of Steamer for Oregon.—Difficulties in the Way of Reaching the Seat of the Oregon Conference. — An All - night Ride in an Open Wagon.—Sleeping on Sheaves of Oats.—Twenty Miles on Horseback, Satchel in Hand.—Reaches the Log School-house in which the Conference is Held.—Great Joy of the People.—Return to Portland.—Journey up the Columbia River.—Perils of Waters and of the Wilderness. —A Night in an Indian Camp.—Journey Home.

XIV.

FROM the time of his election to the episcopate, the conditions of life for Matthew Simpson underwent an entire
change. Having no diocese, and the law of his Church requiring him to "travel at large," he was, of necessity, always in motion. His study of books was intermittent. He
had accumulated an ample library, but the hours spent in
it were the few snatched from the pressure of business. It
was rather a retreat for him when, utterly weary, he wished
to be alone. The careful reading of former years, his habits
of close observation, and his retentive memory supplied him
with the resources for his many sermons and public addresses. He had an open eye for the beautiful in nature
and art, and quickly caught up the historical material necessary for giving art objects their proper setting. In whatever country he travelled he acquired rapidly an intelligent
understanding of its topography, politics, sources of wealth,
looking at it with the eye of a man of affairs. Above all
he talked much with men, was accessible, and had the knack
of drawing from those he met, without seeming to do so,
the information he desired.

His mental activity during his episcopal years was extraordinary. I find among his papers lectures on a great
variety of topics: lectures to young ministers, frequently
delivered early in the morning, before the hour of Conference opening; narrative lectures upon his travels in foreign
lands, some of them carefully arranged as if for publication;
lectures on philosophy, on oratory, on the connection of
commerce with science and religion, and reports enough of

sermons to fill several volumes.* Whenever he travelled in foreign lands he corresponded with newspapers, usually with several. There was arranged for him, in his later years, a correspondence from China, with the *New York Tribune,* but, owing to his illness in California, the trip to China was given up.

I had always supposed that he secured the results of reading by the help of his private secretaries, but the Rev. S. M. Stiles, who was his secretary for years, assures me that he was never called on to look up points. Mr. Stiles's account of the bishop's methods of work is decidedly interesting :

"With reference to the bishop's preparations for lecturing or preaching, my time being divided between him and the office of the Board of Church Extension, I am not so fully informed as if I had been more constantly with him. I simply went to his house or office when he was ready to dictate. I suppose he spent some time in preparation for the pulpit and platform, yet he never dictated anything to me in this line except in preparing one of his lectures, and I never saw any manuscript notes of his sermons except one, and these were brief. He was so constantly occupied in travelling and public services, and the little time he spent at home was so taken up by callers that he had not much left for either study or rest. His study and preparation for the pulpit were principally done in former years. He was too much taxed to do much of either when I knew him; it is wonderful that he could perform the work he did and keep up his reputation as a preacher with so little leisure for study. I do not believe he used a pen much in his pulpit preparation when I knew him. But he could probably do as much thinking in an hour or two as most preachers in a day, and prepare himself as well without a pen as others with one. I remember on one or two occasions being at

---

* A volume of his sermons, made up from short-hand reports, was published by Harper & Brothers in 1885.

<u>"While we look not at the things that"</u>

1. The Christian habit of mind is to look at the unseen.
   1. (To look at). Not (seen committed) us to look a notice more.
   2. To give special attention — gallery of paintings — garden of flowers.
   3. It marks the power of religion other = science — all earthly — mingle strength — all heavenly. Where are you?

II. This habit is in accordance with true philosophy.
   1. The law of progress is ever towards the invisible.
      a) In nature, the beautiful is the order of the unseen.
      b) In art — muscle — water — wind — steam demonstrating electricity.
      c) In science, the palpable only the impalpable — chemistry to relation of the impalpable, electrons protons.
   2. Men of enlarged minds ever contemplate the invisible — Poetry paints it — philosophy revels in it — science ... it — Alexander — Clay.

III. It produces abiding joy.
   1. The eternal is alone unchangeable all joys of earth are fleeting.
   2. The mind relying on earthly things must wholly ... and pass away. View it its tendrils.

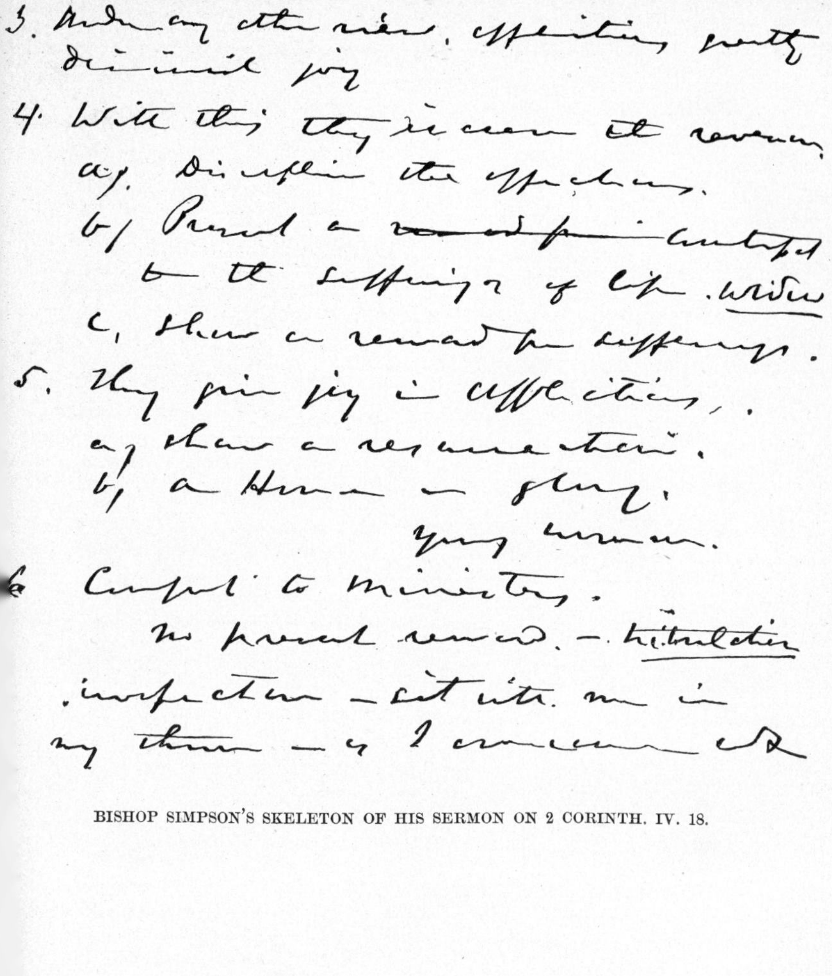

3. Under any other view, afflictions greatly diminish joy
4. With this they increase the reverence
a, Discipline the affections.
b, Present a ~~reward for~~ counterpart to the sufferings of life. Widow
c, Shew a reward for sufferings.
5. They give joy in afflictions,
a, shew a resurrection.
b, a Home in glory.
young woman.
6. Comfort to ministers.
No present reward. — tribulation — imperfection — sit with me in my throne — as I overcame etc

BISHOP SIMPSON'S SKELETON OF HIS SERMON ON 2 CORINTH. IV. 18.

his house when I heard him walking the floor over my head and repeating what I imagine was a sermon that he was soon to preach. I suppose he did his thinking upon a subject in this way more or less. I heard him remark once, as nearly as I can remember, that he did not study any models of preaching, or any work on homiletics, but that his method of sermonizing was his own—such as came to him from the consideration of a subject, and not according to any scientific or school methods. His great lecture on 'The Future of Our Country' was never written or dictated by him. I do not know that he even had any notes of it; though he may have had. All that remains of it, so far as I know, is in newspaper reports. I heard it but once, and then after the war, and it was, in the manner of delivery and the effect, not to be compared with what it was on some former occasions, judging from the accounts I have heard and read of it. I never looked up any points for him on any subject, and do not know of anybody else doing so. I know he had in contemplation some literary work that he wanted to dictate to me, but never had time for it. He did dictate to me a sketch of his life, for his family. I think, however, that even this was left unfinished. The dictations I took were letters. His correspondence was very large."

It may be safely asserted that for instant and overwhelming effect upon an audience, Bishop Simpson was exceeded by no man of his time in America or England. The inquiry into his method of preparing for public addresses is, therefore, worth prosecuting. The testimony of his secretary on this point is confirmed by the written remains of his sermons. One of his favorite themes was the power of the invisible; his discourse thereupon is the thirteenth of the published volume, from 2 Corinthians iv. 18; of two skeletons of this which I find, each is written on a leaf of note paper, and neither fills more than fifty lines. The skeleton is, however, closely analytic, and covers all the points.

Under such circumstances, profound thought is out of the

question, and if popular eloquence moves in the realm of commonplaces, profound thought is not required. A mixed assembly will soon weary of thoughts with which the hearers are not more or less familiar. But to change the familiar into something more than a commonplace, to give clear expression to half-conscious feeling, to say for thousands what they too would say if they only could, and above all to make the spiritual as real to the mind as the sensible, are achievements requiring, for their highest form, nothing less than genius. In this realm of common thought and universal feeling Bishop Simpson was supreme; usually one short hour gave him the mastery over all who listened to the sound of his voice.

He had in his episcopal life a compensation for the loss of the opportunities of studious reflection in the wider spread of his influence as a Christian orator. And it is curious to notice how uniformly the effects of his preaching followed, in the earlier days of his episcopate, when he was in the fulness of his vigor. No matter where, on the Atlantic or the Pacific coast, at home or abroad, speaking directly or through an interpreter, the same accounts of the effects of his preaching are given us. Some of these are absurdly extravagant, others are toned down to soberness, but all alike show the spell he laid upon the minds of men. Now he is in Oregon—a wilderness in 1854—and is preaching to a congregation of Methodist pioneers assembled in the woods. He has been delayed, and only reaches the spot at the close of the Sunday-morning sermon. He is announced to preach in the afternoon. "And the sermon," says the enthusiastic writer, "who shall describe the indescribable or speak the unutterable. Its imagery was celestial, its pathos divine, its power omnipotent. It was more than Bishop Simpson's own; it was God's and Christ's. Years after, when in London, the same sermon that he thought not too good for these Oregon pioneers he thought good enough for one of the greatest audiences in

Christendom." Again, he is in Norway: he is among a people whose language is as foreign to him as is his to them. He speaks through an interpreter. "All the people," says the reporter, "listened and wept." Again, he is in Dublin, among the susceptible Irish Methodists. Even the staid London *Watchman* glows with enthusiasm: "His eloquence has been well compared to a river. At first it is slow and unpretending, but gradually gathers strength and volume, as tributary thoughts flow in, until it becomes a broad, deep, and rapid stream. He brought his admirable discourse to a close by a peroration which, for thrilling power, we have never heard surpassed." And now he is among his friends in his own West, gathered together on the shore of Lake Michigan. "His mind," says one of his hearers of that day, "seems like a huge, well-built cage, filled with mountain birds, all strong-winged and eager to be let loose, confident in their power of battling with the storm and triumphing over opposing tempests. His figures come out clear, strong, and beautifully beaming, like the light of the sun, illuminating the dark places of his logic, making them attractive and easily understood. You feel that a man of genius, a great spirit, is near you, but in him there is a sort of magnetic charm that makes you love the man and have large hopes of yourself." These touches of extravagance in the description of him only show that Bishop Simpson carried men away from themselves; they are unconscious as well as conscious testimonies to his power. "He has swallowed me up," said Father Taylor to me after a sermon preached by the bishop in 1860. It may be readily supposed that the applications for pulpit and platform services poured in upon him in floods. While holding the New York Conference in June, 1856, with another Conference immediately to follow, and an interval of a few days between them, he writes thus to his wife: "As to work between this and the Maine Conference I give you a list of applications: (1) Newark, New Jersey, to aid in a public meeting on Thursday of next week. (2) To dedicate the new Trinity Church in New York on Sabbath week. (3) To preach same day at Hedding Church. (4) To lay the corner-stone of a new church in Brooklyn on Monday week. (5) To spend Sabbath week in Bangor, Maine. (6) To spend it in Boston. (7) To spend it in Lynn. (8) To dedicate a new church in Lynn on Monday week. (9) To preach at Hillside (Mrs. Olin's home) on Friday of next week. I believe these are nearly all the applications I yet have for the three or four days between the Conferences. How many more I shall have I cannot tell."

Nor was he slow to meet these calls for aid; it cost him something to say "No" to an appeal for the help which he best of all our preachers of that time could give. He was literally "in labors more abundant" than other men. In May, 1857, he sailed for Europe, and he gives this account of his manner of preparing for his trip: "Early in the spring I presided at the Kentucky, North Indiana, Western Virginia, and Pittsburgh Conferences; and in three days from the close of the last-named Conference I left my home in Pittsburgh to begin my journey. Having spent the Sabbath in Philadelphia, preaching in Green Street in the morning and in Trinity at night, I reached New York on Monday. Here, in addition to the usual preparations for the trip, I had an engagement to preach a dedicatory sermon on the Scandinavian Bethel ship on Tuesday afternoon and to lecture in Greene Street Church that night in behalf of a new church in Hudson City, New Jersey." On Wednesday he sailed; and in this fashion he worked on, though with more prudence in later years, to the end.

But we are anticipating our story. In 1853 it was arranged that he should go to California—then a long way off from the Atlantic border—and while holding his fall Conferences his mind was busy with the preparations for this trip. His wife was in poor health, and in his correspondence he does his utmost to cheer her up. One is often in his letters reminded of his own account of himself : " I ought never to have been a bishop ; I love my home too well."

September 27, 1853, he writes from Loveland, Ohio, and, after telling her all the news, he expresses his solicitude for her health and spirits in this wise : " Be a good girl—say your prayers—always keep in a good humor—keep every wrinkle off your brow, for time will make them too soon, anyhow—look at the bright side of the picture. Get into the fresh air, keeping good care of your feet—move about a little every day—if nothing else, move the bed round as it used to be, and then, when you have looked at it, move it back again. Change the chairs and the divans and pull the piano cover a little—just a *little*—farther over ; and when you have nothing else to do, think of me, but *don't write too often.*"

Dec. 20, 1853, he set sail, with several companions, among them the Rev. N. Reasoner, in the steamer *George Law,* for Aspinwall. In the party were several ladies, who, under the escort of the bishop, were proceeding to join friends on the Pacific coast. Of this trip, at that time novel, there is a long and carefully written journal, arranged in chapters, apparently with a view to publication. It is said, in abatement of the popular estimate of him, that, though an enchanting speaker, his capability as a writer was small. A few passages from this journal will show how aptly he could express himself with the pen when he had time to collect his thoughts.

The Isthmus of Panama had at that time to be crossed partly by boat up the Chagres River and partly on mules. It was a rough journey, and was sometimes accompanied with exciting incidents. The bishop's party was large, and the care of it taxed him. They had arrived at Aspinwall and were getting ready for the transit :

" Early the next morning all was in commotion. The first note heard on awaking was the shrill cry of runners for the baggage and transit lines. Passing to the town, I went to register and exchange our tickets, as directed by officers of the ship, while the rest of the party agreed to find a place for breakfast. Hurrying up-town, I found my friends waiting, having agreed to breakfast at the 'Gem;' it had been depicted in glowing terms by the runners as the best place in the city. Away we went to the 'Gem;' and a 'Gem' it surely was. Entering a crazy entry, whose floor was of loose boards, we passed to the dining-room, reminded as we went that if we expected to *eat,* we had better not *see* too much. It was rather strange to the ladies to see an old table, with its feet placed on the bottoms of broken glass tumblers (why, I could not tell), set in what appeared to be a bedroom; and yet they were relieved to get anywhere out of the close confinement of the vessel. Breakfast came by and by, for in these tropical climates no one is in a hurry, and it was better than we had expected. We had coffee, fried ham, boiled potatoes, eggs, and bread. All their provisions, we learned, are brought from a distance, for scarcely anything is produced in the neighborhood, notwithstanding the fertility of the soil. Having done ample justice to the breakfast, we paid our fare and hurried to the train. Some seven or eight cars were already filled, and, waiting until another was added, our party found seats, and I sallied forth to view 'the city.'

"At quarter-past nine our train, consisting of eleven cars, drawn by a small engine, started for the interior. So shrill and fine was the whistle of the engine that it called out laughter and responses from the crowd, such as, 'Go it while you're young,' etc. Doubt was expressed whether so small an engine could draw so long a train, but the doubt was silenced by the fact that we were in motion. Part of the way the road is constructed on piles, and shakes much, but the main portions of it are strong and substantial. The clay is generally reddish. There are some heavy cuts, and such rock as I saw appeared to be black or brown sandstone. Much of the stone used in the work must have been found near the surface. Our first station was Gatun, several miles from Aspinwall, where we reached the Chagres River."

The account of the passage up the Chagres River contains some good bits of description:

"Some of us were stowed away with twenty others in a covered barge. But our crew were provokingly patient about starting. Boat after boat shoved out before us, and it was rumored that at Cruces there might be a scarcity of lodging-places, and that 'first come would be first served.' Our boatmen were ready to start, when a violent altercation sprang up between them and the adjoining crew about the rowing-poles. Such swearing and gesticulation and menacing attitudes foreboded some terrible result, but no blows were struck. I afterwards found that these natives believed in Falstaff's philosophy that 'discretion is the better part of valor.' They seem perfectly infuriated, and rage like madmen, until you fancy the battle is beginning; then suddenly they cool down and are as peaceful as pet lambs. At last we were in motion. Our propelling force consisted of five natives, one of whom stood at the stern to direct the barge; and two on each side, fixing their poles in the bed of the river, and throwing thei weight on the poles, resting against the shoulder, shot us up stream, as they walked on the edge of the boat from stem to stern. The costume of these native boatmen consisted of nature's garb, plus with two a pair of trousers apiece, with two others a red flannel shirt, and with one simply a cloth around the loins. Several of them were athletic and exceedingly well formed; one of them had a smile ever on his countenance, as he placed his shoulder against the pole and uttered his boatman's cry. Another made the most hideous and awful faces I ever beheld. It seemed a kind of compound grin, between a monkey's and a hyena's. How they bear the pressure upon their unprotected breasts and shoulders for hours together seemed strange, but they manifested no sense of inconvenience. Their song was a monotonous cry something like 'Ho-a, hesh, hesh, hesh, hevy.' Occasionally they slipped, though remarkably sure-footed, and once one of them, missing his brace against the pole, plunged into the water. As it was near the shore, a few leaps brought him to land, and the boat pulled up to receive him.

"A mile or two up the river we arrived at Gorgona, a village upon the southwest bank of the river, containing a population of about two thousand. From this point are two routes to Panama. The Gorgona route is more level and less stony, but is very muddy in wet weather. As the rainy season was nearly over, some preferred that route. The great majority preferred to go by Cruces, six miles up the river. As we progressed the scene was in many respects exhilarating. In some places the stream was broad and shallow, in others narrow and deep. The dark waters (for the water appeared very dark) were overshadowed by the trees and shrubbery. The palms, of various kinds, reared their tall, slender trunks, and on some hung large bunches of fruit. Innumerable vines and flowers, trees in full bloom, and shrubs of delicate leaf and rich fragrance were constantly in view. Here and there were large fields of plantain; and in the distance upon our right were conical eminences, one of which towered up proudly over two thousand feet. About half-way between Gorgona and Cruces the river, compressed into a narrow channel, turns to the left at a right angle. Upon the right is an elevated plain with a small native town; and directly at the angle, on a high bank, stood an American house. It was readily distinguished by its boards, its glass windows, and shutters, and a cart which stood close by. There was an excavation, showing that the railroad was in process of construction; and it is at this point that the road leaves the Chagres River and ascends towards the high lands. It was about the middle of the afternoon, and in a hammock stretched from tree to tree in front of the house swung probably an engineer or officer of the railroad taking his siesta. The water was so deep that we were compelled to hug the shore, and the boat was propelled by the oars placed against the rock or hard clay of the bank. The scene was so fine, and the high bank seemed so suited for the location of a town, that our company, in true Yankee style, began to discuss the propriety of laying out a city and speculating in town lots.

" We were interested in noticing the ascent of vast shoals of small fish. Where the current was rapid they ascended close by the bank; and meeting some projecting root or other obstacle, they shot out into the water in a ceaseless silvery stream, presenting almost the appearance of spray. It was some time after we noticed them before we could be persuaded it was a stream of fish. Thousands, varying from one to three inches in length, must have passed every few minutes. A little bird, with white breast and brownish back and wings, stole softly along the bank just at the river's brink, watching for the little fish as they came within stroke of its bill. Birds, like meadow-larks and kingfishers, were upon the bank, or skipped among the bushes. Large buzzards winged their slow flight in the distance, or sat, as in grand and solemn council, on the trees. Towards evening a flock of parrots made their appearance, being the first which we had seen in this tropical land, and upon a bank of mud a foot or two above the water's edge lay an alligator some five feet long, occasionally moving his jaw to seize his unwary prey.

" On arriving at Cruces I confess to some little disappointment. I had read of it as being the point at which the old paved road met the Chagres River. It had stood, connected with romantic legends, for some three hundred years. I expected to see something like an American city. Besides, Mr. H., the agent of Mr. Hinckley, had assured me on the cars that we should find accommodations at the 'St. Charles.' And as he was going in advance in a light boat to make necessary arrangements at Cruces, he had kindly promised that he would engage rooms for the ladies of our party. But here stood Cruces, on a high bank, with its native huts, low and thatched, almost without order and without any enclosures. Sure, however, of finding a comfortable house and good rooms at the 'St. Charles,' we hurried on, amid the crowd of passengers. We passed the 'American,' a two-story frame house, with a small addition of three stories, but so rough and uncomfortable in appearance that I almost pitied the passengers who were compelled to tarry in such a place. Congratulating ourselves that we had the good-fortune to have rooms engaged in advance, we made our way through filthy streets, if such they may be called, where mules had tramped the clay into deep holes, and between huts where back and front yards were the same. Finally we reached the 'St. Charles,' another frame still worse looking than the 'American,' but then it was our home, and the weather was so excessively hot we wished to go no farther. Entering the hotel, there were neither chairs nor benches on which we could sit; and on inquiring for rooms, we found there were none empty. Mr. H. had not been there—no room had been spoken for, and there was no place where the ladies could stay. Leaving them, I hurried back to the 'American,' and was just in time to secure the last vacant room, which was in the third story, or, as we should term it, the garret. For the use of this room for the four ladies, I paid eight dollars in advance, and was also required to pay two dollars for breakfast and supper for each of us, at the time of securing the room. Brother Reasoner and myself were furnished cots in the gentlemen's commons for one dollar each. These cots had no covering, and no pillows, and from their appearance they had remained unwashed so long, as it seemed to us, 'that the memory of man runneth not to the contrary.'

"Supper was served in wild confusion. Passengers had arrived from the Pacific. Hundreds were with us from the Atlantic. Provisions were scarce, and waiters were few. Such screaming for coffee, tea, bread, and meat I had never heard. After waiting long, I was served with some tea with sugar, and some bread, and I had no appetite for anything more. Milk is not heard of in all these regions. Beef I had seen cut up into strings at a hut near by, and I had no inclination to try it. Fresh meat is not cut as with us in pieces for roasting or broiling, but the flesh is cut from the bones in strings, and is sold, as I was informed, not by the pound, but by the yard. After tea, Brother Reasoner and myself surveyed the town. Along the bank of the river almost every house had liquors for sale, and gambling-tables were before nearly every door. Natives and Americans of a low class crowded the gambling-places near the river, while upon the street back of the hotel the natives pursued their amusements alone.

"Returning to our hotel and ascertaining that the ladies of our company were as comfortable as could be expected with the accommodations furnished, we repaired to our cots in the sleeping commons. But there was little sleep for us. It seemed as though the refuse of creation had been gathered into one room. There were from one hundred to one hundred and fifty cots and bunks, and many of them were occupied by men highly excited with drink. Now and then, when sleep was about

20

to visit our eyelids, some rude remark was made and responded to, followed by a volley of oaths and obscene utterances of the most disgusting character. To add to the darkness of the picture, some lewd women occupied an adjacent room, separated only by a thin partition. Their jests and laughter and vile language were heard and responded to by men of the baser sort. In the bar-room beneath us men who could get no cots to lie on were drinking, swearing, and carousing, and making night more hideous by their revelry. In the native huts, long after 'the noon of night' had passed, there were alternate singing and hallooing. One shrill voice near us kept up a song in loud vociferation the greater part of the night, as if some one were acting the part of an improvisator for the amusement of company. Add to this the noise of mules and donkeys collecting for our journey, and the confusion may, in part, be imagined. We felt as if we were in the very suburbs of Pandemonium.

" As soon as it was sufficiently light we began to look for mules. Our company needed seven, with side-saddles for the ladies. As these had been but lately introduced, being an innovation on native usage, and as there was an unusually large number of ladies, it was exceedingly difficult to get a supply. We had the first transit tickets taken for this trip, and were entitled, according to the contract, to a preference in choice of mules. But in vain we applied to Mr. Hinckley for our rights. Every man seized a mule as he was able, and it was an hour or two before we were even partially suited. We had, indeed, received sundry lessons before leaving New York as to the qualities of mules and how to make our selection. But somehow these directions were not applicable to the miserable specimens before us, and finally we were glad to seize any that offered. When we fancied ourselves ready to mount, a native laid claim to two of the mules and demanded payment, and I was compelled to refer to Mr. Hinckley again before the matter was settled. The natives frequently combine to impose on travellers. One calling himself the owner of a mule lets it for the trip, receives payment, and disappears. When the traveller is about to mount the real owner comes forward, demands payment, and seizes the mule until the money is paid. The proceeds of the trick are then divided between the parties. No traveller is well mounted without a spur. Not, indeed, such spurs as are worn by horsemen at home, but large ones, with points projecting from half an inch to an inch and a half in length. It seems unmerciful to ride with such spurs, but travellers find them very useful. Boys, and even men, drive quite a trade in this article at Cruces and at Panama, selling to the traveller when mounting and begging from him when dismounting and glad to part with every encumbrance.

"About eight o'clock we mounted and began our journey. But the ladies had never been on mules before, and, to say the least, our mules were *mulish.* Some took it into their heads to go back to the starting-place, while others paused as if considering the difficulties of the journey. Not until spurs had been freely used and sticks applied, and one or two umbrellas had been broken, did we get partly started, and then it required the constant exertions of the rider to maintain anything like a respectable gait."

Their way, when near the Pacific side, led through narrow gorges, which are thus described:

" On either side the hills rose abruptly; the bottom of the pass was so narrow that the slender legs of the mule had scarcely room for motion, and the rider needed to guard with great care his feet and limbs from being bruised. Many of the ascents and descents were exceedingly steep. The feet of the mules had worn holes in the clay or rock, so that the ascent much resembled a stairway. Each mule trod with great care in the 'footsteps of its illustrious predecessor,' and only by its remarkable carefulness was it possible to descend with safety. When approaching the first descent, and observing step below step some eighteen inches or two feet apart, it seemed impossible to maintain my position. But others had preceded me, and then it was a risk to get in the narrow pathway with mules coming tumbling after me; so, trusting to my beast's sure-footedness, I retained my seat, and shortly acquired full confidence in its ability to climb up and get down. And yet one misstep must inevitably have hurled the rider over its head.

" These gorges or narrow ravines are quite numerous and of considerable length. To pass another train in them is altogether impossible, and the native muleteers are heard uttering their shrill cries to give notice from ravine to ravine of their approach. Occasionally these passes are obstructed by a mule falling beneath his load. It is said that in such cases they are killed by the natives and cut in pieces, in order to remove them out of the road. One pass, where there chanced to be a choice of ways, we found thus obstructed. We were also told that when mules laden with trunks or boxes meet others they can scarcely be stopped, but press right forward, their determination strengthening as the obstacles multiply."

A native forest is very prettily pictured:

" The greater part of the way the forests remain in undisturbed grandeur. Many species of the palm tower towards heaven. The manzanilla, mahogany, and varieties of the cedron are also abundant. With these are found an immense variety of trees unknown to the casual traveller. Some stand as giants that for centuries have been spreading out their branches as a home for the multitudes of parrots and monkeys which chatter from the midst of them. Some shoot up slender trunks as if anxious to catch a glimpse of the pure sky, which is almost concealed by their larger neighbors. Then every tree is covered with vines, or with parasitic plants. Sometimes the vines pass from tree to tree, making a complete net-work almost impenetrable. Then, descending from some lofty branch, they swing in mid air, sporting their blossoms, and adding beauty to the magnificent scenery.

"Notwithstanding the fatigue of the journey, the passengers generally were in excellent spirits. Grotesque enough were we in our costumes and equipments. The men wore palm-leaf or chip hats tied with a ribbon to a button-hole of a light coat. Heavy garments were doffed as far as possible, and in our outer appearance—well sprinkled with mud, on donkeys some four feet high, one half the ladies riding after the fashion of men—our friends would scarcely have recognized us. But we were all in the same category, and could afford to laugh at our condition. The donkeys after being whipped and spurred, would occasionally take it into their heads to gallop for a short distance, while the rider would exclaim, after the manner of the natives, '*mucha mula*' at the top of his voice. The poor donkeys seemed to enjoy words of praise spoken in Spanish.

"At last we arrived, and almost exhausted we saw the twin towers of the Cathedral of Panama, and, winding around the base of the Bolivar hill, we shortly entered the suburbs of the city. Little native huts clustered together make a native town outside of the walls. Passing nearly a mile through these, about five o'clock we reached the outer gate, and, entering through a narrow, walled way several rods in length, we passed the inner gate, and dismounted at the 'Louisiana Hotel.' My first task was to visit the steamer office, where our tickets were registered. Our hotel was a French one, and furnished only lodging at one dollar per day, and we must needs visit the restaurant for supper. As the one near by had exhausted its stock when we called for supper, we went to the next, where we had tea, coffee, bread and butter, for fifty cents each. But my stomach refused the food, as fever had begun to rise; on our way back we stepped into a Catholic church where evening service was about closing. A few native boys were singing; a few women were saying their prayers and bowing towards the altar. Returning to our hotel, as it was the last day in the year we spent an hour with the ladies in religious conversation and bowed together in grateful prayer—myself and Brother Reasoner leading—trying to be thankful for the mercies of the past and covenanting that, if spared, the new year should be one of greater devotion to God. We thought of loved ones from whom we were parted, and we lifted also our hearts in prayer in their behalf, and to some extent felt it was pleasant to wait upon God.

"Calling for our beds, Brother Reasoner and I were sent to the parlor, as it was termed, where, after some controversy, I got the last cot of about twenty in the room. It stood directly in a current of air, and Brother R. was allowed to lie on a sofa. Trying to move my cot a little and to close the door, so as to keep off part of the current, I laid me down to sleep, but about eleven my cot gave way, and I came down head foremost. As it was useless to complain, and impossible to get another bed, I lay upon the floor, and rested as well as I could.

"*Jan.* 1, 1854.—In the morning I was weak and feverish; my clothes were with my baggage, which had not arrived at bed-time last night, and I was in a bad plight for a New-Year's Sabbath in a strange land. After a breakfast, of which I was able to partake but lightly, I felt somewhat better, but before I could get my clothes out of my trunk, and dress, church hour had passed. My fever continually increased, but, as notice was given that passengers might go on board at one, and that the ship would sail at six, I took a short walk about the town.

"*Monday morning, Jan.* 2.—Though I rested but little during the night, yet knowing we were farther south than we would be at any other time, and as it was perfectly clear, I rose between three and four, and walked out to look at the stars of the Southern sky. The cross shone in full brilliancy, and I stood for some time looking at a part of the heavens I had never seen before. The north star was some seven degrees above the horizon, but almost lost in a slight haze. All the stars beamed with that soft planetary lustre which is peculiar to tropical climes. The sea was full of phosphorescence, not merely sparkling, as if set with stars, as on the night we ran into Aspinwall; but it seemed as if the waves which broke around our ship were tipped with silvery glow, now and then sparkling into brighter lustre."

While running up the coast, the *Golden Gate* broke her shaft, and was compelled to lie to some days for repairs. Fortunately the sea was calm, but this accident led to other misadventures:

"*Thursday, Jan.* 12.—A bright, beautiful morning, but we are still drifting southwestwardly. I find that there is but little prospect of getting the engine at work for perhaps two days, as a large part of the shaft must be drilled away. The air is still, the sea is calm, and everything is delightful, except that we are not moving in the right direction. We are especially apprehensive that our non-arrival before the sailing of the mail from San Francisco may create great alarm among our friends in the States. We shall probably be on short allowance of food, but that we think we can bear. We are in the hands of Him who orders all things well.

"In the evening we had one of those glorious sunsets for which the Pacific is so famous. The sea was almost as smooth as a plain, save for the ceaseless undulation which ever moves its surface. Not a cloud was in the sky. The sun went down slowly, while a deep ruddy color spread around, and its last line of light suddenly disappeared. The sea from the reflection of light seemed like a mosaic pavement. Its color upon the summit of each swell was a purple shaded with blue; the sides of the swells inclining towards the west were covered with rings of yellow and green, while on the side of each swell eastward the colors shaded into black. I stood gazing at the scene until, under the dimming light, the colors faded away. On the other side the full moon cast her rays from the east, and the undulations were tinged with silver as they sparkled under her beams. It lacked only some fleecy clouds to display the various colors which I had seen a few evenings before to make it indescribably grand.

"I spent the evening chiefly in religious meditation. Here we were resting for forty-eight hours on the bosom of the Pacific. One shaft broken —the probability that a day or two must elapse before even an effort could be made to put our engine in motion, and there was some uncertainty whether it would work. No breeze fanned the sails—and already we were reminded that food and water were growing scarce. Yet He who rules in all space and all time is with us on the ocean's waste, as well as in the busy city, and He will order all things well. Committing myself to His care, I went sweetly to sleep.

"*Friday, Jan.* 13.—Another lovely morning rose upon us. All was peaceful and calm, but there are no indications of getting ready for moving. For two days suppers have been dispensed with, but to-day our dinner was limited to a single course. Passengers express considerable uneasiness."

On his way along the coast he writes a cheery letter to his wife:

"Steamer *Golden Gate*, Jan. 17, 1854.

". . . In my day thoughts as in my dreams, I have been much at home with you and the children. Sometimes fancy would play a little strongly, but generally I have been kept in peace, have looked into the family circle, and have seen your sparkling eye and almost heard your merry laugh, and then again you seemed careworn and exhausted. I have looked at the children in their studies and sports, ——— at his Latin, ——— and ——— at their geography and arithmetic, ——— at her mischief, and little ——— cooing and jumping, while his mother says, 'What a pretty boy!' But then I sometimes ask, 'What if some one may be sick, or—' and I try to look upwards and commit all into the hands of my Heavenly Father, who careth for them. I have never been nervous, I think, but an hour or two one night. It was in Panama. I was bilious when I reached the Isthmus; I had slept little at Cruces the first night; I had had much care besides fatigue in reaching Panama, and fever had already set in. When I sought my bed, I could get but a broken cot, which, the last of about twenty, had been put up in a saloon, and it was precisely between two doors where the night air of that unhealthy spot must blow upon me. I tried to move my cot a little, and, with the consent of others, got the principal door closed where the wind blew, and, turning my head as far from the current as possible, I was soon asleep. But about eleven o'clock, my cot broke down with me head foremost, and the panel of the door blew open so that I could not fasten it. On the hard floor I lay, trying to fix the broken cot so as to protect myself from the current of air. As my head ached, as my mouth and lips were dry and thirsty, and I felt the feverish throb in my pulse, I own to a little nervousness when I thought of the Isthmus fever, and of home, and of the deep, blue sea. But trying to believe that all was right, and that arms of love were around and beneath me, the floor grew softer, the current of air seemed less annoying, thoughts of friends and a home in the upper sanctuary mingled among my imaginings, and I sank into a calm and peaceful slumber."

His perils by the sea were not yet over. The disabled steamer made its way to the harbor of San Diego, and while trying to get out again ran upon a shoal, and came near being wrecked. He describes this unexpected experience in his diary :

" Our steamer seemed to be floating finely out, though worked by one wheel, but as we were eating dinner a sudden jar indicated that we had touched bottom. It was not at first supposed to be serious, but after an attempt or two to get off, baffled by the wind setting in from the southeast and the tide running out, a signal was hoisted, and speedily brought the steamer *Goliad*, the small vessel which I had seen in the morning, to our aid. Vain, however, was the trial, and, after breaking two or three of the largest cables, the *Goliad* lay near us, waiting for the evening or night tide. Low tide is about five to six; high tide, eleven to twelve. We supposed that then we could be pulled off, as our bow swung free.

"As the tide began to come in, the breeze strengthened into a gale, and by seven o'clock we were dashed against by strong waves. Towards nine it was found impossible to make an attempt to get us off, and between nine and ten the *Goliad* made for the harbor, narrowly escaping being driven on shore. Our condition became exceedingly critical from nine to one. The storm raged fiercely; the cordage creaked; the sail, which had been put up, was torn into shreds, it being impossible to get it down; the shrouds cracked like whip-cords, while an occasional squall suddenly striking the sail sounded like thunder. The waves rose high, dashing furiously against the vessel, and every now and then breaking even over the top of the cabin. The foremast was cracked and almost ready to fall, and the cabin-work around the mainmast began to crack and give way. Near twelve, the guards on the larboard side were split part of the way up; those immediately outside my room, which was wholly above the guards, splitting up so that I could not get to it without great risk. A heavy sea striking shortly after burst up the guards in the passageway, so as to throw the surges directly into the cabin, and wetting several of the rooms. At this time there seemed but little hope of the ship outriding the storm, but about one o'clock the squalls of wind were further apart, and from that time till three the surges were less regular and not so strong. After three there was a decided moderation of the weather, and the ship, which all night before had leaned to the larboard, so as to require many of us to stand on the starboard guard, righted up, and we were relieved from that duty. I stood perhaps three hours during the night on the guard, and got tolerably wet. The latter part of the night the sky cleared up, and at daylight the wind had fallen. The majority of the passengers did not lie down during the night, but after four o'clock, and especially after five, some were able to sleep. Though assured by the officers that the ship was strong enough to last several days, it was evident that the best seamen were exceedingly doubtful of the result. The ship leaked so that it became impossible to work the engine, the wheel being so far under water, and the water gathering in the ship put out the fire.

"In the storm the passengers were as cool and as tranquil as could have been expected. All were aware of our great danger, and many had but little hope. Several, who had been in storms around the Cape of Good Hope and in the Atlantic and Mediterranean, said they had never witnessed a night so terrible. Some of the wildest men came to me to converse on religious subjects, and I had an opportunity of pointing several to the mercy of God in Christ, who at other times were utterly careless. The ladies in our company were very quiet, and I did not hear an exclamation from any one of them. Some other ladies were much excited, and some Spanish women were incessant in their prayers to all the saints, calling upon each one by name. About eleven, I proposed to Bishop Kip the propriety of prayer, it having first been suggested to me by one or two of the passengers. We consulted several, but found that it was objected to by several gentlemen, and especially by the physician of the ship, lest it should increase the terror of the passengers.

" The sight of the sea during the storm was sublime. The waves ran high, dashing into foam and spray, and in their mighty rush leaped as if in defiance of any earthly power, while their roar could have been heard from afar. The words of the Psalmist in Psalm cvii. 23–31 have now a fuller meaning to me than ever before. It was a great consolation to remember that 'The sea is His, and He made it,' and that other expression, 'The Lord sitteth upon the flood; yea, the Lord sitteth King forever.'"

Although the *Goliad* was a small steamer, most of the passengers preferred making the rest of the voyage on it to waiting for a larger ship. After their rough night's experience the whole of the company on the *Golden Gate* went ashore.

" About five o'clock, or between five and six in the morning, the *Goliad* left the port of San Diego and was soon out upon the ocean. It is a small vessel, built originally for a tug steamer in New York, and is very strong. Its engine is large, unusually large, for a ship of its size. Its upper cabin is well fitted up and is the dining-room, and some eighteen staterooms are finished in comfortable style upon the deck. The captain has been a physician, is a very gentlemanly man, and he and the purser exerted themselves to make our company comfortable. And though but a coasting vessel from San Francisco to San Diego, and only expecting from fifty to eighty passengers, yet so attentive were the officers that from all the two hundred and fifty I did not hear a single complaint."

As soon as he reached San Francisco he began to work at a prodigious rate, even for him. The first evening in that city was spent in true Methodist fashion in a prayer-meeting. He found travel in this state, so recently opened to Americans, rough beyond all former experience, but he met his adventures with a light-hearted and elastic temper. A little anxiety disturbs him, however, when he thinks of home.   Sailing up the Sacramento River, he writes to his wife:

"Steamer *Antelope*, Jan. 30, 1854.

". . . I have been lodging at Mr. Hillman's temperance hotel.   He is a Methodist, and I have been kindly treated.   I have met several old students. . . . Personally I have but little to say.   God has been pleased to keep me in safety and health thus far, and I try to leave myself in his hands without anxiety for the future.   I have been trying to keep notes of my journey, which, should I return, may be of interest to you and the children.   I have appointments now made to fill up next month in traversing the country, which I must do by stage, on horseback, muleback, steamboat, or on foot, just as I find most convenient.   Brethren have received me kindly, and I think, apart from constant labor, I might have a pleasant visit.   I am trying also to give my heart and life more fully to God and his service, and I trust that, by his assisting grace, I may advance in spiritual knowledge and holiness.   A shade sometimes comes over my spirits when I think of the condition of my eyes, the spots before which have increased since I left home; but perhaps I may not need them longer than they shall serve me.   At any rate all will be right—yes, *all will be right*—for God can do nothing wrong.   I need not say that I think frequently of you and of the children.   I try to think of you in my most sacred moments of devotion, when I present you all at the cross, and plead for your health, your peace, and your safety.   I think of you frequently at other times, and often am ready to count the moments long, but I try to check myself, knowing that my duty is simply to live right the present moment, and to commit all my interests and all my ways into the hand of him who careth for me.   Please to remember me kindly to —— and to ——, as well as to my brethren of the ministry—the glorious ministry of reconciliation.   Oh, how I long to be more useful in the discharge of its duties!   The night of that terrible storm I little expected to see you or the children, or to preach again in the name of Jesus; but God, who is rich in mercy, has allowed me to speak again, and possibly he may permit me to meet my loved ones.   In the meantime meet me at the cross—the blessed cross."

It was not long before he met the Rev. William, now Bishop, Taylor, who was busy in San Francisco, holding open-air services on the Long Wharf and on the city plaza. We draw from the diary a brief notice of Taylor's California life, the beginning of a career which has touched all the continents of the globe:

"Sunday morning I visited the wharf on my way to Brother Heath's church on Folsom Street. Brother Taylor was preaching to one or two hundred men who were gathered around him, but I had not time to stop and listen. Preached at eleven to a well-filled house at Brother Heath's church on Folsom Street, on 'Thus it is written,' etc. After dinner walked to plaza, where Brother Taylor preached to some one or two hundred people, a plain, pointed sermon; very good order was observed; one lady besides Mrs. Taylor present; these services are attended with much good. At half-past three attended sacrament on Folsom Street, and after services addressed the church on Church duties. Tea at Hillman's, and preached at night to a full house in the Bethel. After sermon Brother Taylor invited mourners — three came: one American man; one negro woman, darkest I ever saw; one Peruvian young man — all nations and tongues seem to be congregating in California, and I trust that here is to be the centre of a great good."

His next letter, dated from Sacramento, contains an itinerary, and shows that he did travel " by steamboat, stage, horseback, muleback, or on foot," as he found best for his purpose. One wonders how he came through it all:

"Sacramento, Feb. 14, 1854.

"When the last steamer arrived I hoped to receive at least a line from home, but I was distant from San Francisco, and could only receive my letters at certain points. A few days after the arrival of the steamer, I rode some seventy miles by stage in mud and rain, consoling myself with the thought that I should meet my letters at Stockton; but no letter came. Just as I was leaving Stockton, a friend informed me that a letter post-marked Pittsburgh had been forwarded to me at Sacramento, which I was engaged to reach that evening. Fifty miles staging brought me to Sacramento, but no letter was there. The next evening at Mormon Island, twenty-eight miles farther, I received it, but it was *not from home.* Brother Kincaid had kindly written, but had no news in it from you, except that he had seen you on the Thursday evening after I had left. Again I travelled my round, and this afternoon, after forty-five miles staging through frost and snow and mud, I arrived at this place, where Conference will begin Thursday morning, and where, Thursday evening, I will meet the elders — but no letter meets me. Two months, save three days, have passed since I left home, and no letter yet —

'My friends, do they now and then send
    A letter or thoughts o'er the sea;
To tell me I yet have a friend,
    Who loves to write letters to me?'

But that parody must close this chapter of letter accidents. I send you a few scraps to show you I have not been idle since my arrival here. I have had appointments almost every day, and I have not failed to meet them. I have ridden by stage, horseback, and muleback, and to a few I have walked; and my health is about as good as when I arrived. When I last wrote you I was sailing up the Sacramento River, on Monday night, January 30. I send a sketch of my whereabouts since:

" *Tuesday, Jan.* 31.—Rode forty miles by stage to Ione Valley; visited gold diggings; rode five miles on mule to see parts of the valley; preached and lectured to young men.

Wednesday, Feb. 1.—Rode sixteen miles on horseback; visited quartz mills at Amador; preached in Jackson at night.

Thursday, Feb. 2.—Rode ten miles on horseback; climbed Mokelumne Butte, a high mountain; had a splendid prospect (had a bad fall, tearing the skin off my knuckles, and worse still the knee of my trousers); walked several miles, visiting camp of Digger Indians; preached at Mokelumne at night, and talked to young men.

Friday, Feb. 3.—Rode forty miles to Sonora by stage; immense hills, steepest I ever rode over in stage, at river Stanislaus; no appointment at night, by mistake.

Saturday, Feb. 4.—Walked about country; preached at night.

Sunday, Feb. 5.—Dedicated church at eleven; rode in buggy in rain to Columbia, four miles; preached at three; very hard rain, not *pouring*, but *coming down;* rode two miles in buggy in rain; then walked two miles in dark and rain—the mud not *quite knee deep.*

Monday, Feb. 6.—Rode seventy miles in stage to Stockton; rain part of the day.

Tuesday, Feb. 7.—Walked around Stockton and wrote; preached at night.

Wednesday, Feb. 8.—By stage fifty-five miles to Sacramento.

Thursday, Feb. 9.—By stage twenty-eight miles to Mormon Island; walked over the hills; preached at night.

Friday, Feb. 10.—By stage twenty-three miles to Coloma; preached at night.

Saturday, Feb. 11. — Visited mill-race where gold was first found; walked over high hills to Uniontown and back, three miles; rode to Cold Springs on horseback, five miles; preached at two P.M.; rode horseback six miles to Diamond Springs.

Sunday, Feb. 12.—Dedicated church; a severe snow-storm; rode in storm to Placerville, horseback, three miles; addressed Sunday-school at three; preached at night.

Monday, Feb. 13.—Walked several miles; visited upper Placerville;

rode back three miles to Diamond Springs; saw —— at Placerville,
tending bar in a groggery; —— is a doctor making $1000 a month;
—— and —— are digging gold; walked two miles; preached at night
at Mud Springs.

Tuesday, Feb. 14.—By stage forty-five miles to Sacramento, and am
now writing to you. So much for the diary, and so endeth the second
chapter.

"And now you may rest awhile in reading, as I do from writing—or
rather change to other writing—and so I kiss my hand and, waving it
towards the Rocky Mountains, say, 'Good-night, peaceful dreams to you.
Schlafen sie wohl.'"

He was so delighted with California that he was inclined
to make it his home. In February he writes: "Had I you
with me I could live contentedly in this land for several
years. There is a wide field for usefulness, and there are
few who seem to comprehend the actual condition of things."
And again, the same month: "What would you think of a
home in California? I have been very warmly urged to fix
my residence here, and I confess were you and the children
with me, I think I could spend a few years very pleasantly, in trying to lay the foundations of the Church on the
Pacific coast. It is a strange and a peculiar country. Everything in society is on a grand scale; everything is under
high pressure, and I believe great good might be done by
plans well directed and promptly and vigorously executed.
But I think I almost see you throw down the letter and
say, 'Catch me going to California!' Well, then, pick it up
again, and I will drop that subject."

Steamers from San Francisco to Oregon were very uncertain. He could not find one starting in time to enable him
to reach the Oregon Conference on the day of its opening.
"I have felt very much regret that I have been so long
detained, and it is now questionable whether I shall reach
the Oregon Conference at all—certainly not for several days
after its commencement. To have come so far and yet to
miss my Conference, by reason of the irregularity of the
steamers, is hard to bear; but I must try patiently to sub-

mit." This delay led to a struggle to reach the place of Conference session in the heart of the Willamette valley, which illustrates his nerve and, as well, the perils of travel in the wilderness. On the way up the Columbia River, he writes to his wife :

"Steamer *Peytona,* March 15, 1854.

"I am now on the steamer *Peytona,* sailing up the Columbia River between Astoria and Portland; we expect to reach Portland this evening. . . .

"Last night, while standing on the deck of the vessel, I could but notice the position of the North Star, which seemed to have risen so high above me. We are here in latitude 46½°, or near that, and a few weeks ago I was in latitude 7°, where this star was almost at the horizon. The climate changes, the plains and mountains change, the sea changes, the very stars seem to change; there is above, beyond, around, the Eternal, the Infinite. There is a spirit land, unchanging and unchangeable. In my dreams of the night, of late, loved ones from that sphere have been visiting me. I seemed to be again in their society, and thoughts of the past and the Invisible have been strangely intermingled. I have felt that mind cannot change. The loved ones of my childhood have my affections still. The friends of my youth are bound to me by bonds indissoluble. Loved ones, dearer than life, parted now by mountains and by seas, seem but the dearer for the distance, and, strange as it may seem, I fancy them sometimes as *nearer* for the *separation.* How often does our little family circle rise around me, as if I were in the midst of it, and even our eldest, though long asleep in Jesus, seems not unfrequently one of the group. Strange are the sympathies of our nature, and they point forward as well as upward. They have more than mortal strength, and will be satisfied only when the flock shall be gathered where there *is one fold and one shepherd.* But I forget myself when I begin to moralize. It is a letter of news you wish, and not a page of sentimental prosing. And yet it is so easy for me to glide off from the outward to the inward, from my observations to my fancies. Well, well, you must pardon me, for I have been so constantly in the habit, for these eighteen years and more, of talking my whole heart to you, that the current flows right out of the end of my pen when I begin the sheet with your name.

"To-morrow Conference begins at Belknap Settlement, which is four days' journey from Portland, where our boat will stop this evening. I hope, however, by travelling all night, Saturday night, through a wild, woody country, if I can get a guide, to reach my brethren by Sabbath morning. This missing Conference, or half of it, after coming so far, is for me a great trial, but I cannot help it, and so must submit. To-morrow I expect, Providence permitting, to see Oregon City; Friday evening, Salem; Saturday evening, Maysville; and then by some way, if possible, get through to Conference."

Pushing as rapidly as possible for the seat of the Conference, he took, at Oregon City, a steamer for Corvallis, on the Willamette River, the nearest landing to the place of session. This is what he meets on entering the cabin:

"Passing into the cabin, I found one school-teacher and three or four girls or ladies squat on the floor, busily engaged in playing cards, which appears to be the inward passion of the Western coast. Gentlemen in the cabin, boys on the beach, Indians around their camp, and ladies in their clubs, all may be seen playing cards. On the left side, about two miles below the old mission site, we passed the place of Gervais, a Frenchman, said to have accompanied Lewis and Clark, and at this house Mr. Lee preached his first sermon in the Willamette. Shortly after we tied up until the moon rose, when, again starting, we grounded on a sand-bar some eight or ten miles from Salem. Though exceedingly anxious to hurry on, I found it impossible to land and get a conveyance. The yawl of the boat was employed in taking soundings and trying to procure a lighter. There was an island and a large number of sloughs on our left, so as to prevent our journeying if landed. We finally got loose at nine A.M., but were detained until eleven by various circumstances. We reached Salem at quarter-past one, and hastened to procure some mode of conveyance to Corvallis.

"Governor Gaines met me on the wharf with his usual kind manner and good-humored smile, and pleasantly remarked that when we last met in Indiana we did not expect to meet in Oregon, he as governor and I as bishop. By the help of a friend who had joined me at Portland, Mr. Barnhart, Mr. Campbell's son-in-law, and myself succeeded in procuring a wagon to convey us to Corvallis for $40—I paying $30—with the promise of going through very rapidly. Our vehicle was a light spring wagon, rather frail, with but one seat; and our horses, though promised an excellent team, were very small. Soon after starting our traces got loose several times, and the sides of the wagon-bed, held together by a string, broke the string and let down our seat. Mr. B. sat behind us, on his trunk, and I on the seat, one end of it elevated, the other on the floor. We passed over hills south of Salem, resembling California hills, with thin oak timber, scrubby and orchard-like. The land is rolling and nearly mountainous. Some very fine views were had of the Coast range, the Cascade range, and the snow-peaks of Mt. Hood, Mt. Jefferson, and the Sisters. Passed the governor's residence, eight miles from Salem; came to the top of a hill overlooking the Willamette valley at Humphrey's ferry. Here a beautiful view opened before us. The Willamette winding below our feet, and, in the distance, wide plains with improvements here and there; beyond, prairies, forests, flowers, and fields green with wheat, and the mountain range, all made a delightful prospect; while the evening rays of the sun gently shed a mellow brilliancy over the landscape. We crossed the ferry. The ferrymen landed us with our wagon towards the shore, to the no small consternation of our Jehu, who had been boasting of his Yankee origin and his power of making money. The boat was shoved off and turned, and we were soon under way, passing a mile or so of thick fir woods, with very bad roads. Emerging from the forest, we entered a prairie skirted with a lake, a slough on our left, and missed our way in consequence of the fencing up of claims. This was found to be almost universally the case. . . . It was now twilight, and in a mile or two farther our driver lost his way. After winding to several points of the compass, we brought up at the farm-house of Mr. Collins, with whom we made a bargain to send us on to Corvallis. But the horses had been turned out Saturday evening, and it was pretty dark, and they must be hunted before we could proceed."

Baffled though he was, he was resolved not to fail in accomplishing the object of his long journey by sea and land, and pushed on through the darkness of the night. The narrative continues:

"Finding who we were, we were treated very kindly and furnished with supper. Horses were procured and harnessed to the wagon, leaving our driver and horses. A son of Mr. Collins started with us to Corvallis at ten o'clock at night. Taking advantage of some sheaf oats put in the hinder part of the wagon, I lay down on them, and thus rode a large part of the way, which was down through sloughs and mud, reaching Corvallis at two at night. Here all were in bed. Mr. and Mrs. Campbell were absent at Conference, and I could not learn how I was to get forward to Belknap's Settlement. Lying down, I slept until sunrise, when I was awakened by Mr. B., and found the Indian boy at Mr. Campbell's had been sent to Judge Stewart's, a mile below town, for a horse. Judge Stewart was to have accompanied me, but, despairing of my coming, the horses had been turned out. Before a horse could be caught and brought to town it was a quarter-past eight. Assured, however, it was only fifteen miles away, I was immediately in the saddle, crossed

Mary's River in a ferry-boat, and, over a very muddy road and exceedingly deep sloughs, I rode rapidly, two men being my pioneers.

"Mary's Peak, covered with snow, was visible all the time some thirty miles distant. Five miles riding on a level not far from the Willamette brought us to clumps of trees; ten miles to an undulating ridge—fifteen miles—brought us to Belknap's Settlement, near the junction of the Long Tom and the Willamette. We rode along Long Tom, a dull, sluggish stream in this part of its course, said to have been named from an early settler—Long Tom Barr. Having parted with my guides, I learned that the church was yet five miles distant and situated among the spurs of the Buttes. Riding on and carrying my satchel, I at length came in sight of a log school-house, with a little board shed attached temporarily to it. It stood on the top of a butte, in great measure surrounded by sloughs, and nearly a mile from any house. Horses and wagons were tied up around it. Alighting and divesting myself of my outer wraps, I stepped into the church just as the congregation engaged in prayer at the close of, as I was informed, an excellent sermon by Brother Pearne, who had acted as president of the Conference. At the close of prayer some one announced my name; going forward, an appointment was arranged for half-past two. My place of lodging was a mile and a half off, and, getting my dinner, it was time for preaching. Preached on 'Oneness' and ordained three deacons. At night did not go out."

To reach this log school-house in the woods of Oregon he had journeyed several thousand miles by sea, had encountered the difficulties of river navigation in a new country, and in the last desperate struggle had ridden nearly all the night before, sleeping in his wagon on sheaves of oats, and then had pushed forward twenty miles on horseback to find himself in time to join in the Sabbath worship. And he had his reward. He was among men who were laying the foundations—not of empires, far better than that—of commonwealths of self-controlled and all-controlling citizens. They were in the midst of their struggle with the forces of untamed Nature and bore its marks upon them. I find in a paper of later but uncertain date a description of the scene, written by one who was on the spot. The time is Sunday morning, and preachers and people are assembled for the Conference love-feast:

21

"Reader, did you ever attend a Conference love-feast•on the frontier, where common sufferings and deprivations and trials had moulded all hearts into one? where a universal poverty equalized everything, so that there could be no classes or grades of appointment? If not, we pity you. You have lost the sight of the greenest spot that ever blossomed in the path of an itinerant.

"The love-feast of this Conference was rich with experience and history, with pathos and unction, all finding expression in word and song, in tear and shout, rendering the hour indescribable. At its close the president of the Conference preached a sermon of great power, and just as he resumed his seat the tall form of Bishop Simpson appeared in the door, and Conference and congregation were thrown into a whirl of excitement as they welcomed him to this rustic sanctuary. It was at once announced that he would preach in the afternoon. When two o'clock came, and the bishop arose in that humble desk to preach and gave out,

> ' When I survey the wondrous cross
> On which the Prince of Glory died,'

how the words of that old hymn beat with new life! And his prayer! dews of heaven could not distil more sweetly. And his sermon! who shall describe the indescribable or speak the unutterable?"*

His perils of waters and perils in the wilderness were not all past. His plan of travel included a trip up the Columbia River to the Dalles, where was an important Methodist mission station. Accordingly he retraced his way, going down the Willamette to Portland, and from thence up the Columbia. Returning to Portland, he writes of this trip to his wife :

"Portland, April 10, 1854.

"I reached this city on Saturday morning, after a difficult and somewhat perilous journey to the Cascades and Dalles of the Columbia River.

"I reached my Conference on the Sabbath of its session, after having travelled all Saturday night, my guide missing his way in the woods. Conference closed on Tuesday afternoon; that evening I rode twenty miles on horseback to Corvallis; spent there three days waiting for a steamboat, but it was sunk on its passage up, and I started on horseback for Salem, some thirty-two miles distant; but my horse gave out, and I was compelled to walk part of my journey. There I spent Sabbath, preach-

---

* This sermon is more fully described on p. 298.

ing twice; addressed the church on Monday night; attended to mission-ary business on Monday and Tuesday, and on Wednesday left on a steamer for Oregon City. Thursday from Oregon City to this place (Portland); Friday by steamer to the Cascades, on my way to the Dalles, to look af-ter mission property. There the steamer above the Cascades was broken, and, after having waited for a sail-boat until Monday, I was obliged to hire an Indian canoe, and with Brother Pearne, who accompanied me, to row up the river. About ten o'clock at night we reached the Indian camp, where, as it rained, we were compelled to lodge in a miserable In-dian hut, among the filthy natives, until the morning light appeared. The next evening we reached the Dalles. There spent Wednesday. Thursday tried to get down the river in a schooner, but, the wind being adverse, after struggling for twenty hours, and being nearly capsized, and escaping by a hand's-breath from being dashed upon the rocks, we left the schooner and took a small boat or skiff. We rowed all night, except three hours, when the crew gave out. Making a fire upon the shore, miles from any house, we threw ourselves upon the ground, and I had a good, sweet sleep. Friday reached the Cascades, and Saturday, by steamer, returned here.

"Should Providence spare my life, I expect to reach San Francisco on my return in the next ten or twelve days, and it is now highly probable that I shall sail from thence by the steamer of the first of May. If so, and Providence should see it best to keep me from accident and disease, I may reach New York the latter part of May."

XV.

AN EPISCOPAL TOUR TO TEXAS.
JOURNEY TO EUROPE.

1855–1857.

Many Gaps in Bishop Simpson's Papers.—Episcopal Tour in Texas.—
Travels with Bewley, the Martyr.—Rough Stage-riding.—His Connec-
tion with the Founding of the Methodist Episcopal Church in India.—
The Rev. William Butler's Commission.—Appointed in 1856, with Dr.
McClintock, a Delegate to the British Conference.—Rev. W. H. Mil-
burn Joins the Party.—" You, Dr. McClintock ?"—Reception of the
Delegates by the British Wesleyan Conference.—Their Speeches.—No
Rest at Home or Abroad.—World's Conference of the Evangelical Alli-
ance in Berlin.—Krummacher's Address of Welcome.—Replies on Be-
half of Americans by Governor Joseph A. Wright and Bishop Simpson.
—Entertainment of the Alliance at Potsdam by the King of Prussia.—
A Handsome Reception.—Sermon on Christian Unity by Bishop Simpson in the Garnison Kirche, Berlin.

XV.

In examining Bishop Simpson's papers one has frequent reason for regret that gaps are now and then met with which cannot be filled. Such a gap appears in the correspondence of 1855. In the autumn of that year he made a trip from St. Louis to Bonham, Texas, where he held the Texas Conference. Part of the way his travelling companion was Anthony Bewley, known to us as one of the Church's martyrs. Though a native of Tennessee, Bewley had refused, at the time of the division in 1845, to enter the Methodist Church, South. For a while he preached quite independently of all ecclesiastical fellowship; but in 1848, when the Plan of Separation had been declared null and void, he entered the Missouri, and afterwards the Arkansas and Texas Conference. His connection with a Northern Church subjected him, in that wild region, to constant peril, so that in 1856 he returned to his home in Missouri. In 1860 he started for Texas again, saying to his friends as he left them: "Let them hang or burn me on my return if they choose; hundreds will rise up out of my ashes." His words proved to be prophetic: he was pursued by a mob and hanged on a tree, Sept. 13, 1860.

The perils of the trip to Texas in 1855 were clear to Bishop Simpson's mind, and his letters to his family show much anxiety. Unfortunately we are without any account of the session of the Conference, or of the spirit of the men who were its members. His journey was made by rail to Hermann, Missouri, thence by stage, open wagon, or whatever could be found, now and then on horseback, and

328 LIFE OF MATTHEW SIMPSON.

we suspect, more than once, for short distances, on foot, with saddle-bags hanging from his arm and overcoat on his shoulder. Before starting he thus writes to his wife from St. Louis: "Time hangs very heavily on my hands, and I long to be at home again. But I do not know whether I can hope for much continued domestic happiness while driving over the world as I do. I hardly seem to be made for a bishop. I guess Stevens is pretty near right in that matter." And again, from the same point, Oct. 15, 1855: "I have sent my carpet-sack to Cincinnati; possibly Bishop Janes may take it to Pittsburgh. I have purchased a pair of saddle-bags and prepared an outfit for travelling by horse or mule, as I may be obliged to do for several hundred miles. I shall learn better at Springfield, from whence I will try to write you. May God watch over and protect you and keep you and the children in all your ways."

From Hermann, where the railroad ended, he began to "rough it" in the usual Western style. He writes from Jefferson City: "I took stage, or, rather, a hack sort of wagon. Brother Goode was with me. Nine passengers could sit inside, and there were ten of us. I found it so uncomfortable within that I took an outside seat with the driver. Here, unfortunately, the Utah and New Mexico mail going through, in addition to the ordinary mail matter, so filled the space that I was perched high up, with scarcely a spot to put my feet. In this position I rode the afternoon and all night, and until eleven to-day, save a short change this morning."

Near Springfield he found the home of Anthony Bewley, and with him travelled to the seat of the Conference. He writes again: "Springfield, Missouri, Oct. 18, 1855.— I arrived at Brother Bewley's, four miles from this place, a little after noon to-day. I had to walk and carry my saddle-bags, coat, and blanket some two miles and a half to reach his house. He was just starting for Conference. I go in his buggy, drawn by two young and small mules.

The buggy is narrow and without a top, but it will be comfortable. I am well provided for."

The rest of this interesting journey is a blank; we have only a short note, written on his way back, from Washington, Arkansas: "I left Bonham on Monday morning last, and now, on Friday evening, I am only about one hundred and seventy miles on my journey. Thus far I have travelled as fast as the mail. But, as it will run on Sabbath, and I must lie by, this letter may reach you some days before I get home. When I stop for Sunday I have no chance of stage for three days, but possibly I may get a private conveyance. This is uncertain. It is right, however, that you should know my route in case of any accident."

It was his privilege during the period from 1853 to 1856 to take part with Dr. Durbin in preparing for the planting of the Methodist Episcopal Church in India. In the first year named $7000 had been appropriated for opening the India Mission. Bishop Simpson, by appointment of his colleagues, had episcopal supervision. The letters written to him during the three years by Dr. Durbin, all of them repeating the question, "Can you find me a man for India?" become, as one reads them to-day, pathetic. No man offered himself, though we know now * that the Rev. William Butler was ready to accept the call, but was restrained by fear of snatching away an honor which, in his judgment, belonged of right to some American-born Methodist preacher. Dr. Durbin, reduced to despair by the silence of the Church, published an appeal in the *Christian Advocate* of May 10, 1855; his state of mind may be inferred from the title of the appeal—*The Crisis.* "We suggest," he writes, "that the presiding elders cast about them and see if the men are not in their ranks whom God is moving to this work, and who need but to be called out in order to manifest their

---

* See Dr. Butler's volume: "From Boston to Bareily and Back," pp. 63 to 72.

readiness to go. . . . We sincerely trust that we may be put in communication with the brethren chosen of God to found and execute what we deem to be a great work of the Church, viz., to take a worthy part in the evangelization of India." With what feelings Bishop Simpson, after such delay, wrote the commission of the Rev. William Butler may readily be imagined. We reproduce it here as a memento of a historic event, for out of this unpromising beginning have grown three Annual Conferences, superintended by a bishop for India and Malaysia, with more than eleven thousand adherents to the Christian faith, and all the appointments of a well-organized Church.

Immediately upon his return from his long tour to Texas, he entered again upon the excessive labors so characteristic of him. In the following fashion he spends a Sunday during the General Conference Session at Indianapolis, May, 1856: "I visited New Albany and Jeffersonville on Saturday evening. Went to Wesley Chapel Sunday-school on Sabbath morning and opened it with prayer; visited Roberts Chapel Sunday-school and addressed the scholars; preached at Centenary Church; helped to administer sacrament at Roberts Chapel at half-past three, and preached at Wesley Chapel at night. Rose at four next morning; at half-past four got in omnibus, stopped at Jeffersonville to breakfast. Dined at Dr. Cunan's, and left at quarter-past three for this place, where I arrived at eight. So much for the journey."

Another note from the seat of the General Conference gives a hint of the purpose to send him as delegate to England:

"Indianapolis, May 21.

"There is nothing done as to districting the bishops, and nothing I think will be done. I suppose I have pretty deeply offended the Northern brethren by saying I thought their proposed action against slavery unconstitutional. But this will likely work well and please you, for before this a large number of them said they were going to send me to England. Now I think it will not be done, and, if spared, I shall be the more with you."

7.

Rev. William Butler.
Dear Bro

You are hereby appointed as Superintendent of the Mission about to be commenced in India by the Methodist Episcopal Church. Your services will be appropriate to this region until the close of your present Conference year, at which time you will be under the direction of the Missionary Board. Instructions as to your duties, and information in reference to your assistant will be communicated hereafter.

Yours in Christ
M. Simpson

Pittsburgh Jany 8th 1856.

He was, nevertheless, appointed a delegate to the British Wesleyan Conference, with Doctor McClintock as an associate. This was for him a most memorable journey; it extended to the Continent, where he attended the Conference of the Evangelical Alliance at Berlin, and from thence to the Holy Land. His letters, while abroad, to his family are no longer brief itineraries, but are full of life and enthusiasm; they will best tell the story of his sickness and health, of the traveller's pleasures and mishaps. He left New York in May, 1857, crowded to the last moment before his departure with engagements for sermons and addresses. His son Charles was on shipboard with him; Dr. McClintock and the Rev. Mr. William H. Milburn, who became one of the party, joined him in Liverpool. The first letter is from that city:

"May 25, 1857.

"Many thanks to a kind Providence for protection amid the dangers of an Atlantic voyage. And here, sure enough, I am in Old England, the land of story and of song, the land of brave men and fair women for centuries past. And yet I am in a kind of bewilderment. Am I really here? I am ready to ask myself; for everything is so much like what I have seen elsewhere, and so many marks of a common civilization and a common Christianity are about me, and the same language which I have always heard I hear still. I can scarcely feel that I am abroad, and yet there are differences. But you want no essays; well, then, to my story.

"That last white handkerchief I saw waved, was it yours? I fancied so; I know you did wave, and I waved, and Charles waved, and we all waved. But when you and we quit waving our pocket-handkerchiefs, and you turned homeward on the train, we kept *waving* away, sometimes a great deal more than we wished. At least Charles thought so, and so thought about one hundred and fifty or one hundred and eighty out of the two hundred passengers who went through all sorts of grimaces, and gyrations, and gesticulations, and utterances. But the waters are safely crossed, and once more we are on dry land.

"Somehow I get to the end of my story too soon; I scarcely start from America but I find myself landing here. It was not so in reality, for the days seemed long, very long, as we tossed on the ocean, with the thermometer, as it was two days, down to 32°. I said the days were long—so they were, for the sun did not set till after eight, and it was bright twilight until ten. And the daylight broke at half-past two, and the sun was up again about four, while we were on our Northern passage—for we passed north of Ireland. But here I am again across the sea before my story is done. Well, then, besides Mr. Holmes, we had on board Mr. Wandell, of New York, a merchant going to China for tea, a member of our church, and Mrs. Havemeyer, also a member, whose husband was formerly Mayor of New York. Then we had Mayor or ex-Mayor Brady, with his wife and two daughters, and a number of others with whom I became well acquainted. The ladies generally were very sick, but one old woman from Louisiana talked so incessantly from morning to night that she had not time to be sick. As for myself, though I had some headache and a little nausea occasionally, yet as Bishop Ames says of me, 'I had not sense enough to get sick.' On Sabbath I was invited to preach, and did so to an attentive audience. This is rather unusual on this line, but the captain was very polite. I had written a letter on board, hoping that I might reach this city in time to send it by the steamer of Saturday, but I was too late. But on arriving we got thinner paper, and I began to write the letter over again, but somehow it would come out a very different one.

"We arrived about three on yesterday (Sunday) afternoon. About five we got the custom-house officers and came ashore. We stopped at the Adelphi Hotel, and at six I heard Milburn preach. Having learned that his party was at the Union, I changed our lodging to the Union, and now we are all together. They had a delightful passage over, I suppose much more pleasant than ours, having arrived on Friday night. To-morrow I expect we shall go to London. From thence it is uncertain what our course will be."

Never did a more brilliant company of men go abroad to represent a Church or a people than were now happily met together in the Union Hotel, Liverpool. Mr. Milburn's almost total blindness gave an additional interest to his oratory; Dr. McClintock was in the maturity of his powers; grace, polish, and strength were revealed in every public address delivered by him. And Bishop Simpson was, during this trip, at his best. The trio travelled much together, enjoyed life together, and together delighted the thousands who thronged to hear them. In those days, English audiences listened more critically to Americans than they do now. America was, in some sense, on trial before them; and American Methodism, in the presence of English Wesleyans, was expected to give an account of itself; to prove, not so much the legitimacy of its derivation—that was conceded—but its faithful adherence, in every point of detail, to the Wesleyan ideas of Church order. It seems to us, of this day, incredible that it should be so, but so it was. Our visitors, in 1857, felt themselves to be, without fault of their own, in precisely this position.

Mr. Milburn gives an account of one of the first adventures of the party in Liverpool:

"Here is a droll bit over which we had a hearty laugh.

"The Sunday after Doctor McClintock and I reached Liverpool, while we were waiting for the bishop, the doctor went to a Wesleyan Chapel, dressed as he had been on the ship, and at the close of the morning service entered the vestry-room. The preacher who had officiated, a tall, dignified person, was, after the manner of the time, taking a glass of wine which had been deferentially handed to him by a chapel steward.

"The courteous doctor approached, and said, in his bland tone, 'The Reverend Mr. ——, I believe.' 'That is my name,' answered the other, with some asperity of manner, 'have you business with me? If so, pray state it at once.' 'None whatever,' said the doctor; 'I simply called to pay my respects.' 'Respects indeed,' said the Englishman, somewhat tartly, 'and what may be your name?' 'McClintock,' said the doctor. 'McClintock,' exclaimed the other, with a slight touch of contempt in his tone.

"'Irish, I see.' Then, musing a moment, he added, 'Do you happen to be related to the Rev. Dr. McClintock who is shortly expected in this country with the American deputation to the Wesleyan body?' 'That is my name,' said the doctor, bowing. 'You, Dr. McClintock?' exclaimed the Briton, as he held the half-emptied glass in his hand, and a mingled expression of incredulity and amazement overspread his features, as he rapidly ran his eye over the doctor from head to foot, surveying the slouch hat in his hand, his blue body-coat, his brown waistcoat showing the shirt-front, the brown trousers, pausing longest upon the black neck-tie, and adding, ' You, Dr. McClintock ? I never could have believed it !'

"Recovering a little from his astonishment, the Englishman went on, ' Really, if you are the Rev. Dr. McClintock, one of the American deputation, you must preach for us at our evening service ; but where is the Right Rev. Bishop Simpson ?' ' He hasn't arrived yet,' said the doctor. ' We expect him this afternoon.' ' Then, certainly,' said the other, ' if the bishop should reach here in time, we shall wish him, as the head of the deputation, to preach ; otherwise, we shall insist upon your doing so.' ' It will be quite impossible for me,' said the doctor, pointing to his throat, which, by the way, was so seriously affected that he had not spoken in public for many months. ' Oh, that can be easily managed,' said John Bull, totally misapprehending his meaning ; ' you must certainly have a clerical suit in your baggage, and as to the white cravat, I will lend you a fresh one with great pleasure.' "

A trip to Norway helped to fill up the interval of time between Bishop Simpson's arrival in England and the meeting of the British Wesleyan Conference. In June, in company with Dr. McClintock, he visited the Irish Wesleyan Conference, where they received " a thousand welcomes " as only Irishmen can give them. They were both near their ancestral home, the father of Dr. McClintock having been born a few miles on the one side of Omagh, in County Tyrone, and the father of Bishop Simpson a few miles on the opposite side of that town. Dr. McClintock said afterwards, laughingly, that while in Ireland he had received a certificate of his nationality. After having preached on a certain occasion, a venerable old minister to whom he was introduced asked him when he went to America. The doctor replied that he was born there. " Dear, dear," responded the old gentleman, " he talks as well as most any one of us." In July the two delegates were presented to the British Conference. We will draw again from Mr. Milburn's narrative: "The Conference sat with closed doors until the day on which the bishop and the doctor were received, when time-honored precedent was thrown aside, the doors opened, and an almost suffocating crowd thronged every part of the building. The bishop, who was the first to speak, could not but be conscious, as he looked over the vast assembly, that, kindly disposed as they might be, there was a barrier to his success, for the hospitality of mind in his hearers was tinctured by a slight distrust and undervaluation of him as an American; undefined it might be, but none the less real and potent.

"It was a trying moment for the great orator who had achieved so many triumphs in his native land, and he, at first, seemed almost to falter, while the doctor and I, who sat near at hand, were tremulous, even feverish, dreading lest our champion might fail for the first time in his life on a great occasion. For ten or fifteen minutes we were kept in most painful suspense; our breath came hard and fast, for the bishop was hampered and ill at ease, or appeared to be so. It may have been his art, but I think it was genuine embarrassment. Just as we were giving up all for lost, the speaker seemed to forget himself for a moment or two, as a happy illustration fell from his lips; his face lighted up, his eye flashed, and every eye in the multitude answered him, and there was a murmur of 'Hear, hear!' from all over the house. The bishop's legs were no longer unsteady; he seemed to erect himself above himself; his voice lost its wavering inflections and uncertainty of tone; his sentences flowed freely, in clearer and higher form. The speech became earnest, effective, poetic, impassioned, thrilling. The silence was at times oppressive, but relieved at the end of every paragraph, sometimes of a few sentences, by deafening, overwhelming shouts of 'Hear, hear! good, good!' English reserve is proverbial, and the mercurial stranger from this side of the water is sure to feel it, as a chill most repressive, well-nigh paralyzing. This is true of individuals, as well as of great assemblies; but if there be power and heat enough to melt the ice, when the thaw comes it is accompanied by a flood. As there is no private hospitality in the world superior, if equal, to that of England when one has gained a welcome, so there are scarcely any audiences on earth so responsive, demonstrative, enthusiastic, as the English when they once yield themselves to the spell of a great master. Bishop Simpson has made many great and powerful speeches in the course of his long and brilliant public life, but I doubt if his marvellous strength and magnetic sway over thousands of his fellow-men were ever more signally displayed than in this speech in Brunswick Chapel, except upon one other memorable occasion, when he preached before the Wesleyan Conference, some years later, at Burslem, when the effect upon the congregation was indescribable, unparalleled in this generation. As the bishop took his seat the dignitaries upon the platform, the ministers upon the floor, the laity, and the ladies were in a tumult of excitement, and it was many minutes before the thunders of applause ceased.

"It was no easy task to follow such a speech. It was a tide which, taken at the flood, would not lead on an ordinary man to fortune, but to be bound in shallows and miseries; and as Dr. McClintock arose I could not but feel the deepest solicitude. My anxiety for him, however, was soon relieved. His singularly handsome person and engaging manner, noble head, beaming eye, attractive face, mellow and beautiful voice—for he had regained the use of his throat—enlisted the audience on the instant. The rhythmic flow of his perfect English; the luminous statement of his subject — 'The State and Prospects of Higher Education in the New World;' his vivid and masterly presentation of it; his melodious tones, rising to full sonorous power, every accent, inflection, modulation, controlled by an almost infallible taste, delighted the ear, while every mental faculty was charmed and the emotions stirred by the spells of this most accomplished scholar, orator, human-hearted man. There could scarcely be a greater contrast than that between these two speakers—each admirable, almost perfect, in his way. The effect of the doctor's speech was as satisfying and profound as that of the bishop; nothing more can be said. I could have hugged both my friends for joy, and never on English soil felt prouder of my country and my countrymen."

Even the scrupulously decorous London *Watchman* (alas, poor ghost!) was stirred to something like enthusiasm, and had visions of a strengthening, by means of such deputations, of the bonds of national friendship. It draws quite a charming picture of what might be hoped for in the years to come:

"The people of this country and of America are sensitive, proud, and occasionally have, on minor matters, a conflicting policy; so that it requires all the influences arising from a common ancestry, language, and literature, and all their real identity of material interests to prevent occasional quarrels. Nay, they do quarrel and sometimes half draw the sword; though the reception given to Mr. Dallas here, and to Lord Napier there, shows how quickly, how gladly, and how thoroughly they can be reconciled. It is a great and providential fact, influencing the destinies of both these great peoples and of the world, that among each of them every religious communion feels such interest in one of the same name existing in the midst of the other, that a war would seem to entire Christian fellowships, which count their communicants by the hundred thousand, the most awful and Cain-like of crimes. In no denominations is this feeling stronger than in the youngest—the two communions of Methodism; that in England being the youngest here, yet second in number only to the Established Church; that in America being the youngest there, the daughter, in fact, of British Methodism, but far more prolific than her mother, and with a larger family of spiritual children than any other Church in the United States. A deputation every four years from each to the other of these great communions must assist in perpetuating and vivifying the feeling of kinship between the two countries."

Bishop Simpson found that there was no more rest for

22

him away from home than at home. He writes from Ireland to his wife: "I have but little hopes of hearing from home for another week at least. I leave for the Lakes of Killarney this evening; Thursday evening I speak at Limerick, and next Sunday I have two appointments in Dublin; Monday evening I speak in Belfast, and then visit the Giant's Causeway, Coleraine, Londonderry, etc. The latter part of the week I cross over to Scotland. When shall I have rest? But I will not ask it. If prepared for the union of the blessed on high, there will be time enough to rest in heaven. And if not prepared there will never be rest—no, never. In my visions of the day, as I wander over hill and dale, as I gaze on silver streams, clear lakes, wild mountains, beautiful edifices, or old ruins, how often I feel that my delight would be almost perfect could I have you to enjoy those scenes with me. And when I sit, as I now do, by a window overlooking the city, and hear the noise of wheels in the street and the busy tread of feet in adjoining rooms, I almost involuntarily look around to catch a smile from you."

Strange to say he barely mentions in his letters to his wife his extraordinary oratorical triumphs. The only notice of them from himself that I have found is a brief passage in a letter from Paris: "You will see by the *Watchman* I sent you how matters went off in England. I suppose I ought not to desire more favor than I received in expressions of kindness and satisfaction. But all these things are empty, and so full am I of conscious imperfections that I only wonder why my efforts are so well received. At my last sermon, though it rained hard, every foot of standing-room in every part of the house was packed, and hundreds were unable to gain admittance."

When the autumn of 1857 drew near, and it was time to think of returning home, the life-long wish of Bishop Simpson to visit the East began to shape itself into a purpose. He writes thus to his wife, towards the close of July:

"I shall finish my official work about the 20th or 25th of September, and I could be home in October. But if life, health, and circumstances should permit, I would be pleased to visit the East. Yet it seems so long to be away from you. This morning I awoke from a dream that I was at home, and you were sitting near me, and you looked up and smiled, and I awoke, and it was all a dream. Time seems long. If ever I get home again it seems to me I would wish never to leave it, but with you to pass in domestic quiet, if I could, the rest of my days."

First, however, he must attend the World's Conference of the Evangelical Alliance, which was to open in September, at Berlin. This meeting of the Alliance was memorable for many reasons: first, for the interest taken in its proceedings by the King of Prussia, who, besides being present at its sessions, entertained the Alliance at his palace in Potsdam; memorable also for the service rendered to the Americans in attendance by Governor Joseph A. Wright, at that time our Minister to Germany. Governor Wright was not a mere looker-on, but rather an energetic promoter of the purposes of the Alliance and a frequent speaker at its meetings. The Conference was memorable, too, for its vindication of Methodism before assembled Christian Germany, by Doctor William Nast; and last, but not least, for the eloquent plea for Christian unity made by Bishop Simpson, in the Garnison Kirche of Berlin. We shall make up our narrative from the letters of Doctors McClintock and W. F. Warren, who were present, and who say more of the bishop than his modesty would ever have permitted him to say of himself.

The Conference was opened by an address of welcome from the court preacher, Krummacher; the replies to this in behalf of the Americans were made by Governor Wright and Bishop Simpson. "Krummacher's address of welcome," writes Doctor McClintock, "was exceedingly well-conceived; he embraced every nationality and almost every

Church, hitting off the characteristic features of each in a few compact and pregnant sentences. Speaking of Methodism, he said: 'It is the angel flying through the midst of heaven, summoning the dead churches to a new Christian life.' Much of his address was taken up with refutations of the objections that have been made here to the meeting of the Alliance in Berlin. 'They say that this gathering of Christians will be a flood of waters desolating Germany. Nay, rather, it will be the Nile flood, which covers the banks, indeed, and only recedes to leave behind it the seeds of richness and fertility.' Altogether, in matter, manner, and spirit, this speech of Krummacher's was a most masterly and appropriate one.

"Governor Wright, American Embassador to Berlin, spoke first in reply; and no speech, in the whole course of the meeting, has been more apt and telling than this brief address, which was delivered with great force and earnestness of voice and manner. The vast audience was fairly taken by surprise. It was a great gratification, too, to Christians of all lands, to see a man occupying so high a public position identifying himself with this movement of Christian brotherhood.

"Bishop Simpson followed Governor Wright. His remarks were, in substance: He, too, as an American, was glad to respond to the cordial welcome that had been given to Christians of all lands and of all churches, and to offer to the assembly the greetings of Americans and of American Methodists. While he was listening this morning to the manly voice of Dr. Krummacher, it seemed easy to fancy that Luther had again appeared to rally the Christians of his native land. So far as he understood the views and feelings of the great body of American Christians, they sympathized with the objects of the Conference as a union, not of creeds, nor of organizations, but of heart and Christian activity. Types of this union lay all around us in nature. The little streams, rising among the hills—some flow-

ing faster, some slower—might, indeed, singly, quench the
thirst of the passing traveller, but only by union could they
bear the treasures of commerce, and so bring the ends of the
earth together. As in Germany, so also in the United States,
the independence of the several sovereignties secured freedom of thought and action, while the confederation gave
strength and power to the whole; and it was so with the
Church: singly, the churches did great good, but when
united in heart and activity, they offered a sublime spectacle to the world. He believed that it was the desire of
American Christians that all Christians, in all the earth,
should be one in Christ Jesus."

The Episcopal Methodist Church of America, was, in 1857,
a novel name to German ears; and the announcement to
the Alliance of one of its bishops as a speaker, Dr. Warren
tells us, created a genuine feeling of surprise.

"After Governor Wright's address," says Dr. Warren,
"was heard the announcement of 'the Rev. Dr. Simpson,
Bishop of the Episcopal Methodist Church of America.'

"'Who is that?' said a German gentleman near me.

"'Bishop Simpson, of the Bischöflichen Methodisten
Kirche of America.'

"'Bischöflichen Methodisten Kirche?' repeated he, dubi-
ously; 'Episcopal Methodist! why, that is a contradiction
in terms! What do you mean?' and he turned for enlight-
enment to another. How he succeeded, I do not know."

At Potsdam, whither the members of the Alliance went
upon the invitation of the king, they found royal hospitality. We draw again from Doctor Warren's lively report:
"At three o'clock we betook ourselves to the Potsdam depot,
white-cravatted and white-kidded, according to the irre-
fragable postulates of court etiquette, whence two extra
trains conveyed us gratis to the 'Prussian Versailles.' As
I was whirled along the familiar way, I could but smile to
think how little I expected, when I came to Europe a year and
a half ago, to ever ride around the country at the King of

Prussia's expense, and how little I thought, the last time I had seen the new palace, of ever being entertained therein by the same august personage.

" We found our American representation amounted to no less than thirty - two, among whom were Governor Wright, Bishop Simpson, Doctors Baird, McClintock, Patton, Dwight, missionary at Constantinople, King, of Athens, and others almost equally worthy of mention. Governor Wright was unanimously chosen to present us. At length, after an enormous amount of consultation and anxious amendments of different parts of the arrangements, during which the chief of the English tribe approached ours, and respectfully begged to suggest whether, instead of boisterous hurrahing, it would not be better to adopt the resolution which the Englishmen had taken of shouting 'God save the king!' it was heralded, 'Behold, the king cometh!' Surrounded by his ministers, he descended the steps of the palace, amid the 'hurrahs' of all the 'nationalities,' and was met by Pastor Kuntze, who presented to him the committee in a very pretty speech, reminding his majesty that, though he had reviewed many an imposing army, the one now before him was unlike any of them; their weapons were the sword of the Spirit, etc., etc.

" His majesty, with uncovered head, listened, and then replied that he was too much affected by the peculiar and moving circumstances of the occasion to be able to find words to express himself (rather an old formula of his, by the way), but he was rejoiced to see his visitors, to bid them most heartily welcome. Advancing then towards the Americans, and seeing Governor Wright, he hastened forward, shook his hand most cordially, and expressed his lively pleasure at finding him there. After a little conversation the governor proceeded to present his countrymen. The king expressed great satisfaction in seeing his old friend Doctor Baird, held Dr. Dwight's hand a long time, inquiring about his missionary success, did not forget to greet the na-

tive Armenian preacher who was in his company, begged
to know of Bishop Simpson the name of his see (!), in a
word, 'did the polite and handsome' by us all ; so much so
that he excited the jealousy of more than one ' nationality,'
among the rest his own.

" Gliding around in the crowd at the station, while waiting
for the train back to Berlin, I tried to gather up the various
impressions which might be prevailing. All seemed to think
the king's conduct worthy of the highest praise ; they laud-
ed his hospitality, condescension, etc. ' But,' said one old
German, setting down his great beer-pot with emphasis,
' how came his majesty to show such particular regard to
those Americans? I really became quite jealous of them.
He showed to them more attention than to his own people.'
' The king ye always have with you,' replied a gentleman
near by, who had heard the remark ; and, looking up, I saw
my humorous friend, Mr. E., from my own state. ' That is
true,' returned the German, in a tone which made it sound
very much like ' too true.' "

While in Berlin Bishop Simpson preached in the Garnison
Kirche, which was under the direct control of the king.
We gather from the reports that there was some—not loudly expressed—opposition to the occupancy of this pulpit by
a representative of " a sect," as the phrase runs among those
who ought to know better. If there was opposition, it was
gently put aside.

" It was the first time," writes Doctor McClintock, " that
an established church in Prussia had been opened for the
preaching of the gospel by an Evangelical minister of the
English or American churches, and now it was opened for
a Methodist bishop. I was surprised to find a good audience in attendance, notwithstanding that other services in
English were going on at the same time. The reputation
of the bishop, doubtless, drew many Church-of-England
people from their own chapel, and the rest of the audience
was made up of Presbyterians, Congregationalists, and

Methodists. The service was opened by the reading of a hymn and prayer by Doctor Patton, of New York. The Scripture lessons were read by Doctor Dwight, of Constantinople. The bishop's text was John xvii. 22, and the sermon was admirably adapted to the occasion and the audience. He showed, first, that Christian unity was possible, from the prayer of Christ; secondly, that it was desirable; and thirdly, that it was essential to the world's conversion. These were the subdivisions of the first head; the second was occupied in showing that true Christian union consists not in unity of belief, for this is not possible as long as minds and nations differ so widely; not in uniformity of worship, which is equally impracticable, even if desirable; but in union of fellowship with Christ, and of Christian activities and labors for the advancement of Christ's kingdom. The sermon was masterly, both in the structure and the filling up, and the lucid neatness of its statement and exposition was only surpassed by the pathos and tenderness of its exhortation to Christian unity and fidelity. Many an eye was dimmed with tears, and many a heart formed new resolutions for the service of God under that sermon.

" An Englishman, who had listened to the bishop, said to me, ' Ah, sir, that was preaching; what a backbone of hard, stout thinking was behind all that tenderness and unction !' I don't see that a sermon could well get higher praise than this."

XVI.

JOURNEY TO THE EAST.—ILLNESS AND RECOVERY OF HEALTH.

1857–1860.

On the Way to the Holy Land.—His Travelling Companions.—At Constantinople.—Taken Sick on the Voyage to Smyrna.—" Twenty Years Ago. "—Slow Recovery.—The Traveller's Enthusiasm.—Last Look at Palestine, and Homeward.—Alexandria, Cairo, and the Pyramids.— Prostrated again at Naples. — Reaches Marseilles, Paris, and London.—At Home, and at Work again.—Removal from Pittsburgh to Evanston, Illinois.—Reaches his Fiftieth Year.—Growing Old.—The Troubles in the Church.—The Nation and the Church in Sympathy with Each Other.—The Aggressions of the Slave Power in the State.— Aroused Anti-slavery Feeling in the Church.—The New Chapter on Slavery.—Unrest of the Border Conferences.—*The Methodist* Established.—The Last Struggle between Freedom and Slavery Coming on.

XVI.

It had long been a question with Bishop Simpson whether he would ever be able to visit the lands of Bible story. He had hoped and waited, and now that he was in the heart of Europe, should he turn eastward or westward? The journey to the Holy Land was a more formidable undertaking thirty years ago than it is now. Steam conveyance was to be had, but the conveniences of travel were fewer and the fatigues greater. Palestine was not then as well known to us, in its every-day life, as it is to us of the present time, and active imaginations could make lively pictures of the perils from wandering Bedouins and conscienceless Turks. It cost the bishop, however, an effort to decide upon an eastward course, for he was homesick. He thus writes to his wife from Dresden, September 25, 1857:

" You will see by the address of this letter, that I am on my way South and East. And yet the weather is becoming very cool; where I now am it is almost like November. This I presume is but temporary. Since I wrote you from Berlin, I have been visiting the spots made interesting by the labors of Luther and Melanchthon. I have seen the house in which Luther was born, and the house in which he died. I have seen the table at which he wrote, the gown which he wore, and the beads which he counted while yet a monk, the room in which he first studied the Bible, the castle in which he was lodged for safety, and the wall at which he threw the inkstand to hit his Satanic majesty. I have also been at Hernhutt to see the Moravian colony which Mr. Wesley visited, and from which he drew some practical plans. I have returned from it this afternoon. Battle-fields, too, I have seen, and palaces, and paintings, and ornaments, almost without number. But how much more would I give to see your bright eyes and cheerful face; to tell you all about my journeyings, and to have one hour's real romp with the children. If it pleases God to grant me a safe return, and to spare to us all the children, I hope to have a delightful home again. How sweet is that word 'home;' what recollections, what associations cluster around it! In the graveyard of the Moravians, which I visited to-day, instead of the inscription 'Dead,' were the words 'Gone home' such a day. It was quite touching. 'A home in heaven.' How sweet to think, to know, there is a world of bliss with a home in it, a quiet resting-place for the soul when life's journey is over."

His travelling companions to the East were the Rev. Dr. W. F. Warren, now President of Boston University, a son of Governor Wright, our Minister to Berlin at that time, and a Lutheran minister from Pennsylvania. His letters written on the way are full of the tenderness which marks all his home correspondence. We select a few of them:

"Dresden, Sept. 25.

"One more letter, Providence permitting, you may expect from me next week, written at Vienna just before parting from the regions of railroads and of regular communication. After that you must not look for anything for two weeks at least, and probably for three weeks, as I shall be getting farther away, and the communications will be much more difficult. But be of good heart; two or three months more will take me to the farthest point, and then I shall turn homewards. How do you like my letters in the *Advocate* of late? It is at least a consolation, if I cannot get time to write, they cannot criticise. I see so much that I really do not know where to begin writing. I have despaired of making any readable letters. But possibly I may try my pen again."

"Constantinople, Oct. 16, 1857.

"After a tedious voyage on the Danube, we reached the Black Sea on Saturday last. But, as a severe storm was prevailing, our ship did not venture out. We lay at Sulina until Monday, and arrived in this city on Tuesday evening. I have been busily engaged since, almost night and day. Our missionaries, Long and Prettyman, with their families, are here, and in consultation with them as to our mission, in reading what I can to aid in determining their course, and in consultation with the American Board, my evenings have all been spent, and two days have been fully occupied in sight-seeing. Yesterday I was at the Seraglio (the old one) and the Church of St. Sophia, now a mosque. The Greek and Armenian women look like our own. The Turkish are veiled in a kind of way, but, with two or three exceptions, all I have seen are pale, feeble, and cadaverous."

"Steamer *Germania*, between Constantinople and Smyrna, Oct. 21, 1857.

" How I wish you could just peep into the cabin of the ship, and see me as I sit writing at the table. I think you would know me, a tight match, too, for I have a low, soft, white hat, which I wear tied by a ribbon to my button-hole to keep it from being blown away, and then my long beard; yes, my beard. It is as white as a patriarch's of seventy years upon my chin, brown upon my cheeks and whiskers, and strongly threatening to be sandy on my upper lip; that is about as many colors as the rainbow. What would you say to that? Now don't curl that lip of yours, nor even draw down your eyebrows, nor let your eyes flash too brightly with virtuous indignation, because, if ever permitted to see home, I expect to find a barber before I reach civilized land again. I have a notion, however, to get my daguerreotype taken just before, to preserve for you as an Oriental antiquity."

" October 21, 1857.

" The American missionaries here treated me very courteously, and I had several pleasant interviews during my stay in Constantinople. Brothers Long and Prettyman left to seek a home in Bulgaria just before our vessel sailed. Sabbath I preached to a fair congregation, and on Monday aided in an Alliance meeting. I suppose these will be my last public services until I reach England again, if a kind Providence permits me to return thither. You think I am now far away, and so I feel that I am, yet three weeks more will pass, possibly four, before I reach the Holy Land, the great object of my journey. When I reach that I shall then get no farther away, and in a short time will begin to turn my face a little homewards. But I must be cautious how I begin to say ' home,' lest I become too impatient to return."

" Beyrout, Nov. 3, 1857.

" Twenty years ago this evening—yes, this very evening. Do you remember the little group which met in that parlor in Penn Street, and do you remember the neat young woman, with the blush of health upon her cheek, who stood trembling beside a tall, awkward-looking young man, and there and then, before God's minister, those solemn vows—irrevocable—were said? Yes, how long then to look forward, how short now to look back; an eternity past, an eternity to come, how different. And where is the little group now? Father, mother, and a youthful sister have, I trust, found a fulness of joy in the presence of God.

" Then there are Mr. and Mrs. ——, and, if I mistake not, Mrs. ——, gone too—gone well, too, doubtless. Such is life. And now here in Beyrout sits the same lank man, not now young, and sends across the Mediterranean and the Atlantic the greetings of unchanged, undying affection to the same woman, not now quite so roseate, but more thoughtful, and even more worthy to be beloved, who dwells still in the same city and in the same street. How strange to whisper affection from Asia to America, though Europe is right in the way. Need I say I would like to see you? Vain would be the wish, and yet I have had many strong reasons why I would have been glad to see you in the last few days. And yet I did not wish you here. On parts of my trip I have said, and said, and said again and again, ' Oh, if I had Ellen here how she would enjoy it.' But I have not felt so for several weeks, as there are few conveniences and comforts to be obtained.

"I have been sick, very sick, not, I suppose, in any immediate danger, but I have suffered extremely. I had some pain at Constantinople, but I thought it would pass away, some unpleasant symptoms at Smyrna, which warned me to be careful, but on the way from Smyrna to this place, by steamer, I was again seized with pain. The day before I arrived here, and especially the last night, was one of excruciating agony. It seemed as if my strength was almost gone. On reaching the port, Mr. Wright hurried on shore for a physician, by whose aid I came to the hotel, where, by anodynes, twenty leeches, mustard plasters, blisters, and poultices, etc., the disease was subdued. I think that never in my life have I felt more grateful for returning health. To-day I have sat up several hours, for the first time, and my first moments of holding a pen for nearly a week are consecrated to you. I cannot tell you what has been my trouble. I feared fever, but I had very little. It is enough for me to know that, through the mercy of God, I have now good prospects of recovery in a few days. Praised be his holy name! How differently matters turn out from our calculations! Under any common circumstances I should almost have leaped for joy to see the bold front of Mt. Lebanon, the very Lebanon where Solomon got the timber for the temple. Yet here rises that old ridge, and I have never yet seen it, except one glance I gave it as I was rowing ashore, and then my eyes fell, heavy with pain. To-morrow I hope to get out of doors. The young men started this morning for Damascus, and that part of the trip I shall be compelled to lose, as I cannot detain them longer. They expect to return in about eight days, and then it is supposed that I can join them.

"They were very kind and attentive as to sitting up, etc., but, unfortunately, none of them knew anything practically of nursing a sick person. Still I have had every attention I needed. My landlady, a nice, sprightly Greek woman, came into my room the third day, and put it in order, and right glad I was to see her. She has since been quite attentive. But the misfortune is she talks only Greek and Italian, neither of which I can use. By a few stray words of French, however, we can make out to understand each other a little. The landlord, a Greek, talks a little English."

"Nov. 4, Wednesday.

" Last night I had the best rest I have had for a week. This morning I have had a cup of tea and some arrow-root, but not such arrow-root as you make. And now I am up again. It is raining, however, and I cannot go out. I will add a few lines each day until the mail goes, which, I learn, is on Saturday.

" *Nov.* 5.—Last evening I was not quite so well, but to-day I have sat up since nine o'clock, and this afternoon walked out about half an hour. Mrs. Ford, the wife of a missionary here, sent me some jelly to-day, very good. I think I shall go to see her to-morrow. May I ?"

" *Nov.* 6.—Still on the ' dauncey ' list; you know when I get a little down I am long getting up; still there is nothing dangerous. I sit up, and yesterday I read a good deal. I shall have, I fear, to quit reading and writing, and let my mind be entirely free. I don't think Mrs. F.'s jelly did me any good. Are you glad ?"

" *Nov.* 7.—Mail goes to-day, they say. Better this morning. I rode out a short distance yesterday, and bore it very well. I cannot tell when I can write you again. If I am detained here, will write you next week. But if I leave this, as I hope to, I shall have no chance for at least two or three weeks. Write me at Rome, care of the American Minister, and now, one kiss and then farewell."

Dr. Warren, who, as already stated, was one of the bishop's party, has sent me some reminiscences, especially of the bishop's enthusiasm and of the severity of his illness :

" In our passage down the Ægean the bishop was at his best. The sight of the Trojan shore, of Scio's rocky isle, and, more than all, of Patmos, stirred his soul. He could hardly leave the deck for food or sleep. Great was his gusto as he told me of the blunder of a Scotch professor who had ventured a Latin question to a Greek priest on board, and mistook his ' I do not know '—*Nescio*—for the name of an island.

" On the passage from Crete to Beyrout he became seriously sick, so that when we landed we had to carry him for the most part, though, to avoid creating a panic, he was dressed and was supported in an upright position, with his arms extended over the shoulders of a courier on each side. Fortunately we found good friends in the American Board mission, and a skilful physician in the Rev. Dr. Van Dyke. For some days the symptoms were very alarming, but at last he began to mend. Then he insisted that the rest of our party should improve the time by making the tour of the Lebanon and Damascus, returning thereafter for him. This was done, but when we returned he was by no means fit for travel on horseback, though he insisted that he would improve by this means. Of the kindness which the bishop experienced in the mission-house he could never say enough.

"We went down the coast to Sidon, where we spent a Sunday in rest. Here he was too weak and ill to ride farther, and we (he and I) engaged boatmen to row us to Haifa. Thence we went to Nazareth, the Sea of Galilee, ascended Mount Tabor; thence proceeded down to Jerusalem, Dead Sea, Hebron, Bethlehem, Jaffa, etc., etc. Thence to Alexandria, Cairo, the Pyramids, etc. From Alexandria to Corfu; thence through the Isthmus of Corinth to Salamis and Athens; thence to Marathon and a few other points; thence to Naples; thence to Civita Vecchia, where we parted, he to return home as fast as steam could take him, I to visit Rome and what remained of Italy.

"During all this time the bishop was wholly unfit for travel, especially in so rude a country and with food so wretchedly unpalatable. Not one day was he well. The physicians consulted at different points did not agree in their diagnoses of the difficulty, but I think there is little doubt that a malarial fever was originally at the bottom of the trouble. I presume it was contracted on the Lower Danube. Twice he despaired of living till the morning, and began to give me his farewell messages to his family and friends. Once was in Athens, the other time in the Holy Land. Nothing but a marvellous constitution and a mighty faith in God ever carried him through such a strain.

" Often he considered the question of our immediate return home, but whenever well enough to think of undertaking it, he would hope to continue to improve and so to complete the dream of his life, a thorough tour to the sites of Biblical history. Much of the time, too, every stage of his journey was a stage homeward.

"Through all these trying experiences his serenity of spirit, his faith, his consideration for others, never forsook him. He believed that his Heavenly Father had led him thither, and that everything his gracious providence permitted to come upon him was ordered in infinite wisdom and love. Despite his bodily condition he was very keen and observant. His conversation was often a great delight to me. His broad mind found room for all good things wherever encountered, or with whatsoever religion or nationality associated. At Prague we attended an open-air service with processions and banners, culminating in exhortation and prayer before the statue of St. Nepomuck in a public square. When it was over, the bishop expressed himself as renewedly impressed with the conviction that our Church, as a Church of the people, must hold fast to its camps and groves and Sunday-school celebrations—to its free and unconventional life of song and worship—while adding, in their places, all fruits of age and culture.

" In Buda-Pesth, in a delightful social evening with the former pastor and other patriotic friends of Kossuth—enjoyed only with closed and guarded doors—we saw, as perhaps nowhere else, the intensity of the flame with which the love of liberty was ever burning in the bishop's soul. In Constantinople, and everywhere under the Crescent, he acquainted himself with the work of the missionaries, and was always recognized as a welcome and cheering visitor. In Athens, in the school of Dr. and Mrs. Hill, it was touching to see the little girls reverentially kiss his hand as he parted from them."

Of the fatigue of the land travel from Beyrout to Sidon,
23

Dr. Warren gives this account in a letter written at the time. It was a sharp experience for a sick man, just up from his bed, to go through:

"After a day or two spent in rest and preparation for the trip before us, we set out for Sidon—at least the bishop and myself—leaving the rest of the party to complete the preparations and follow at a better speed than a recent invalid could well bear. Our road lay along the coast, almost due south from Beyrout, across great tracts of sand and gravelly shingle, where the heat was intense. Twice we came to shade and gladly dismounted, to stretch ourselves under the leafy covert. It was quite late when we had started, and now noon was far past, but back along the glowing beach, as far as we could see, quite to the outskirts of the city we had left, no sign of our companions was visible. Hunger came upon us, but we had nothing to eat; heat tormented us, but we had nothing to drink. We dared not wait for them to come up, lest something had happened to prevent their coming, and then night would overtake us far from any shelter. If we pushed on with all our might to reach Sidon, there was no hotel to go to, nor did we know a single man who could talk an European language. The dilemma was very unpleasant, but, after holding a convention upon the subject, and concluding that it would be impossible to reach Sidon that evening, under any circumstances, we resolved to make for the little mosque of Nebi Yunas, and see if we could not, by hook or crook, obtain admittance for the night. This mosque stands upon the spot where, according to Mohammedan tradition, the prophet Jonah was cast up by the great fish. We reached it just after dusk, but were happily relieved from the necessity of making our petition by signs, as our dragoman and the rest of the party came galloping up just before we arrived. We were soon comfortably quartered in a large upper room, and there, over the long white shore, with the gentle beat of the rippling surges falling in measured cadences upon our ears, we read the story of the recreant prophet, who thought to flee from the face of the Lord."

At last he is on the sea again, with his face towards home; he writes, on his way to Alexandria:

"I have at length taken my last look at the Holy Land. I have said in my heart 'Farewell,' for I shall never again see its mountains, its valleys, and its plains. On Wednesday morning we left Jerusalem, and that evening reached Ramleh. Yesterday morning we started for Joppa, and about noon took our passage on the French steamer to Alexandria. It did not, however, start until eight o'clock last night. There, at Joppa, was my last view of Palestine, where Peter dwelt, with one Simon, a tanner, by the seaside. They pretended to show the precise house, but in this I have no faith. Last night we had a pleasant run. This morning breakfast, which is at half-past nine o'clock, is over, and I have time to write a few lines, though the steamer, a propeller, shakes and rolls considerably. We have pleasant weather, about as warm as the month of June with us. It would have charmed you yesterday, on entering Joppa, to see the large orchards hanging full of bright golden oranges, some of which were the largest I have ever known. On the table for breakfast the average size was about three to three and one half inches in diameter, but the landlord assured me that sometimes they were double that size. Everything, too, is green. Fresh lettuce, etc., is regularly served in the steamer, as in early summer. From all such things, however, I almost entirely debar myself.

"My health is, I think, now decidedly improving, and you need have no further fears of the Arabs. I have left the whole Bedouin region. I shall be among a class of Arabs in Egypt, but they are poor and inoffensive. I shall now be wholly at your command to return just as soon as it shall be deemed best, though I could have enough to occupy me very busily two or three months more. Especially write me when and where my Conferences begin. You see by this that I have wholly abandoned the purpose of going through the desert of Mount Sinai. Much as I should like the trip, my health will not permit it, nor do I think I would be justified now in incurring the expense."

His next is from Egypt:

"Alexandria, Egypt, Dec. 19, 1857.

"I arrived in Egypt a week ago this evening. Spent that day and the Sabbath in this city, and on Monday went to Cairo. I visited the pyramids, ascended to the top of the highest, though for me it was a hard task, which I could not have accomplished without the aid of the Arabs, who are perfectly familiar with the best way of ascent, and who help strangers in hope of 'baksheesh.' I also visited the catacombs, and wandered over the ruins of old Memphis, went to the lonely obelisk that marks the site of Heliopolis, once a city of renown. The petrified forest, as it is called, I have also seen in part. This, with a view of some of the mosques of Cairo, and palaces, etc., occupied my whole time. My present plan is to sail in the next steamer, Monday or Tuesday, for Corfu, and thence to Athens. Then my Asiatic and African journey will have been finished, and I shall feel that I am much nearer to you and to home."

At Naples he was prostrated again; he writes from this city:

"January 19, 1858.

"I have been quite ill again, and have been under the doctor's hands since the day after my arrival here, now about a week. I find also that my Conferences begin in Arkansas in March. This will not allow me time to lie by with sickness, and then to complete my route. Consequently I put it all aside, and, though here in Italy and obliged to pass within eight hours of Rome, I must give it all up. My health and strength are so nearly gone that I must try to get home if I can."

From Naples he journeys by sea to Marseilles, and from Marseilles by rail to Paris, where he begins to enjoy the sense of getting near home, though the Atlantic still intervened:

"Paris, January 24, 1858.

"I arrived in this metropolis of France last night, which I left a few days more than five months ago. I found at Naples that my health would not bear completing my contemplated tour in Italy in time for my return to my Conferences. And as I know you must be lonely, and I feared also sad, I concluded that my duty was to omit Rome and all else, and to turn my face homeward. I stop in this city a few days to gather some books and maps and plates, which I may need if I should write anything, and then I shall go to London and spend a few days there for the same purpose, and especially to purchase some Methodist materials which I need. My health, though not as vigorous as when I left home, is now better than for some time past, and I hope in a few weeks more, God willing, to be on American soil, and, above all, in the bosom of my family. How I would enjoy a month of undisturbed domestic quiet! but it will be long before I can hope for this. Indeed, perhaps it is wrong to wish for rest in this world. There is rest in the grave—there is joy in heaven, yet I do hope for some more calmness and settled habits than I have had for a long time."

In London he was sick again, but his indomitable will still carried him forward. Short trips were taken to places in England of interest to American Methodists. He is forming plans of labor at home; more than he can execute:

"London, Feb. 5, 1858.

"I send you a paper which has a slight note of myself. That day I had a chill, which had been troubling me some time before, and I was obliged to take to my bed. The doctor has kept me in bed or in my room ever since, as he said both my liver and right lung were in great danger unless I rested wholly and took medicine.

I am now much better than I have been for two months. I greatly needed a little rest. This has detained me here, as I have not been able to look after any books or any business as yet. But yesterday I rode in a carriage to the Crystal Palace, and was able to spend there an hour or two. I think I shall soon be able to commence looking after such books, etc., as I want. But I cannot yet fix the time of my sailing, for I am well assured that it is better for you and the family and the Church, as well as for myself, that I should not attempt any labor or undergo any more exposure until I have fully conquered my disease and gained more strength. In the meantime be perfectly easy. I have a very comfortable home, kind friends, and Charles is with me in good health."

All through the year 1858 Bishop Simpson was sick, much of the time at his home in Pittsburgh. Though able to attend sometimes to official duty, he was wholly unfitted for preaching. Now and then the report was spread that he could not possibly get well; his friends waited for his recovery with alternations of hope and fear, and sent him frequent expressions of their affection for him. The strain of his prolonged exertions, while abroad, to keep himself up to his work as a traveller, told upon him, and was followed by a long reaction of weakness and pain. His thoughts dwelt much upon the possibility of a speedy death, and his anxieties for the future welfare of his family expressed themselves in his letters.

By the spring of 1859 he was able to hold his Conferences, but with that which the people most wished from him—his preaching—omitted. By July, he reports himself as preaching again, and that "out of doors, without much injury."

Starting late in 1859 upon his fall tour of Conference visitation, he writes to his wife the day after their parting: "Look upward, and I pray that God may give you the rich consolations of his grace. Life at best is short, its scenes will soon pass away, eternity will be our home—our *only* home, our *permanent* house. All we need be anxious about is to do our duty to ourselves, each other, and to those intrusted to our care. Let us act as if God saw us and heard us constantly, and does he not? Are not his presence and his power always about us? Take courage to leave all your cares and anxieties in the hand of him who careth for you."

He recurs to this topic again in a letter written a little later on. He is at Brockport, New York, holding a Conference, and in the midst of the troubles with the Nazarites,* so called:

"I have great confidence that God will take care of you in my absence, as I believe that I am necessarily absent, engaged in his work. But we are not far apart when we meet at a throne of grace. When I look up at the moon these clear nights, I can fancy that it shines also on my loved ones, on the shores of Lake Michigan, as brightly as it shines on me here, not far from Lake Ontario. And if that moon, so low comparatively, has such a view, how much greater has *he* who sits upon the circle of the heavens. He is really very near us, and then he careth for us—yes, even for us. Thanks be to his holy name for the revelation that he careth for us. I can—yes, I do—commit to him my dearest on earth, my own loved wife, and to his arms, for they are wide and strong, I can commit my children also."

---

* Subsequently the Nazarites seceded from us, and formed the Free Methodist Episcopal Church.

He is now occupied in the old way, that is, to the last atom of his strength. Writing from Brockport again, October 9, 1859, he says: "I have been exceedingly busy. I have sat in Conference from eight to twelve and from two to half-past five; and in cabinet from seven to ten or eleven at night. And all the intervals engaged in interviews and examining papers for decision." In his very brief notices of the Nazarites, he sketches a scene in the Conference-room not often witnessed: "Women have come by troops—one crowd by a canal-boat, others from Utica, and some, it is said, from St. Louis. They are in attendance in the galleries, and some have their knitting busily employed. They are all Nazarites, and use, in their conversation, many epithets denunciatory of the Conference."

In this year he changed his home from Pittsburgh to Evanston, a suburb of Chicago. A town had been laid out by his friend Doctor, afterwards Governor, Evans and his associates, the Northwestern University had been planted, and the bishop was greatly desired as neighbor, counsellor, and leader. Still his presence was almost as much demanded in every part of the country, and he was, as usual, flying from point to point as fast as trains could carry him. In the middle of December, 1859, he wrote to his wife from New York: "Unexpectedly I have agreed to stay here over next Sabbath to preach. I have an engagement at Altoona, but have postponed it. My engagements are to-day (18th of December) in Seventeenth Street Church; Monday evening at Newark; Tuesday evening at St. Paul's; Thursday at Mamaroneck, and Thursday night at a meeting for the Home of Aged Women; on Sunday following at Hanson Place, Brooklyn." At times he wearies of such excessive exertion. In January, 1860, he writes: "And now ten thousand wishes for your health and happiness. I do not regard my own hard work, nor my own exposure, but I feel anxious for my family. Were it so that I could remain at home consistently with duty, how glad I would be. But

God can take care of my loved ones in my absence. I some-times say, 'What if God had removed me altogether when I was sick? What then for my loved ones?' Is it not bet-ter to live a little longer with them, even if at home only occasionally. God grant to have my dear wife and chil-dren in his own embrace, and may his Holy Spirit give light and peace and comfort to every one." At times he writes in a playful vein, but always with the same sweet affectionateness. From Manchester, New Hampshire, where he was holding Conference in April, 1860, he sends this message to his new home: "To-day is bright and beautiful after the rain. How I wish you were here, or that I could look in upon our home on Lake Michigan. How are you? Is your health improving? Are all well? Did you buy that new bonnet Charlie spoke of when he wrote, and does it please you? Are the ribbons 'greenish-blue,' or 'bluish-green'? Is it the new 'coal-scuttle' pattern, or is it of the old 'kiss-me-quick shape'? I think the latter is my preference."

Meanwhile the hard work goes on. One wonders that he ever lived beyond his threescore and ten years. He is hold-ing his fall Conferences of preachers, and writes from Ionia, Michigan: "My health is about as it was. My feet troubled me some at the Ohio Conference, but they are better now. Preaching in the open air to a vast crowd, and speaking at the morning meeting, and reading the appointments in a grove at night gave me some hoarseness, which has bothered me a little. The grove was lighted up by the 'Wide-awakes.' I left in a hack at half-past nine, rode twelve miles, stopped and rested till four in the morning, and rode fourteen miles more to catch the train at nine. Thence to Cincinnati at half-past five P.M.; thence to Toledo at four A.M; Detroit at seven, and here at one P.M. So you have my journal."

He is now in his fiftieth year, and thinks himself growing old. Of this he speaks in a very tender strain. He writes from Ionia again, September 28, 1860: "How blest is it that hearts once joined may be united forever. Other things are changing—scenes change—our bodies grow old, our eyes weak, our limbs infirm, but the heart remains ever young. Its affections are ever fresh. It may not love so passionately, it may not throb so violently, but pure and changeless as a fountain of life are its outgushings of sympathy. And then why should we not love more truly and strongly as we grow older? We have fewer to love. The scenes of our childhood are fled; the sweet flowers and birds are gone. Our playmates and schoolmates have, one by one, passed away, or have parted from us. We have ourselves yet and our children to love. They, too, will leave us. We started down the river of life together, and we shall sail on together until we reach the great ocean, or one of us drops from the other to perish in the waters. If so, how lonely will the voyage be to the other! It seems to me I shall look forward to a speedy arrival at the end of my voyage. But why do I moralize? Were this heart silent, other hearts would beat on; were these eyes closed, other eyes would still smile, and soon the very waves that cover me would sparkle back the starlight of heaven. Be it so. The world need not mourn for me when I pass away. A few hearts will bleed, a few eyes will weep, and then all shall be as though I had never been."

We must now turn to other scenes and other events. Every intelligent American living between the years 1840 and 1860 carried in his heart an apprehension of the possible overthrow of our national union. The unending slavery controversy could not and would not be settled; adjustments failed to adjust, and compromises failed to satisfy. Our own Church had incurred the loss of nearly all its slaveholding territory in 1844. We still retained Delaware, Maryland, parts of Virginia, and had a precarious footing in Kentucky, Missouri, and Arkansas. The ministers and members of the Conferences in slaveholding territory who still adhered to us looked for considerate treatment, in view of their fidelity to the ancient anti-slavery convictions of Methodism. They stood upon the declarations of the Discipline, as it was in 1844, which affirmed slavery to be an evil to be extirpated, and refused office to slaveholders in all states where emancipation was permissible. As we look back upon those years from this distance of time, it is clear that it was impossible for the Church to stand still. The repeal, in 1854, of the Missouri Compromise, which had forbidden slavery to pass north of a certain parallel of latitude, and the consequent opening of the Far West and Northwest to slaveholding settlers, had destroyed the confidence of the country in the stability of any legislative adjustments. And when to this was added the contention that the National Constitution, by its inherent virtue, protected slaveholding in all territories until such time as each one became a state, the indignation of the citizens of the East, West, and Northwest burned with a heat that had never been known before.

As citizens were church members and church members citizens, the Church was as much affected by this rising anger as the State itself. On the one side it was felt that, inasmuch as slavery was assailing the integrity of the nation, a new and stronger testimony should be delivered by the Church against slaveholding; on the other that, as the fidelity of the Conferences in slave states still with us in 1860 had been put, in 1844, to the severest test, they should not be subjected to further trial. It was not a question of slavery or freedom. Rather it was a question of the best measures to be applied to members of the Church who had been faithful to us; faithful, too, in the presence of a pressure which, if it could have had its way, would have forced them into union with the pro-slavery South. It seemed good to the General Conference, in 1860, to record anew its condemnation of slavery and slaveholding. In order to give this act, as far as could be, the sanction of antiquity, it was couched in the terms of the first declaration upon slavery made by

American Methodism in 1780. Like the testimony of 1780, too, the New Chapter (as it was called) was admonitory and advisory only, not statutory. Its passage was followed by great excitement in Delaware, Maryland, and Central and Western Virginia. Shall we secede or stay? was the question which the Methodists of this region at once asked themselves. Bishop Simpson was strongly anti-slavery in opinion, but he deprecated another rupture of the Church. The letters of his correspondents, in my hands, express many varieties of opinion, but the expression is always intense. His faithful friend, Gordon Battelle, writes him from West Virginia in September, 1860: "With our present prospects, even if there should be no immediate or actual revolt of our members, some of the most efficient laborers in our community will leave, I fear, at the end of the year." In Baltimore a convention of Methodists was held to determine what was expedient to be done. And there was a foreboding of trouble when the Baltimore Conference should meet in the spring of 1861. In order to prevent the threatened disruption *The Methodist* was established in New York. Its first editorial, July 14, 1860, was a declaration of its purpose to maintain the unity of the Church.* Dr. McClintock, its corresponding editor, wrote to Bishop Simpson from Paris: "The troubles of the Church at home pierce me through. *The Methodist* has done and will do much to prevent secession. This is now its mission."

I have in my possession none of the letters of Bishop Simpson on his side of this animated correspondence. He heard much, thought much, was in hearty sympathy with the good men and true who were struggling to preserve the

---

* In this editorial *The Methodist* said: "The mere advice of a party in power, whether in Church or State, has never been, and never can be, considered a sufficient cause for revolution. And we are satisfied that secession, for such a cause, cannot be vindicated, either before him 'who is head over all things' or before the general Christian public."

unity of the Church, but beyond this I have no information. His correspondence here again fails, just at the points where the record of his opinions would be most interesting to us. But another and greater conflict was impending, in which he was to be a conspicuous actor. To his part in this, the last struggle between freedom and slavery, we must now direct our attention.

XVII.

THE CIVIL WAR.

1861–1865.

The Contest over the Spread of Slavery Transferred from the Church to the State.—Attitude of Political Parties in 1860.—Effect on the South of Mr. Lincoln's Election.—Bishop Simpson and the President.—Testimony upon the Bishop's Relations to Mr. Lincoln.—Bishop Bowman's Narrative.—Testimony of General Fisk and Doctor Lanahan.—The Bishop becomes the Evangelist of Patriotism.—His great War Speech. —Effects produced by its Delivery.—Scenes in Cincinnati and New York.—Not a Line of this Address Written by him.—Despondency of the Country in 1864.—The General Conference Sends a Deputation to the President to Assure him of the Support of the Churches.—Mr. Lincoln's Reply to the Conference's Message.—Removal of the Bishop to Philadelphia.—Address, in Behalf of Mr. Lincoln, at the Sanitary Fair, Philadelphia.—The Death of Mr. Lincoln, in 1865.—Bishop Simpson's Address at the President's Grave.—Another Closing Scene. —The Last Meeting of the Christian Commission in February, 1866.— The Bishop Speaks the Final Words.

XVII.

THE seventeen years from 1844 to 1861 sufficed to bring the contest, which in the former year shook the Methodist Episcopal General Conference, to a broader field, and to a decision by other weapons than the weapons of logic. In fact, Church and State, on either side of the dividing line, were keeping pace with each other. It required a longer time to tear the nation apart than sufficed for dividing the Church, but the same convictions, the same passions, were at work which had sundered the ties of Christian brotherhood. In the State, as we have seen, the concession in the Compromise of 1850, which permitted the territories acquired from Mexico to be organized with or without slavery at the option of their inhabitants, was boldly applied to all the remaining territories of the nation. In December, 1853, President Pierce declared that the Compromise legislation of 1850 " had given new vigor to our institutions and restored a sense of repose and security to the public mind." * In January, 1854, one month thereafter, a bill was brought into the national Senate, repealing the Missouri Compromise of 1820, and opening the vast region from the northern line of Arkansas to the British possessions to settlement by slaveholders. This repealing bill was passed, and Nebraska and Kansas were organized, with the result of an actual but suppressed civil war. Bands of energetic settlers went out to the plains of Kansas, resolved on the one side to establish freedom, on the other, slavery, if necessary, by force of arms.

---

* Quoted from Mr. Blaine's "Twenty Years in Congress," Vol. I., p. 110.

When, in 1860, the two parties met once more to select candidates for the Presidency, the lines of separation between them were drawn more strongly still. The Democratic convention was hopelessly divided, and two candidates of that party were named for our highest office. Mr. Douglas and his friends stood firmly on the ground of non-intervention by Congress with slavery in the territories; Mr. Breckenridge and his followers just as solidly on the affirmation that it is the duty of Congress to give slavery in the territories national protection. Mr. Lincoln represented the immovable opposition to any further extension of slavery. His pithy phrase, "The Union cannot exist half slave and half free," was caught up and repeated all over the free states. It put in the concisest form the conviction to which the country had come, and strengthened the purpose to resist, to the bitter end, the schemes of the Southern extremists. The effect of his election was instantly felt. By the close of 1860 South Carolina had declared itself out of the Union; and when he was inaugurated in March, 1861, he was met by the spectacle of states seceding and preparing for war.

Bishop Simpson's life had been a long preparation for the service which he was now to render his country. He had been, as a delegate, a hearer of, if not a sharer in, the important debates of 1844; as editor of the *Western Christian Advocate* he had, in 1850, discussed, with vigor, Mr. Clay's scheme of pacification. In carrying on this controversy he had won the confidence of Mr. S. P. Chase, Mr. Lincoln's Secretary of the Treasury; with Mr. Stanton and Mr. Lincoln he soon came to be on terms of intimacy; he compelled the respect of Mr. Seward and Mr. Montgomery Blair.

The president discovered very quickly that, the issues of the war being moral, the support of the churches was of the last importance to him. He knew well that no men understood the people so thoroughly as the Methodist bishops, who, being without dioceses, were continually passing over the length and breadth of the land. With Bishop Simpson his relations became especially close. Most unfortunately again the bishop's letters and private memoranda fail to shed such light as we might wish upon this important period of his life. I have, however, gathered from the reports and reminiscences of friends, sufficient material to supply this defect.

As usual, the old uncle, now greatly advanced in years, was one among the first to discern the character of the conflict. He writes to his nephew, from Iowa, April 23, 1861: " The great, the irrepressible contest between liberty and slavery has at last broken out in war, and a war of no ordinary magnitude it may yet be. But the Lord reigns; let the earth rejoice. Bad as war is, he can cause good to follow; therefore it may be that the agitation of the slavery question, both in Church and State, is about to be put to rest forever by the destruction of the peculiar institution." The bishop's steadfast and courageous friend, Dr. John Lanahan, then stationed in Alexandria, Virginia, kept him advised of the state of affairs in the national capital, and conferred much with him upon the events now following one another with startling speed. There was a likelihood of the secession of the Baltimore Conference from our Church. A convention of laymen was held simultaneously with the assembling of the Conference in Stanton, Virginia, March, 1861. The laymen and ministers there organized in two separate meetings acted and reacted upon each other. Many clamored for instant secession; but the proceedings ended in the passing of a protest against the " New Chapter " on slavery. What was to come of all this aroused feeling no one could tell. The probable effect of the decision of the Conference upon the attitude of Maryland and Virginia towards the Union was, however, present to every mind, and gave additional keenness to the debate. It was, in point of fact, if not consciously, a struggle for position in the greater contest

24

yet to come. Bishop Scott, who held the Conference, wrote to Bishop Simpson, March 14th: "The prospect is stormy. The convention, it is said, will close this afternoon, having recommended a conditional plan of separation—to separate if by fall there is no prospect of relief." And he adds, pathetically: "I have never felt the loneliness of official position so much as I have done here. How painful the suspense in which we are held." Dr. Lanahan, who showed unusual clear-sightedness in his prevision of the future, wrote to Bishop Simpson as early as Feb. 8, 1861: "Maryland will remain in the Union in any event. The fact is, the incoming administration will not let her go." And so it came to pass.

Thus the events which marked the opening of the civil war appealed to Bishop Simpson as they did to very few men of important position in the country. First, it was his duty, as a loyal citizen, to do what in him lay to preserve the Union in its entirety. Next, it was of the utmost moment to maintain the unity of the Methodist Episcopal Church by resisting the secession of the parts of it lying below the free-state line. To save this region to the Church was, in good part, to save it to the Union. It was a region of divided opinion, and Church relations largely determined opinion. Still further, it was incumbent upon him to sustain the faith and courage of the people with all the resources of his eloquence. Mr. Lincoln very quickly recognized the importance of his co-operation. Both were at that time Illinois men, and I am informed that conferences between them took place in Springfield, Mr. Lincoln's home, during the winter of 1860–61. While the war lasted the bishop was very often sent for to come to Washington for consultation with the president and with Mr. Stanton. Mr. Stanton was the son of a Methodist, had been reared in the Methodist faith, and, under his hard, official manner, carried a heart surcharged with feeling. Bishop Simpson's advent to the war-office was usually followed by an invitation to the secretary's private room, where long conferences were held, ending sometimes, at Mr. Stanton's request, in earnest prayer.*

It is not the purpose of this volume to trace the vicissitudes of the war from 1861 to 1865; to depict, if that were possible, the alternations of hope and despair. Nor need we dwell upon the slow growth, in many minds, of the conviction that the struggle, instead of being a holiday parade of ninety days, was to task all the resources of the loyal people. In the main the citizens of strongest moral feelings had the clearest vision of coming events. Especially was this true of those who kept aloof from political jugglery, and had small faith in the efficacy of political combinations for the repairing of the great schism. The religious mind of the country comprehended, better than the political, the true nature of the conflict. And among the far-sighted men Bishop Simpson may be set down as one of the most sagacious.

I can best show his relations to Mr. Lincoln by putting on record here the narratives furnished me by his personal friends. Besides their bearing on the point in hand, they are interesting as memorials of the period of the war.

The Rev. Dr. Thomas Bowman, now senior bishop of the Methodist Episcopal Church, was chaplain of the United States Senate during the latter part of the war. He writes thus of the intercourse of the president and Bishop Simpson, as it fell, at that time, under his observation:

"In 1864–65, as I spent several months in Washington, I often heard members of Congress and other distinguished visitors in the city say that they had heard the president frequently express his great respect for, and his confidence in, Bishop Simpson. It was well known that the president occasionally sent for the bishop, in order to procure infor-

---

* My authority for this last fact is Mrs. Simpson, who had it from the bishop himself.

mation about the affairs of the nation. The president said, in substance, 'Bishop Simpson is a wise and thoughtful man. He travels extensively over the country, and sees things as they are. He has no axe to grind, and, therefore, I can depend upon him for such information as I need.'

"On one occasion, with two or three friends, I was conversing with Mr. Lincoln, near the distant window in the 'Blue Room,' when, unexpectedly, the door opened, and Bishop Simpson entered. Immediately the president raised both arms, and started for the bishop, almost on a run. When he reached him he grasped him with both hands and exclaimed, 'Why, Bishop Simpson, how glad I am to see you!' In a few moments we retired, and left them alone. I afterwards learned that they spent several hours in private, and that this was one of the times when the bishop had been specially asked by the president to come to Washington for such an interview.

"At another time, under very different circumstances, I had an opportunity to witness the kind feeling which the president evidently cherished for the bishop. Simpson delivered his wonderful lecture on 'Our Country' in one of our churches in Washington. Lincoln, without any mark of distinction, was in the great crowd of hearers. I happened to be near him, and could see his every movement. I never saw a hearer who gave more marked evidence of a personal interest in a speaker than the president gave that evening. He joined most heartily in the frequent, and sometimes prolonged, applause. At one time, as the bishop was speaking of the wonderful opportunity that our country affords to young men, he paused for a moment, and said, 'Why, it is commonly reported that a rail-splitter has been elected president of the United States!' This, of course, brought down the house, and I was particularly pleased to see with what almost boyish enthusiasm the president joined in the tremendous applause. At the close of the lecture Mr. Lincoln stepped out into the aisle and strode down towards the pulpit. I followed, for I was anxious to hear what he would say. Taking the bishop warmly by the hand, he exclaimed, in a voice that could be heard all around, 'Bishop Simpson, that was a splendid lecture!' Then, in a low tone of voice, and with an expression of face which indicated a little surprise, a little curiosity, and a good deal of humor, he said, 'But you didn't strike the ile!' I did not see the point, but the bishop did. So he replied, 'Mr. President, I am surprised at myself to see that, while I have thought so much about the great resources of our country, I should have entirely overlooked our great oil interests. I shall not do so again.' The next time I heard the lecture the bishop struck 'the ile.'"

From General Clinton B. Fisk, one of the bishop's most intimate personal friends, I have this narrative:

"In April, 1861, after the call for seventy-five thousand men, the bishop met Lincoln in the president's office. Several members of the cabinet dropped in, Bates, Blair, Cameron, and Seward. The bishop expressed the opinion that seventy-five thousand men were but a beginning of the number needed; that the struggle would be long and severe. Mr. Seward asked what opportunity a clergyman could have to judge of such affairs as these. Judge Bates replied that few men knew so much of the temper of the people as Bishop Simpson; Montgomery Blair sustained the view of Judge Bates. A cabinet meeting followed. After it was over Lincoln and Simpson remained together quite a long time. The bishop gave him, in detail, his opinion of men throughout the country whom he knew.

"After Mr. Stanton came into the cabinet the bishop's relations with the president became more intimate. The bishop was used by Mr. Lincoln to modify the War Secretary's views, and to gain points which he wished to reach. For instance: Stanton was disposed to treat with great severity the border rebels who stayed at home and gave aid and comfort to the enemy. Lincoln was inclined to treat them leniently. The bishop was of the same mind as the president, and was sent to Stanton to bring him over to the president's way of thinking.

"Early in 1862 Mr. Lincoln was meditating the issuing of an emancipation proclamation, though, in answer to public appeals, he declined to take the responsibility of such a measure. Bishop Simpson had said to him, as far back as 1861, that that would need to be done. He believed from the first that emancipation would come out of the war. In discussing Frémont's proclamation, he said he would have done the same thing.*

"In the summer of this same year—1862—after the seven days' fighting and McClellan's repulse, the bishop had another interview with Mr. Lincoln, confined to the point of the president's duty to issue a proclamation setting the slaves free in the rebellious states. Subsequently Mr. Lincoln showed him the proclamation; the bishop was delighted with it. When it was read in the cabinet meeting Mr. Chase suggested its last sentence. 'Why,' replied Lincoln, 'that is just what Bishop Simpson said.' In their interview prior to the meeting of the cabinet the bishop had suggested that there ought to be a recognition of God in that important paper."

The Rev. Dr. John Lanahan, during the war a resident of Alexandria and Washington, was in close correspondence with Bishop Simpson, and sends these reminiscences:

"I received many letters from Bishop Simpson about government matters and the churches, none of which I can now find. I was often with him in his visits to, and interviews with, the leading men of the country in Washington, and often received from him the substance of his conversations about public matters when I was not present. Mr.

---

* General Frémont, in August, 1861, issued an order emancipating the slaves of all persons in arms against the government throughout his district, the Western. This order was annulled by the president, and Frémont was relieved of his command.

Lincoln held him in the highest esteem, and attached much importance to his counsel. He never failed to attend upon his ministry. The same is true of Mr. Stanton; he not only manifested great respect, but even love; he was invariably present to hear the bishop preach. At one time during, and I think near the close of the war, Mr. Lincoln and Stanton wanted him to serve as one of an important commission, which he declined as not the best for him as a bishop of the Church. I only remember the fact, but cannot recall the subject.

"Bishop Simpson's arrival in Washington was always the occasion of interest and courtesies from the chief men of the government and of Congress. I was often surprised to see how quickly his arrival was known. During my residence of some fifteen years in Washington I have known of very few who received more attention and manifestations of respect from leading men. But Mr. Lincoln and Mr. Stanton took him to their bosoms. Mr. Stanton, you know, was not a man to be free and easy with many persons— with very few indeed. In one matter Bishop Simpson was very peculiar. When in Washington he always asked how 'our people' were being treated by the government. They had not been dealt fairly with immediately prior to Mr. Lincoln's day, and he was ready to lend an ear to such as were in trouble and needed help, it mattered not how humble the person. He was a man of unusual sympathy, and, while receiving attentions from the great, never forgot the lowly.

"In the midst of the hurry and rush of the affairs of the War Department, Mr. Stanton always gave the bishop willing and deferential attention. That I saw when with the bishop; many interviews were had when I was not present. I never was present when they conversed specifically about 'public affairs,' but have no doubt, from my conversations with the bishop, that such talk was had.

"I know not that Lincoln consulted the bishop upon the

emancipation of the slaves. Leading Republicans were much dissatisfied with Lincoln's apparent slowness to proclaim emancipation, and among them was Bishop Simpson. Dr. Morgan just now told me that Moncure D. Conway went from his (M.'s) house to see Lincoln and urged emancipation upon him just after the Bull Run defeat. Lincoln said, ' Go and educate the people up to it, and I will issue the proclamation.' I don't think Simpson ever urged upon Lincoln such a proclamation, although he desired it. I judge they must have talked about it. Lincoln seems to have kept his views on that subject to himself, largely, till he reached his ultimate conclusion."

These reminiscences, although given after the lapse of a quarter of a century, confirm each other on the point of the close personal relations existing between the president and the bishop. It has, however, become clear to us of the present time that Mr. Lincoln's mind acted with unusual independence. He delighted, as he himself expressed it, in " an opinion bath," which saturated him with the thoughts on public affairs of all manner of men. With a few he was, as with Bishop Simpson, unreserved, and listened to them with entire respect for their knowledge of affairs. Perhaps, too, in weighing the considerations for determining the time of doing what he saw he must ultimately do, he had in mind the effect of his proclaiming the emancipation of slaves upon the partly loyal border states. He was in the forepart of 1862 advising these states to accept a scheme of gradual abolition, with payment to loyal owners of the value of their slaves. Congress also appropriated $600,000 for colonizing such of the slaves thus set free as wished to migrate to other lands. This measure failed. September 22, 1862, Mr. Lincoln issued his declaration of purpose to set free, on January 1, 1863, all slaves in rebellious states, if by that time the states were still in arms against the national government.

But the war was growing to greater and greater proportions. It is difficult to convey to the minds of the Americans who have come to manhood since 1865 the apprehension, universally felt, that the struggle, if carried on beyond a year or two, would exhaust our resources. The people, though loyally calling upon Congress to increase taxation, felt the weight of their ever-increasing burdens. A debt was accumulating beyond all precedent, for the rapidity of its growth, in the experience of nations. Trade was for a time depressed; values were uncertain; the best blood of the country was flowing freely. Still the cry came from Washington, more men, more money, more help, in this hour of supreme trial, from the people.

In 1862 I attended, by the invitation of a friend, a private meeting of loyal men in the city of New York — editors, lawyers, clergymen, and two generals: Hunter and Mitchell —called to consider the question, "What should be done in case the Confederate army should at that time capture Washington." Much later on in the war Mr. Greeley publicly advised the president to continue the struggle ninety days more, and if the rebellion was not then suppressed, to make peace on the best terms possible. " Ninety days!" said Grant, when he heard of this, " he should have made it ninety years," and went on with his fighting. Unquestionably the despondency of thousands of our best citizens was real, and its paralyzing effects could be sensibly felt. It was in this juncture that men of the stamp of Bishop Simpson were indispensable, to rally hope, to sustain faith, to point out to us that we had ample strength for our day and trial. He was not the only public man who did this service, but he did it more eloquently, more effectually than any other. He became for us the evangelist of patriotism, having the whole land for his field and pleading for the loyal cause with such power that where despair had reigned, he left hope and confidence in God. He travelled from city to city, from town to town, from East to West, and from West to East again, till he had wrought the people up to the tension of his own enthusiasm. It is as impossible to explain the power of these addresses analytically as it would be for a spectator to analyze a whirlwind, for they swept like a whirlwind over the hearts of their hearers. Men clenched their hands, shouted, stamped, stood on their feet, and were left at the end in a tumult of patriotic excitement. His peroration was usually an apostrophe to the old flag, which, with consummate art, he grasped in his hand and held up to view. As a specimen of the effect of its delivery, we take the following from an Ohio Methodist minister:

" It is said that Bishop Simpson's speech on ' The State of the Country,' delivered in Walnut Street Church, Chillicothe, at the reunion of the Ohio and Cincinnati Conferences, was one of the greatest of his life, and certainly the surrounding circumstances did much to give it interest. The war was raging; the whole country was in a white heat of excitement. Two large Conferences and many citizens were before him. Many of them had near relatives in the army, or in prison or hospital. No pen can adequately describe the speech; no person present can ever forget it. If some Daguerre could have taken the likenesses of the audience showing their attitude, faces, hands, and feet, it would have been a very ludicrous picture, for such was the power of the bishop's logic and eloquence that his hearers seemed to be wholly unconscious of themselves. Ladies threw away their fans and handkerchiefs; men threw their hats in the air, stood erect, and mounted the seats, and stretched out their necks and their hands. When the bishop closed, it was as if a great storm at sea had suddenly ceased, but leaving the billows still in commotion—requiring some time for them to settle down to quiet.

" The large and imposing form of Rev. Wm. Simmons, of the Cincinnati Conference, was seen rising; he had a written resolution to offer. On the other side of the house was the tall figure of Granville Moody, with the quicksilver up. Both were trying to be heard. Being pastor of the church at the time, I was endeavoring to give an important notice of an arrangement for dining the Cincinnati preachers. Great preparations had been made by the good people of the city, who are so noted for their hospitality. But such was the wild excitement that it was impossible to be heard, and I had the disappointment of seeing the great congregation slowly move out without knowing that entertainment had been provided for them. I well remember, in the midst of the scene, to have heard Moody, just behind me, say, 'Never mind, Simmons.' Many a grand dinner had no eaters that day."

The Rev. Dr. Lucien Clark, assistant editor of the *Christian Advocate,* was present at the same meeting, and since the first publication of this book has sent to me his own recollections of the effect of the bishop's eloquence. He writes: "Your correspondent states that Drs. William Simmons and Granville Moody both arose at the same time to offer a resolution or read a paper. This could not have been. No one arose after the bishop concluded his address, for no one was sitting. In the midst of the bishop's peroration all the people sprang to their feet, as they had done twice before during the speech, and such was the uproar that no word of his closing paragraphs could be heard. We could see him holding up the tattered flag and addressing it. The effect was electrical. Some cried, some shouted, some laughed, and others stood in blank amazement and were dumb with excitement, but all stood and continued standing. The audience was not again brought to order. Utter confusion prevailed, and the confusion seemed to be entirely appropriate. An attempt to restore order, or announce a hymn, or offer a resolution would have seemed out of place. The first intelligible sound I heard proceeded from the lips of Granville Moody, who, standing on one of the seats, his tall form towering above us all, tried to sing the doxology. But no one joined in the song, and his own voice, choked with emotion, completely broke down.

"I had never heard the bishop before, and a member of the Cincinnati Conference with whom I walked to the church said to me: ' He will draw you to your feet. I have been magnetized by him several times, and compelled to get on my feet.' 'He will never do that with me,' said I. ' I shall keep my seat if the whole congregation gets up.' Being early, I selected a position from which I could easily see the audience. When the bishop reached his first great climax the people rose to their feet, but I sat still as though I were an unmoved observer. Very soon all was calm again, and I congratulated myself that I had kept my word and had won a victory. The second climax was mightier than the first, and when the whole audience arose with noisy demonstration I had no little difficulty in keeping my seat, but I remembered my pledge and secretly resolved to stubbornly sit still if the roof of the building should fly off. It appeared to me that the orator had completely exhausted his resources, and that from this to the end my task of sitting still would be comparatively easy. But when he reached his third and last climax, and held aloft the battle-torn flag, and began to apostrophize it in his own inimitable way, and the people sprang to their feet as if impelled by some magnetic force, I forgot all about my promise, ceased to resist the impulse that moved me, and rose with the rest. It seemed to me that no one with human feelings could withstand that torrent. The effect on the bishop himself was very manifest; the strain on his nervous system made him sick. He did not complain, but, returning with the Cincinnati Conference to Greenfield, he attempted to hold a cabinet meeting that evening. The extent of his exhaustion appeared when he tried to fix his mind on the business of making appointments. After a few minutes he dismissed the presiding elders, saying, 'Two conferences of Methodist preachers and a battle-torn flag have been too much for me to-day.'"

One of the most important occasions of the delivery of

this war speech was Nov. 3, 1864, in the Academy of Music, New York city. The presidential election was but a few days off,* Lincoln and McClellan being the candidates. Of the mass of people assembled the *Tribune* of November 7th says : "Such an audience gathered at the Academy of Music as seldom or never before was crowded within its walls. Long before the time announced for the lecture to commence the spacious building was crowded from pit to dome—the seats were soon filled, the standing-room all taken up, and still the crowd poured in till no more room was left in which to squeeze another person."

With much tact the bishop began by saying that he did not appear there as a partisan. " I would stand," he said, " far above all party ; I have no epithets for any of my fellow-citizens." Looking at the immediate situation and expressing his confidence in God, he continued : " One great thought now occupies every mind, and one feeling moves every heart. All eyes are turned towards the front, and the ears of anxious men listen for the latest tidings. Loving wives wait for husbands, and mothers long to see their sons, now on the battlefield. Many weep and mourn, and all are asking, ' When shall the end of these things be ?' I have no gift of prophecy, but in history we learn of the rise and fall of nations. And the one lesson of history is that God reigns, that he rules for the good of mankind, for their ruin never, except when they combine to plot against the Lord and against His Anointed." As it was his purpose to give his discourse a firm body of logic, he outlined four possible issues of the war. "*First :* It is a possible result of this conflict that we may become a prey to some foreign power and be reduced

---

* The delivery of the address immediately before the presidential election was purposely so arranged. Mr. Mark Hoyt, who had the preparations for the meeting in charge, writes to him : " All your friends agree that you should speak before the election. Speaking at that time, with the full report, promised, in the *Tribune, Times, Herald,* and *Evening Post,* is equivalent to speaking to the nation."

under their control. There is a second possible result of this contest: that the nation may be divided into two or more separate confederacies. There is a third possible issue: that the nation may remain united, but with its present institutions overthrown, and Southern institutions and Southern ideas established. The fourth and last possible issue is that our nation, having passed through this fiery ordeal, may come out of it purer, stronger, and more glorious than ever before. At this point I will simply say that I believe it to be the design of Providence to secure the last result." Taking up the first topic, he proceeded to say: "No great nation has, in all history, risen and fallen in a single century. [Illustrated by examples.] Moreover, there are indications to show that this is destined to be a great nation in the earth. The discovery of America by Columbus, at the time thereof, was opportune. This nation has done more than any other to fulfil a great destiny. One thing it has done towards the accomplishment of its work is the education of the masses. In this land all may rise to the highest offices. The humblest cabin-boy may lead our armies, and the poor hostler may sit in the Senate. Who has not heard of Henry Clay, the Mill-boy of the Slashes, and Jackson, the child of poor Irish parents; and some may have heard that even a rail-splitter may become president. [Applause.] Again, this nation is an asylum for all the nations of the earth. There is no large migration to any other land, but men come here from all parts of the world. I have no feeling of sympathy with any person who will seek to exclude from free national association all who may come. We have broad acres for them to cultivate, schools for their children and churches for themselves, and a Constitution broad enough, thank God! and strong enough for all the world to stand upon. This nation has the sympathy of the masses all over the earth, and if the world is to be raised to its proper place, I would say it with all reverence, God cannot do without America.

"Then comes the second question—Shall the nation be divided? If we divide, where shall we divide? We have no mountain-chains, no great natural landmarks, to separate us into two, and if we divide must it not be into several confederacies? If you allow the South to go, then the Northwest will become a separate confederacy; and when the Northwest undertakes that, the people of the Pacific coast will set up for themselves, and you will lose all that gold-bearing country. I tell you here to-day, I would not give one cent on the dollar for your national liabilities if you allow a single dividing line to be run through your country from the Atlantic to the Pacific. [Applause.] I deprecate war, it is terrible; much of the best blood of the nation has flowed, and more, possibly, will moisten the earth; but if we should divide this land into petty sections, there will come greater strife, which will waste the blood of your children and grandchildren, and there will be sorrow and wailing throughout the generations to come. When I look at this dark picture, much as I dislike war, I yet say, better now fight for twenty years and have peace than stop where we are. [Tremendous applause.] If any peace is had, I want a peace which shall be lasting, so that I can leave my wife and children safe when I die, and that can only be by our remaining a united nation. We have glorious boundaries on the north and the south, on the east and the west, and when I look at those boundaries I say: 'Palsied be the hand which shall try to wrest from us one foot of this great domain.' [Applause.]

"Then the question comes, 'Shall our form of government be changed?' This is what Mr. Davis expects; he can hardly suppose the South will live in separation. They at the South expected that this great city would declare itself independent; but this city has a heart that throbs in sympathy with the nation, and stands out, as it ought, as the national metropolis. The South hopes for a monarchy, but this nation will never tolerate a monarchy.

"If these three results are not likely to happen, then shall we, as a people, emerge from this contest purer and more glorious than before. The nation must be purified, and for that we are going through the war. The war is nothing new; the South has been preparing for it for thirty years. At the same time a series of providences has appeared, which shows the hand of God." (The bishop here gave a review of the timely discovery of fresh resources for the increase of national wealth, and dwelt on the incidents of the war which appeared to him to have a Providential meaning. A high tribute was paid to Grant and his tenacity of purpose. He then turned his attention to slavery.)

"I have one more impression, that if this war lasts much longer slavery will be damaged. [Loud applause.] It is seriously damaged now, and I hope and desire that it may pass away quickly and let us see the last of it. [Loud applause.] Do you ask what has been accomplished? The District of Columbia has been made free [Applause], and this week—on last Tuesday—the sun, as it rose, shone for the first time on the glorious free State of Maryland. [Great applause.] West Virginia, from her mountain home, echoes back the shouts of freedom. But this war ought not to be carried on for the purpose of destroying slavery, or for any other than the single purpose of restoring the authority of our government. But if, while we are striking blows at the rebellion, Slavery will come and put its black head between us and the rebels, then let it perish along with them. [Applause.] Our children can look back to the battles of the Revolution and assure themselves that their fathers were worthy of freedom. Let the children of these poor slaves have the chance to look back not only to Fort Pillow, but to battles fought and won in front of Petersburg and Richmond, and they will feel that they, too, are worthy of freedom. It has been demonstrated in this war that a blue coat can make a hero even of a sable skin. The black men have long ago learned to follow the stars; they have followed the North Star successfully, and now it is shown that they can follow, as well as any others, the stars that are set in our glorious flag. [Loud applause.]

"Your Fifty-fifth Regiment carried this flag [taking up a war-worn, shot-riddled flag, which was greeted with tremendous cheers]; it has been at Newbern, and at South Mountain, and at Antietam. The blood of our brave boys is upon it; the bullets of rebels have gone through and through it; yet it is the same old flag. [Most enthusiastic applause, the audience rising and giving three rousing cheers.] Our fathers followed that flag; we expect that our children and our children's children will follow it; there is nothing on earth like that old flag for beauty. [Long and loud cheering.] Long may those stars shine! Just now there are clouds upon it and mists gathering around it, but the stars are coming out, and others are joining them. And they grow brighter and brighter, and so may they shine till the last star in the heavens shall fall! [Great cheering and waving of handkerchiefs and hurrahing.]"

Such is a meagre outline of an address which usually occupied in its delivery some two hours. It was one of the stirring events of the time, and was worth to the nation thousands of men. Its sublime trust in Divine Providence was a part of Bishop Simpson's religion, and he infused a large measure of his own faith into the hearts of all who heard him. There is not, however, a written line of the address among his papers, and this lack makes us dependent on hurriedly written reports, none of which give more than broken fragments of it. Its intensity reflects the spirit of the loyal citizens, especially at the precise moment of its delivery. It was feared that a verdict against Mr. Lincoln's administration might be given by a disheartened people; for the first time, too, an election for a president was to be held during a civil war; could it be orderly and in exact conformity to the requirements of the law?

25

In that trying hour the men of lofty faith became the true leaders of the nation, and Bishop Simpson was one of them. He fully realized Mr. Webster's ideal of a great-souled citizen in the midst of a national crisis: "Then self-devotion is eloquent; the clear conception outrunning the deductions of logic, the high purpose, the firm resolve, the dauntless spirit, this, this is eloquence; or, rather, it is something more than all eloquence: it is action, noble, sublime, godlike action." Had it been possible for Mr. Webster to take the bishop for his original, the likeness could not be more exact.

But it is time to return to the events of the war period in their order, as far as Bishop Simpson was connected with them. Instead of going to California in 1861, as he had intended, he gave his time to the Methodist Episcopal Missionary Society, whose collections of money were imperilled by the unsettled condition of public affairs. In 1862 the trip to California and Oregon was undertaken, and consumed nearly six months. As usual, he was half homesick while abroad, and counted the days which must elapse before he could return. Only three weeks of the twenty-two gone," he wrote back, while he was yet on shipboard, but nearing his destination. The trip to Oregon was made from San Francisco by sea, but the return to California by land, the bishop using · saddle or private vehicle or stage as he found it most convenient.

He came over the plains eastward by stage, tarrying at Carson City, Nevada, Denver, and other points. So much was he disabled during this long journey that he could preach but once a day. Occasionally his tone in his letters is despondent. Thus he writes to his wife: "Sometimes I have visions of years of usefulness; and then a shade comes over me, and I feel as if my work were about done, and that you ought to select the home where you will be happiest, should I not be with you." At Carson City he notices the utter extinction of religious life in many who had been trained in Christian homes. "I preached," he says, "on

Sabbath to a crowded house, and the tears moistened the eyes of many a strong man. In the evening I received a pressing invitation, signed by a large number of leading citizens, requesting me to remain and preach again on Tuesday evening; but my health and other duties did not permit." Despite his weak condition his old love of enterprise and adventure still possesses him. He writes from Oregon to Mrs. Simpson: "How greatly I miss you! Were you here I should be willing, if our family could be comfortable, to remain some time upon the coast, or, what would please me more, take a trip to China and India. Men are going constantly as merchants, sailors, and soldiers—why not as ministers?"

In January, 1863, the government expressed its confidence in him by asking him to perform an important service. "Secretary Stanton," he writes to his wife, "sent for me, was about telegraphing, wishing me to be chairman of a commission to visit Fortress Monroe, Newbern, Port Royal, and New Orleans, to examine the condition of the colored people and make suggestions. He wanted three public men apart from politics. He offered transport, subsistence, a clerk, and fair compensation. I have, however, declined any such position. Called on Mr. Lincoln this morning; very friendly."

After his return home he drove his work forward again, taxing his strength to the last point of endurance. He writes from Ashtabula, Ohio, July 20, 1863: "The labors of the Sabbath are over, and I have not, as I believe, sustained any particular injury. We had an immense concourse, and preaching was in an orchard. I have been very busy, as I try to talk a little in the morning to the young men; but the old men and the women also attend, and the large church is nearly full at six o'clock. Whether any good will be done I cannot say." These morning "talks" to young ministers were, in fact, carefully outlined lectures on homiletics. He continued this practice for some time at his Conferences, always meeting the young men before the morning breakfast-hour. It is not surprising that there came of all this a temporary collapse of health. He writes to his son from Jackson, Michigan, in September of this year: " I was seized with a bilious attack on my way to the Detroit Conference; chills and fever set in. I was prostrated from Friday till Tuesday, but I had kind friends who watched me night and day, and the Lord was pleased to raise me up. On Wednesday I had a bed put in a stage, and rode eighteen miles to a railroad; thence, by train, to this place. Yesterday I presided part of the forenoon, and to-day the whole of it." Though enfeebled he attended his Conferences, and was moving on at full speed. October 22d he wrote again to his son: " I dedicate a church at Kittaning, Pennsylvania, to-morrow, and start for Evanston, Illinois, where I preach on Sunday at the Biblical Institute Commencement. On Tuesday I dedicate a church at Niles, Michigan, and then hasten home to attend the bishops' meeting, not being able to wait for commencement."

He was beginning, however, to think more than before of securing a home of his own, and, if possible, east of the Alleghanies. There was in his mind a strong persuasion that the climate of the West did not agree with him. He was invited to Baltimore; to Stamford, Connecticut, by his friend Oliver Hoyt; and, by the faculty of Dickinson College, to Carlisle, Pennsylvania. His Chicago and Evanston friends were loth to lose him. Dr. Evans suggested the plan of a house on the lake shore, and urged its acceptance. Meeting him early in 1863 at the home of Oliver Hoyt, and ascertaining, from his conversation, that he was inclined to settle in Baltimore, I urged upon him the greater desirableness of Philadelphia, at least as long as the war lasted. The suggestion of Philadelphia was accepted, and a house was in a short time purchased by the Methodist laymen of that city, and presented to him. His friends in New York claimed for themselves the privilege of furnishing his new home. The change of dwelling-place brought him nearer the centre of national affairs, at that time a matter of prime importance, and gave to Philadelphia one of its most eminent citizens. That he was beloved and revered in that city, as few men were, goes without saying.

The parting with his Evanston and Chicago friends was full of regrets on both sides. Miss Frances E. Willard has furnished me with a very pretty picture of the bishop's Evanston life, as she saw it in her early days: " He lived in Evanston when I was a school-girl here, and among all the gifted men who made the earlier days of our university so brilliant that the later ones can only hope to compete with, but not excel them, he was chief. In the heroic years of the civil war, among all the wonderful experiences that are impressed so plainly on my mind, none are so deeply stamped as the prayers of Bishop Simpson in our plain old church among the trees. When the Union cause seemed least prosperous the bishop's faith was strongest, and as he prayed for the success of our armies it seemed as if the presence of God was veritably with us. He is one of the few persons I ever watched during prayer, but at these times, reverently as I had been taught to bow my head, it was lifted involuntarily, not out of curiosity, but from the fascination of that man's face while he talked with God. As I recall it now there was at such times something in his voice as well as in his words, and certainly something in his presence, that approached the supernatural.

" When he went to California all of our young people from the schools marched to the station in his honor, to wave their farewells, and when he returned they gathered under his window and sang ' Home again, home again, from a foreign shore.' His speech to them on both occasions was like that of a father to his children."

Our civil war began at a period when the utility of voluntary efforts for the relief of sick and wounded soldiers was fully recognized by Christian nations. The lessons of the Crimea had not been forgotten. The mortality of the British soldiers, in camp and hospital, from 1854 to 1856, rose, at one time, as high as one hundred and seventeen per cent. per annum, a rate rapid enough to destroy the entire army in less than one year. The change wrought by the well-directed energy of Miss Florence Nightingale and her company of trained nurses was such that the death rate in the active service was no more than that of soldiers in comfortable barracks at home. The thought, so the testimony runs, that they were remembered at home, quickened the energy of the soldiers, helped them to resist the attacks of disease, and to recover when stricken down.*

Our army was an army of citizens; it was emphatically the people in military array and engaged in military service. The farmers, lawyers, doctors, merchants, mechanics, laborers, clerks, and men of letters had gone to the front to help to save their country. Even clergymen marched at the head of regiments recruited by their eloquent appeals. A people addicted to peace devoted themselves four years to the study and practice of war. It would have been impossible to restrain the citizens at home from following, with their love and devotion, their fellow-citizens in the field. The experience of England in the Crimea suggested, directly after the call of Mr. Lincoln for 75,000 men, the idea of "A Nightingale Band." Before a blow had been struck, after the fall of Sumter, Ladies' Aid Associations had been organized in Philadelphia and New York. Out of these grew the Sanitary Commission, and the formation of the Christian Commission followed in November, 1861. As the women of the country had originated the one, so the Young Men's Christian Associations had originated the other. In the year of which we now write—1864—we were in the midst of the most desperate part of our struggle. Gettysburg had then

---

* See the Introduction to the "Annals of the Christian Commission," by the Rev. Lemuel Moss, pp. 42–61.

been won; Vicksburg had been taken; Grant was fighting in the Wilderness of Virginia, and our best blood was flowing freely. A battle nearly every day, with indecisive results, was sending the wounded soldiers in thousands to the rear. The year had begun with the holding of fairs, for the benefit of the Sanitary Commission, in the great cities East and West—that in New York resulting in the gathering of over a million of dollars. That of Philadelphia was to have been opened with an address from President Lincoln, but, being unable to attend, he requested that Bishop Simpson take his place, saying that there was no other man in the country by whom he would prefer to be represented.*

The speech was so characteristic, and the occasion so extraordinary, that the reader will relish some of its passages:

"At the request of the President of the United States, and in his behalf, I accept from the honored Executive Committee the vast treasures contained in these buildings—the generous offerings of the citizens of New Jersey, Delaware, and Pennsylvania—to be dedicated, in the name of the people, to the use of the sick and wounded in our army and navy. No one, more than myself, regrets the absence of our honored chief-magistrate. [Applause.] The noble ends in view, the unparalleled magnificence of the arrangements, and the character of this assemblage combine to form an occasion worthy of his presence. Delighted would we have been to hear from his own lips the expression of his sympathy, and to catch the inspiration of his heart, which swells with strong confidence in the glorious results of our present national struggle. [Applause.] But he could not be with us; his eye was upon Richmond. [Applause.] He is listening for tidings from our brave generals, and from our equally

---

* Mr. John Welsh thus wrote in regard to the president's request: "Mr. Cresson, Mr. Cuyler, and myself, a few minutes since, waited upon you to communicate to you a wish, expressed in writing by President Lincoln, that you should represent him at the opening ceremonies of the great Central Fair, on Tuesday next. Finding that you were absent, Mr. G. W. Childs, one of our Executive Committee, has kindly consented to be the bearer of that request, which, I earnestly trust, it may afford you pleasure to comply with. We had assigned you a position in our services, but your acquiescence in the wish of President Lincoln will render it unnecessary to allude to it."

brave advancing hosts. He is waiting to furnish such aid and to give such orders as the interests of the hour may demand. But while he is not with us, he is of us. He sympathizes with the suffering sailor and soldier, and is deeply moved by their distress; and all that the government could do to assist this great enterprise he has, from the beginning, promptly done for the officers of the Sanitary Commission. [Applause.]

"But why all this outpouring of treasure? Why this universal stirring of the national heart? We are in the midst of war—earnest, terrible war; war with a people of the same race—with our former brethren, who have breathed the same air of freedom; who have been educated in the same schools of learning; who have been inspired by the noble deeds of the same ancestry. But the leaders of the South have torn them from us. They were weary of our constitutional forms. They murmured at, and feared, the growing spirit of freedom, and they broke the bonds of our ancient covenant. They seized a part of our heritage, and have sought to found a government whose corner-stone should be human slavery. They have erected their altar to this dark Moloch, and verily they have made their sons pass through a terrible fire; and more victims have been laid already on this dark altar than were ever sacrificed on that of the angry deity of old.

"But the injury stops not there. The friends of the Union have risen, and have rushed to the rescue. The farmer has left his plough, the mechanic his shop, the man of letters his desk, and the merchant his office. The noblest of young men have been foremost in the thickest of the fight; and though, amid the smoke and carnage of battle, some of the stars have been dimmed, and some of the stripes have been torn, yet the star-spangled banner still waves, and the millions rally round the flag! [Long-continued and deafening applause.] But, alas! how many brave men have fallen! How many are wounded! To-day, in camp, and in hospital, and on the battle-field—perhaps at this very hour—multiplied thousands of husbands, and brothers, and sons are lying among the sick and helpless. Shall their comrades cease from the strife to care for them, or shall other hands, less able and less skilled in war, perform these offices of kindness? Shall they be left to suffer and to die neglected, or shall every attention which humanity can suggest be freely given them? This question you, with others, are answering by your donations and by your labors.

"This land of ours is wonderful. The government has called for men, and they have come from every plain, and from every mountain, and from every valley, until more than a million have stood in martial array. And yet our crops have been sown and gathered; the sound of the hammer is heard in the shop, and the hum of machinery in the factories. Our wharves are laden with goods; our trains are crowded with passengers; every village and town is enlarging its limits; our city streets are full; whole blocks are added to our buildings, and still the crowd of population cries for room. Money has been called for, and though the government has asked hundreds of millions, its loans have all been eagerly taken. We have been taxed, and the taxes have been unmurmuringly paid. And, in addition to all this, the people come forward with their free offerings by millions to aid and comfort the wounded and the dying. [Applause.] This Sanitary Commission has already collected, in money and values, more than ten millions of dollars, and the Christian Commission has also received, and is receiving, large sums for its work. Nor are these sums merely the offerings of the wealthy. Many of them have given nobly. But the poorest vie with the richest in devotion to this cause. Families of narrow means—the laboring-man, the working-woman, teachers and children in our schools, artists and amateurs—all have given freely. The old grandmother, with failing eyes, has sat up, on long winter evenings, busily knitting for the poor soldier-boy, and the little prattler has gathered a flower to add to your collections of beauty. All have given, for all have felt. All have friends who have suffered or who may suffer, and the images of loved ones cheer them on. God has touched every heart. He has written a lesson which the ages may read, that great wrongs must terminate in great catastrophes; and the people have resolved that, cost what it may, the system which could not live within the Constitution shall die beyond it. [Applause.]

"I remember, when I was travelling on the Pacific coast, to have seen a river taken from its bed, half-way up the mountain-sides, and its waters distributed all over the hill-slopes and plains. At the side of every rill the miner stood, and gathered, with eager care, the precious particles of gold. That same river, before it was parted thus, had been formed by hundreds of springs from near the mountain-tops. So it is with your benevolent agencies. You have gathered all the little rills from country and from village, until they have swelled into a deep, broad stream. Chicago and Baltimore, New York and Brooklyn, St. Louis and Pittsburgh, all gathered from their tributaries and combined their vast supplies. Philadelphia comes last, but not least. Here are the gathering rills from Delaware and from New Jersey, and from the mountain heights of Pennsylvania, pouring their waters into this great reservoir. Here they shall be commingled and distributed until some little rill shall flow beside every sick and wounded soldier in the camp and hospital, and returning life and health and joy shall far outweigh all the golden sands on California's coast. And who that remembers the scenes of a year ago; who that listened for the step of the invading enemy; who that looked for the devastating fire that should mark his pathway; who that held his breath as tidings came, hour by hour, from Gettysburg, can wonder that Philadelphia pours out her treasures for those brave men who stood as a living rampart around her? [Much applause.]

"While much of the credit is due to the gentlemen of the various committees, we must not yet forget to acknowledge that much belongs to the ladies. [Applause.] And yet why should I mention this? Who would suppose it to be otherwise? Who here will deny that woman is foremost in every good work? For woman hath a nature to be kind. She is full of sympathy everywhere. When, with ceaseless care, she plans and labors for the poor and suffering; when, by example and persuasion, she gathers resources from every quarter; when, as I have seen her, she moves, with silent step, among the couches of the sick and dying in the hospital, giving now the cordial, and now the word of comfort and of hope—it is then she becomes in her mission an angel of mercy, a worthy sister of the beloved Mary whom angels hailed. [Applause.]

"As we turn to descry the signs of the times, I think I can see the light dawning over the mountain-tops. Our resources seem yet undiminished, while the resources of the South are fast becoming exhausted. Its borders are contracting, its vitality is declining, while with us new fields of wealth are ever opening. Our vast territories, from Arizona to Montana, from California to Colorado, are unveiling their mines of boundless wealth, and are waiting only for the miner's toil. We have resources, too, in brave men. 'Tis true that many of them sleep in the dust. Lyon and Baker and Sedgwick and Wadsworth, and others, rest in their glory. But we have heroes still living. Sherman is just now showing, from his onward career, that he is a Northern man with Southern proclivities. [Cheers and laughter.] We have a Thomas who never doubts. [Cheers.] We have a Hooker who pushes his forces amid the clouds. [Cheers.] New England has given us her Howard, who, one-armed, is still within himself a host. [Cheers.] Pennsylvania has in her Hancock a tower of strength [cheers], and near her heart she bears her Meade of honor. [Cheer upon cheer.] While the giant West, from the shores of her broad Mississippi, sends us a Grant of unconditional victory! [Tremendous outbursts of applause, culminating in a "three times three," given with full emphasis.] Nor are the seamen less brave. A gallant Foote has ended his labors, and peace be to his memory. But Porter, Dupont, and Farragut still marshal our fleet. [Cheers.] Our monitors have changed naval warfare, and have taught the world the value of hearts of oak in breasts of iron.

"And now, in the name of the people who have furnished these generous gifts, whose sympathies are with the brave men in the field and on shipboard; in the name of the people who ordained that Constitution under which we live, and who have sworn to defend and uphold it; in the name of the people who are determined to live or die under the stars and stripes, I dedicate these treasures and their proceeds to the sick and wounded soldiers and sailors of our army and navy—to those brave men who for us and ours have perilled their lives, and driven back the hosts of the enemy. May God, in his infinite mercy, restore them to health and to their friends and to their country! And may the donors realize that 'it is more blessed to give than to receive.' [Amen! Amen! shouted the audience. Three cheers were proposed and given for the eloquent bishop, as he sat down.]"

But in all he expressed of devotion to the cause of freedom, throughout this stirring address, Bishop Simpson but echoed the voice of the Methodist Episcopal General Conference, which had adjourned from its place of session in Philadelphia, only a few days before the opening of this Sanitary Fair. In maintaining the national unity he kept no more than equal step with the Church of which he was a trusted leader. As soon as it assembled in the Union Church, of Philadelphia, the Conference ordered the national flag to be raised over the building; appointed a day of prayer for the deliverance of the country, and observed the day with impressive services; named a committee to wait upon President Lincoln, and to carry to him the assurance of the unfaltering support of loyal Methodists.* "Say to him," so the Conference directed, "that we are with him heart and soul for human rights and free institutions." As the visit of this deputation drew from Mr. Lincoln a reply so deeply imbued with religious feeling that it arrested at once the attention of the country, we have requested a brief account from its only surviving member, the Rev. Dr. Joseph Cummings. He thus writes: "On May 14th, Joseph Cummings, Chairman of the Committee on the State of the Country, presented an address prepared by him and ap-

---

* The committee were: Bishop E. R. Ames, Joseph Cummings, George Peck, Charles Elliott, Granville Moody.

proved by the committee, and the nomination of a deputation to bear the address to Washington, and, in behalf of the Conference, to present it to the Chief Magistrate of the United States. The address was adopted, and the nominated delegation was confirmed. The committee was organized by the appointment of Bishop Ames as chairman and Joseph Cummings, secretary. Before reaching Washington, Dr. Moody requested the secretary to let him have a copy of the address, which he would present, as soon as practicable, to the president. On our arrival he went immediately to the president's house, and represented to Mr. Nicolay, Mr. Lincoln's private secretary, that it was important he should see the president immediately. He said that on the next day a delegation of a Conference of ministers assembled in Philadelphia, representing the largest, most loyal and influential Church of the country, would call and present an address. Mr. Nicolay was much interested, and went immediately to consult the president, and secure an interview for Dr. Moody. This was soon granted, and he made to the president similar statements to those made to the secretary, and presented a copy of the address. Mr. Lincoln thanked him, and said he would think about his reply. On the next day, by previous arrangement, Mr. Seward, the secretary of state, introduced the committee, and the address was formally read and presented. In his reply the president playfully remarked, much to the surprise of those members of the committee who knew nothing of the arrangement, that he had seen the address before, and had prepared his reply. He then took from his desk and read to the committee the answer that is so highly and justly prized. The existence of this paper is due to the arrangement giving notice to the president that the address would be presented. As we took leave of the president, Dr. Moody, in his usual style, said, ' Mr. President, we all hope the country will rest in Abraham's bosom for the next four years.' This produced a general smile, and the interview closed.

Gentlemen.

In response to your address, allow me to attest the accuracy of its historical statements; indorse the sentiments it expresses; and thank you, in the nation's name for the same promise it gives.

Nobly sustained as the government has been by all the churches, I would utter nothing which might, in the least, appear invidious against any. Yet, without this, it may fairly be said that the Methodist Episcopal Church, not less devoted

...than that the Methodist Church sends more soldiers to the field, more nurses to the hospitals, and more prayers to Heaven than any. God bless the Methodist Church—bless all the churches—and blessed be God, Who, in this our great trial, giveth us the churches.

A. Lincoln

May 18. 1864

"While we waited for a copy to be made, which should be kept by the president, there was a general conversation relative to public matters and on the state of the Methodist Church in the South ; and it was amusing to see how Mr. Lincoln evaded a direct answer to Bishop Ames's request for an opinion relative to our rights to the Methodist churches in the South."*

But, alas! for us, the resting of the country for four years "in Abraham's bosom," as it was playfully expressed by Granville Moody, was not to be. It was ordered far otherwise. After giving to the country a second inaugural address, which the London *Spectator* characterized as the loftiest, in its moral tone, of the political papers of this century, Mr. Lincoln was assassinated. The rejoicing over the capture of Richmond, and the still heartier rejoicing over the surrender of Lee's army, was changed into a sorrow which sought every conceivable form of expression. Bishop Simpson was at once summoned to Washington to render such service of consolation as he could to the distressed family. And when the prolonged funeral processions, which accompanied the body of the president from city to city, were over, he spoke, in Springfield, Ill., the last words at the grave of his friend. Something of this address should be given here, as part of the record of the times :

"FELLOW-CITIZENS OF ILLINOIS, AND MANY PARTS OF OUR ENTIRE UNION,—Near the capital of this large and growing state of Illinois, in the midst of this beautiful grove, and at the open mouth of the vault which has just received the remains of our fallen chieftain, we gather to pay a tribute of respect and drop the tears of sorrow. A little more than four years ago he left his plain and quiet home in yonder city, receiving the parting words of the concourse of friends who, in the midst of the droppings of a gentle shower, gathered around him. He spoke of the pain of leaving the place where his children had been born, and where his home had been rendered so pleasant by many recollections. And as he left he made an earnest request, in the hearing of some who are present

* We give, on the preceding page, a fac-simile of President Lincoln's reply to the General Conference.

at this hour, that, as he was about to enter upon responsibilities which he believed to be greater than those which had fallen upon any man since the days of Washington, the people would offer up their prayers that God would aid and sustain him in the work they had given him to do. His company left your city; but as it went, snares were set for the chief magistrate. Scarcely did he escape the dangers of the way or the hand of the assassin as he neared Washington. I believe he escaped only through the vigilance of the officers and the prayers of the people; so that the blow was suspended for more than four years, which was at last permitted, through the providence of God, to fall.

"How different the occasion which witnessed his departure from that which witnessed his return! Doubtless you expected to take him by the hand, to feel the warm grasp which you felt in other days, and to see the tall form among you which you had delighted to honor in years past. But he was never permitted to return until he came with lips mute, his frame encoffined, and a weeping nation following. Such a scene as his return to you was never witnessed. Among the events of history there have been great processions of mourners. There was one for the patriarch Jacob, which went out of Egypt, and the Canaanites wondered at the evidences of reverence and filial affection which came from the hearts of the Israelites. There was mourning when Moses fell upon the heights of Pisgah, and was hid from human view. There has been mourning in the kingdoms of the earth when kings and princes have fallen. But never was there, in the history of man, such mourning as that which has attended this progress to the grave. If we look at the multitudes that followed him, we can see how the nation stood aghast when it heard of his death. Tears filled the eyes of manly, sunburned faces. Strong men, as they clasped the hands of their friends, were unable to find vent for their grief in words. Women and little children caught up the tidings, as they ran through the land, and were melted into tears. The nation stood still. Men left their ploughs in the fields, and asked what the end should be. The hum of manufactories ceased, and the sound of the hammer was not heard. Busy merchants closed their doors, and in the Exchange gold passed no more from hand to hand. Though three weeks have elapsed the nation has scarcely breathed easily. Men of all political parties, and of all religious creeds, have united in paying this tribute. The archbishop of the Roman Catholic Church in New York and a Protestant minister walked side by side in the sad procession, and a Jewish rabbi performed a part of the solemn service. Here are gathered around his tomb the representatives of the army and navy, senators, judges, and officers of all the branches of the government. Here, too, are members of civic professions, with men and women from the humblest as well as the highest occupations. Here and there, too, are tears—as sincere and warm as any that drop—which come from the eyes of those whose kindred and whose race have been freed from their chains by him whom they mourn as their deliverer. More races have looked on the procession for sixteen hundred miles—by night and by day—by sunlight, dawn, twilight, and by torchlight—than ever before watched the progress of a procession on its way to a grave.

"A part of this deep interest has arisen from the times in which we live, and in which he who has fallen was a leading actor. It is a principle of our nature that feelings, once excited, turn readily from the object by which they are aroused to some other object, which may, for the time being, take possession of the mind. Another law of our nature is, that our deepest affections gather about some human form in which are incarnated the living thoughts of the age. If we look, then, at the times, we see an age of excitement. [These thoughts were copiously illustrated.]

"The tidings came that Richmond was evacuated, and that Lee had surrendered. The bells rang merrily all over the land. The booming of cannon was heard; illuminations and torchlight processions manifested the general joy, and families looked for the speedy return of their loved ones from the field. Just in the midst of this, in one hour—nay, in one moment—the news was flashed throughout the land that Abraham Lincoln had perished by the hand of an assassin; and then all the feeling which had been gathering for four years, in forms of excitement, grief, horror, and joy, turned into one wail of woe—a sadness inexpressible. But it is not the character of the times merely which has made this mourning; the mode of his death must be taken into the account. Had he died with kind friends around him; had the sweat of death been wiped from his brow by gentle hands, while he was yet conscious—how it would have softened or assuaged something of our grief. But no moment of warning was given to him or to us. He was stricken down, too, when his hopes for the end of the rebellion were bright, and prospects of a calmer life were before him. There was a cabinet meeting that day, said to have been the most cheerful of any held since the beginning of the rebellion. After this meeting he talked with his friends, and spoke of the four years of tempest, of the storm being over, and of the four years of content now awaiting him, as the weight of care and anxiety would be taken from his mind. In the midst of these anticipations he left his house, never to return alive. The evening was Good Friday, the saddest day in the whole calendar for the Christian Church. So filled with grief was every Christian heart that even the joyous thoughts of Easter Sunday failed to remove the sorrow under which the true worshipper bowed in the house of God.

"But the chief reason for this mourning is to be found in the man himself. Mr. Lincoln was no ordinary man. I believe the conviction has been growing in the nation's mind, as it certainly has been in my own, especially in the last years of his administration, that, by the hand of God, he was especially singled out to guide our government in these troublesome times, and it seems to me that the hand of God may be traced in many of the events connected with his history. First, then, I recognize this in the physical education which he received, and which prepared him for enduring herculean labors. In the toils of his boyhood and the labors of his manhood God was giving him an iron frame. Next to this was his identification with the people, his understanding of their feelings, for he was one of them, and connected with them in their daily life. His education was simple. A few months spent in the school-house gave him the elements of knowledge. He read few books, but mastered all he read. Bunyan's 'Pilgrim's Progress,' Æsop's 'Fables,' and the 'Life of Washington' were his favorites in the time of his boyhood. His early life, with its varied struggles, joined him indissolubly to the working masses, and no elevation in society diminished his respect for the sons of toil. He knew what it was to fell the tall trees of the forest and to stem the current of the broad Mississippi. His home was in the growing West, the heart of the republic, and, invigorated by the winds that swept over its prairies, he learned lessons of self-reliance which sustained him in seasons of adversity.

"His genius was soon recognized, as true genius always will be, and he was placed in the legislature of his state. Already acquainted with the principles of law, he devoted his thoughts to matters of public interest, and began to be looked on as the coming statesman. As early as 1839 he presented resolutions in the legislature asking for emancipation in the District of Columbia, when, with but rare exceptions, the whole popular mind of his state was opposed to the measure. From that hour he was a steady and uniform friend of humanity, and was preparing for the conflict of later years.

"If you ask me on what mental characteristics his greatness rested, I answer, on a quick and ready perception of facts; on a memory unusually retentive; and on a logical turn of mind, which followed, sternly and unwaveringly, every link in the chain of thought on every subject which he was called to investigate. I think that there have been minds more comprehensive in their scope, but I doubt if there ever has been a man who could follow, step by step, with more logical power, the points which he desired to illustrate. He gained this power, in part, by the close study of geometry, and by the determination to perceive the truth in all its simplicity. It is said of him that, in childhood, if, when listening to a conversation, he had any difficulty in understanding what people meant, he could not sleep, after retiring to rest, till he had tried to make out the precise points intended, and, when made out, to frame language to convey them in a clearer manner to others. Who that has read his messages fails to perceive the directness of his style? It was not, however, chiefly by his mental faculties that he gained such control over mankind. His moral power gave him pre-eminence. The conviction of men that Abraham Lincoln was an honest man led them to yield to his guidance. As has been said of Cobden, whom he greatly resembled, he made all men feel a sense of himself. They saw in him a man who, they believed, would do what is right, regardless of all consequences. It was this moral integrity which gave him his hold on the people, and made his utterances almost oracular.

"But, after all, by the acts of a man shall his fame be perpetuated. What are his acts? Much praise is due to the men who aided him. He called able counsellors around him—some of whom have displayed the highest order of talent, united with the purest and most devoted patriotism. He summoned able generals into the field—men who have borne the sword as bravely as ever any human arm has borne it. He had the aid of prayerful and thoughtful men everywhere. But under his own guiding hands, wise counsels were combined and great movements conducted. The great act of our dead president, on which his fame shall rest long after his frame shall moulder away, is that of giving freedom to a race. We are thankful that God granted to Abraham Lincoln the decision and wisdom and grace to issue his proclamation of freedom.

" Abraham Lincoln was a good man; he was known as an honest, temperate, forgiving man; a just man; a man of noble heart in every way. As to his religious experience I cannot speak definitely, because I was not privileged to know much of his private sentiments. My acquaintance with him did not give me the opportunity to hear him speak on those topics. This I know, however: he read the Bible frequently, loved it for its great truths, and he tried to be guided by its precepts. He believed in Christ the Saviour of sinners, and I think he was sincere in trying to bring his life into harmony with the principles of revealed religion. Certainly if there ever was a man who illustrated some of the principles of pure religion, that man was our departed president. Look over all his speeches; listen to his utterances. He never spoke unkindly of any man. Even the rebels received no word of anger from him. As a ruler, I doubt if any president has ever shown such trust in God, or in public documents so frequently referred to divine aid. Often did he remark to friends and to delegations that his hope for our success rested in his conviction that God would bless our efforts, because we were try-

26

ing to do right. To the address of a large religious body he replied: 'Thanks be unto God, who, in our trials, giveth us the churches.' To a minister who said that he hoped the Lord was on our side, he replied that it gave him no concern whether the Lord was on our side or not, for 'I know the Lord is always on the side of right;' and, with deep feeling, added: 'But God is my witness that it is my constant anxiety and prayer that both myself and this nation should be on the Lord's side.'

"Let us pause a moment and consider the lesson of the hour before we part. This man, though he fell by assassination, still fell under the permissive hand of God. What more could Mr. Lincoln have desired of life for himself? Were not his honors full? There was no office to which he could aspire. The popular feeling clung to him as to no other man. He appears to have had a strange presentiment, early in his political career, that some day he would be president. You see it indicated in 1839. Of the slave power he said: 'Broken by it I, too, may be; bow to it I never will. The probability that we may fail in the struggle ought not to deter us from the support of a cause which we deem to be just. It shall not deter me. If ever I feel the soul within me elevate and expand to those dimensions not wholly unworthy its Almighty architect, it is when I contemplate the cause of my country deserted by all the world besides, and I standing up boldly and alone, and hurling defiance at her victorious oppressors. Here, without contemplating consequences, before high Heaven and in the face of the world, I swear eternal fidelity to the just cause, as I deem it, of the land of my life, my liberty, and my love.' And yet, secretly, he said to more than one: 'I never shall live out the four years of my term. When the rebellion is crushed my work is done.' So it was. He lived to see the last battle fought, and to dictate a despatch from the home of Jefferson Davis; lived till the power of the rebellion was broken, and then, having done the work to which God had called him, he passed to his reward.

"Standing, as we do to-day, by his coffin, let us resolve to carry forward the policy so nobly begun. Let us do right to all men. Let us vow, before Heaven, to eradicate every vestige of human slavery; to give every human being his true position before God and man; to crush every form of rebellion, and to stand by the flag which God has given us. How joyful that it floated over parts of every state before Mr. Lincoln's career was ended. How singular that to the fact of the assassin's heel being caught in the folds of the flag we are probably indebted for his capture. The time will come when, in the beautiful words of him whose lips are now forever sealed, 'the mystic chords of memory, which stretch from every battle-field and from every patriot's grave, shall yield a sweeter music when touched by the angels of our better nature.'

"Chieftain, farewell! The nation mourns thee. Mothers shall teach thy name to their lisping children. The youth of our land shall emulate thy virtues. Statesmen shall study thy record, and from it learn lessons of wisdom. Mute though thy lips be, yet they still speak. Hushed is thy voice, but its echoes of liberty are ringing through the world, and the sons of bondage listen with joy. Thou didst fall not for thyself. The assassin had no hate for thee. Our hearts were aimed at; our national life was sought. We crown thee as our martyr, and Humanity enthrones thee as her triumphant son. Hero, martyr, friend, *farewell.*"

There was another closing scene, memorable in its way, awakening other feelings than those aroused by the death of Mr. Lincoln, yet equally a part of the history of the war —the last meeting of the United States Christian Commission. In this, too, Bishop Simpson took part. Through the courtesy of Mr. George H. Stuart, the president of the Commission, I have been put in possession of the bishop's address on this occasion.* The time was February, 1866;

---

* In the course of conversation, Mr. Stuart gave an account of the presentation of a home to General Grant by citizens of Philadelphia, which is well worth preserving:

"General Grant had sent his children to Burlington, New Jersey, for schooling, and wanted to place his family in Philadelphia, but found rents so exorbitant that he could not afford it. He wrote to Mr. Stuart to find him a house. Mr. Stuart suggested to his friends that the people of Philadelphia give him one. No sooner said than done, for the subscriptions were quickly made. It was then determined to furnish the house—one on Chestnut Street. When all was ready, the Grants were invited to lunch with some friends. The place was the new house; the hosts, the subscribers and their families. General Grant and his family, when they arrived, were puzzled to know who their host and hostess were. Whose house are we in? they asked, and were not a little mystified.

"Very soon, as the general was seated on a sofa, Mr. Stuart handed him the deed, informing him that the gift of the house was made by his friends in Philadelphia to express the sense of their obligations to him. Grant's eyes filled with tears, and speech failed him. Stuart quickly relieved him, saying, 'General, you are a man of deeds not of words,' and again gave expression to the great debt of gratitude due him for saving the country. The party then sat down to an elegant entertainment; and the company of friends left, leaving the house furnished with ample stores for housekeeping."

the place the Hall of the House of Representatives in Washington; the presiding officer, Speaker Colfax; the audience was largely composed of the men who had carried the nation through its trials. The bishop rose to the demands of the occasion, and fitly said the last words, which were in his tenderest vein. The concluding passages, at least, are worth preserving:

"But I must not delay. The record of the Commission is made. Its accounts are closed. Its workers are about to scatter, and we have only to say 'Farewell.' Let me congratulate you, brethren of the Commission, on closing your work in such a place and in such a presence. It was fit that you should meet in the Capitol of the nation, in this Hall of Freedom, where the nation meets through its chosen men; in this chamber, where the light shines so sweetly and so softly through those emblems of peace and national glory, as typifying the light of heaven, which shines on every mortal enterprise. We rejoice also in the associations of the evening. We have in the chair our honored speaker, who presides over the House of Representatives, and who has shown a deep interest in our work. And I may be allowed to say that while he presides over a body eminent for wisdom and eloquence, he never presided over more patriotic and loyal hearts than those of the workers in the Christian Commission. We are here also in the presence of the army and navy, in the persons of so many honored officers of high rank, who well know what the association has accomplished; in the presence of distinguished members of the cabinet, and of the learned and accomplished chief-justice of the Supreme Court. Around us we recognize many senators and representatives who gave us their sympathies and their prayers. In such a presence, and with such benedictions, it is meet that our Commission should pass gently away. Are there not some that have been more glorious in death than even in life? I think that Moses, though he had led his people triumphantly through the sea, and had been on Sinai in the Divine presence, was never so honored as when, having stood on Pisgah's summit and glanced at the distant hills and plains, it is simply said that God 'buried him.' The Christian Commission has led a noble life. It was baptized in prayer, worked amid suffering and affliction, leaned on the affections of the wise and pure, received aid from all classes, and ministered to multiplied thousands. Its dying moment has come, and it breathes its last breath sweetly and gently as the fabled notes of the dying swan. The nation draws near, utters its benediction, and 'buries' with honor.

"But, beloved workers, as we part we go to other fields. The spirit of the Commission will still live. We shall not be an organized body, but we shall be active laborers. There are other fields. Vice in many forms is to be encountered and vanquished. Cities are to be evangelized. Freedmen are to be educated. The ignorant everywhere are to be instructed. A great work is before us. The nation is to be reconstructed. The theoretical and political work, and the exercise of power, we leave to statesmen, officers, and wise men assembled here. But when the law and the sword have accomplished their utmost work, they cannot change unwilling minds. The moral work remains to be done. We must carry the gospel to men of all ranks, classes, sections, and prejudices, for one thing alone can make us truly one,—the love of God through Jesus Christ our Lord.

"Ere we part it is proper to return our grateful acknowledgments to the officers who have conducted the affairs of the Commission. I have seen their labors, having been slightly identified with them. Diligence, system, economy, earnestness, and deep devotedness have marked their varied movements. From the headquarters at Philadelphia, from the offices at Boston, New York, Pittsburgh, Cincinnati, Chicago, St. Louis, and elsewhere, immense stores have been issued and vast labor has been performed, without confusion and without ostentation. As I look upon the whole band of laborers, I am reminded that the expression is not too strong, for it is written of all active laborers, 'They that be wise shall shine as the brightness of the firmament, and they that turn many to righteousness as the stars forever and forever.' Workers of the Commission, continue to shine as stars. Your light cannot be hid. If the mite which the widow cast into the treasury remains before the eye of the great Master, surely the cups of cold water, the messages of mercy, the words of holy comfort, ministered by the delegates, shall never be forgotten.

"But the workers are not all here. Scattered over the land they are with us in spirit. They are not all visible. Some fell on the battle-field, whispering with their dying breath the name of Jesus. Some fell by disease contracted while ministering in the hospital. May they not be here also? May it not be that brave soldier boys, comforted in their anguish and death by your ministrations, join you in spirit also? These galleries are densely crowded. Are there not higher galleries? Above this light, beaming so softly upon us, may they not be purer and brighter lights? May not the unseen be very near us? In my youth I was taught to repeat:

> 'Angels now are hovering round us,
>   Unperceived amid the throng,
> Wondering at the love that crowned us,
>   Glad to join the holy song.'

And if angels come, may not redeemed and glorified spirits come also? While the benedictions of officers and statesmen fall upon your ears, may there not be gentle tones whispering love and joy within? May it not even be that he, our martyred one, whose seat is vacant here, but who cheered us twelve months since, looks lovingly upon the scene? Be that as it may, there is a far greater among us, who hath said, 'Lo, I am with you always, even to the end of the world.'

"Brave workers, go to your fields. They are ripening to the harvest. Work for Jesus, and what your hands 'find to do, do it with your might.'"

XVIII.

LAY DELEGATION.

1852–1872.

The History of Methodist Lay Representation a Long One.—Origin of the Ministerial Power.—Dissatisfaction with the Sole Government of the Church by Ministers.—The *Wesleyan Repository.*—Merged in the *Mutual Rights.*—Mr. William S. Stockton and Dr. Thomas E. Bond.— The Report of 1828 on "Petitions and Memorials."—The Philadelphia Movement.—Return of Dr. Bond to the Chair of the *Christian Advocate.* —The Wolves and the Sheep.—Petitions to the General Conference.— Popular and Ministerial Vote on Lay Delegation in 1861.—Lay Delegation Defeated.—The Cause Taken Up by *The Methodist.*—Prejudice against its Supporters.—The Right to a Free Press Asserted.—Bishop Simpson becomes a Helper of the Laymen.—Letters of Daniel L. Ross to Him.—The John Street Meeting, March, 1863.—The Bishop's Counsels.—The Convention in St. Paul's Church, New York, May, 1863.— The Bishop's Address.—Angry Opposition.—The Opposition not Surprising.—Succeeding Conventions.—Co-operation of Leading Official Editors.—The Minority becomes a Majority.—Completion of the Work in 1872.

XVIII.

THE history of the effort to secure lay representation in the Methodist Episcopal Church covers a period of fifty years. Originally, as is well known to Methodists, the government of the Church was wholly in the hands of the ministers. This was, however, more an accident than the result of design. In England, John Wesley exercised autocratic power over the societies which he had gathered; after his death his power was inherited by the company of preachers to whom he had conveyed it by deed of trust. In America the same plan of organization was followed; neither Mr. Wesley, who drew up the scheme of government, nor the preachers in America, for whom it was provided, thought of any other system than that which had been adopted in the mother country. The preachers met once every year, and passed rules for the regulation of the Methodist societies. They had created the Church by their missionary labors, and felt, naturally enough, that the care of its interests pertained to themselves alone.

In the nature of the case such a system could not last. To begin with, it was contrary to the instincts of Protestantism, which, by affirming the priesthood of all believers, restored the laity to their proper place in the Church. It was contrary, also, to the genius of Methodism itself, for in nothing is Methodism more remarkable than in the extent to which it uses lay activities. Dissatisfaction with the sole control of the Church by the ministry appeared very early in the present century. By the year 1821 it began to be outspoken. Mr. William S. Stockton, a layman of Trenton,

New Jersey, established a monthly periodical, known as the *Wesleyan Repository*, which advocated the admission of lay delegates to the ministerial assemblies. In 1824 the *Repository* was merged in the *Mutual Rights*, and transferred to Baltimore. By this time the contest had become very bitter; it was, unfortunately, involved with an assault upon episcopacy as unrepublican and despotic. Crimination was followed by recrimination; members of the Church in all respects excellent were expelled on the charge of inveighing against the Methodist system of government. Ultimately a new Church was organized, which took the name of the Methodist Protestant. The bitterness which accompanied the controversy lasted far into the next generation. In Methodist speech, to be a radical was to be counted unfit for church fellowship.

It is a remarkable fact, too, that the champion on the conservative side was also a layman. Dr. Thomas E. Bond was, in his day, easily the first controversialist in our Church. Master of an admirable style, keen to perceive every weakness of his opponent, energetic in expression, incapable of writing a dull paragraph, he added to all these qualities an extraordinary power of satire. Had he devoted himself to literature he would have been the peer of any prose writer of his time in America. On this question he became the Church's chief authority, and wrote for the committee on "Petitions and Memorials" of the General Conference of 1828 the report which virtually concluded the debate. There was not force enough nor intelligence enough in the Conference to answer the arguments of the report; yet it rested on the assumption that the divine call to the ministry carries with it the equally divine right of the ministers to the exclusive government of the Church. Our Church was thereby virtually put on Roman Catholic ground, and the people were remanded to a state of pupilage. In this position American Methodism — the seceders excepted — remained until 1851–52. For a preacher to be known as a promoter of lay delegation was as much as his ecclesiastical life was worth. For him there was no hope, no preferment, no peace. An amusing incident, of which I was myself a witness, will illustrate the universal feeling. An applicant for admission to the Philadelphia Conference, in the year 1847, was objected to on several grounds. While the case was pending, a respectable member of the Conference arose and said, " Mr. President, I am opposed to the admission of this brother ; I am told that he is a lay delegation man, and I had as lief travel with the devil as with a lay delegation man !" *

In 1852 affairs took a turn for the better. The laymen of Philadelphia, who keenly felt a dissatisfaction which was shared with them by many intelligent Methodists, summoned a convention to meet in that city. They profited by the experience of the past, and resolved to proceed in a peaceable spirit and by the use of peaceable means. They called into counsel with them the champion of the old system, Dr. Bond, now mellowed by age, and, as I believe, convinced that some concessions should be made. He was ready to waive the question of right, and to treat the subject in a wholly practical way. He even approved of a scheme of lay co-operation which had been adopted by the Tennessee Conference of the Southern Methodist Church. The earliest champion on the other side, Mr. Stockton, was also still living, and became a frequent, though an anonymous,

---

* Dr. George Brown, one of the patriarchs of Methodist Protestantism, tells a similar story. He was a presiding elder in the Pittsburgh Conference, and was privately circulating the " Mutual Rights of the Ministers and Members of the Methodist Episcopal Church." His people, however, supposed him to be on the other side. While travelling his district, he says, this " periodical was kept out of my sight, wherever I went. When dismounting from my horse at the house of Thomas Maple, a valuable local preacher, to whom I had sent the paper, I heard Sister Maple call out to one of the girls, ' Run, Sal, run ! take them " Mutual Rights " off the table ; there comes the elder.' And ' Sal ' must have taken and concealed them in some by-corner, for they were not to be seen during my stay."

contributor to the organ of the laymen, the *Philadelphia Christian Advocate.* But how changed the men! The two antagonists, possibly unknown to each other as disputants in this newly ordered battle-field, retained the intellectual keenness, but had outlived the fiery zeal, of their earlier years. Friend and foe were alike welcome to the columns of the *Philadelphia Advocate*, and the foes of lay delegation used their opportunity to the utmost. As the fruit of the convention, a petition was sent to the General Conference of 1852. This, as we have stated already, was kindly received,* but the prayer of the petitioners denied, on the ground of the inexpediency of the change asked for. But a step forward had been taken. The question of right was put aside, and the other question of the utility of a representation of the laity was brought to the front.

To secure the Church against what was supposed to be a threatening danger, Dr. Bond was recalled to the chair of the New York *Christian Advocate*, but died before the expiration of his term of office. He still, however, during these closing years, relied upon the old arguments, republished his famous "Appeal," and claimed the authorship of the "Report on Petitions and Memorials" of 1828—a point which, up to this time, had been in doubt. He still continued to hold the Church fast in the logical puzzle which is the principal feature of the report, and out of which there was for many minds no possible escape. †

---

* See chap. XI., p. 248.

† I refer to the second paragraph, beginning, "As to the claim of right to the representation contended for, if it be a right which the claimants are entitled to demand, it must be either a natural or an acquired right," etc. Dr. Bond, being a layman, was not a member of that General Conference; the chairman of the committee on "Petitions and Memorials" was Dr. John Emory, afterwards bishop. Dr. Bond denied his own right to be a member of the General Conference, but exercised the prerogative of intellectual energy to control its deliberations. Taken altogether, it was a curious situation. As to the effect produced upon the Conference of 1828 by the reading of the report, I was told by the Rev. Solomon Higgins, of

But the temper of the times was rapidly altering for the better. Laymen and ministers could now say that they favored lay delegation without instantly becoming objects of suspicion. Yet there were many who trembled with apprehension whenever this change in the constitution of the Church was named. A little incident will show the susceptibility of Methodist feeling in 1852. The convention of the laymen in Philadelphia was followed by a counter convention of the opposition in the spring of the same year. The venerable Dr. Bond presided. There were gathered about him as officers and promoters of the objects of the assembly some of the best-esteemed laymen of that day. The excellent brother who opened the devotional service read out the hymn beginning—

> "Jesus, great Shepherd of the sheep,
>   To thee for help we fly;
> Thy little flock in safety keep,
>   For, oh! the wolf is nigh."

The innocent wolves were sitting quietly in the congregation, and were highly amused by the turn that had been made on them. The reader of the hymn was, however, one of the lay delegates elected to the General Conference of 1872.

The laymen appeared also before the General Conference of 1856 with a petition very much in the terms of that of 1852. The Conference, however, was absorbed in the discussion of the project of a new chapter in the Discipline on slavery, and gave little time or thought to anything else.

In the General Conference of 1860 the subject was brought forward by the bishops, who said in their address, " We are of opinion that lay delegation might be introduced in one form into the General Conference with safety, and perhaps

---

the Philadelphia Conference, himself a delegate, that Nicholas Snethen, a leader of the lay delegationists, pronounced it to be unanswerable.

advantage, that form being a separate house." After much discussion the Conference declared itself ready to sanction the measure whenever it should appear that it was demanded by the people and the ministers. A test vote of both ministers and people was ordered to be taken in the year 1861. But in the period from 1856 to 1860 the country had been more absorbed than ever in the anti-slavery struggle. In 1861 the war began; the result of the vote taken that year was the total defeat of the lay delegationists. From the ministers there were 3069 votes against to 1338 for, and from the people 47,885 votes against to 28,884 votes for. The number of votes in favor was, however, too large to be overlooked. At this point the movement was espoused by *The Methodist* (edited then and for years after by the present writer), which had been established in 1860 for the purpose of doing what in it lay to preserve the threatened unity of the Church. The task set before us was to take up a defeated cause, to inspirit its friends, to obtain a rehearing from the Church, and, if possible, to achieve success. There was, besides all this, a serious difficulty in the way. The ministers and laymen who were united in sustaining *The Methodist* were in a minority on the question of the proper treatment of the so-called border Conferences.* In fact, it would not be extravagant to say that they were under the ban of the Church. All their movements were regarded with distrust. It was supposed that they had an ulterior object, for which the advocacy of lay delegation was a mere cover; sometimes it was said that their aim was purely personal, and that they wished to use the laity as a means of gaining power. To tell the truth, freedom of thought and of speech, even on matters not of the faith, was grudgingly allowed in those days. It is strange that the

---

* These were the Baltimore and Philadelphia, lying in both free and slave territory, and the Kentucky, West Virginia, and Missouri and Arkansas Conferences, lying wholly in slave territory.

founding of a newspaper, one of the commonest occurrences of American life, should bring upon its founders so
much detraction, but so it was.* It seems never to have
occurred to the ruling majority that men who were cut off
from such representation, through the organs of the Church,
as they deemed indispensable to themselves, had the right,
if they were strong enough, to provide means of representation of their own. The correspondence of Bishop Simpson
discloses some remarkable facts. Thus he writes to his wife
from Ohio, in 1863 :

"I find an overwhelming opposition to *The Methodist*.
They seem determined to have nothing to do with any
movement in which it is engaged. I scarcely know how
matters will turn." Dr. Eddy, then editor of the *Northwestern Christian Advocate*, writes to the bishop at nearly
the same time : "The fact is, bishop, lay representation has
a heavy load to carry in being in some sort placed under
the patronage of the once 'Ministers' and Laymen's Union,'
and the disloyal corps of *The Methodist*." Dr. Whedon partook of the prevailing distrust. In his *Review*, the same year,
he asks the question : "Is the founding and support of periodicals for private objects trenching on the territories of

---

* In my reply to Dr. Whedon, who attacked us with great severity on
this point, I said : "The press is *for* the people. It is their only effectual
check upon those who are selected as the depositaries of power. Through
it they give utterance to their wants, their grievances, and whatever else
concerns them. A system of government, civil or ecclesiastical, which
would permit only the expression of its own (that is, of official) opinion
would be a sheer despotism. In the normal development, therefore, of
the press, under the conditions of freedom, it will come at length to be
the organ of the people, by means of which they hold their rulers closely to their responsibilities, and keep alive in them a sense of their ac-
countableness to public opinion. Especially will it be likely to develop
in this direction under a hierarchical system, where the press is, originally, the property of the ministry, and where the people have an interest of their own to represent and promote."—*The Methodist*, Sept. 5,
1863, p. 276.

the periodicals of the Church, and infringing upon our legal system, loyal?" * These promoters of lay delegation were, like the ancient Christians, a sect everywhere spoken against.

In taking his position with us, Bishop Simpson showed uncommon courage. It was contrary to the traditions of the Church for a member of the episcopate to take a leading part in the discussion of debated questions. The bishops were expected to act as mediators between contending parties, and to maintain the existing system in its integrity. It was unusual, too, for a bishop to separate himself from his colleagues, and to stand alone in the advocacy of measures whose acceptance by the Church was a matter of doubt. His mind had undergone a great change since 1852, when, as chairman of a committee of the General Conference, he had reported against the expediency of lay delegation. From 1852 to 1860 he had been a careful observer of events. The liability of the General Conference to be swept by storms of passion alarmed him; he felt the necessity of some means of arresting precipitate action. No plan seemed to him so feasible as that of having the important measures of a Conference voted upon by two classes of delegates, the lay and the ministerial. For this purpose, I am inclined to believe he preferred a Conference composed of two houses. These were his convictions; but in his determination to take an active part in the discussion which must inevitably precede such an important change, he was greatly influenced by a few close personal friends. Among these, no one, perhaps, did more to decide him than the gentle but resolute Daniel L. Ross, of New York. Mr. Ross was one of the earliest friends of lay delegation, and also one of the trustees of *The Methodist.* Early in 1863 he wrote to the bishop as follows:

---

* It is but fair to say that we came very soon to a good understanding with Dr. Eddy, and that Dr. Whedon's objections to the managers of the lay movement were in time withdrawn.

"After reflecting a good deal on the subject, I cannot see what objection there can be in your taking a decided stand on the subject of lay delegation. We understand you to believe it to be for the interest of the Church, and if it is it ought to be advocated. On other subjects you would not hesitate for a moment, if it was convenient for you to attend a meeting. We need some distinguished name, and the desires of all the brethren point to you. It seems to me nothing can be lost, and very much gained by your casting your influence with the laymen. Besides, the more good and true men are found in the movement, the more it will go on to the interest of the Church. I know it is not Methodistical for a bishop to enter into a progressive movement, but it seems to me that we must carry on the thing bravely, or it will fail of success. Do give your consent to speak, unless you see grave objections, which, if you do, I must give up my opinions for yours."

And, again, in a letter before this : "Believing it (lay delegation) to be for the great good of the Church, I do think your name should be used, and your influence given, openly and ardently, for it. In a brief time it will succeed ; and I am sure you will stand first in the hearts of a hundred thousand laymen, which may go to balance some opposition you will of course meet."

These letters were written by Mr. Ross to Bishop Simpson while our first public meeting was preparing; I mean that held in the John Street Methodist Church, New York, March, 1863. The correspondence with Mr. Ross must have had some effect on the bishop's mind, for he accepted the invitation to address the laymen there assembled. His address shows that he felt the perilousness of his venture—and it was perilous for him—for he dwelt much upon the importance of preserving a pacific temper while meeting opposition. A happy illustration expressed what he wished to see. Closely connected with this was a well-deserved tribute to the fidelity of the laymen who had been engaged in promoting lay delegation since 1852 :

27

"I have admired the patience, the brotherly kindness, the watchfulness of the men who have been engaged in this movement, and whatever I may have felt, at any time, of doubtfulness with regard to the attachment of any advocating this change to the great interests of the Church, the very fact of their continued labor for the Church must have completely removed any such notion from my mind. And when I look abroad, I see the churches which, I think, are most deeply imbued with this spirit to-day among the most active in all the great operations of Methodism. Well, now, I desire to see this state of things continue, and I trust that it is the will of this assembly, of these brothers here, not to destroy a single element of Methodism, not to impair or to overthrow, but simply to strengthen, to perfect, to adorn. I live out in the West, where a city has grown up with almost magical rapidity. As I walk along the streets of that city, I sometimes notice a whole block undergoing a process of elevation. A little opening is made, a beam, a screw inserted; all along the foundation, and all around the buildings there are placed hundreds of these screws, which are made to turn in perfect harmony together, and to raise the edifice. Whole blocks of buildings are elevated, and, sirs, merchants are selling their goods all the time, the families are taking their meals and sleeping quietly in their homes all the time. There is no disturbance, and yet you pass along after a while, and the house has gone up one story higher, beautified, and made more capacious. So, that is what I want to see you laymen do. I want to see the whole edifice raised up without jostling or jarring one single arrangement. Let us live in the edifice, labor, pray, preach, watch, save souls; but at the same time I shall be very much pleased to see it enlarged, beautified, and made worthy of the age in which we live."

To this *The Methodist* promptly responded: "Nothing could be better timed than Bishop Simpson's counsel to the laymen to carry on their reform movement concurrently with a peaceful administration of all the interests of the Church. This, since 1852, they have done, and this we know they mean to do to the end. They will raise the edifice of Methodism a whole story higher, by giving it a new substruction, while the busy throngs that people it are plying their appointed tasks. The calmness, the patience with which the advocates of lay representation have pressed their reform upon the conscience of the Church are the best guarantee that they will labor in the same spirit till they reach the consummation of their hopes." *

The John Street meeting was, however, intended to be preliminary to another; it was a trial, if we may say so, of the temper of the Church. The result of the trial was favorable, and on the 1st of April, 1863, a call was issued for a convention to be held in St. Paul's Methodist Church, New York. The convention was accordingly held, May 13th and 14th, and was addressed, among others, by Bishop Simpson. His tone in this speech is more decided, and he avows in it his conviction that only the concession of lay representation will give peace to the Church. Some of its passages are of historic value:

" Now we look from this Church of ours into other churches. Take the Presbyterian Church. It has had its difficulties, but they have always been on points of doctrine. If we look at the Episcopal Church, it has had its difficulties, but they grew out of questions of church order —the high and low. But if we turn to our Church, the difficulties seem, whatever questions may arise, before they pass away, to touch the other question of lay and clerical influence. I ask myself: ' Why is this? Why should this peculiar difficulty recur, and repeatedly, in Methodism?' As thoughtful men we must meet it. To myself the solution is found here: Methodism was from its beginning, and is in its nature, the uprising and development of lay influence. What were the laity in the churches prior to Mr. Wesley's great movement in England? I speak of the English churches. What did they do? What part did they take? The minister conducted the services. There were no church officers in the sense of our modern church officers to exercise anything like spirit-

---

* *The Methodist*, March 21, 1863.

ual functions. Mr. Wesley's great movement called lay influence into exercise in the Church. Class-leaders were appointed, stewards were called into action, exhorters were licensed, local preachers were selected, and there came up out of the ranks of the Church a body of laymen to spread personal holiness through the Church. And what was the nature of the attack made on Methodism? It was attacked on this very ground —that it was profaning holy things; that it was calling laymen to the exercise of ecclesiastical functions—and if you read the records of those times, and the history of the contests of those times, you will find that Wesley and the early Methodists were charged with this special crime of intruding men into the sacred office who were unfit for the position, and of giving to laymen a part of the conduct of ecclesiastical affairs.

"Methodism not only did this, but it came to the people teaching every man to work. It called upon the men to pray; it called upon the women to speak; and long before the days when women's rights were talked about, Mr. Wesley had our mothers talking in the prayer-meetings and in the class-meetings, many of them becoming burning and shining lights in the Church. And, sir, I believe there is many a man among us who owes much of what he is to the fact that his mother had learned to talk in the Methodist Church. Methodism is, in its essential action, an uprising of the popular element. Wesley selected many of his preachers from laymen. He called them to go and preach the unsearchable riches of Christ. He gathered those preachers around him, and he counselled with them in reference to carrying on his great work. So much for the usages of the Church.

"The first contest of Methodism, then, was to secure to the people this position—this working position in the Church. Then again, sir, it came with a charm to the people in another way, and that was in its doctrines. It was a contest with exclusiveness in religious opinions. It set forth the universality of the atonement—the mode in which every man might become a child of God by faith in Christ Jesus. But such a system, producing a working people, giving them the consciousness of their position, necessarily leads men on further. And where you place a barrier, and say, 'Thus far, but no farther,' there may be expected to be some restiveness at that point; and Methodist people taught to work, to pray, to sing, to exhort, to lead class, to preach, very naturally argue, 'Why should we not also have something to do in planning in the great arrangements of the Church?' Is it a natural feeling? and will it not gush out from the very constitution of the Church? And can it be otherwise than that there should be an almost perpetual friction?

"Sir, I believe from the depths of my heart that we never shall have permanent quiet, I believe that there will always be periods of agitation and threatened schism, until the laity are admitted into the highest assemblies of our Church. But when they are placed where the Church has its directing centre, I think that the whole friction will be done away. Our wise men and our good men, ministers and laymen, will sit down together, with delightful harmony in all departments of the Church, and I think, sir, we shall be free from friction for all time to come. This, sir, is one of the strong reasons influencing my mind. I want peace for my children. Is it said, 'Why then do we meet here if we want the Church to be quiet?' I answer, it is best for us to move when there is a time of quiet. If we do not move while we have time and while there is peace, there may come up some vexed question before we are aware of it, some excitement may arise, and we may have the scenes of '28 and '43 re-enacted among us. We have no security for the permanent peace of our Church but in the introduction of the lay element; and I believe that will give us peace.

"There is another reason why I favor lay representation that may seem a little novel at first to you. It is this—I favor lay representation because I am opposed to conventions. It has been said that conventions are dangerous. I admit their danger. There is danger in all irregular action. There are sometimes words uttered and there may be acts performed that are not in harmony precisely with the spirit of our institutions. But how are they to be prevented. May I ask these my brethren, and through them friends who possibly may hear, has it occurred to you there never has been a call, so far as I know, for a convention of the people of the Protestant Episcopal Church? I have never heard of a call for a convention of Baptist laymen in this country. I have never heard of the calling of a convention of Presbyterian laymen in this country; I have never heard of the calling of a convention of laymen in any Church that I know of in the United States except in the Methodist Church. But we have had our conventions—we have had them from the beginning of the century every now and then. Conventions in the days of radicalism, conventions in the days of 'Scottism' (I use the expression simply as expressive), conventions of anti-slavery men, conventions of this and that form. Why is it? Simply, as I understand it, because there is no other way in which the laymen can give expression to their views. [Applause.] Why is it that other Protestant churches have not had these conventions? They have laymen associated in council with the ministry, and they can express their views so that there is no need of their going outside to do so, and they do not go outside. But when an excitement arises and a question comes up in our Church, either the laymen must keep silence or they must go outside to discuss it. So long as the present order of things continues we are perpetuating conventions in the Church. And instead of being opposed to conventions, by opposing lay delegation, I think I destroy the necessity of conventions altogether by saying to the laymen, 'Come inside and counsel with us, and let us act together and not separately.' [Applause.]

"I have another reason for lay representation. I am opposed to all innovations of any magnitude in our Church economy. And yet I know that this very movement is termed the greatest of innovations. But, sir, what is there that can give us greater security than the introduction of the lay element? Is there any organized government that is safe with a single legislative body, composed of a single order of men of the same employments, and chosen in the same way? What means this almost universal conviction of our race as to government, of the propriety of what may be termed an upper and a lower house, of a house of commons and a house of peers? What means this disposition to have separate bodies—a House of Representatives and Senate? Is it not that they wish to examine matters from different points of view? Men elected at different periods, men elected from wider districts and having different interests, come together; they see subjects in different aspects and throw new light upon them. Now the wisdom of such combination is shown in the fact that all governments prosper better with two elements. I care not what the form may be. Ministers necessarily, as a body of men, are moved by a common impulse. Looking at things as we do from one point, we are liable to sudden excitements, moving us just as other classes of men are moved. We seem to require that there should be some other element in some way to come in and give us the kind of stability that mankind look for in a perfect legislative body. Bring in the lay element —it is composed of men no wiser and no better than ministers, but they are trained to look at subjects in a different light. They are business men, and when missionary or educational or financial questions come up, as they must in our great bodies, they will help us to look at them from all points of view. And while as ministers we are more competent to discuss theological questions than our brethren in the laity (shame on us if we were not when we give our time and hearts to these subjects and claim a divine call), they are far more competent than we to discuss financial and business questions. In my own business I consult these lay brethren rather than rely on my own judgment. As a minister of the Church of Christ, I want, in great financial measures, to go to my lay brethren; I want to ask them what they think upon these great subjects and great plans. I want them side by side with the ministry, and I would defer to their judgment in business as they defer to mine in theology. [Applause.]

"Now, brethren, in bringing this second element into the Church—and especially if, as was suggested in the Episcopal Address, at the last General Conference, or if, as is done in the Protestant Episcopal Church in our own country, on all questions of moment the vote of the ministry is taken separately, and the vote of the laity separately, and there must be a concurrent majority to pass any measure, what will be the effect? Here are the ministers who compose the General Conference. No measure can be passed through unless they vote for it. Here are the laity whom you introduce into the General Conference. No measure can be passed there unless they vote for it. Now in a moment of sudden excitement my ministerial brethren might go for a measure which my lay brethren might not approve, and my lay brethren might be in favor of a measure which my ministerial brethren would disapprove; but if I could find a majority of both my ministerial and lay brethren in favor of the same measure, I think I should feel that that measure would be more likely to be right than if either laymen or ministers alone had adopted it.

"Take the General Conference, composed, as it must be, of so many ministers. Whatever they are opposed to being done now they could forever prevent being done. In the General Conference nothing could be done without the consent of the same body of men who now make the laws. Will any point of our economy be in danger? It never can be touched but by a vote of the ministry; but in addition to that the ministry might want to change something, and a majority of the laymen might be unwilling to consent to it. The result would be that the laity might lock the ministry, and the ministry might lock the laity, and the Church be kept more permanently just where it is. It might be opposed to progress, but it would certainly be opposed to innovation. I want to leave this Church in its great outlines to my children as my parents left it to me. I look with deep interest to this very element of lay representation in our General Conference to guard against possible changes in the future.

"Such are my feelings on this subject. I look at this question in the light of expediency. I am not disposed to discuss, brethren, the question of right at all. If this Convention would bear suggestions from me, I would say in my career through life I have noticed that the bitterest contest comes up when you undertake to talk about being deprived of rights or about making demands. I doubt whether it is wisdom for you to come up to me and say in strong language, 'You shall do so and so, you are withholding from me my rights.' There is something in my nature—whether it ought to be there or not is another question—that says you ought not to talk so, and I will not hear you; but if you come up to me and reason with me as to the effect of my conduct, I will be disposed to listen, and you will be very likely to bring me to your views.

Hence I would say to my brethren, be cautious in expressing yourselves on this subject; whatever may be abstract principle or abstract right, the great question with us all is what can we do to promote the efficiency of the Church of the Lord Jesus Christ? ['Amen' and applause.] That is the simple question.

"Had I my brethren of the ministry here to-day, as I have taken the liberty to counsel you on the one hand, I would counsel them on the other. I would say to them, Why intimate that there is any danger to arise from introducing the laity into the general council of the Church? Why is it? Is it because the laity have not wisdom enough to plan general measures? That cannot be. Is it because the laity do not love the Church? We were all laymen once. I know I loved the Church just as dearly before she set me apart for her ministry as I ever have since, and I believe our lay brethren love the Church. Is it said that our itinerancy is in danger or anything else in danger from them? Why so? How have they learned their attachment to Methodism? It was through the influence of Gospel teachings. What a commentary will it be upon our labors, if, after one hundred years of toil in this country, we have not been able to gather a laity together who love the economy of our Church! It seems to me it would be a reproach upon our labors to say so.

"The laymen have been taught and indoctrinated by us; they have imbibed our spirit, and if they do not love the Church, pray, who ever will? Must it be that a Church shall be afraid of its members? Sir, I am not afraid of the members of the Church. [Applause.] I should feel that my fathers, my brethren, and myself had been doing but a poor work if we had not a Church around us in whose judgment and whose piety we could trust. But is it said there is no distrust of them? Why not let them sit by our side? Hide it as we will, cover it over with specious words as we may, there is at the bottom of this, though not confessed to the heart, the feeling that there is danger in trusting the people. Is that to be forever so? Does Christianity rest on such a feeble foundation that you cannot trust Christian people with its institutions? Is Methodism afraid to trust the people? Are the people too ignorant to comprehend the value of its system? or is the system so defective that we fear the people would change it? If it is unsafe to trust the people with the system, either the people or the system must be in fault. So monarchs thought that people could not be trusted; but the great idea of the age is, in civil government, the people, educated, intelligent, and trained, ought to have power in their hands. In the state there may be a question sometimes whether the inebriate, the wicked, the vicious, and the degraded ought to have power. That might seem to be a possible question; but when you stand side by side with your brethren, and say, 'These are the sons of God by faith in Christ, these are men who have hearts united to God by living faith, these are men who are washed and purified by the blood of Christ, these are seals to our ministry,' are they not men who can be trusted with all the institutions of our Church? Now I would say to my brethren in the ministry, if I had their ear, Why stand in such an attitude that the people feel that you distrust them? What is the consequence?

"If I understand human nature, it is this: if a man distrusts me, or if I fancy he distrusts me, that man loses just so far his influence over me; if he distrusts me, he cannot take me to his heart so fully as if I felt he considered me to be true, and that I would not betray a trust. If the laity of the Church feel from any cause that the ministry cannot fully confide in them; if they think that the ministry look upon them as a body of men who would overturn the foundations of the Church, who would sweep away the old landmarks, whose sympathies are not with the Church, does not this beget mutual distrust? Do not ministers and people become alienated? Do not these manifestations of distrust prevent the full power of our Church from being exercised on the world? I think when the whole ministry shall feel as the Maine Conference felt and acted, there will be a great change. A year ago the Maine Conference voted upon the question of lay delegation. Thirty were for, and forty-nine against, lay representation. At the recent Conference which I attended, a committee was appointed upon this subject. Professor Vail, of the Biblical School at Concord, was chairman of the committee. He brought in a report, which many of you have read, taking the ground that the membership ought to be urged to come in, and share with us in our labors and responsibilities. I expected to see a division in the Conference, and a debate. The report was read, a number of brethren said 'Amen' in different parts of the house, the matter was put to a vote, a large number of hands were uplifted, and when I called for the contrary vote there was not a single hand raised. [Applause.] You could not say that Conference did not do its part. The General Conference simply say, 'You may come in.' That Conference went further, and said, '*Brethren, you must come in and help us.*' I speak of that simply to show what is moving in the mind of the Church.

"I must say, Mr. President, one other thing to these brethren—don't be in a hurry. God moves slowly in his providences. Great changes require time. Be in no hurry, do your duty, work earnestly, stand firmly, bear obloquy if necessary, don't be afraid of censure. The man who is in the right can bear censure for a time; the future will vindicate him, but even if there is no vindication in this world, all is clear light on high.

If your motives are impugned, it is only for a few days at most; all will be clear by and by, and the great Head of the Church will know what was the motive that influenced men to take whatever course they did. If it was any selfish motive, his curse will rest upon them; if it was simply to promote his glory, the one smile from Jehovah's countenance in eternity will more than repay for all the censure heaped upon them. Then stand firmly, but be patient.

"And yet, for myself, I would say that if the matter could be carried speedily I should rejoice. How speedily it can be carried, I do not know. I have heard my brethren say, it is a question of time; it will come some time, but it is not best just now. I sometimes say, If it must come, why not now? Why have all the agitation which must attend delay? If it is a change that must come, why not make it when we can arrange it most calmly? If it must come, why not make the time now, and bring it near. It seems to me it is wisdom to do so. Yet, this very point is an encouragement to you to wait. If it must come, you can afford to wait."

I do not know whether Bishop Simpson really expected that the antagonism to lay delegation would be either without force or free from angry expression. His kindliness of heart did disarm much antagonism, but he himself became the object of attack as well as the rest of us. The opponents found an organ in the *Christian Advocate*, then, as now, the chief representative of the Church. Its amiable editor, Doctor, afterwards Bishop, Edward Thomson, was completely helpless in the hands of the men by whom he was surrounded. A correspondent of that paper, who signed himself "Timothy," distinguished himself for scurrility. Dr. Whedon, in the July *Quarterly Review*, made an assault on the movement as an effort to wrest from the itinerant the honors, a title to which he had earned by toil and sacrifice. He represented such an itinerant as saying, "I did once hope that by faithfulness and perseverance and patience under penniless toil I might purchase a good degree, and even one day take a seat with my honored brethren in the General Conference. But, alas! that honor is now claimed by Judge Such-a-one, or Ex-Senator Such-a-one, or Governor Such-a-one. My unpaid labors have at last made the place honorable, and they are now ready to snatch its honors. One would think that they had routes to dignity and emolument enough without running me off the track. I wish that folks who so adore the itinerancy had a particle or two of sympathy for the itinerant. But I, poor fellow, am to be crowded out." " Yes, dear brother," answers the editor of the *Review*, "your chance is slim; for these metropolitans are millionaire and you are all sixpenny." Throughout the long years from 1861 to 1872, the *argumentum ad invidiam*—the appeal to odium—was plied to the utmost, but it failed, as it deserved to fail.

Enough, however, of all this, and perhaps the reader will be ready to say, more than enough. The picture of the Church as it was in 1863 would not be complete were these facts suppressed. Old prejudices were shocked; old traditions were threatened; the distribution of powers in the Church was to be changed; the ministers, honest to the core, and persuaded that the settlement of 1828 was both scriptural and final, were amazed to hear it questioned by brother ministers. The itinerancy had, in many minds, taken the rank of a divine institution, and the saying, as old as Bishop Asbury, that itinerancy and lay delegation are incompatible with each other, was repeated with as much confidence as if it were one of the verities of Christ's gospel. Even the candid personal confession which Bishop Simpson made in his St. Paul's address did not quiet the fears nor check the harangues of the alarmists.

"Allow me a word or two personally. I had thought upon this subject for years; I had looked over it until my mind was satisfied, and I expressed it to my most intimate friends that lay representation was the greatest want of the Church. As you know, I went abroad a few years ago, and was taken ill. I doubted whether I should get home. I reached my home, however, and lay sick for a length of time, on a bed from which my friends thought I would never rise. I looked over the Church. I determined, God helping me, if I had strength enough before the dying moment came, to issue an address to the Church on this question of lay representation. I went so far as to prepare the outlines of it, designing to have it filled up while I had sufficient strength. God was pleased in his mercy to spare me a little longer to my family. I was raised again from my bed of sickness. I laid the matter aside, waiting until in the providence of God there should be occasion for it, and I said no more. I crossed the Rocky Mountains last summer, after having had a very sudden and severe attack, which my friends feared would terminate my usefulness and active labor. I found myself in travelling exposed to danger and disease, and I knew not whether I should return or not. While on that Pacific coast, I resolved to send back to the church papers of our denomination the declaration that I believed that lay representation was needed for the benefit of our Church. [Applause.]

"I did it, sir, for the purpose of putting myself on the record, and if I had aught of influence among my friends, to say to them, if I never should have a chance of speaking to them personally again, 'If you wish for the unity, the prosperity, and the perpetuity of our Church, admit lay representation.' Well, sir, I am here among you, spared, in the providence of God, to labor a little longer, with health in which I am able to do something more for the Church, whether it shall please the Church to keep me where I am or to use me in any other way. In my youth, I gave myself to that Church in a covenant never to be forgotten. God helping me, I shall live for that Church, and tell it what I think best for it, according to the light given to me, as long as God lets me live. ['Amen.']

> "'For her my tears shall fall,
> For her my prayers ascend,
> To her my cares and toils be given,
> Till toils and cares shall end.'"

"And I can say more, that as sure as God reigns in heaven, and we are faithful to our charge, God will give us a gloriously increasing heritage. We have the doctrines, the usages, and the general economy; and all we want is more unity, more efficiency, and more power to take hold, shoulder to shoulder, and accomplish the great work we have on hand."

This confession, the fruit of much meditation and of his conferences with the lay delegation leaders, was a committal to the cause of the minority, which he never shrank from repeating whenever an occasion called for its repetition.

Here is not the place for a history of the lay movement. It is enough to say that the resolutions of the St. Paul's convention contained a call for another convention to meet simultaneously with the General Conference of 1864. This was a daring step for the time; its purpose, however, of bringing the laymen and the General Conference face to face, was accomplished. The personal hostility to Bishop Simpson for his connection with us culminated at this Conference, and then broke, never to rally again. Threats had been made to bring him to judgment for his advocacy of a revolutionary measure, but the leader of the assault found, when the General Conference assembled, that he was barely able to take care of himself. Franklin Rand, of Boston, always upright and downright, wrote to the bishop, May 31, 1864: "I was at the laymen's convention; sorry I had no opportunity of seeing you. Indeed, I was almost afraid that my intimacy with lay representationists would compromise you with some of the opposing brethren. The question has the elements of a mighty agitation, if such an alternative should ever become inevitable." After 1864 the efforts of the bishop in behalf of lay representation were less conspicuous.

He was still a most active friend, but other men came forward to help with pen and voice; his own attention was largely occupied with the centenary of American Methodism; the calls for his war speech alone absorbed all the time and strength he could spare from the routine duty of the episcopate. The subject was now fairly before the Church. The *Western Christian Advocate*, under the charge of Dr. John M. Reid, and the *North-Western*, under Dr. Thomas M. Eddy, and the *Zion's Herald*, under Gilbert Haven, were speaking strong words for the laity, and were moulding the opinions of their constituents. Dr. Abel Stevens discussed the subject with his characteristic energy and brilliance. But the burden of planning, arranging, carrying forward, and bearing the brunt of the opposition fell to the supporters of *The Methodist*. With scarce an exception all the documents issued by the laymen were prepared in its office. On the eve of the taking of the popular vote, two hundred and fifty thousand tracts were issued by its publishers, and were eagerly called for by the seekers for information. The circle of laymen of which *The Methodist* was the centre sent out Dr. James Strong and Mr. Charles W. Bond as secretaries. These two gentlemen occupied the field for three successive years. Between 1868 and 1872 the Church turned over; the minority grew into a majority; the judicious men, who meant to take no personal risks, came to the winning side. In the Conference of 1872 the lay delegates quietly took their seats beside their clerical brethren; the wounded itinerancy uttered no groans, and the heavens did not fall.

XIX.

THE YEARS OF PEACE.

1865–1881.

Peace Restored. — Reunion of the Northern and Southern Methodist Churches.—Visit of Bishops Janes and Simpson to the Southern Bishops.—A Friendly Meeting.—At what Point shall the Restoration of Fraternity Begin?—Demand that the Church South shall be Recognized as Legitimate. — A Deputation to the Southern General Conference of 1874.—Speeches of our Fraternal Delegates. — Fraternal Messengers from the South to our General Conference of 1876.—Doctor Lovick Pierce Unable to Attend in Person.—His Address Read.—Its Beauty and Christian Spirit.—Appointment of a Commission to Settle Pending Questions.—These Questions Difficult.—Order of Secretary Stanton, in 1864, in Relation to Southern Methodist Churches.—The Order Modified.—Its Operation.—The Case of McKendree Chapel.— Some Good Results of the Order.—General Fisk's Pacific Policy.— "Disintegration and Absorption."—Terms of Settlement Unanimously Agreed to by the Joint Commission.—Anxiety of Bishop Simpson for the Success of Lay Delegation.—His Letters on that Subject.—Letters to his Family Abroad.—Trip to Mexico in 1874 and to Europe in 1875. —Preaching through an Interpreter.—The Yale Lectures on Preaching. —Starts for Japan and China in 1880, but is Taken Sick at San Francisco.—The Methodist Œcumenical Conference, London, 1881.—The Garfield Memorial Meeting in Exeter Hall. — Wonderful Effect of Bishop Simpson's Address.

XIX.

Never was peace more welcome to any people than to the loyal Americans of the United States in the year of grace 1865. What they had undertaken to do was now completely done. Rebellion had been suppressed, the national authority had been vindicated, the Confederate armies had surrendered, and the paroled Southern soldiers had gone to their homes. There was no reason to fear that the war would linger on in aimless efforts to maintain a lost cause. It was not forgotten in that hour of thankfulness that they with whom we had fought were our brethren—of the same nation—and many of them of churches holding the same creeds. To reunite the churches of the North and the South was the first thought in the minds of Northern Christians. Slavery had torn them apart from their Southern brethren, and, slavery now gone, why should they not all come together again? Among Northern Methodists this desire for reunion was peculiarly strong. Only twenty years had passed since the Church had been cut in twain, and many of the men who had been conspicuous in the General Conference of 1844 were still alive. The *Methodist*, immediately upon the cessation of the war, took the ground that a reunion of the Northern and Southern churches would be the readiest mode of settling all disputed questions, and the best assurance they could give of the future repose of the country. Our bishops were of the same opinion, and in April, 1869, appointed two of their number — Janes and Simpson — to visit the bishops of the Southern Church at their meeting in St.

28

Louis. They had for authority the appointment, by our General Conference in 1868, of a commission empowered to treat with a like commission of any other Methodist body that might desire to unite with us. Of this commission our bishops were members. They had, also, as early as 1865, published a declaration, saying, "The great cause which had led to the separation from us of both the Wesleyan Methodists and the Methodist Episcopal Church, South, has passed away, and we trust that the day is not far distant when there shall be but one organization, which shall embrace the whole Methodist family of the United States." The letter of our Episcopal board borne by their colleagues notes the fact that the Methodists led the way in the separation of the churches, and should lead in restoring their unity. "It is fitting," say the bishops, "that the Methodist Church, which began the disunion, should not be the last to achieve the reunion. And it would be a reproach to the chief pastors of the separated bodies if they waited until their flocks prompted them to the union, which both the law of comity and religion invoke, and which the providence of God seems to render inevitable at no distant day." Our two fraternal messengers were received with all courtesy by the heads of Southern Methodism. Janes was well known to most of them, having been elected by the last undivided General Conference. Once more they prayed together, which was a good beginning. The Southern bishops—very properly, as we think—put forward the point that restored fraternal relations should begin where the effort on their part had been left in 1848.

To understand this request, it is necessary to remind the reader that at our General Conference of 1848 we declared the Plan of Separation null and void, and had declined to receive the fraternal messenger of the Southern Church, Dr. Lovick Pierce. The annulling of the Plan of Separation made the Southern Methodist Church, in our estimation, a seceded body, and, so far, an illegitimate family of Meth-

Eng.d by H.B.Hall's Sons, New York.

odists. It was claimed by the Southern bishops that as we had rejected their offer of fraternity, it could be only renewed by us. In regard to the mode of separation of the two bodies, they reminded our messengers—Janes and Simpson—that they had separated from us in no sense in which we had not separated from them: "The separation was by compact and mutual, and nearer approaches to each other can be conducted, with a hope of a successful issue, only on this basis." *

Here, then, on the very threshold of the negotiations, was a bar to further progress which only right Christian feeling and good sense could remove. It was effectually removed. Without tarrying to argue with the Southern Church the question whether slavery was or was not the cause of the division, Bishops Janes and Harris visited the Southern Methodist General Conference, which met in Memphis in May, 1870. By this time it had become clear to our leaders that immediate reunion of the two churches was impossible. In a very admirable address to the Southern delegates, Bishop Janes said, "My understanding is that the commission was deputed to bear a message, not to negotiate. I judge that it was expected by the General Conference that if information was wanted by the General Conference of the Church, South, as to the views of the Church that we represent, the commission could afford it. I don't think that any of us anticipate that a perfect organic union can be effected at once. It cannot be done without prayer and without magnanimity and concessions on both sides. The history of the past twenty-five years would not justify us in entertaining such expectations. But I do believe that the prayer of Christ will be heard, and that the time will come when his people shall be one. Anything to hasten that end should be done. I am not willing to lead this General Conference to any action not fully justified by the action of

---

* See "Formal Fraternity," p. 11.

the Conference which I represent.   It would do injustice to my feelings did I not express the fact that it affords me great pleasure to look on the countenances of so many whom I knew many years ago.   Thank God for his preserving kindness to you all."

Most admirably said.   Never did the sweet spirit of Bishop Janes shine out more beautifully than on this occasion. In saying "nothing can be done without magnanimity and concessions on both sides," he struck the right thought.   In the persons of its representatives—Janes, Simpson, and Harris—our Church appeared in its proper character as a peacemaker, ready to heal the wounds which war had made.   In further explaining the objects of the commission, of which he was one, Bishop Janes also said: "Perhaps we have transcended our bounds in coming at the present time, and not waiting to be first approached on this subject.   But we did not think so highly of ourselves as to suppose that all these churches should first knock for admission.   We judged it proper to inform them of the appointment of the commission, and that it would give us pleasure to meet them."

The result of these two timely visits was the passage of a resolution by the Southern General Conference expressing a sincere desire that the day might soon come when fraternal relations between Northern and Southern Methodism should be permanently established.   It remained now for our own General Conference to make the offer for the re-establishment of fraternity.   Let us thank God that our beloved Church had the magnanimity to yield this concession.   It sent a deputation to the Southern General Conference, meeting in Louisville, May, 1874, bearing the Christian greetings of Northern Methodism.   After the soreness which we felt when we discovered, in 1848, that in agreeing to the Plan of Separation we had been out-manœuvred, outwitted, and, as we said then, duped; after repealing the Plan as null and void; after having declared for nearly thirty years that Southern Methodism was a secession, and not legitimately derived from the parent stock; after having fought out, as Methodist citizens, by thousands and ten thousands, in the national armies, the one issue which had divided both Church and State, we asked for a restored fraternity with the brethren from whom we had long been severed.* We sought, in point of fact, that the formal peace of the country might become a true peace, and that Christian love might begin to flow once more in its accustomed channels. No brighter chapter in our ecclesiastical history than this has been written; no brighter chapter than this can be written.

Our fraternal delegates, Dr. Albert S. Hunt, Dr. Charles H. Fowler, and General Clinton B. Fisk, were well chosen. Had any one said upon their departure to fulfil their mission, "How beautiful upon the mountains are the feet of him that bringeth good tidings, that publisheth peace," he could not have been accused of extravagance. Dr. Fowler said very aptly: "The speeches we make this day may not be very great nor very weighty, but I hope they are worth something. There are a church and fifteen hundred thousand believers back of them, and peace and good-will in them. In receiving us you receive not us, but them that sent us." General Fisk told the Conference that a friend had offered to give him a full account of the events of 1844, especially of the Plan of Separation, and he had replied that he preferred to consider the wonderful plan of redemption. Dr. Hunt most cordially saluted, in the presence of the Conference, the now venerable Dr. Lovick Pierce, who had borne, without result, a fraternal message to our General Conference of 1848. Times had changed, and men had changed

---

* The Plan of Separation had been passed on the assurance of Southern delegates that it would be used only as a last resort, if they found on returning home that their people would no longer remain in Church fellowship with the North. It was charged that, instead of waiting, they began at once, in the city of New York, making preparations for separating from us.

in them; it was proper for Dr. Hunt to say in 1874, "I bless God that he has spared you until this morning."

The way was now clear before both churches for the establishment of a lasting peace. On our side we claimed that our presence in the Southern States was an unchangeable fact, a fact which we would not alter if we could. On the Southern side it was claimed that their legitimacy as a Methodist body must be recognized. Fraternal messengers to our General Conference were appointed; and a commission was created to meet a similar commission from us to settle all pending disputes.

The appointed messengers came to us at Baltimore in 1876; and in their number was Dr. Lovick Pierce. But the weight of ninety years was too much for him; after starting upon his journey, he was compelled to desist and to let his colleagues go on without him. He had served two generations in the Christian ministry, and had the spirit to begin service with a third had that been possible. His address was, however, read to the Conference by its secretary. There are in this address beautiful passages, which should be long preserved. He called the visit of Bishops Janes and Simpson to St. Louis, in 1869, "a star of hope rising above the gloomy horizon." The address speaks thus of the appointment of Messrs. Hunt, Fowler, and Fisk: "The action of your General Conference in Brooklyn we regarded as the official recognition of the Methodist Episcopal Church, South, as a legitimate organization of the Methodist Episcopal Church, as provided for in 1844. Here began our official intercourse. These brethren came to us in love. We received them with loving hearts. They did their work nobly and well. That General Conference determined to send to you, at this meeting, a like delegation, and, by the blessing of God, we are here. How we may do our work will be for you to say. We will never be outdone by you as far as Christian comity and effort are involved. Neither can we, in this good work, ever come in ahead of you. Your delegates were sent to us without plenary powers in regard to the pending issues. So, likewise, have we come to you. On both sides it seems that we, in our humble spheres, have been sent, like John the Baptist, to prepare the way of the Lord." Of the matters in dispute between the churches, he remarked, very wisely: "They are delicate, sensitive things—never to be settled by chafing speeches, but, as we believe, can be speedily prayed and talked to death by a joint board of discreet brethren intent upon Christian peace."

These "delicate, sensitive things" form a part of the history of the period. They date back to the years of the war, and to the occupation of the South by both Northern and Southern armies. In Virginia many of our congregations had seceded to the Southern Methodists; in East Tennessee many congregations under jurisdiction of Southern Methodism had come over to the Northern Church. In the part of Virginia occupied by us up to 1861, loyal pastors had been dispossessed; in East Tennessee the pastors were, in the main, Southern in sympathy, and upon the occupation of the country by us retired with the Southern forces.

Still further, as our armies penetrated the slave states, many churches were abandoned and left wholly untenanted; in still others disloyal ministers remained as rallying-points of disloyal opinion. Secretary Stanton, therefore, at the instance of Bishop Ames, issued an order, November 30, 1863, placing at his disposal "all houses of worship belonging to the Methodist Episcopal Church, South, in which a loyal preacher appointed by a loyal bishop does not now officiate." Considering that it is the usual fate of churches within the field of the operations of hostile armies to be turned to account as hospitals, storehouses, and what not, and considering, too, that the use of abandoned churches by loyal ministers might be, and was, in many ways useful to the national cause, the order was well enough. It must be borne in mind that we were in the midst of war, and that its issue was still uncertain. To encourage the expression of loyalty in the partially conquered states, and to repress disloyalty, were the obvious duties of both civilians and soldiers. But the order was extreme in its terms and worked injustice. Mr. Lincoln, who, to use his own phrase, had declined "to run the churches," was greatly dissatisfied with this measure of his war secretary. He wrote to Mr. Stanton, February 11, 1864, saying that he was embarrassed by having had brought to him what purported to be a formal order of the War Department for the delivery of these churches to the Northern Methodist bishops.* This remonstrance had its effect. On February 13 the secretary of war modified his order so as to limit its application to states designated by the president as being still in rebellion.

Bishop Simpson's part in the application of Secretary Stanton's order was, as far as I have been able to see, limited to Tennessee. Here, for instance, in Nashville, the McKendree church, which the army was using for its own purposes, was put in order for the occupancy of the Rev. M. J. Cramer as a loyal pastor. He visited this, to him, new field of labor in January, 1864, and here met, in Nashville, for the first time, General Grant. He wrote to his wife: "We had an interview with General Grant. He is not very communicative, but I have no doubt is both an able general and a talented man. I purpose to spend next Sabbath here, and then to visit Chattanooga. It is doubtful if I can reach Knoxville, as the river has fallen." Later in the month he writes: "I had an interview with General Johnson this morning. He is true Union; but all these Southern people have a deep prejudice against the North. To-morrow morning I have agreed to preach in the hall of the House of Representatives. But my congregation will be small. The citizens care nothing about us, except to dislike us."

---

* "Life of Abraham Lincoln," by Nicolay and Hay, in *Century Magazine*, August, 1889, p. 566.

As to the bishop's appointee—the Rev. M. J. Cramer—he was in the midst of "a sea of troubles." The McKendree Chapel had been dismantled when the army took possession of it; the seats were gone, carpets had disappeared—in fact, the entire interior had to be reconstructed. All this was to be done by the quartermaster of the forces in Nashville. Mr. Cramer thus writes to Bishop Simpson: "I have just now received an order from General Grant to have McKendree Chapel refitted for worship. I shall immediately proceed to the chief quartermaster to have the order executed as soon as possible." Several weeks later he writes: "The order of General Grant to the Quartermaster's Department to repair McKendree Chapel and the German church is at last in progress of execution. The carpenters are at work to make new seats, and to do the other necessary repairs. The master-carpenter told me that the audience-room of the chapel will be ready for occupancy in two weeks. The walls need either to be repapered or frescoed; the latter would be preferable, for I desire to make the church as attractive as possible. . . . I have no doubt we shall have large congregations when it is known to be ready for occupancy, for many temporary sojourners here desire to attend a Methodist Church." Still later, after more delays: "I have had to superintend the repairing and do a great deal of the work myself, especially in refurnishing the church. I had trouble in finding the whereabouts of the furniture, and, when found, the keeper thereof refused to deliver it, but I procured an order from the post commander. The walls are newly papered; new seats put in, painted, and grained; the ceiling whitened—in short, the church is entirely repaired and thoroughly renovated. On June 12th it was opened for divine service."

Our occupancy of this church was strongly resisted by the Methodists of Nashville. But worse results than opposition followed in various parts of the South. Some of our Northern Methodist ministers, holding Southern Methodist pulpits, conceived the idea that their occupancy gave them title to the churches which were, for the time being, in their hands. They were led to this opinion the more readily because our General Conference had rejected, in 1848, the Plan of Separation by which church property had been divided between the North and the South. When reminded that the Plan of Separation had been pronounced valid by the Supreme Court of the United States, they would shake their heads and answer: "That was in pro-slavery times, and was done by a pro-slavery bench of judges." True to the letter, but law is law, and legal decisions can be traversed only by established legal methods. All lands and buildings in the South which in 1844 were the property of the undivided Methodist Episcopal Church were no longer ours, as little as we relished the decision of the Supreme Court.

In numerous cases our temporary use of these places of worship as centres of loyalty was of great advantage to the nation. An excellent instance of this is given by a report of the Rev. Dr. Newman to Bishop Ames. His field of labor was New Orleans, and he thus writes in October, 1864: "When the president of the United States appointed August 4th as a day of national humiliation and prayer for the success of our arms, I at once determined to have the day properly observed. I was, however, repeatedly assured by leading citizens that any such attempt would be futile, as such days are never kept by the people of New Orleans. Believing the time had come when social reforms should commence, I immediately applied to the editors of our leading papers to prepare a strong leader on the importance of all good citizens suspending business and giving themselves to reflection on the grandeur and responsibility of the events through which we are passing; and, calling upon the mayor, I was assured that a proclamation would be issued worthy of the occasion. Subsequently, at a meeting of all the loyal clergy, it was resolved to hold divine service in each of the churches in the morning, and to have Union prayer-meetings in the afternoon and evening at two central points. The day dawned in unclouded beauty, and a cool breeze from the Gulf tempered the heat of an August sun. To our delight, the secular press not only suggested the propriety of a general suspension of business, but exhorted the people to attend church; the proclamations of the mayor and governor were not merely formal documents, but were simple, earnest, and devout. At ten A. M. the Union merchants commenced to close their stores, their secession neighbors soon followed, and by eleven o'clock every store of any importance was closed; all the banks, all the civil and military offices were shut, and the press suspended for the day, so that the public were without a paper the next morning. In the evening the mayor presided at one of the Union meetings, and I commenced my remarks by congratulating him on the general and respectful observance of the day."

It would have been better if at the close of the war we had surrendered the churches occupied by us more promptly. When General Fisk was appointed Commissioner of Refugees, Freedmen, and Abandoned Lands, he greatly aided the cause of peace by his friendliness to the Southern Methodist leaders, and by doing all that lay in his power to secure to the Southern Church the restoration of its property. The large powers intrusted to him were used in establishing relations of confidence between the national government and the people of Tennessee. In performing this service the chiefs of Southern Methodism co-operated heartily with him.

Another cause of irritation which the Southern bishops had noticed was the cry that the destiny of Southern Methodism was to " be disintegrated and absorbed by the Northern Church." This cry left out of account the lesson of history, that to no institutions do men cling more tenaciously than to their churches. To disintegrate churches has, except in a few rare cases, been beyond the power even of conquerors. The scheme was a favorite one with the editor of the *Christian Advocate* of New York, the Rev. Dr. Curry;* he reasoned that the members of a once disloyal Church could never become loyal again. But he made no account of the softening influence of time, and of the fact of experience that community of interest does in the end create community of feeling. What the future may have in store for us, no one of us knows; but of one thing we may be confident, that we have done wisely thus far in following the things that make for peace.

With all these events fresh in their minds, the commissioners of the two churches met at Cape May, New Jersey, August, 1876. A basis of fraternity framed partly in the terms suggested by Dr. Lovick Pierce was determined upon; rules for settling conflicting claims to church property were laid down; and contestants were advised to amicably compose their differences, irrespective of strict legal title, and to settle the same according to Christian

---

* Some passages from the *Christian Advocate* will show its reasoning on this subject. On February 22, 1866, the editor says: "The Church of the South, not less than the State, was built upon and fashioned to the institution of slavery; and as with the State, so with the Church, the removal of slavery necessitates a disintegration and reconstruction. This general remark applies more fully to Southern Methodism than to any other Southern ecclesiastical system, on account of its denominational unity and common pastorate." The offer of lay delegation to the laity by the first Southern General Conference held after the war seemed to Dr. Curry to foretoken a dissolution of the Southern Church. On April 25, 1867, he says: "We doubt whether the [Southern] laity are prepared to accept this degenerate bastard Methodism at the hands of their ministers. Let us be ready to give them that which they will require—the Methodism of the fathers of the first century of our history, in spirit and form, as it ever has been. With this we may not only maintain our place in the South, but certainly disintegrate the rival body, and absorb whatever of it shall be found worth preserving." Dr. Curry was sincere in all this, but the results of history show that he was mistaken in his judgment of the course of events. Nor do I think that his opinion was generally entertained by our Church.

principles.* May the future historian of Methodism be able to write: "Then had the churches rest and were edified; and walking in the fear of the Lord, and in the comfort of the Holy Spirit, were multiplied."

The bishop's letters to his wife during this period give us the best impression we can now have of his multifarious activity. To-day he is here, to-morrow gone, and in a week he is a thousand miles or more from the first point. In 1866–67 he goes to the South and to Havana, in company with his eldest son, who is in failing health. While on this journey he receives all possible courtesies from our government. We quote from his letters to his wife and his friends, mostly brief passages: "Conference is nearly over. It will close to-morrow, and I have seen not the slightest cause for alarm. General Sheridan told me to-day that he had sent a staff-officer several times to ride near the church, and to see that all was quiet.

"How I wish you were here with me, that we might talk together, and say so much more than it is possible to write! Pen and ink are indeed a great convenience and comfort to distant friends in aiding correspondence, but how fast the moments would fly could we only sit down by our quiet study-room fire and talk over the events of the past and the prospects of the future!"

Bishop Janes to Bishop Simpson:

"New York.

"Your lectures are great successes. I am glad. Your success is my success. You cannot very well rise without lifting me too. The episcopacy is a unit. Getting possession of churches by military authority has a great deal of odium attached to it, especially since the close of the war."

The following order from the War Department was intended to secure for him a protection during a tour through the Southern States.

---

* The names of the commissioners were: For the Northern Church, M. DeC. Crawford, J. P. Newman, E. L. Fancher, C. B. Fisk, E. Q. Fuller; for the South, E. H. Myers, T. M. Finney, R. K. Hargrove, D. Clopton, R. B. Vance. The final action was unanimous.

"Washington, D. C., Nov. 24, 1866.

"To Commanders of Military Departments and all Officers and Persons in the Military Service of the United States:

"The Reverend Matthew Simpson, bishop of the Methodist Episcopal Church, having occasion, in company with his son, to make a journey through the Southern States, it is the desire of this department that they receive assistance, courtesy, and protection from all commanders of military departments and posts through which they may pass or in which they may sojourn. Edwin M. Stanton, Secretary of War."

Bishop Simpson to Mrs. Simpson:

"Philadelphia, Oct. 28, 1867.

"And now, having given you the gossip, I naturally look up to see your sparkling eye, and to hear you ask, 'And what did he say then?' 'And what did you say?' But I see no eyes, I hear no voice.

"Well, well! the world is a scene of toil and care; we must work while it is called to-day at whatever our hands find to do. There is a land where there is no sickness, no anxiety, no pain, no separation. May we be ready for that bright land."

Bishop Simpson to Bishop Ames:

"Philadelphia, May 29, 1869.

"I have returned and speak again upon the subject in Pittsburgh, for which I expect to be taken to task by ―――― as a partisan bishop; but as he has all the bishops on hand at present, possibly he may think I am too small game. I feel an intense interest in the subject growing out of the attitude of the Church South. If we are to have a union with other Methodist bodies, it can only be on the basis of admitting the lay element, as they all have it. But if we are not to have it, then all along our border, as well as through the South, we must stand face to face with the Church South, which, when the slavery question is settled, will have no point of difference with us excepting this lay element, and I fear they can so use this question as to greatly retard our progress."

The vote given on lay delegation by the people was so overwhelming in its favor that the ministers could not honorably do otherwise than concur. The General Conference of 1868 had pledged the ministry to concurrence. On the probable result of the ministerial vote, Bishop Simpson, during the autumn of 1869 and the spring of 1870, expressed great anxiety. The attitude of the four surviving bishops towards the measure can be described in a few words. Bishop Simpson was heartily committed to it; Bishop Ames was fearful of its effect upon the stability of the episcopate; Bishop Janes, though not favoring lay delegation on its merits, was extremely solicitous that the pledge of the ministry should be redeemed by the casting of the necessary three-fourths vote in the Annual Conferences; Bishop Scott was in opinion opposed, but was passive. Bishop Janes thus describes his position in a letter to Bishop Ames from Lynchburg, Va.: "Since I saw Bishop Simpson I think I can trust you on the lay delegation question. He understands that you have made up your mind to give your influence in favor of it. I am very glad to hear it. Though, *per se*, I am not in favor of it, from the present state of the question I am very anxious it should carry. I think I see very severe conflicts before us if it does not carry. But the point of painful anxiety with me is the '*keeping faith with the people.*' I do feel that the Methodist ministry will be dishonored before the world if we fail to keep our declarations to them on this subject good. On this point my feelings are very anxious. But enough till I see you."

Yes, our honor as ministers was involved. And this fact Bishop Janes put before the members of Conferences in such clear light (yet always in private interviews) that they felt the call of honor to be imperative, and obeyed it. They thus added another to their many claims upon the gratitude of their people. Before this date Bishop Simpson had written to his wife from Indianapolis: "Indiana and Northwestern Indiana Conferences have gone so badly on lay delegation as almost to destroy hopes of success." Early in 1870 he informs Mrs. Simpson that he may go to Germany, and advises her to get ready to accompany him. The vote on lay delegation, he thinks, will be very close, and the help of the Conference in Germany may be necessary. His letters written while holding his Spring Conferences show the fluctuation of his feelings:

Springfield, Mass., April 20, 1870: "Lay delegation will be so close that it is impossible to say how it will go. I have both hope and fear." Augusta, Me., May 4, 1870: "Arrived safely last evening. Matters look squally here for lay delegation. The opposition is strong, active, and determined. I will let you know the probabilities early." Augusta, Me., May 5, 1870: "Matters look very badly here—we shall be beaten, and I think that lay delegation is probably lost. My heart is sore and sad. I fear I shall be almost as nervous as you are. May God direct us." May 7, 1870: "So I think we shall have a majority in this country that will give a good start for Germany, and may discourage the opposition. Still, on Germany it will turn."

It is due to the *Methodist* company to say that we were not so apprehensive of defeat as Bishop Simpson was. We were confident that the ministers would keep faith. It was our determination, however, even if we did fail, to begin again, and that without appeals to passion. Our conviction of the thorough integrity of the ministry was too strong to be shaken by any untoward event. In his next letter Bishop Simpson writes more cheerfully. He is still at Augusta, Maine: "I am satisfied we are past danger on the lay delegation question. We were in great peril here, and everything was against us for two or three days, and looked very dark. We may not, however, get a sufficient majority to make us safe without my visiting Germany. With this there can be no question."

After finishing his Conferences in the spring, of 1870 he started for Europe, taking with him Mrs. Simpson and his daughters. A daughter and son-in-law were then living in Antwerp. In August he returned home alone. His letters to his family during this absence are among the most interesting of his entire correspondence. A few are here added. The first is written on the way to New York:

"Steamer *Scotia*, Aug. 21, 1870.

"This is a wonderful trip. I have wished a thousand times that you could have been with me to enjoy it. From the time you left us until now we have seen or felt nothing of storm or roughness on the sea. Not only have there been no racks upon the tables, but there has been scarcely a perceptible roll of the vessel. Occasionally there has been some swell of the sea, and a gentle heaving up and down, but I do not believe you would have missed a single meal. Our tables have been crowded all the time, though I have learned that a few ladies complained of sickness.

"I scarcely allow myself to think of the long dreary days that must pass before you return. But I will try to do the best I can to employ myself profitably, if God gives me health and strength. I pray that you may have a happy and profitable sojourn abroad, and be for time to come healthier and happier among your loved ones on your return.

"The captain read prayers and a sermon to-day, not inviting any minister, though four Catholic bishops and three Presbyterian ministers were on board. This Episcopal exclusiveness is abominable. The more I see of it, the more thoroughly I detest it. I hope it will not be many years until the Church of England shall be disestablished, and all denominations shall be on equal footing. But we must patiently wait for the 'good time coming.'"

"Elmira, N. Y., Aug. 28, 1870.

"How glad I am, after the labor of the Sabbath, to have, even across the ocean, a little chat with you. How strange it seems that only two weeks have passed since I kissed you good-bye on the steamer, and then saw you gradually receding as you went back into the harbor, until I could no longer discern features or form, or see even the waving of the white handkerchief. And yet here I am in Central New York, with the work of an Annual Conference almost over. Should no unforeseen delay occur, we will close to-morrow evening, and I hope to leave on Tuesday morning for Indiana, calling by Erie on the way.

"To-day I preached in the Opera-House. Twenty-five hundred people were in the room, by count, and the halls, vestibules, etc., were crowded down to the street, and many hundreds were unable to get admittance. My theme was, 'Prophetic pictures of Christ.' The people were very attentive, and there was much feeling, but the sermon was quite slipshod. After preaching I ordained eleven deacons.

"With all I have written, and with all that the Church knows of my labors, I am receiving constant applications both for lectures and dedications. The dedications are all *critical* cases—would not ask me, only for *extreme* necessity, etc. I have declined all engagements, however. Now I have spun out a pretty long letter. The family have come home

29

from church, and I must close. How I wish you were here, or I were with you! But so it cannot be, and we must as cheerfully as possible abide our time. As to going over this fall, I cannot see my way clear. I could not go until the meeting of the Missionary Board and the Bishop's Meeting, to fix our places in November. And I would be compelled to return in February. It is a very stormy month, and you would not wish to cross then, so I could not be of service to you, and as I have been twice on the ocean in storms that month, I dislike the thought of being out again. So it seems, at least, at present."

"Bloomington, Ind., Sept. 4, 1870.

"Three weeks ago I bade you good-bye, and how long it seems! I have crossed the ocean, been at home, at Elmira, and now here in Indiana, almost at the close of my second Conference. How much labor can be crowded into a few days. It seems almost as if God was giving us power to condense thought and action. And yet we pay for all this in the wear and tear of muscle and of brain.

"To-day I preached to an immense concourse of people in the court-house yard. I did not want to do it, and had declined unless it was a very favorable day. It however turned out to be so, and special trains came both from New Albany and Greencastle; about four hundred it was said came in the New Albany train. This afternoon Dr. Merrill, of the *Western Christian Advocate*, preached in the same place. I did not receive any injury, as I was quite careful.

"It is a bright moonlight night—it is pleasant to think you may have seen at an earlier hour the moon which now looks down on me. It has passed from you a few hours since. How I wish it were a carrier-pigeon, to have in its wings some message for me. But that moon is only the reflection of a brighter sun now hidden from view, and that an emanation from the eternal fountain of uncreated light and joy. How delightful to be assured that we are remembered at the great centre of the universe, that our names are recorded there, and that a heart of infinite compassion is 'touched with the feeling of our infirmities.' Yes, not with the feeling of our thoughts of beauty, or our grand resolves, or noble purposes, or unutterable joys—but 'of our infirmities.' Are mine known in heaven? Does the creator of all worlds, the eternal Word—the Lord of light and glory—share them with me? What a glorious revelation has God given us, that tinges with a border of glory even the dark shadows of earth. If the shadow be so brilliant, what will the substance be?

"But I hear you say, enough of this moralizing—leave the sermons for the pulpit and the press; letters ought to be personal, lively, chatty, full of tender thoughts and life pictures of the hour. Well, so be it—and yet time and eternity will have a point of contact, and all around us hang the curtains of the invisible. How near the border none can tell. I can almost hear the sweet chant to-night, 'I am nearer my Father's house than I've ever been before.'

"But they are coming from church; the footfalls sound on the board walks which serve here for pavements; the crickets sound in the house; the alternation of murmur and of silence tells of the hour of rest, and away in the distance I hear the sound of lively song in the church in the strain, 'Oh, how I love Jesus!' That sweet sound of music faintly heard in the distance is like an echo from a far-off camp-meeting, and tells of earnest Christian hearts. But then, again—there is my pen running back again to a half-homily, when it ought to be a colloquy. But, as Bishop Morris used to say about his appointments, 'What is writ will stay writ.' There goes another strain in the distance, 'Oh, bear me away on your snowy wings!' What an odd thing that Bishop Morris's song should come just as I had his name on paper!"

The interest of the people in his preaching is greater than ever, and he is compelled to speak out-of-doors Sunday after Sunday. There is no public building within reach large enough to hold the eager congregations. He writes to Mrs. Simpson from Lebanon, Ill., September 18, 1870: "Last night I read the appointments here, as we had finished Conference business, and to-day preached to an immense congregation on the college green. For three Sabbaths I have been compelled to preach out-of-doors, as the crowd is so great as to be utterly unmanageable otherwise. The weather has been very fine, only so warm as to be considerably oppressive."

"Warsaw, N. Y., Oct. 9, 1870.

"At last, this evening, I have got away from company to my room, to talk a little while with you. For two days I have been exceedingly busy, and to-day have not had a moment to myself since preaching. I was obliged to talk in a tent and to those around it (for the curtains were up) to the number of about four thousand persons. The sermon was only moderate. I am glad that this is my last Conference. I am getting very tired. Other duties will gather about me, but I will be free from Conference anxiety. Everybody seems kind and loving. How thankful ought we to be for friends. One old man I never saw before gave me two *nice apples* from his pocket yesterday.   It was a token of his love, simple as it was.

"I listened to-day to a good sermon from Dr. Wentworth, on sacrificing for Christ.   I fear I have not done enough of it.   My service has all been repaid a hundredfold.   It is no reproach, no pain, now to work for Christ. Occasionally my head aches, and my heart has its strange sensations that tell me some day it will be weary and stop; but these I would have anywhere.   They are not borne for Christ's sake.   What are my crosses? What am I doing to show the world my love for Christ—a love that costs me something.   I think I am willing to do all that my strength will permit—but if I were not a minister, would I not have to labor as much for my daily bread?   How I abound and am at ease while my Master suffered!   I fear that none of us are thankful enough."

Here is a pretty glimpse of home:

"Philadelphia, Oct. 14, 1870.

"Have got safely home, and how I wish you were here!   It will not be home without you.   But we must do the best we can, and hope for the best.   By and by fall and winter will pass away, and sweet spring will come again—sweeter for your return.   By the way, Mrs. Stiles said she knew I was coming last evening, by the way the birds acted.   She said the evening before I came the canary had been unusually lively, and yesterday not only was the canary lively, but the mocking-bird, that had been mute, began to whistle and sing.   That was a pretty welcome, was it not?"

"Philadelphia, Nov. 27, 1870.

"Again it is Sunday afternoon—to me it has been for the first time for weeks and months a day of rest.   I had no service to-day.

"We are like children playing 'make believe.'   We are trying to 'make believe' that we get along right pleasantly without you.   But it is terribly hard work to play at it successfully.   We catch ourselves being lonely in spite of ourselves, and saying, 'Wonder where is ma,' and yet the time of return is so far ahead that we dare not begin to count. I had a letter from ———— last Monday, but the week has passed without one from you.   Possibly it may come to-morrow."

"Cheraw, S. C., Dec. 18, 1870.

"Dear me!   how times have changed since I was young.   I never crossed the mountains but once till I was over forty years of age, and here my children, in their *teens*, are rambling over Europe.   Well, well!   times change, and we change with them."

To his daughter:

"Pittsburgh, Pa., Feb. 12, 1871.

"I am thankful that God has enabled me to give you all a visit to Europe, and that your feet have been in the garden of Gethsemane and on the Mount of Olives; that you have looked into the cave at Bethlehem; seen the lofty pyramids; walked among the ruins of the Parthenon at Athens, and tasted the honey of Hymattus. And then you have seen the choice scenery of Europe, and visited so long in the British Isles. Has it occurred to you that you have been longer in the Old World than I have been by nearly four months?"

To Mrs. Simpson:

"Philadelphia, Pa., Feb. 17, 1871.

"I saw in Monongahela City, the other day, the small house in which you and I commenced housekeeping. It is the same little building, but it looks smaller, as larger houses are around it. How many memories of the past came clustering round me as I looked upon this scene of our earlier labors and love, and how short seems the interval between those days and these! But years have intervened—years of sunlight and of shade—years of great joy and of deep sorrow. I am older. I would fain hope that I am wiser and better, but how little we learn, as we should learn, of life's great mission and of life's great duties!"

"Stamford, Conn., Feb. 19, 1871.

"Drs. ———, ———, and ——— are down pretty severely on the bishops for their part in ——— ———'s trial, and are going to elect us every four years, and curb our power generally. I rather enjoy the hackling, as this time my colleagues share it with me. For myself they may elect me *out*, just as soon as they please. I have no care on the subject, but I fancy they will change their tune at next General Conference."

"Alexandria, Va., Feb. 26, 1871.

"And now, I hope you are still in good health, and enjoying all the pleasures of the trip. In those old homes of art and culture, the past bends over you, teaching its lessons, and human life seems to be almost insignificant in the great march of the centuries. The individual is almost lost in the nation. Then, too, in those vast cathedrals how small does man seem!—the majestic, the strong, and the vast encircle him, and he feels dwarfed in the presence of giant forces. Yet, with all this, how sweet are the words of our Saviour, 'The hairs of your head are all numbered!'

"I have tried to fancy where you may be this last Sabbath of February, and I have thought it possible that you might be in Dresden."

"Steubenville, O., March 19, 1871.

"Sunday night finds me again at the table to chat awhile with you. Oh, were you here, how much more delightful it would be to talk face to face, than this slow way of talking by pen and paper! I tried to preach to-day on 'Glorying in the Cross;' a very large assembly, and I trust some good was done. Bishop Clark is wholly unable to preach, and is a failing man. How thankful ought I to be that with my heavy labor, and such draughts on my time and strength, through the blessing of God, I am kept in fair health!

"Wherever you are my heart travels with you. Few minutes of the day are you absent from my thoughts, and I try to invoke Heaven's rich blessings upon you. I trust God will have you in his holy keeping, and preserve you from all accidents and dangers; and when the time comes for you to return, that he may give you a safe and comfortable passage over the waves. If it pleases him to allow us as a family to meet again —all of us in health and happiness—how devoutly thankful ought we to be! We have been separated and scattered long and far; others have fallen and many have suffered, yet thus far his hand has been over us for good. May it so continue for our dear Saviour's sake."

"Morristown, N. J., March 26, 1871.

"Time is growing shorter, and I feel more and more the value of eternity. Often I wish I had no cares, no business, no lectures, and had only to preach the gospel, the glorious gospel! But I must address myself to work as it comes to hand, and hope for more leisure by and by."

"Peekskill, N. Y., April 9, 1871.

"It is a bright, beautiful day—Easter-day. I ought to be glad in the day in which Christ rose triumphantly from the tomb, conquering death and hell. And yet my heart is sad. Bishop Clark lies dying in an adjoining room. He may live till to-morrow, but it is quite doubtful. He was too weak to leave home, but so much had been said in the papers about superannuated bishops that he was determined to work. I was deputed to be with him, and attended the Pittsburgh and New England Conferences, and then came here. Here he opened the Conference, and presided near an hour on Thursday morning. Since that he has been confined chiefly to his room. How strange that the three bishops last elected should all die, and away from home!

"To-day I tried to preach to a very crowded house from 'Charity never faileth.' I trust some good was done, as a divine influence seemed to rest on the congregation. The weather is very warm for the season, and the hot air of the house made me feel the fatigue.

" God's will ought to be everything to us; to work with *him* our constant aim. If we only could know just what would please him, how often it would relieve us from perplexity! And yet we are not always willing to yield our desires, and we do not always ask, ' Is this just what God likes?' It seems to me that if we lived up to this point, we should know more of the will of God. The nearer we come to this standard the happier we shall be.

" Now that you are all together once more, even if you are on the other side of the sea, it seems more as if you were home than when travelling so far apart. I trust that you are happy together, and if you are at Antwerp, how glad I would be if I could look in and see you all!

" How strange is memory!—above all, the memories of affection! They do not die. Loved ones across the sea—loved ones across the great sea of the invisible—seem to come near. Back yonder, in Greencastle—in that small house—I can see our little boy climbing on my knee. How plainly I see him now, as I write with the tears falling from my eyes!—his round, rosy cheek; his soft voice; and then—and then—that forehead, so smooth and cold, that we kissed before we laid him away! And how often I think of him, too! Often and often that last hour with him is so vivid, when I lie down at night. And my mother, and your mother and father, and our little daughter. How the circle widens! How many friends we have in that upper sanctuary! But sweetest and best of all, Jesus loves us, and calls us his *own*. How near heaven earth sometimes seems!"

Some one has wittily said that there are three stages in Methodist Episcopal life. In the first the bishop enjoys the novelty of fresh scenes, and travels with a sense of pleasure; in the second, he wearies of so much unrest and change; in the third, he travels because he cannot keep still. Be this as it may, Bishop Simpson, as he advanced in years, much as he loved the quiet of his home, was as ready as in his prime to take long tours abroad. He considered himself bound to obey every call of the Church he possibly could, and never to shrink from any duty. In 1874 he made a trip to Mexico, by way of New Orleans and Havana, for the purpose of inspecting our newly established missions there. The overthrow of the political power of the Roman Catholic Church in that republic had been followed by an inflow of Protestant missionaries from the United States. Our own undertakings in Mexico were growing in importance, and called for episcopal supervision. In 1875 he visited our missions in Italy, sailing from Philadelphia, and going by way of London, Antwerp, and Paris to his destination. "The last Saturday evening in June," he writes in his narrative, "I arrived in the city of Florence, where I spent the Sabbath. I had some difficulty in finding the place where the Methodist service was held, as it was not opened in the morning. In the evening I had the pleasure of hearing a sermon from one of our Italian preachers, and of meeting the superintendent, Dr. Vernon."

At last he reaches Rome, and has the full realization of another of the dreams of his life. Early in 1854 he was as near the Eternal City as Naples, but was prostrated by sickness, and had in his mind's eye a Conference in Arkansas, beckoning to him to hasten homeward. I doubt if he tarried long over the antiquities of Rome, for he writes: "The next day after my arrival I spent in examining the general interests connected with the Protestant churches in the city, visiting the headquarters of the Wesleyans, of the Free Church, and of the Waldenses." It was, however, the feast-day of St. Peter and St. Paul. "I had the opportunity of visiting St. Peter's Church, and of observing the peculiarities of worship at Rome. Multitudes were kissing the great toe of a brass statue, said to be that of St. Peter, but believed to be the statue of one of the old Roman gods." From Rome he proceeds to Milan, stays there two days with the assembled missionaries, and then is off to Germany.

In Germany he meets the Conference of German Methodist ministers. What strikes us as surprising is the number of persons who come to hear him preach in a tongue not their own. He writes again: "On Sabbath a large Turner's hall was offered for divine worship, where I preached through an interpreter to between two and three thousand people." From Germany he moves on (one is tempted to say rushes on) to Denmark. He jots down only a fact or two: "I reached Veile in the afternoon, and preached in the evening, in our hall rented for public worship, to a crowded congregation, Brother Scon acting as interpreter." He now crosses the Channel to Gottenburg, in Sweden; reaches Christiania, the capital of Norway; meets the assembled missionaries, and once more preaches through an interpreter "to a large concourse of people." Still on to Stockholm and to the island of Gottland, where he meets the sixty Swedish preachers. Again he records: "On Sabbath I dedicated the new chapel building, the crowd being so great as to fill the yard and the adjacent street as well as the church. I preached through Brother W. as interpreter. I have seldom seen a people more earnest and more deeply devotional than the congregation at this place." From Gottland he turns his face towards Copenhagen, where he is the guest of the Rev. Dr. M. J. Cramer, then our American minister to Denmark. Now homeward bound, he tarries for a short space of time at the meeting-place of the British Wesleyan Conference at Sheffield. "Under the blessing of Providence," he says in his itinerary, "I had a safe return home in the month of October, in time to participate in the fall meetings of the various charitable organizations."

In the winter of 1878–79 the Yale Lectures on Preaching were delivered. They made a deep impression on those who heard them, as will be perceived from the press notices of that date. They were delivered to full audiences, which increased in numbers to the end. The lectures were, however, read, and in reading he was not at his best. But the exhibition in them, always modest, of his own personality, gives them a beauty peculiarly their own. In 1881 a Congregational minister wrote to him: "I was talking, not long ago, to a brother-minister, in his eighty-second year, and we both expressed a wish that we were just beginning our ministry, with the light you had shed, showing us our path. I thank God for your work, and I pray that all our young ministers may follow, in all respects, the directions you were guided to give."

All during 1880 he was interested in the preparations for the Œcumenical Methodist Conference, to be held in London, September, 1881. Full as ever of hopefulness and courage, he started early this year for Japan and China. He was nearing threescore and ten, but I doubt if this fact was taken into account by him for a single moment. Our missionaries in those fields were counting much on the pleasure they would have in showing him their work; they had found out in our foreign stations that he was a sympathetic supervisor. Our chief magistrate, Mr. Hayes, wrote a letter commending him to the courtesies of our national representatives abroad. The secretary of the navy, Mr. R. W. Thompson, directed the admiral of our Asiatic squadron to give him transportation in the Chinese and Japanese waters. I do not think that there was the slightest political significance in this exhibition of personal interest. It was a spontaneous expression on the part of the president and his secretary of their sense of the value of the bishop's services to the country. It was their assurance that they regarded him as one of the first of American citizens, to whom something was due for his unselfish devotion to the national welfare. Never did a journey open under better auspices, but all its hopes were dashed by the illness of Mrs. Simpson in California, and not long after by the illness of the bishop himself. In truth, he was nearing the end, and these reminders of failing strength, I doubt not, were understood, but, as far as appears, seemed to have the effect to make him more solicitous "to finish his course with joy."

In September, 1881, the Conference of Methodists assembled in London. All the bodies of the common family name were well represented by delegates. Bishop Simpson preached a thoughtful opening sermon; it is one of the few discourses which he read from manuscript to his audience.* He also delivered, while in England at this time, addresses

---

* This sermon will be found in the volume published since his death.

and sermons which were full of his old power. But no one of his speeches so deeply stirred the people of England as that spoken in Exeter Hall to an assembly of Americans and Englishmen met to pay suitable honors to the memory of the President of the United States, General J. A. Garfield. All through the sessions of the Œcumenical Conference the Americans present were subjected to the alternations of hope and despair, as they received day by day from home the news of the wounded president's condition. On Sept. 24th a meeting, chiefly of Americans, but largely made up of Englishmen, was held in Exeter Hall, under the presidency of James Russell Lowell, minister of the United States. About three thousand persons were present.*

Mr. Lowell, in opening the meeting, said in part: "The object of this meeting, as you all know, is to testify our respect for the character and services of the late President Garfield, and in so doing to offer such consolation as is possible to a noble mother and a noble wife, suffering as few women have been called upon to suffer. It may seem a paradox, but the only alleviation of such grief is a sense of the greatness and costliness of the sacrifice that gave birth to it, and this sense is brought home to us by the measure in which others appreciate our loss. It is no exaggeration to say that the recent profoundly touching spectacle of womanly devotedness, in its simplicity, its constancy, and its dignity, has moved the heart of mankind in a manner without any precedent in living memory. But to Americans everywhere it comes home with a pang of mingled sorrow, pride, and unspeakable domestic tenderness that none but ourselves can feel. This pang is made more poignant by exile; and yet you will all agree with me in feeling that the universal sympathy expressed here by all classes and conditions of men has made us sensible, as never before, that, if we are in a

---

* These extracts from the addresses delivered at this meeting are taken from the memorial volume published in London.

strange, we are not in a foreign land, and that if we are not at home we are at least in what Hawthorne so aptly called 'The Old Home.' On an occasion like this, when we are met together that we may give vent to a common feeling so deep and so earnest as to thrust aside every consideration of self, the wish of us all must be that what is said here should be simple, strong, and manly as the character of the illustrious magistrate so untimely snatched from us in the very seed-time of noble purpose that would have sprung up in service as noble; that we should be as tender and true as she has shown herself to be, in whose bereavement we reverently claim to share as children of the blessed country that gave birth to him and to her."

Bishop Simpson's address on this occasion *was* "simple, strong, and manly," and did rise to "the lofty level" of a self-forgetting sympathy, which sought only to comfort the sorrowing and to express the sense of bereavement which all Americans felt. "They all joined," he said, "in thought and sympathy, the funeral procession which was then wending its way from the capital of their nation, over plain and mountain, through country and city, to the former home of the late president, on the banks of Lake Erie. Wherever that procession moved thousands of heads were bowed in tears. They likewise bowed their heads and dropped tears of sympathy as they thought of the illustrious citizen who had been taken from the land of his birth and his glory. The ocean is between us and our home, but the American, in sympathy and in thought, is never far from home. He may love the land in which he sojourns, he may be delighted with the voices and the sights around him, but, after all, he turns back to the land of his birth—to his home—and his sympathies gather round the fireside there.

"There is good reason to-day why we should participate in the general sorrow which afflicts our people. A great citizen has been cut down in the strength of his manhood and of his matured intellectual power. He has

THE GARFIELD MEMORIAL MEETING AT EXETER HALL, LONDON.

been smitten without provocation, and seemingly without motive.

"I take no exception to the habits or customs of other lands; it would neither be fair nor generous to do so, but I do feel that in our land a poor young man has opportunities which no other under heaven can afford him. President Garfield rose from a boyhood of poverty to a life of culture, and did not stop until he was placed at the head of a great nation. When he falls it is not America alone that mourns. Kings and princes gather round his bier, and the queen of the greatest empire in the world drops a tear of sympathy with his widow, and lays a wreath upon his tomb. God bless Queen Victoria for her womanly sympathy and her queenly courtesy." (The whole meeting at this point rose spontaneously and responded to the sentiment of the speaker by giving three prolonged cheers.)

"But it is not only a lesson that young men may rise that I read in the life of General Garfield. I read a lesson also as to the steps by which permanent fame can be gained. Our lamented president was no demagogue. As a young man he did not aim at a political life, he sought no popularity. He aimed to make himself a man, to cultivate the intelligence which God had given him, and for this purpose, working with his hands, he found his way to college, and spent years in close study. From college he turned to teaching the youth of his native land, and sought to impart to them the knowledge which he had gained. His associates perceived his power and placed him in office, and you have heard how both in war and peace he showed himself worthy of their confidence.

"It has seemed to me that in inflicting upon us this suffering, God has been teaching the nations of the earth the strength of our republic. As you are aware, this is the fourth time a president has given way to a vice-president under peculiar circumstances. Two of those presidents died of disease; Lincoln and Garfield fell by the assassin's hand.

Nevertheless, amidst these trying circumstances, there has never been a single voice raised against the succession which the Constitution of the United States prescribes.

"The death of President Garfield is a loss to every one of us, and yet, somehow, I have faith that it will be a gain to the world. 'The blood of the martyrs,' as it has been said, 'is the seed of the Church.' And I believe that is true in politics as well as in religion. General Garfield crowned his virtues as a soldier and a statesman with the virtues of a true Christian life. After his nomination as president, he was the same plain man that he was before — with the same manly bearing, and the same regularity of attendance at the church of his own people. He made himself the centre of his household. He was the pride of his mother — he was her darling boy, and, perhaps, some of you may remember that when the news reached her that some one had shot him, she cried, forgetting all about his presidency, 'Who could be so cruel and so wicked as to kill my baby?' He was her all in all. It is strange how an all-absorbing feeling will sometimes reflect itself in our surroundings. I passed to-day the monuments of Wellington and Nelson, and it seemed to me the heads of those heroes were bowed in grief. As I passed Westminster Abbey, also, it seemed to me that the holy dead of past ages looked down with a greater solemnity, and were waiting to be joined in that upper circle by the hero of the Western land."

Here were cheers at a memorial service, yet they did not seem to those who were there incongruous. Tears flowed freely while the bishop was speaking. All hearts were melted. As if moved by a sudden impulse, the audience sat down as quickly as it had risen up. The bishop waited quietly, and then went on as before in the same tender strain. This was one of the last flashes—as far as I know, the last flash—of his peculiar electric power.

XX.

LAST DAYS.

1882–1884.

Serious Nature of the Attack of Illness at San Francisco.—The Bishop's
Hopeful Spirit.—Solicitude of his Family and Friends.—His Last Ser-
mon in Boston, in the Winter of 1884.—Giving Way of his Strength.
—General Conference Meets in May, 1884, near his Home.—Opens the
Conference.—Unable to Preside more than Once.—Occasional Visits to
the Conference Sessions.—Closes the Conference with an Address.—A
Rallying of his Strength, Followed by Relapse.—Last Words.—Death,
June 18, 1884.

XX.

The attack of illness with which Bishop Simpson had
been seized while in San Francisco, during the autumn of
1880, meant more than I think he was willing to confess.
On that occasion he was, for the first time in his life, unable
to go on with his sermon. It was on a Sunday morning in
September. He had taken for his text the forty-fourth verse
of the second chapter of Daniel: "And in the days of these
kings shall the God of heaven set up a kingdom, which
shall never be destroyed; and the kingdom shall not be left
to other people, but it shall break in pieces and consume all
these kingdoms, and it shall stand forever." His exposition
had been completed, and he was about to enter upon the
discussion of his theme, when he suddenly stopped and
placed a handkerchief to his lips. His face became white,
and he said, after a pause of a few moments, "I am not sure
I shall be able to finish this sermon." He soon became very
ill, and grasped the pulpit for support with both hands. He
explained to the congregation that he had suffered from
pain in the night, but thought that once started he would
warm to his work and get on. Requesting them to sing a
verse or two, he waited, but only grew worse. During the
singing a physician came to him, felt his pulse, warned him
that he was threatened with a congestive chill, and directed
his removal to a place of rest.

Of a hopeful temper, he could not be persuaded that this
was the beginning of the end. He always found, if that
were possible, the bright side of every event; he had been
ill before, and had recovered—why might he not recover
30

fully again? In peril and disaster he had always committed himself to the care of Providence, and had given himself up, without anxiety, to the keeping of his Father. Years before he had told the congregation, which he had reached belated in the woods of Oregon, that while threatened with shipwreck on the Pacific he had thought with comfort of the lines of Henry Kirk White:

> "Once on the raging seas I rode;
>> The storm was loud, the night was dark,
> The ocean yawned, and rudely blowed
>> The wind that tossed my foundering bark.
> Deep horror then my vitals froze—
>> Death-struck, I ceased the tide to stem:
> When suddenly a star arose—
>> It was the Star of Bethlehem."

This cheerful confidence was the habit of his mind; and so he went on, during the year 1881, doing the splendid service in England which has already been described. Friends were watching him, however, with an increasing solicitude. He travelled less alone than he had before. After his return from England he still continued in his usual routine of official duty, holding Annual Conferences, and answering, too liberally, the calls of the churches for his services. His last sermon, delivered at the dedication of the People's Church in Boston, in the latter part of the winter of 1884, was full of his old-time power. The text was from Isaiah ix. 6: "For unto us a child is born, unto us a son is given; and the government shall be upon his shoulder: and his name shall be called Wonderful, Counsellor, The mighty God, The everlasting Father, The Prince of Peace." As he spoke of the sureness of the coming of a reign of peace, he exclaimed, "I think I see the light shining now on the hill-top. Christ's kingdom is coming, and the song shall arise, 'Hallelujah! the Lord God omnipotent reigneth!'"

Surely hope sprang eternal in this man's breast. But the trip to Boston and the exertion of preaching were followed by a reaction. Shortly before the meeting of the General Conference of 1884, at Philadelphia, the bishop's strength wholly gave way. The uneasiness of all who loved him— that is, of the whole Church—was much increased. Greater than the fear that he would not be able to attend the Conference, which would sit so near his own house-door, was the fear felt by his friends that his iron will would bring him to its sessions, and that this effort would result in a fatal relapse. However, as before, his determination and hopefulness enabled him to rally; although feeble, he presided at the opening session. But he could take little part in the proceedings; an occasional appearance in the hall of assembly, which was always the signal for an outburst of applause, was the only sign he could give of his interest in the debates.

He was also able to take part in the consecration of the bishops elected by this Conference, and, to the joy of all and the surprise of many, he made the closing speech at the end of the session, Friday evening, May 28th. I think he was conscious that this might be his last public address, and he put into its simple, touching words all the kindliness of feeling he cherished for his brethren. He said: "Brethren of the General Conference, at this closing moment it is fitting I should give utterance only to a very few words. I wish to express my regret that I have not been permitted to mingle more intimately with members of this body during their session in this place. But I have been very much gratified with such association as I have been permitted to enjoy, and I desire to express the pleasure I have felt in witnessing occasionally your deliberations. It has been my privilege to see a number of General Conferences. My first was forty years ago, in the city of New York. Wise and great and good men were there, of whom only one, I think, remains in this body, Dr. Trimble. I believe he and Dr. Curry are the only two members who were present in 1848 that still remain. I have seen the composition of the body change from time to time, and I want to say this—that my conviction is that there never has assembled a more distinguished, a more able, and a more cultured body of delegates in the Methodist Episcopal Church than now. It is true. that there is a larger proportion of youthful members than we have had in former General Conferences; but it is exceedingly gratifying to me, as I feel that the shadows are gathering around me and others, to see young men, truly cultured and devoted to the cause of Christ, able to come forward and take the reins of the Church and guide it so successfully onward. May God be gracious to them and make them greater than the fathers.

"I desire also to say that I have been pleased with the results of your deliberations. While there is a diversity of opinion upon some subjects, and must always be in a body of this kind, yet I think that the results of your deliberations have been for the good of the Church and for the glory of God. Some very important measures, I think, have been enacted, and I believe the Church will go forward with increased strength and power from this time.

"And now, brethren, a word personally. I have no words to declare the gratitude of my heart for the many courtesies and the kindly utterances you have made. They will be embalmed in my heart forever. Whatever the future may be, whatever of time and strength I may have, all belong to the cause of Christ. And may we go forward from this time, dear brethren, to try to do more vigorous work than we have ever done. May we have the spirit of deep consecration. May we pray for a more powerful outpouring of the Holy Spirit. May we look for revivals all over our country, until multiplied thousands shall be converted to God. And now, dear brethren, in closing this service and bidding you farewell, I pray that God may be with you and protect you in your journeyings to your respective homes. May you find your families in peace and safety and prosperity, and may God ever pour upon you the riches of his grace."

After these words he pronounced the benediction, and so closed the Conference and his ministry.

Bishop Foster speaks very beautifully of these visits of his colleague to the Conference: "When, but a few days ago, he came in among us, at the closing hours of the recent General Conference, to pronounce the few parting words which so many loving hearts waited to hear, his pallor frightened us, and his tremulous voice and emaciated form filled us with distressing apprehensions; but we little thought the dreaded time was so near. And yet, as we look back now, we realize how, in each of his few brief visits during the session, welcome as they were, making our hearts to leap within us, he seemed even then not to be of us, as he was wont; but rather as one perceptibly withdrawing himself. There is no mistaking it now—he was already consciously loosening the strong ligaments which had so long bound him to the earthly Church, and quietly transferring its care to other hands after he should depart. As we see it now, and as we are now conscious of dimly seeing it then, there was something in his manner of coming and going which denoted that he was even then being parted from us. He seemed to be saying, as indeed he did in every word, 'My work is done,' and he was as one surveying the situation ere he departed. There was a beautiful serenity, a dignified repose, in his manner and in his communications which we all felt; noticeably the absence, not of interest, but of all anxiety and all desire to mingle any more in the struggle which had been his very life. It was so when he conferred with his colleagues in their frequent visits at his home. He was feeling still sympathetic interest, but he was as one who had fought, and was content and assured of the victory without putting his hand any more to the conflict."

Notwithstanding the great effort it cost him to deliver his address, he continued to improve for several days after the adjournment of the General Conference. He even rallied so far as to plan and prepare for a journey to Clifton Springs. "But," says Dr. Kynett, whose narrative we shall now follow, "within a day or two of the date fixed for his departure, his strength utterly gave way, and his physicians were constrained to say that there was no reasonable ground to hope for any improvement, and thought that the hour of his departure was at hand. During most of the time he suffered greatly, and could converse but little. That little, however, showed clearly that he possessed the full control of his intellectual faculties. In this condition, for nearly a week longer than his physicians thought possible, his remarkable vital power struggled with death.

"Only the immediate members of his family were admitted to his room, as the utmost possible quiet was important. On Wednesday, June 11, in answer to the inquiries of his son-in-law, Rev. Charles W. Buoy, he replied, in terms often used when in health, 'I am a sinner saved by grace. O, to be like Him! O, to see Him as He is!' To the question, 'Is Jesus precious?' he answered, 'Precious! precious!' and quoted the text, 'To you which believe, he is precious!' And again he exclaimed, 'O. the wonderful possibilities beyond!' Thursday, June 12, he exclaimed, with tender pathos, 'My Saviour! my Saviour!' and quoted the glorious promise now being fulfilled in him: 'When thou passest through the waters I will be with thee; and through the rivers they shall not overflow thee!' Friday, June 13, in the midst of suffering, he exclaimed, 'Father, thou knowest! When the verse was quoted,

"'O would he more of heaven bestow,
And let the vessels break,
And let our ransomed spirits go
To grasp the God we seek;
In rapturous awe on him to gaze
Who bought the sight for me;
And shout and wonder at his grace
Through all eternity,'

he repeated the last two lines,

> " 'And shout and wonder at his grace
> Through all eternity.'

" Sunday, June 15, at about daybreak, he roused up with unexpected strength, for his death was hourly expected. Mrs. Buoy, who was watching with him, read Psalm ciii., one of the bishop's favorites, commencing, ' Bless the Lord, O my soul; and all that is within me, bless his holy name.' During the reading he responded frequently in a quiet way. Mrs. Simpson repeated the first verse of Charles Wesley's hymn, ' Jesus, lover of my soul,' and to the last line, ' O receive my soul at last,' he responded distinctly, though in feeble accents, ' My Saviour! my Saviour!' These were the last words which fell from his lips. He lingered on in silence until Wednesday morning, June 18, at 8:40 o'clock. Had he lived three days longer he would have completed seventy-three years upon the earth."

Of the sorrow which was felt at home and abroad, when the news of his death was announced—of the funeral and memorial services—this is not the place to speak. A typical American life has been delineated in these pages—a life beginning under lowly conditions, and ending in honor. As to eulogy—the record of what he did, of what he said to his fellow-men, and of what he was, is the best eulogy of Bishop Simpson that can be written.

APPENDIX

I.

THE PUBLISHED WORKS OF BISHOP SIMPSON.

1. Cyclopædia of Methodism. Embracing Sketches of its Rise, Progress, and Present Condition, with Biographical Notices and Numerous Illustrations. Philadelphia. Everts & Stuart. 1878. (Containing a Bibliography of Methodist Works in England and America.)

2. A Hundred Years of Methodism. New York. Phillips & Hunt. 1876.

3. Lectures on Preaching, Delivered before the Theological Department of Yale College. New York. M. E. Book Concern. 1879.

4. Funeral Address Delivered at the Burial of President Lincoln, Springfield, Ill., May 4, 1865. Pamphlet. New York. Carlton & Porter. 1865.

5. Sermons. Edited from Short-hand Reports by George R. Crooks, D.D. New York. Harper & Brothers. 1885.

II.

PRESIDENT SIMPSON'S INAUGURAL ADDRESS.

GREENCASTLE, IND., SEPT. 16, 1840.

WHEN a celebrated Grecian artist was asked why he spent so much time and labor in finishing the productions of his pencil, his simple and laconic reply was, "I paint for eternity." And were we to inquire why this noble edifice has been erected—and why, on this first literary anniversary within its halls, there is such a congregation of the talents and beauty of our enterprising, though youthful state—and why such a deep interest is felt in the exercises of this day, doubtless the friends of the institution would respond, "We paint for eternity." This thought of interminable effects, of ceaseless consequences flowing from every important event, confers an inexpressible interest upon every effort to cultivate the intellect. The brightest colors of the canvas will fade, and the fabric itself decay; even the sculptured monument will crumble into dust; but imperishable, as the mind itself, will remain every lineament, feature, and color imprinted upon it in time, and eternity's pure light shall only serve to exhibit still more conspicuously its excellence or deformity. Fountains, oftentimes, burst forth to spread their enlivening waters upon the surrounding land; yet in the lapse of time they may cease to flow. But here is a fountain now opened, whence shall issue an uninterruptedly flowing stream. Tall trees shall grow upon its banks, and luxuriate in the richness of the soil, fertilized by its waters; but whether their fruit shall be for the healing of the nations, or, like the fabled Upas, become a source of pestilence or death, must be principally determined by the arrangements adopted and carried into perfection.

Your speaker cannot be insensible to the interest of this moment. The surrounding circumstances, the eloquently impressive charge, the high trust committed to his care, and the almost immeasurable responsibility connected with it, stand vividly before him. Insensible to feeling must he be, did he not tremble at the magnitude of the trust, and yet recreant to true principle, did he not entertain some hope of being able to discharge its duties with fidelity. The great cause in which we are engaged, which has convened this assembly, is of the utmost importance. It is no less than directing the efforts, and in some degree forming the character of immortal intellects. And it may be profitable for us to consider some of the reasons which should excite us to vigorous exertions.

1st. Man is the creature of education. By this we do not mean that either colleges or common schools give the entire direction to a man's life, nor yet, that they supply what is naturally deficient in intellect; but we do mean that all his actions are under the influence of education. This term, in its most extensive signification, includes the development and strengthening of man's powers, physical, intellectual, and moral, together with the accumulation of all the varied information which he may be capable of receiving. The truth of our proposition will be manifest if we consider his circumstances. In infancy, he is the most helpless of all animals. Furnished with senses in perfection, he knows nothing. Passive, he waits upon the kindness and attention of others, and is scarcely able to perform an intelligent action. It is not so with other animals. They need not education. Knowledge to them is intuitive. The young nursling of the forest instinctively springs to his feet. The merry warbler of the grove pours fourth its soul in melody, unconscious of the effort to learn, and, though separated from its entire species, as natural as to mount on sportive wing is it for the lark or nightingale to strike its enchanting notes. But man learns everything. The use of his limbs is acquired only after long repeated efforts; every word he utters, every musical note which he sounds, is the result of imitation. And yet, when his powers are developed, he makes all animated nature serve him. He harnesses the fleetest to his chariot, and subjugates the strongest to his service.

The same difference is perceptible in their various operations. The architecture of animals is regular and uniform. The fowls of the air construct their nests, each after its kind, and not so constant is the color and plumage of each species as the order they observe in all their arrangements. The beaver builds his dam as his sires did before him, without alteration or improvement. The bee, for nearly six thousand years, has regularly built and inhabited his hexagonal cell. But man varies his work as he is taught. The wigwam of the Indian and the subterranean hovel of the Laplander stand in striking contrast to the pyramid of Egypt, the rock-hewn palaces of Petra, or the hundred-pillared domes of Thebes.

The lion may be caged for years, he is a lion still. The blood-thirstiness of the tiger is not abated by confinement or discipline. But how different is man! With the same form, he is another being. As a savage, he roams the forest, feeds on beasts of prey, or greedily devours the flesh of his enemy; has no bed but the forest leaves or the river's sand, and, save the skins of beasts scarcely wilder than himself, no protection against inclement seasons. He drags out a miserable existence, oblivious of all the past but wickedness, careless as to the present, save what will gratify appetite, and thoughtless of the future but to perpetrate crime. View him, civilized, instructed, illuminated by the word of God and the agency of the Holy Spirit—he has all the treasures of history as examples, a knowledge of the world, himself, and his God. Nature is tributary to his designs, the elements wait on his bidding. He surrounds himself in this world with multiplied comforts, and, in the next, he stands amid bright and holy intelligences, and bows only to the throne of God.

2*d. He is perpetually receiving an education.* Were the mind inactive but when urged by effort, we might be more careless upon this subject. It would then be as paper upon which no characters were traced and prepared for a future penman. But it is not so. A ready penman is unceasingly at work, and the sheets are being filled with characters of virtue or of vice. In his waking moments the mind is perpetually active. The eye is never satisfied with seeing, nor the ear with hearing. The youth may not be at school, no means may be employed to give him instruction, but he is ever learning. In childhood he acquires the elements of all subsequent knowledge. He learns to speak, to think, and to feel. His teachers are indeed in the nursery, but they are no less efficient for teaching unintentionally. From childhood upwards, whether at home or abroad, silent or in conversation, at labor or amusement, something is occurring to furnish new ideas to the mind. Every sight produces an impression, the nature of which varies with the cause; every sound suggests thoughts; and lessons, determining future character, are every moment furnished either from good or from evil sources.

3*d. Our only power is to choose in what the youth shall be educated.* This is the only question which can, strictly speaking, be proposed to the parent or guardian. We have already seen that a youth is continually acquiring some education, and the only power we have is to give it proper direction. We may not attempt to stay the current, but we may prepare the channel. The father who neglects or refuses to send his son to school or to college, only chooses for him an education at home. He intrusts him not to men of intellectual attainments and high moral worth, but he permits him to associate with the licentious and profane. He is taught no science but the science of wickedness. He learns the foolish jest, the impure song, and the profane exclamation. His teachers are the drunkard and the debauchee; with them he joins in revelry and crime, and bids fair to disgrace his friends and injure community, if not to bring himself to an untimely grave. Yet how many fathers choose precisely such an education for their sons, under the impression that they are not educating them at all. In this matter a fearful responsibility rests upon parents. A responsibility which even in this world is felt, by sometimes bringing down their gray hairs with sorrow to the grave, and the effects, in the invisible world, nought but the pencil of God can portray, no canvas but eternity contain. We have said the question never can arise, whether our youth shall be educated, but in what shall they be educated? In his creative wisdom, God has placed some things beyond the control of human volition. As the heart waits not on the will to give its pulsation, or the nerves to convey sensation, so the mind waits not to receive intelligence. Vital action depends not on a principle so fluctuating as volition. Nor is it merely a capacity for knowledge, but a desire for it, which God has implanted in man. The desire for happiness contains a thirst for knowledge. Happiness is but an expanded flow of agreeable consciousness. This is greatly dependent upon the healthy operation of the senses, which are the inlets of knowledge; and these must be in ceaseless activity to secure perpetual happiness. Hence, whenever the desire for happiness is found, there is a thirst for knowledge. This in our common language is termed curiosity. It is manifested alike in the politician who eagerly waits for news, the child that, with breathless anxiety, listens to the thrilling story, or the gossip that longs to hear the slanderous tale. It cannot be eradicated by art, and its strength can only be estimated by observing what it has done. It was the strength of this principle to which an appeal was made by the subtle tempter when seducing our first parents. "Ye shall be as gods, and knowing good and evil." The temptation, we too well know, was a fatal one. With the obscuration of the other powers, in the fall, this retained its full force. To gratify this desire, men had recourse, anciently, to omens, auguries, and oracles. Impatient of being denied the knowledge of the future, they sought with unhallowed hands to tear away the veil, and seek that from demons which God, in his wisdom, had withheld. We need hardly say the attempt was vain. Yet, baffled a thousand times, again they turned to any impostor who pretended to be endowed with prescience. The same disposition is still manifested, in modes slightly different. The entire machinery of fortune-telling, interpreting dreams, omens, lucky and unlucky occurrences, are but a part and parcel of that system which was devised to scale the battlements of heaven—a part of that Babel from which it is intended to look into the invisible world in despite of Jehovah's authority. Strange to tell, among professed Christians some of them are still found, but their origin is easily described. They have been purloined from pagan superstitions, as Rachel stole the gods of her father. But though frequently misapplied, yet Christianity does not seek to destroy this principle, she only purifies and directs it to its proper objects. Some of her most powerful motives are addressed to it. She has drawn in part the veil from futurity. Light and immortality are brought to light in the gospel. The glories of a heavenly inheritance stand forth in bold relief; and when looking farther and farther into the abode of bliss, Nature sinks overwhelmed with the excessive brightness of the eternal throne, Christianity whispers, "When He shall appear we shall be like Him, for we shall see Him as He is. Then shall we know even as we are known." The desire for knowledge then existing, and being intended to exist, boundless and insatiable, restricted only by God's eternal law, our only duty is to direct it to proper objects.

4th. Individual character depends upon the kind of instruction received. While the mind has power to understand almost every subject, it will improve only in those things in which it is exercised, and in those it will assuredly excel. For this reason early and close attention should be paid to the tuition of children. No habit is acquired without practice. Practice requires effort, and effort attention. Yet a small circumstance frequently determines that attention, and thus forms the character for life. A noted duellist traced his course to a declaration made by his father to him when he was a little boy, that he would chastise him if he should tamely receive an insult. This fired his bosom with passion, and he became a deliberate murderer. The remarkable equanimity of Washington has been ascribed, and not improbably, to the influence of parental instruction. The genius of Hannibal, while he was yet a child, was fired against the Romans by his father, and he became their most successful antagonist. Perhaps the influence of education can scarcely be more clearly exemplified than in the well-known instance of the Spartan boy, who, having been taught that it was honorable to steal, but dishonorable to be detected, thrust a stolen fox under his cloak, and lest it should be discovered, stood unmoved until it gnawed into his vitals, and he fell a sacrifice to his firmness. Nothing is so foreign to the mind but it may become familiar. Proof of this may be found in the ancient gladiatorial exercises. The most delicate and refined females, whose bosoms had else swelled with tenderness and love, delighted, day after day, to crowd the immense amphitheatres to witness men fighting with wild beasts or murdering each other. And those voices, which were attuned to sound in unison with Heaven's own minstrelsy, were heard to swell the deafening shouts of applause at the gracefulness and dexterity of the stroke which brought the life's blood gushing warm from its hidden fount.

Excellence is the result of continued exertion. This principle accounts for the acute hearing of the Indian when listening for game or an enemy, for the agility of the mountebank in balancing in difficult attitudes upon his wire, and for the deep researches of the mathematician, who seems to have reached the very boundaries of human thought. The youth who is now seen sporting in the streets, and foremost in every species of impiety, had he been properly educated, might have become the pride of his parents and the glory of his country.

Since man is thus influenced by his associations, and is the creature of education, we see the wisdom and goodness of the Creator in subjecting him to a long and guarded pupilage. Were he able, in a few moments from infancy, to mingle in the busy scenes of life, and behold the enormities daily perpetrated, deep corruption would be the inevitable result. But mark the order of Providence! He must lie in the arms of an attentive mother. Her watchfulness guards him from danger. And if she be, as Heaven designed her, an exemplification of amiability and grace, " if heaven be in her eye, grace in her step, in every gesture dignity and love," if she have the spirit of her station, a heart deeply imbued with the riches of the gospel, she will cultivate in her offspring a spirit of tenderness and affection, a spirit of piety and love. And if in after-life he should be tossed upon a tempestuous sea, and fearful ruin, amid conflicting elements, threaten his destruction, if he should even be agitated by the ragings of passion, his soul will ever and anon return to that peaceful calm which a mother's prayers and tears have inspired in his bosom. The same principles extend to a more advanced period of life. The studies pursued, and the teachers from whom instruction is received, must in a great degree determine future character. Who would send a son to be reared among savages, or would wish his companions to be licentious and profane? If, then, the kind of instruction determines character, the prosperity of our youth depends upon their parents, their teachers, and their friends. If we wish them to grovel in ignorance and crime, let us permit them to associate with those already proficient in iniquity, but if we wish them to be virtuous and honorable, if we wish them to aspire to places of usefulness and distinction, we must sedulously promote their improvement.

5th. National character depends upon the same cause. This we might deduce by argument from the previous position. Nations are but combinations of societies, societies aggregations of families, and families a union of individuals. Whatever, then, affects individuals, must be expected to exert its influence upon nations.

The ancient Greeks devotedly aspired after physical excellence. By athletics they improved the bodies of their youth. The honors bestowed upon victors in the games were well calculated to excite ambition

31

From childhood upwards they sought to develop every muscle, and give to every feature its full expression, and modesty itself was sacrificed to this all-absorbing passion.

The legitimate consequence was, that under such training the human frame attained its maximum of development. Their beauteous forms still stand unrivalled upon the painter's canvas, and swell in full symmetry from the sculptured marble. And at present, artists never think themselves capable of excellence until they have first studied those productions of antiquity. Critics have thought and affirmed that these productions were not copies from nature; but if not, they clearly manifest the prevailing taste of that age, whose ideal forms have never been surpassed. Praxiteles and Apelles still live in their works as master spirits in this department of design. Patriotism also was early taught their youth, and everything dishonorable and disgraceful was associated with the coward's name. And their plains and mountains have long been celebrated in song, as the theatres of their valor. In the later days of Rome wealth was substituted for honor, and for bravery, intrigue. Scarcely had the maxim "Omnia venalia sunt Romæ" been adopted, until her youth burst the barriers of law, and trampled upon rights human and divine. In our own age, the dauntless bravery of the Swiss, the enterprise of the English, the inextinguishable love of home felt by the Chinese and by the Laplander, the ardent love of liberty in Columbia's sons, and the abject submission of the Hindoo, are all the result of early education. The elements may be found in the language of the nursery. An eminent physician has attributed much of the difference between the volatility of the French, and the gravity of the German, to their treatment in infancy. Be this as it may, the German is taught to respect the opinions of antiquity, and he plays his music, smokes his pipe, and dwells as his fathers did before him. The French are taught that glory consists in innovation, and with them a government is prostrated, and a new one erected in less time than many would determine upon the structure of an edifice.

6th. True fame and prosperity depend upon intellectual and moral culture. However famous some men may have become without personal culture, they could never have received that fame but through the culture of others. The heroes of Troy had long since been forgotten but for Homer's song, and the noble exploits of ancient worthies live only upon the page of history. But those who became famous even as heroes excelled their associates in erudition. Nestor, Ulysses, and others are represented as eloquent as they were brave. Alexander enjoyed the instruction of Aristotle, and received those enlarged and comprehensive views which enabled him to sweep as the spirit of the storm over the habitable world.* Great men are, indeed, generally the birth of great times. Men as splendid in intellect, as courageous, as patriotic as ever breathed, frequently are unknown, because the times demand not those qualifications. In a young Alexander is personified the spirit of the times, when he complained lest his father would conquer the whole world, and leave no brilliant achievement for him. It was this spirit that Alexander directed, and this led him to triumph; yet none but a master-spirit could have presided in such a tempest. But passing from heroes, whose names are those which stand conspicuously on the roll of fame? The good, the wise, the great men of splendid intellects and refined feelings, men who were beloved by their country, their age, and the world. The names of Cincinnatus, of Luther, of Bacon, Newton, and Howard shall never die. Though ages may roll away and myriads perish, yet phœnix-like they shall rise afresh from the ashes of each generation, and in memory's record "their youth shall be renewed as the eagles."

The position may be more fully illustrated by a reference to national history. The fame of no nation has been transmitted to us but by records. And just in proportion to the number of writers do we perceive the character of the times. Athens and Sparta were rival cities. Both aimed at dominion, both strove for excellence. At Sparta, learning and science were prohibited. Her youths were taught war, and the bravery of her soldiers has never been surpassed. At Athens they taught philosophy; her temples rose in splendor, and her academies were crowded with students. What has been their fate? Athens was burned, but still she flourishes. There Euripides, Sophocles, and Æschylus sung, and the air sweeping over Attica's sacred soil, and visiting those revered ruins, still brings to our ears the dying strain. There, too, Demosthenes spoke —and eloquence was his. Before him stood breathless multitudes, who hung upon his lips. Rage and indignation against tyrants were kindled by his words, and Philip dreaded the power of his voice more than the array of fleets and armies. His voice yet rings. Many a youth has felt the impulse of liberty waked by his words, and many a tyrant has turned pale when he has heard the mountains reverberating with those echoes of liberty, marshalling her heroes to glorious conflict. Xenophon and Herodotus wrote, and Sparta is known, but in the page of the Athenian historian. Socrates, Plato, and Aristotle philosophized, and while the modern philosopher rejects their errors, he yet bows before the strength

---

* In one of his letters to his preceptor, he remarks, "For my part I had rather surpass the majority of mankind in the sublime parts of learning than in extent of power and dominion." Julius Cæsar, though a distinguished hero, has always been justly admired for his perspicuous style and extensive erudition.

of those intellects which pierced the surrounding gloom, and towered, like the white-topped mountains, above the dark and pendent cloud, displaying their beauties to a cloudless sky.   Sparta is gone, but Athens is immortal.

Carthage was once the rival of Rome.   She had wealth almost incalculable; the daughter of the "merchant lady of the East," she inherited her treasures.   Her palaces rose in gorgeous architecture, and her citizens were brave.   Once in the terrible conflict, her sons scaled the mountain's height, and came down on Italy's fair plains as a devastating torrent, and the "eternal city," as an aspen leaf, trembled upon her seven hills. Then the Carthagenians might have been victorious, but, alarmed at an unusually terrific storm, they delayed to prosecute their advantages, and their ignorance was the salvation of Rome.   Where now is Carthage? Gone! forever gone.   Her palaces are in ruins, her splendor exists but in song, and even her warriors are principally indebted to the history of her enemies for their posthumous fame.   Rome still exists, though not in modern Rome.   Wander among her broken columns and ruined edifices, she is not there.   Gaze upon her crumbling statuary and her dimmed paintings, she is not there.   All is lifeless.   Then open the treasures of mind.   Tully still speaks in his enchanting strains.   Horace, Ovid, Virgil, and Juvenal, alternately, depress and transport us with their songs. Livy, Tacitus, and Sallust present us living Rome.   We hear her orators and poets, and her most glorious triumphs are enacted before our vision. Her laws still flourish in other lands and other climes.   Rome said "Carthago delenda est," and she fell, without distinguished sons to transmit her name to posterity.   But while science flourishes and literature survives, Rome can never be forgotten.

We have another striking contrast in the Israelites and the Egyptians. The princes of Egypt had large dominions; their land was fertile, and, watered by their celebrated river, brought forth abundantly.   They also paid considerable attention to education, but their trust was in their wealth and power.   They aimed at immortality, and the broad-based pyramid was erected, towering with its mountain structure towards heaven.   Each rocky eminence was carved into a Sphinx, and catacombs, in endless succession and vast in extent, were formed deep in the mountain's side.   Their bodies were embalmed to resist the corrosion of time, and the latest posterity was expected to do them honor.   The enslaved nation had no such monuments, but their history was written. Moses, whom Lord Bacon quaintly styles "God's first pen," formed that record which still speaks of the beginning of ages.   In that history alone ancient Egypt truly lives, all else is impenetrably enveloped in mist and obscurity.   The builder of the pyramid has for ages been unknown, and the name of the embalmed has long since been forgotten. And when those pyramids shall have crumbled into dust, and the last trace of the embalmed shall have forever vanished, that history shall still live to tell the thrilling story of Israel's triumphant disenthrallment from the yoke of bondage.

We need not dwell upon ancient history to prove that national prosperity depends upon intellectual and moral culture. Why is modern Europe now the centre of civil power? The soil is not more productive, the climate is not more delightful than those of regions in Asia and Africa, and yet everything good and great upon the eastern continent, in modern times, has had its origin there. One answer only can solve the mystery. They are enlightened. Take a single example. Place yourself in the army of Julius Cæsar, cross with him the British Channel, stand on Albion's shore, and view the chalky cliffs of that romantic isle. Who are there? An ignorant and degraded race, savages and idolaters, blessed indeed with fair complexions and muscular forms, but dark and debased in intellect and morals. Then Italy thought the conquest of such an isle an insignificant occurrence. Small was it in territory, and placed on the verge of creation. Go there now. Britannia would smile at the thought of Italy sending an invading force. Though her territory is but little larger than that of our own state, her sails whiten every sea and crowd every port; and millions in foreign lands bow at her name and call her mistress. Her possessions are extensive in every quarter of the globe, and, small as she is, she wields an almost omnipotent influence. What has produced this mighty change? Education is there. "The schoolmaster is abroad." Her venerable universities have illuminated her sons, and widely diffused the spirit of enterprise. They have discovered, and practically applied the maxim, "that knowledge is power." The arts flourish in unprecedented vigor. The hoarse voice of her steam-engines and the ceaseless hum of her machinery are heard in every part of the island, and every effort is made by her philosophers and laborers to bring the useful arts to perfection. Consequently wealth flows into the bosom of the nation, and every land becomes tributary to England's felicity.

Contrast the former with the present condition of Russia. Two centuries ago she was a vast uncultivated territory, her population were principally peasant slaves attached to the soil, the absolute property of their masters, and so ignorant that they dreaded to receive offered liberty lest they should be wholly ruined. She had no ships and consequently no commerce, no science and consequently no arts of a refined nature. But Peter the Great, by his mighty efforts, changed her entire system. He introduced the arts from abroad, commenced commerce, founded colleges, and encouraged learning in every manner, and Russia awoke as from a dream.. Now she has become the rival of England. Her commerce is increasing, her resources are daily being developed, and her wealth is accumulating. Already the haughty Ottoman shrinks from her glance as she wistfully looks towards the Black Sea, and, tremblingly alarmed, he calls upon England and France as his only hope against encroachments upon his territory. Let us take but one example more. What has so wonderfully changed America in the last two hundred years? Why now smiles in fruitfulness this western valley, so recently a gloomy wilderness? Enlightened man has been there. Our less enlightened brethren in South America have waded through seas of blood to attain liberty, which is as often wrested from them by the chieftain's grasp. And even at this moment they are suffering from opposing and contending factions. They lack intelligence and virtue. But our Union has arisen as the sun in its strength, her internal order scarcely disturbed, her external rights esteemed sacred. Her commerce is wide as the earth, and she presents the sublime spectacle of a free nation, unembarrassed by debt, uncontrolled by religious monopolies, at peace with all the world, rising in intellectual and moral grandeur, and throwing open her territory to receive the distressed immigrant as he flies from despotic power. Many of her sons have become eminent in science, and even for excellence in the fine arts; some have worn the laurels in foreign lands. Do we inquire the cause? Go to the rock of Plymouth and look upon those venerable men. Their first care was to plant churches and schools, to promote intelligence and virtue. I trust I shall be indulged in quoting one of their acts as early as 1647 upon this interesting subject. It is as follows: "To the end that learning may not be buried in the graves of our forefathers, in church and commonwealth, the Lord assisting our endeavors: It is therefore ordered by this court and authority thereof, that every township within this jurisdiction, after the Lord has increased them to the number of fifty householders, shall then forthwith appoint one within their own town to teach all such children as shall resort to him, to write and read, whose wages shall be paid either by the parents or masters of such children, or by the inhabitants in general, by way of supply, as the major part of those that order the prudentials of the town shall appoint; provided that those who send children be not oppressed by paying much more than they can have them taught for in other towns." Sec. 2. "And it is further ordered that when any town shall increase to the number of one hundred families or householders, they shall set up a grammar school, the master thereof being able to instruct the youth so far as they may be fitted for the university." Here we see the beginning of that system which has been followed by so happy consequences. America is happy because she is enlightened and virtuous.

7th. Colleges and universities are essential to the improvement and diffusion of education. Many who agree with us in extolling the advantages of common schools are somewhat doubtful as to the necessity for colleges. They are viewed as aristocratic institutions, imparting only the unnecessary refinements. These opinions, however, we conceive arise wholly from mistaken views. In order that we may perceive the true tendency of colleges, it may be remarked that society is interested in having individuals talented, learned, energetic, and useful; and whatever contributes to the formation of such characters contributes to the happiness of society. That a person may be rendered in the highest degree useful, four things are especially necessary, the mind must be well stored with general knowledge, there must be a capacity for close and thorough investigation, ability to communicate information in an interesting and successful manner, and a disposition to use the utmost exertions for the amelioration of the condition of mankind. Our only question then is, have colleges the tendency to form such characters?

They furnish the outlines of general knowledge. The relations of the elements of matter are taught in chemistry, their combinations in all their varied forms, and the laws which govern them in forming those combinations. Mineralogy teaches the character and qualities of the various substances composing the earth's structure, and the uses to which they may be applied. Geology unfolds the structure and arrangement of the earth's surface, and the position of the various strata in reference to each other, with the various fossils found among their masses. Natural philosophy explains the laws of motion, and the mechanical action of bodies, one upon another; it describes the fundamental principles of mechanics and the structure of machinery, and teaches how to estimate the effect of different powers variously combined. All the motions of nature are observed, from the movement of the birds in the air, to the ship upon the mighty deep. The propagation of sound and the flash of lightning —the colors that sparkle in the dew-drop as it glistens on the trembling leaf, or display their lustre in the bow of peace that triumphantly spans the heavens—all are the subjects of philosophy. Astronomy leads us still further. She takes the student, already acquainted with our own world, on a tour of discovery through the universe. Visiting each planet, he becomes acquainted with the laws that govern those mighty orbs as they move perpetually around the great centre of the system. Then he careers with the comet, through unmeasured space, nor stops until, far beyond the visible creation, ten thousand times as many worlds are brought to view.

But the student is taught not only the nature of the world in which he is placed, and its associated orbs, he is also taught the history of man, the various principles that have elevated and overthrown nations, the different events that have transpired, and the period of their occurrence. The actions of the good and great are held up as examples, and the conduct of the bad as warnings. He is taught to know himself. The phenomena of mind are unfolded, with the laws of our being, and he is taught to think with accuracy and precision. And history, the gray-headed chronicler of years, towering with Alpine grandeur, shows those laws exemplified in their consequences, and is thus an ever-bidding monitor to lead to truth. And last of all he is led through every department of nature to view the grand designs of the Supreme Creator. With such knowledge the person is no longer a stranger in a strange land. Wisdom, power, benevolence, and justice are everywhere displayed. All nature hath a tongue to tell of wisdom, there is "music in the spheres." And as he walks abroad in the fields, he views "books in the running brooks, sermons in stones, and good in everything."

Colleges are places of severe mental discipline. The student is secluded from the business and perplexities of life, and consequently the mind is not distracted by those cares which ordinarily disturb the train of meditation. His associates are all engaged in study—he has examples of application in his preceptors—honor is enjoyed only by the successful student—in his studies he becomes acquainted with the characters and actions of the wise, patriotic, and virtuous; he admires and imitates—and all incline him to improve every fleeting moment. The studies at which he is engaged require strong and continued mental effort, and their tendency is to produce habits of close and profound thought. Among these the mathematical course stands pre-eminent. So fully were even some of the ancient philosophers apprised of this, that Plato inscribed over the door of his academy, "Οὐδεὶς α γεωμετρικός εἰσήλθο" —"Let no one who is ignorant of geometry enter." In our own country the distinguished Hamilton was so sensible of the effects of geometry upon the mind that, in preparing his celebrated state papers, he read Euclid regularly once a month. Algebra also, especially in its higher branches, is well calculated to discipline the mind. These are not only essential to prepare the student for active life, but by giving him habits of thought and examination they prepare him for extensive usefulness. His intellect is expanded and his powers developed. He is neither deceived by specious pretences, nor does he shrink from arduous investigation, and when in after-life he is consulted, his judgment will be respected.

Colleges impart qualifications for communicating information in an in-

teresting and successful manner. And this is one of the grand objects of a thorough education. Without it knowledge is comparatively useless. The individual, it is true, enjoys a pleasure which sensual gratifications can never afford. Rittenhouse swooned at beholding the transit of Venus. Newton was so overwhelmed with rapture, when near the completion of his immense calculations that demonstrated the planetary laws, that he was unable to proceed. And Archimedes, going into a public bath, while intent on solving the problem of Hiero's crown, suddenly discovering the method, sprang from the baths and rushed naked into the streets, crying, "I have found it, I have found it." True, it elevates the intellect and makes the individual sit "upon the Alps, the Apennines, and weave his garland of the lightning's wing." But still the great object is to communicate truth to others. Powerful orations may sway the opinions of listening thousands, may turn the majority of a community upon subjects of immense importance. Mary, queen of England, is said to have dreaded John Knox more than all her other subjects, because she feared the effects of his popular oratory. But a written work of strong sentiment and happy expression can do still more. It speaks not to one community, nor country, nor age. Its dominion is the world, its duration that of the earth. For the press has almost secured to valuable productions ubiquity and eternity. Elementary knowledge and habits of thought can never exert their full influence without the power of language, and this is particularly taught in a college course. Attention is directed to the structure and analysis of language, mode of expression, and formation of style. For this purpose rhetoric and logic are taught. Exercises in writing and oratory are periodically required. And a critical knowledge of the Latin and Greek languages is imparted.

We are aware that it has become fashionable to declaim against the study of those languages, and to exalt at their expense the natural sciences. We are not willing to yield to others in an attachment to the study of nature, but we must enter our protest against the neglect of those ancient languages. And as this is a subject upon which considerable discussion has taken place, it may claim our passing notice.

That the study of those languages is necessary for the finished scholar, few are found to deny; and we are at a loss to conceive how any, aspiring to elevated situations, can voluntarily deprive themselves of such advantages. When a student is unable, from uncontrollable circumstances, to give himself a full education, there may be a propriety in his paying but little, if any, attention to them, but circumstances should be imperious to warrant such a course. The study of the languages has been by the imprudence of friends exposed to unnecessary opposition.

There is a great tendency to run into extremes upon any subject, and as a mote near the eye covers a large field of view, so any subject upon which the mind is intently fixed is in danger of being unnecessarily magnified.

Some have attributed to the ancients all excellence, and to the moderns merely imitation. If specimens of oratory are required, they refer immediately to the ancients. Beauties of composition, strength of sentiment, to them only shine upon the classic pages. Nor is the reason difficult to be discovered. They have studied the ancients to the exclusion of the moderns. Their minds were wholly engrossed in youth with classic lore, and the whole current of thought has flowed in that direction. The former system of education was such that nearly the whole time was occupied in studying these languages, and it is not astonishing that the judgment should be biassed by such a course. Others, perceiving the folly of such assertions, have run to the opposite extreme, and condemned the languages as wholly useless. The truth to our minds appears thus. We find many beautiful examples of composition and many addresses of finished oratory among the ancients, but more beauties and stronger oratory are found among the moderns. They have a wider field of illustration, and a greater number of powerful motives. Neither extensive science nor the all-absorbing truths of Christianity were understood by the ancients. In originality, love of nature, and abstraction, they manifest considerable excellence. Their times favored this. They had few works but those of nature from which they could copy, and, not expecting great practical results, sublime sentiments and abstractions were their chief delight. Yet our English poets love nature as ardently; and the abstractions of a Newton and Laplace are superior to any found among the ancients. Besides, the greater part of what is excellent in the writings of the ancients we find embodied in those of the moderns. If we are asked why then we advocate the study of the ancient languages, we answer, 1st. Because there are many turns of expression which lay open the springs of thought, which never can be translated. And this was probably the origin of the famous expression of Charles V. that " he who learned a new language acquired a new soul." These turns of expression frequently suggest new ideas to the mind, and cause it to examine the subject more closely and thoroughly. 2d. Because professional men must understand the technicalities of their science, but these being nearly all derived from those languages, a previous knowledge of them is required. 3d. Because there are writings of peculiar interest to the accomplished physician, attorney, divine, and general scholar which have either never been translated, or yet possess peculiar interest in the original. The physician wishes to read after Galen and Hippocrates just as they wrote, and the attorney to have the gradual formation and expansion of that system of jurisprudence which is the glory and safeguard of our country. The divine must also long to read the word of life just as it dropped in all its richness, freshness, and power from the lips of him who spake as never man spake. He thus seems privileged to stand in ancient company, and to view those sublime scenes transpiring around him. But, 4th. Our strongest reason is that such knowledge is necessary in order to obtain the perfect mastery of our own language. The great object of the scholar is to persuade and convince. For this all the powers of language should be exhausted. Its strength, its beauty, richness, copiousness, should all be the subjects of continued study and investigation. Words are the instruments of the writer and the orator, and if expected to do execution, they must be well chosen, expressive, and polished. If we examine the prose and poetic writings of the last century, we find most that excel are the productions of classic pens. True, some wrote well by forming their style after classic authors, and by severe study imitating their method, but already their works are nearly forgotten, and soon, with but few exceptions, they will have passed from the memory of men.

Who that has any aspiration to leave behind him a name will wish it to be written in other than imperishable characters. Yet, comparatively few can be writers, but all may be orators. It has not appeared strange to us that an opposition to the study of the languages should have arisen in France and Germany. There a popular orator is regarded with jealousy. The tyrant wishes the populace to sleep. He dreads the first symptoms of waking, and consequently wishes not to see the elements of agitation accumulated, lest they should explode with volcanic violence, and upheave the foundations of their governments. But why should opposition be indulged in this country? Here every man is by birthright an orator; he is invested with the attributes of sovereignty, and the affairs of state are subjects of daily discussion among the humblest citizens in the community. Our only security is in the intelligence and virtue of our citizens, and every man who aspires to eminence should seek such an acquaintance with language as shall enable him to pour forth truth in all its strength and beauty; to clothe it in its own heavenly habiliments of loveliness, and to acquire the power of holding thousands entranced with the resistless magic both " of thoughts that breath and words that burn."

But it may be objected that some of our best orators never studied these languages. We admit that to all general rules there may be exceptions, but in this case they will not at all invalidate the general principle. To obtain their eminence, these men have employed their whole time; they have labored assiduously, and formed their style according to the model of those imbued with classic lore. By industry and perseverance they have excelled, and they merit praise; but there is one grand distinction between the accomplished linguist and such speakers and writers. In the linguist, oratory is but a small part of his powers, it appears rather as an incidental circumstance. His language is the natural expression of his thoughts. With the other, oratory is everything; for this he has studied night and day. His writings will be few and ephemeral, for his whole efforts have been employed to obtain the use of language, as it would have flowed almost spontaneously, if he had thoroughly studied that department. But is the example of those who thus arrive at eminence to be a model for others? How frequently do we see men raised in obscurity, destitute of means, rising from one degree of wealth to another, until they proudly place themselves upon a standing of equality with the oldest families in the land. Will they therefore wish their children to commence destitute of means? Do you find them giving away their fortunes to others, and turning their sons penniless upon the world, because in this way they commenced? Do they seek the humblest associations for their daughters, because their mothers made such selections? They wish, and wish properly, to place their children on vantage-ground, and this they should do, in education as well as in wealth. And if we refer to those orators, we find them the most ardent advocates for the thorough education of youth, because they well remember the difficulties through which they were compelled to struggle. But we are told that but few become orators. We admit that but few, comparatively, attain to excellence in any department. Few of the sons of the wealthy continue to amass wealth. The man who fares sumptuously has a son in a few years reduced to beggary; while the poor rises to opulence and splendor. Energy, ceaseless energy, is necessary. Indolence, whether found on a farm, in a shop, an office, or college, never can succeed. But of those who succeed in completing a college course, but few are indolent. Such, generally, tire by the way; to them discipline and close application are irksome, and they gladly leave their studies to engage in business, where they will have greater opportunities for irregularity. There is an additional reason why the languages should be taught. By means of commerce the different parts of the world are in rapid approximation. Men of different languages must commingle, and hence the importance of understanding, especially, the languages of modern Europe. But as many of them are derived from the Latin and Greek, the easiest and best method to acquire them is first to study their originals.

Colleges cherish and cultivate dispositions for enlarged efforts to amelio-

rate the condition of man. The student is taught the relations he sustains to his fellow-men of his own country, and of the whole world, and the obligations arising from those relations. Political economy exhibits the propriety and policy of active exertion, while moral science occupies still higher ground, and shows that man to be criminal who does not employ himself in labors of benevolence. The conduct of the brave, the patriotic, and the philanthropic are held up as examples, and every motive is brought into requisition to stimulate to honorable enterprise. With such convictions of duty, the thorough scholar, bursting the barriers of prejudice, views himself no longer living to himself alone; lays broad plans for future usefulness, and, in whatever profession he may labor, the principles which guide him are those that dignify and ennoble humanity.

8th. Colleges are not only thus useful in furnishing such individuals to act their part in community, *but they also elevate the standard of professional attainments.* How many men rush unqualified into all our responsible professions. Scarcely has a young man completed the acquisition of the simplest elements of an ordinary education, when he assumes a title, and the lives or property of his fellow-men are trusted to his care. And when once entered upon the profession, so far from developing his powers, he looks around, and finds associates as ignorant as himself. They "measure themselves by themselves," and aspire for no higher excellence. While they are yet grovelling in the basement, they fancy they have attained to the summit of the temple, because from the obscurity of their vision they can perceive nothing above them. There is scarcely a more pernicious influence operating against our learned professions. The young man fancies that he can gather laurels to decorate his brow, and that unless he hastes they will all be worn by others. He counts the days as years until he engages in active life. And even sometimes, by a strange mixture of self-esteem and benevolence, he imagines the world will plunge into ruin unless *he* springs to the rescue. The ancient athletæ could spent years in preparation, every muscle was developed, every expedient tried, a long course of training endured, and when admitted to the lists, instead of entering hastily, they deliberately commenced the contest. All this was for a fading laurel. But when property and life, when the dearest interests of men are at stake, our youths rush unprepared upon the course, and, as might be expected, fall exhausted ere they reach the goal. If young men but know the advantages of a full preparation, they would count themselves happy, if at twenty-five or thirty they were prepared to commence a public career.

9th. Colleges are essential to the prosperity of common schools. They furnish writers to explain and illustrate the various branches of an ordinary education. And they furnish competent teachers, to take charge of schools and seminaries. Too frequently, for the welfare of community, is the education of immortal minds committed to those who have neither capacity nor disposition to communicate useful knowledge; who, themselves wrongly taught, perpetuate errors more difficult to be removed than the inscription from the plate of steel; who, without any sublime sentiments or noble aspirations, undertake to direct the development of that intellect designed to scale the topmost battlements of nature. Look where we may, no truth is more clearly taught than that common schools never flourished without colleges. The history of France, England, Scotland, and Prussia might all be cited in proof. And, in our own country, where is common education most generally diffused? Just where the first colleges were established, as radiating points of literary light. Massachusetts and Connecticut, the seats of Harvard and Yale, have in this respect furnished an example worthy of imitation. On this subject many have improper views, regarding colleges, if not injurious, at least as unnecessary to common schools. A distinguished secretary of a neighboring commonwealth, in one of his illustrations, remarks that the proper objects of attention are common schools; for as heated air always rises, so common schools prepare the way for colleges. It is true that this connection is reciprocal, and that colleges will generally not continue to flourish where common education is neglected. But although heated air will invariably rise, yet blot out the sun from existence, or direct its rays from the earth, and thick-ribbed ice would hold universal dominion. Blot out colleges, and a Cimmerian darkness would overspread the land, and the huge icebergs of the frigid zone would but faintly represent the more intense induration of all the feelings and powers of mind.

10th. *Colleges, or high institutions of learning, have always been the precursors of great improvements, whether in government or in the arts of civilized life.* In every land remarkable for intellect we find them in existence. Even in the captivity at Babylon, the Jews sustained high institutions for that age of the world. Shortly after Constantine, a university was established at Constantinople, which served as the depository of Eastern literature; but colleges, resembling those at present in existence, were not established until a much later period. In the ninth century Europe produced two distinguished individuals, Charlemagne in France, and Alfred in England. Each used every means to encourage education, and seminaries were founded, which were the swelling buds that afterwards unfolded into the universities of Paris and Oxford. And is it not remarkable that the land of Charlemagne and of Alfred, after a lapse of one thousand years, still retain a proud pre-eminence over the rest of Europe. At what period college honors were devised and degrees conferred it is now difficult to determine; but their origination is by many ascribed to Irnerius, a distinguished jurist of the twelfth century, and a professor at Bologna. Mention of them was made by Robert de Courcon in 1215; and the term Bachelor of Arts occurs in the Bull of Pope Gregory IX., in 1231. At this period a new impetus was given to collegiate instruction, and in the same century, in addition to the universities of Paris and Oxford, we find those of Toulouse, Bologna, Naples, Padua, Salamanca, and Cambridge; and in the next two centuries between twenty and thirty additional ones of eminence were established. Shall we ask, was their establishment followed by any remarkable events? History points to those centuries as the time of the awaking of mind, and the formation of those very systems now completely developed. That age was a dark one in political relations. Tyranny was absolute and unrelenting. The common people were in a state of abject slavery, attached to the soil, and transposable as goods and chattels by the power of the nobility. The code of jurisprudence was lamentably defective, but in it the first great change was produced. The Roman law was revived and introduced into the universities. The youth crowded to the lectures, and by their means more correct notions were generally diffused. Trials by single combat, by signs and charms, by the "Judgments of God," as they were termed, were gradually abandoned; and order and regularity were established in the courts of judicature. As ideas of justice prevailed, the condition of the peasantry was ameliorated. Princes enfranchised their serfs, and exhorted their nobility to do the same. Cities and villages acquired freedom, and a spirit of enterprise and industry became widely diffused. Notions of individual rights were soon extended to national, and the claims of the monarch were regarded with jealousy by his subjects. Even Louis X., as early as 1315, declared publicly, when manumitting his serfs, that "all men by birth should be free and equal." Such sentiments exercised a powerful influence, and republics sprang up throughout Italy, Spain, and other parts of the south of Europe. But principles were not sufficiently settled, the mass of the people were not yet enlightened, and morals were grossly defective. These infant republics were soon torn with factions, and gradually immerged into monarchies. In the fourteenth century the cantons of Switzerland founded their government, and have since been independent of regal power. The same sentiments spread rapidly in England, and early in the thirteenth the memorable Magna Charta was signed, as an acknowledgment of popular rights. Since that period liberty has been progressive, and has but developed the same principles in greater maturity and beauty in the formation of the American Constitution, that noblest work of man. Yet some there are, even in this favored land, so ignorant of history, and so grovelling in all their conceptions, that they publicly declaim against colleges as fostering aristocracy. Such men, had they lived in other days, would have been the first to strangle liberty in her cradle, and, bowing their own neck to the foot of the despot, to swear allegiance to his throne.

All the parts of truth are intimately connected. The discovery of one leads to the discovery of others. As universities promoted the knowledge of popular rights, so those rights being understood, and having been even partially enjoyed, produced a buoyancy and elasticity of mind which reacted upon the universities. Each supported the other, and as the desire for information increased, the course was extended. Formerly the branches taught were the *Trivium*, embracing rhetoric, logic, and grammar, and the *Quadrivium*, including arithmetic, geometry, music, and astronomy. But with the new arrangements new studies were introduced, the writings of the ancients were eagerly consulted, and nature became a subject of investigation. Astronomy began to throw aside its astrological character, and natural history and chemistry, though yet very imperfect, began to attract attention. Men thought more freely, and consequently more was written. At this juncture commenced the great improvement of the arts. Something was needed upon which to write, parchment was too costly, and bark too fragile. It is said that the manufacture of paper from linen was first devised in the ninth century, but it was not generally known until the early part of the fourteenth century. A suitable substance being prepared, writings were multiplied, but still, owing to the labor of transcription, books were exceedingly costly. A copy of the New Testament was sold in 1429 for £40, being at that time the annual salary of a professor in Oxford. It required an immense fortune to purchase a library. To remedy this inconvenience, the art of printing was invented, and probably about 1431 the press began to work. This constituted a new era in literature. Information spread rapidly, a knowledge of history and geography awakened a desire to visit and trade with other countries. Commerce was extended, navigation practised, and America discovered. Wealth flowed into Europe, the arts were encouraged, and the refinements of life multiplied. Until near this period the roofs of the houses, even of the wealthy, were thatched and without chimneys, and glass windows were almost unknown. But from this period, invention after invention, and discovery after discovery, added happiness to man. We do not wish to be understood as affirming that all these improvements were devised in colleges. But it is certainly remarkable that the establishment of colleges preceded all splendid improvements in those early ages. They were as radiating points, as suns in the universe dispensing light and heat. In them was inspired a thirst for enterprise. Their alumni went forth, and acted on community. New facts were carefully reported, and these again were disseminated, so that, with telegraphic facility, information spread from mind to mind, and from nation to nation. Although many discoveries were made by men not attached to colleges, they were not made independent of the light and interest with which colleges had invested those subjects. The discovery of the laws of mechanics, the principles now embodied in machinery of all kinds, was the result of patient and laborious investigation. To show how such investigations affect community, let us select but a single instance, the refractive power of glass. The fact that light is bent a little out of its course by passing through glass appears but a trivial discovery. Yet in the hand of Galileo it gave rise to the invention of the telescope. And what are its trophies? It has made man a citizen of the universe—spread before his vision neighboring worlds—expanded his intellect by suggesting data for new calculations and matter for profound reflection—revealed additional evidences of the wisdom and power of God, and enabled man, lost in astonishment, more feelingly to exclaim, "The heavens declare the glory of God, and the firmament showeth his handiwork." He has with this measure spanned the surface of the sun, and passed with the velocity of the "swift-winged arrows of light" from centre to circumference of celestial systems infinitely distant and infinitely multiplied. The microscope, constructed upon the same principle, reveals a new world around and beneath us. Each particle of matter seems to teem with life and happiness. Organized beings are seen to sport in a drop of water, with as little sense of confinement as a whale in the ocean. The dust of a plant, which we carelessly brush away, is but a crowded city of living beings, imperceptible to the unassisted vision. Nature thus speaks a new language, and is resplendent with indescribable lustre. The same principle, practically applied, has produced the spyglass for the mariner, and furnished an indispensable part of the theodolite. And who that has attained to the age of forty or fifty has not availed himself of the same principle to remedy impaired vision. This application alone has been of incalculable benefit to man. The short-sighted are enabled to take an extended view, and the dimmed eye of age beholds once more the beauties of creation as it beheld them in youth. Nearly one half of human life is thus made available, to an extent formerly unknown; age is preserved as a counsellor to youth, and the declining moments, when formerly "the grasshopper was a burden," are cheered with new sources of instruction and delight. Dr. Rush remarks that cases of fatuity are much less frequent among the aged since the introduction of glasses, and the well-known history of Dean Swift would seem to confirm us in this impression. Yet all these are the trophies of but a single discovery in modern science.

32

The connection of colleges with religious reformation is by no means to be overlooked. The fifteenth century beheld the European universities in full vigor, and with their strength the Reformation gained ground. Mind, taught to investigate, was not to be shackled by the dictates of assumed power. Nor were the pretensions of any individual considered too sacred to be examined. Go to the University of Erfurt. Behold that youth as he enters the library, and in his search for something interesting takes from the shelves the Scriptures of the Old and New Testaments. It was the first copy he had ever seen. Curiosity prompted him to read, his attention was arrested, and that volume transformed that youth into Martin Luther. That volume may have been the donation of some pious Christian, and, if so, who can estimate the consequences of such a benevolent act. Calvin received his serious impressions while pursuing his studies, and Oxford's classic retreat has had the honor of producing a Whitefield and a Wesley, whose names shall ever stand connected with what is pure in morals, spiritual in religion, and benevolent in enterprise. In our own land, also, revivals of religion frequently occur in colleges, and many who enter, designing merely to study their own pleasure, are induced to commence a life of usefulness. Yet the impression is firmly fixed upon many minds that colleges are unfavorable to religious influence. Why, may we ask, is this impression prevalent? If colleges were destitute of religious instruction, if young men were left unguarded at the most critical period of life, there would be some cause of apprehension. Such institutions would in all probability be nurseries for vice and infidelity. But this is not the case with colleges in general. Students are strictly required to observe the duties of the Sabbath. A portion of Scripture is read every morning, and devotional exercises performed in the chapel. The text-books are avowedly religious in their tendency, and the morality of the Bible is rigidly inculcated. The associations also are generally favorable; for though there will always be exceptions, yet viciously disposed young men cannot generally be found engaged in college pursuits. If trustees have done their duty, the preceptors will always be men of irreproachable habits and unblemished piety. And all the force of attachment will incline young men to copy their example. And who does not know—who has not felt the power of example?

Since, then, the peculiar regulations of a well-arranged college are favorable to piety, if any further objection be urged, it must be against the acquisition of knowledge under any circumstances. The maxim that "ignorance is the mother of devotion" has long since passed away; yet there are some who still think that extensive knowledge is unfavorable to personal religion. If, however, we seek for the foundation of such an impression, we find it wholly baseless. The better we become acquainted with individuals of high moral worth, the more we admire and love; so the more we know of the works of God, the more reason we have to worship and adore. As we have already seen, science wonderfully enlarges our views, and consequently gives us clearer ideas of the glorious perfections of the Deity. Those individuals who have made the greatest discoveries have powerfully felt the influence of this principle. Galen fell upon his knees to adore, when he discovered the admirable perfection of the human frame. Newton, when he had almost measured the immensity of nature, turned all the powers of his disciplined intellect to understand and explain the word of God; and Baron Napier, who by his discoveries in mathematics had in some degree prepared the way for Newton's splendid discoveries, engaged in the same noble employment. The only idea we can have of infinite holiness, of spotless purity, is inseparably associated with infinite wisdom. Man, in the creation, was made in the image of God, in distinction from animated nature, not that he was purer, for all was pure, but he was wiser. He had knowledge for government, power to control himself. And if it be a command that a Christian should in his sphere be like God, he must seek not only for spotless purity, but also for extensive knowledge. The harmlessness of the dove must ever be united with the wisdom of the serpent. As if to impress this truth on the mind of man, God has ever chosen such as his most honored servants. Moses was learned in all the wisdom of the Egyptians, and who was so highly favored as he? Selected to lead Israel and to stand before God, he beheld the exceeding brightness of his glory as it beamed from the burning bush, shone in the fiery pillar, or clothed itself in darkness when upon the cloud-capped mount, amidst the flashing of lightning, the deep-toned thunder of his voice shook the earth when declaring the majesty of his law, so that surrounding millions tremblingly plead that they might hear his voice no more. Yet in this terrific scene was Moses introduced, and for forty days was pavilioned upon Sinai's top with the Omnipotent Ruler of the universe.

View that young prince, the royal heir of Israel's sweetest psalmist. Deity, in a vision descending, bids him utter his desire. See his bosom heave. Does he ask for wealth, for honor, or for long life? Not one of them. His single petition is for wisdom, and what does Deity respond? "Because thou has asked this thing, and hast not asked for thyself long life, neither hast asked riches for thyself, nor hast asked the life of thy enemies, but hast asked for thyself understanding to discern judgment, behold I have done according to thy word; lo! I have given a wise and understanding heart, so that there was none like thee, before thee, neither after thee shall any arise alike unto thee. And I have given thee also that which thou hast not asked, both riches and honor; so that there shall not be any among the kings like unto thee all thy days." And he who penned his wise sayings, who wrote of animals, and of plants from the hysop that springeth out of the wall to the cedar of Lebanon, he only was permitted to build and dedicate a temple for Jehovah. And while he prayed the glory of the eternal descended, and He whom the heaven of heavens cannot contain blessed with his presence that sacred edifice. When Christ was about to appear upon earth, the joyful intelligence was first given to the *wise men* of the East, and they first brought their offerings of myrrh and frankincense and gold, to lay at the humble shrine of an incarnate Deity. The apostle who was brought up at the feet of Gamaliel, and taught in languages and sciences above his colleagues, was especially made the honored instrument of extending God's peculiar kingdom among the Gentiles, and was favored with such ecstatic visions and enjoyed such rapturous emotions that whether he " was in the body or out of the body, he could not tell."

We have endeavored to consider some of the advantages of education, the necessity of the establishment of colleges, and the influence which they exert upon the political, social, and moral condition of the world. And however hasty and imperfect the sketch has been, we are very confident that the reflecting mind cannot dwell upon the subject without being fully satisfied that such institutions are necessary for the prosperity of any community. Deeply impressed with these sentiments, the patrons of this institution have exerted themselves in the noble enterprise; and now the INDIANA ASBURY UNIVERSITY, erected wholly by the munificence of citizens of Indiana, having no patronage from the government, or assistance from abroad, opens her halls for the admission of students. She stands wholly an Indiana institution, and on independent ground; and desires to spread broadly her banner, inscribed with " Universal and thorough Christian education essential to national prosperity." Yet she assumes no attitude of rivalry. As a new state entering our illustrious union detracts nothing from the glory and riches of the previous confederates, but rather increases their influence and power; so entering as a new member into the literary confederation, she will strive to promote, by all honorable means, the general interest. As a star hitherto invisible, when it suddenly shines brightly in the heavens, robs not other luminaries of their glory, but only augments the splendor of the sky; so, while endeavoring to radiate truth and science, she will rejoice in the brilliancy of sister stars in the effulgent galaxy of literature. The spirit of the times is a spirit of peace. The bitter jealousies and rancorous enmities that have subsisted between communities are changed into treaties of friendship and alliance; and nations have at last learned that the prosperity of one contributes to the prosperity of all—that the interest of each is intimately connected with the honor, influence, and improvement of others. So it should be in colleges; and so it is among men of comprehensive intellects and liberal views. None but the illiberal and bigoted—none but minds scanty by nature or contracted by prejudice—can look with envy upon a rising institution, or attribute to her increase the diminution of others that have any well-founded claims upon public patronage. Nor can it with propriety be objected that we had already a sufficient number of colleges in Indiana. The bare fact that sufficient interest has been felt to erect these walls is evidence that many felt the need of another institution. And the more we examine this subject, we shall the more clearly perceive that yet there is no superabundance.

The states of Massachusetts and Vermont, with a territory scarcely more than a fourth of ours, each supports three colleges. Connecticut, with a little more than an eighth of our extent, also supports three, together with academies and seminaries almost without number. It may, however, be said that that state is much more densely settled, and that we have more institutions in proportion to our population. This is also a mistake. Our population is nearly double that of Connecticut; and yet she has at least five times as many college students. This is in a great degree attributable to the fact of her institutions having long been in existence, and having created a spirit of enterprise and emulation among her citizens. Our state is becoming more densely settled, and its wealth is accumulating, and parents anxiously desire to give their sons a thorough education.

The only question is, shall this be done at home or abroad? Every principle of political economy, every feeling of attachment and consideration of interest, invite to educate them at home. Our wealth is then retained in our own borders, instead of flowing into other states. The personal acquaintance of parents with professors exerts a powerful control over the conduct of students. They are frequently cheered by visits from their friends, and their entire education is more immediately under parental supervision. During their collegiate term they are forming such friendships and connections as will be of essential service to them, in whatever profession they may engage in after-life. Eastern parents, who intend their sons to reside in the West, fully convinced of this principle, are beginning to send their sons to the West to be educated. Here they become attached to our customs, and identified with our interests. They are not, when their collegiate course is completed, to be placed like polished marble pillars, isolated objects of attention, and perhaps admiration; but like the young and vigorous tree, deep rooted in the soil, and intertwining its branches with those of a kindred growth, they mount upward, enlarging and strengthening with their age. The proper time to found literary institutions is in the infancy of a community. Their influence is more decidedly felt in all the ramifications of society, and although they sometimes struggle with difficulties incident to a new country—though for a time they labor almost without means, yet their prospect of permanence is much greater than if commenced at a later period. The strongest institutions in the land were once exceedingly feeble. Yale for a length of time was unable to support a regular president, and the neighboring ministers alternately officiated in its supervision. Yet Yale grew, because it had the affections of the people. Its sons, wherever they went, inspired attachment to its interests, its funds gradually accumulated, and it rose to eminence and distinction. Time is always requisite to prosperity and improvement. The order of Providence was a gradual creation, though His Omnipotence might have founded this fair fabric in the twinkling of an eye. And the same order is established in all things in that creation. Every institution must gradually increase. And when the friends of this university refer to its short history and its present standing — when they contemplate how deeply it is seated in the affections of the people in all parts of the state —and with what a noble liberality they have determined to sustain it, they must feel satisfied with its prosperity, and adore the beneficence of a superintending Providence, who hath surrounded its commencement with such auspicious circumstances. A more rapid increase would have been as the unseasonable germination of buds, only to be nipped by the recurring frost—a precocious development of some particular portion, at the expense of the symmetry and proportion of the entire system. As to the course to be pursued in the institution we have but little to say. Our plans will generally be similar to those of all well-regulated colleges. Without claiming for ourselves, as professors, any superior talents, or assuming motives of a higher order than actuate others, our aim shall be to labor indefatigably, and to promote the interests of education in the West. Whatever measure conduces to this, whether it has the sanction of years, or the freshness of youth, we wish to pursue. We are not of those who wish to change established customs merely for novelty, nor yet would we pertinaciously cling to antiquated forms, as the Mussulman to his crescent, merely because our fathers did so before us. Our course of study is designed to be extensive and thorough — equal to that of older institutions; for the literature of the West ought to be equal to that of any other land. Every element of intellectual greatness is here, independence of thought, firmness of purpose, frankness of expression, and noble daring of soul are the characteristics of our Western population. And when to these qualities shall be added high culture of intellect, there is no ascent so steep, no eminence so lofty, no enterprise so laborious as to damp their ardor or cause them to shrink from the undertaking. These elements of character are the same which shone so conspicuously in our brave sires, whose gigantic intellects planned the colossal fabric of our Constitution—whose hands toiled in its erection—whose blood cemented its parts, and calls upon us to preserve uninjured its massive pillars and its encircling dome. To every observer it must be evident that all eyes are turned towards the West. In selecting candidates for the highest offices in the nation, no ticket can hope for success which has not one of its candidates from our wide-spread valley. In our national councils, the voice of the West is heard with delight; it may not have the elegance of the East, but it has the boldness of native sublimity. The Eastern orator may resemble in his intonations, his manners, his thought, the lovely birds of plumage, whose brilliant colors and charming sounds command admiration. The Western has no such claims. Beauty is not his element. He may be unpolished and severe as the eagle, but like him he mounts with undazzled eye and tireless wing, until overpowered vision fails to follow him in his ethereal flights. The celebrated Cousin, in his History of Philosophy, remarks, "Give me the map of any country, its configuration, its climate, its waters, its winds, and the whole of its physical geography; give me its natural productions, its flora, its zoology, etc., and I pledge myself to tell you, *à priori*, what will be the quality of man in that country, and what part its inhabitants will act in history." And if these principles be true, our scenery, surpassingly grand and magnificent, must produce exalted sentiments and emotions. To preserve this character in its greatness, the defects alone being removed, should be the object of the faithful preceptor.

Nor are the circumstances of our young men unfavorable to intellectual improvement. It is true that many are obliged to labor for their own support during the period they are acquiring knowledge, while had their lots been cast in the East, their expenses might have been defrayed by the sympathizing directresses of religious fairs. Still they will lose nothing. They may be longer acquiring a thorough education, but it will be more valuable. Instead of the petty cunning, artful intrigue, and deep dissimulation, produced by such servile and unnatural dependence, there will be the proud consciousness of a greatness which was not thrust upon them. They will have a spirit to brook difficulties—a dauntless energy to urge them perpetually forward, till they stand upon the pinnacle of the temple of fame; while their supported colleagues will be lingering around the basement, waiting for fair hands to open each bolted door, and sweet smiles to cheer them at each ascending step. But while the course of study is designed to be extensive, there are some whose circumstances will not permit them to accomplish it. Some wish to be prepared merely for business pursuits; others to engage in teaching elementary schools; and such desire instruction in some particular branches. To all such our classes are cheerfully opened, and our only requirement is, that what they study, they should study thoroughly. Yet we are by no means disposed to encourage haste to engage in professional business; and where a young man's circumstances will at all permit, our earnest advice is to pursue the entire course. For we are well satisfied that young men, by commencing a professional course too early, injure their own habits, the character of the profession, and the interests of community.

The government is designed to be firm and strict, but parental. The student will be treated as a friend, and every effort used to make him perceive his relations and feel his obligations. But if, unfortunately, his habits should be vicious, and if after proper admonition they cannot be corrected, he must be dismissed from the institution. To such an individual education can be of no service, and he would be as a spreading plague among his associates. The precepts of the Bible is the standard we adopt in morals, being fully convinced that, apart from the influence of the Christian religion, no truly great or virtuous character can be formed. The observance of the Sabbath, attendance at public worship in such churches as may be selected by the students or by their parents, together with such other religious exercises as are instituted in connection with the college, will be strictly enjoined. We are well satisfied that such a course will be approved by the enlightened and liberal citizens of our state. But the startling cry of "Sectarianism" may perhaps by others be echoed throughout the land. Nay, we expect it, because it has always been the favorite resort of infidelity. Eighteen hundred years ago Christianity was the sect everywhere spoken against, and from that period to this "Schism and Sectarianism" have ever been the cry of its relentless opponents.

If by sectarianism be meant that any privilege shall be extended to youth of one denomination more than another—or that the faculty shall endeavor to proselyte those placed under their instruction—or dwell upon the minor points controverted between the branches of the great Christian family—then there is not, and we hope there never will be, sectarianism here. Indeed, our college charter secures equal privileges to all students, without reference to religious peculiarities; and it is ever to be hoped that in collegiate instruction only the grand essentials of Christianity will be taught. But if by sectarianism be meant that the professors are religious men, and that they have settled views upon Christian character and duty, then we ever hope to be sectarian. And what institution is not? Where can the line be drawn? If it be sectarian to differ from one man's religion, then it is equally sectarian to differ from that of another. Where shall we pause? We must not believe in a future state of rewards and punishments, for that is sectarian. We must not teach that the Messiah has appeared, or the Jew cries out "sectarian." We must not claim the Bible as inspiration, or the Deist is shocked at our illiberality. We must not deny the existence of pagan gods, or Nero's torch is the brilliant argument against sectarianism. Nay, we must not admit the existence of a God, or the Atheist will rail at our want of liberal feeling and sentiment. What then shall we do? Whether professors are Pagans or Atheists, Mohammedans or Jews, Deists or Christians, still they are sectarian. The only persons who are properly free from sectarianism are those who either believe *all things,* or who believe *nothing.*

Our own course is fully determined. Education without morals is pernicious, and to have morals without religious instruction is impossible. Taking then our stand upon the grand and broad platform of evangelical truth, passing by all minor and non-essential points, we shall ever strive to cultivate the moral as well as the mental faculties of those intrusted to our care.

With those who differ from us we have no dispute. Freedom of opinion and freedom of expression are the grand bulwarks of American liberty. And if there should be, even in our own country, men who reject the truths of revelation, and wish their sons to be so educated, they can doubtless elsewhere obtain the privilege. Let them have what sentiments they may, if they even deny the existence of a creator—if they believe with the Athenians that they sprang from grasshoppers—with the Egyptians that they grew like mushrooms from the mud of the Nile—or with more modern infidels, that they are monkeys slightly modified—while they suffer us to pursue our own course, we shall never dispute with them as to their *paternity.*

Permit me to suggest a few things, and I have done. The patrons of the university have acted nobly in bringing it to its present condition; and for what they have done doubtless posterity will rise up and call them blessed. But still something more is necessary. The library and philosophical apparatus require large additions, to render the character and influence of the institution what its founders have ardently desired. Other professorships should also be endowed. A noble example was set in the endowment of one of the professorships during the last year, and it is much to be desired that those whom God has blessed with property should imitate such disinterested benevolence, and place the institution upon a lofty eminence. Such persons would experience during life an ample reward in witnessing the beneficial effects produced, and, when their voice is hushed in the silence of the grave, "being dead" they would " still speak." Nor can we conceive of but few more interesting scenes than the return of the disembodied spirits, after the lapse of ages, to revisit the place of their former benefactions. As hovering over these classic halls, they should witness the preparations for noble action—and should gaze intensely on those bright intellects, which even in their youth sparkle with celestial fire, and ardently burn to subdue the world to Christ, and to usher in the millennial glory—overwhelmed with the resistless rush of holy feeling, they would fly back to the palaces of bliss, to join in still more enrapturing anthems of praise unto Him who had enabled them, while on earth, to perform such illustrious deeds, and bear such a noble part in advancing the Redeemer's Kingdom.

III.

THE CENTENARY OF AMERICAN METHODISM.*

WHEN I survey this audience, so large and so representative in its character, the question forces itself upon me, Why are we here? Why have these men and women left their homes; the service in their own particular churches; why have these men of business laid aside the cares and the anxieties connected with their pursuits; and why, sir, have you, laying aside for the hour, the cares connected with your responsible position in our government, met here to enjoy the evening hour and to confer with us? It may be very briefly said: We are here because the first hundred years of Methodism have passed away. But there is more than this. Why should such an event bring us together? What is there in the completion of this period to call for such an assembly? What is there in it to stir our hearts and to prepare us for action? I assume that all who are here present feel a deep interest in Methodism. They have witnessed its past history, they understand its doctrines, its spirit, and its aims, and they are in sympathy with its high purposes and its vast objects. And is it not wise, taking our stand at the passing moment of one century and the beginning moment of another, to ask on the one hand, What has Methodism done? and on the other, What can it do?

The time will not allow me to go into a review of the past; the history is before us. Call to your mind a little gathering a hundred years ago of six poor, obscure persons, in the lower part of the present city, meeting to sing and pray, little thinking that so great a Church would spring out of their efforts. Contrast its present condition. Look at our commodious churches, our large congregations, the wealth, the influence, the refinement, the great enterprise, and we see that a mighty work has been accomplished, and we can well exclaim, "What hath God wrought!" And now is it proper for us to make any expression of our feeling? It is certainly proper for us to utter thanksgiving to Almighty God, for it

---

* Delivered at the Centenary meeting, held in St. Paul's Methodist Episcopal Church, New York, January 25, 1866.

is not by might nor by power that the work has been accomplished, but by the Spirit of the Lord of Hosts, and our hearts ought to ascend in thanksgiving to him because of what he did for our fathers, and of what he has done for us. I think that no heart in this audience can feel unmoved at such an hour as this. The thoughts of the past crowd upon us, the century gone, with its toils, its anxieties, its sorrows, its strifes, its persecutions, its glorious triumphs. The hundred years of the past! Those who fought and those who fell. Those on earth and those in heaven; for while I gaze upon this assembly it seems to me as if in galleries a little higher, and away beyond this beautiful roof, there comes before me another congregation of glorified millions who have gone up from our ranks, and who, to-night, are joining with us in thanksgiving to God for the proclamation of that gospel which saved them as it saves us. But while we utter thanksgiving and our hearts swell with gratitude, is it not proper to give some expression to such feeling? Ought we not to do something to note the passing of time? I may remark that I think there is a natural feeling in the human breast that yearns to note the time of great events. It is a feeling sanctified of God in the human heart.

Thus when Jacob had the vision, when as a youth he was going out and God gave him audience, and the angels came down from heaven to commune with him, he set up stones to mark the place. It was to be to him Bethel, the house of God, to mark the spot where God had communed with him. And so at each victory, at each triumph, at each fresh manifestation of the power of God in the history of the old Church, there was some visible mark set up. If the Red Sea was passed over, there was not only the shout of deliverance, but there was the altar erected. If Jordan's waves were divided, and the host passed over in triumph, large pillars were set up. If the devastating angel was stayed in his course, the threshing-floor was purchased and an altar erected whereon should stand, in time, the temple of the living God. The feeling is not only thus marked by pious hearts, but I think there is something of the kind to be found everywhere. Does a man escape shipwreck? if he is a heathen, he hangs up a votive offering in the temple of the gods; if one is delivered from some terrible danger, he desires to make some outward expression of his gratitude. We notice the history of the churches. How often has the Christian Church marked a great epoch by some great work! And not only churches, but nations. The people of Holland established the University of Leyden to commemorate their remarkable deliverance. Now, is it not proper for us to follow such precedents? May we not even add that God himself has sanctioned it? He has given expression of the material along with the immaterial: while he creates spirit, he creates matter. When he sent us into the world to have pure thoughts and affections, he made the glorious outer world to mark the expression of his loving-kindness. When the old world was destroyed, he gave a promise that it should be destroyed no more; and it was not merely his promise he gave us, but, that we might have an outward symbol, he hung the bow in the clouds to be a sign of his goodness—a monument, as it were, of his saving mercy. When he led the people of Israel he sent the cloud, the pillar of fire, to show his presence. So, when he came on Mt. Sinai, he caused darkness and the flashing of lightning to attest his coming. Though he gave his law as a guide, he gave the tables of stone on which that law was written. So that God has sanctioned external expressions of his spiritual kindness and love, and the Church of to-day is but following the precedents that God and the ancient Church have set. When, at a point of its history, it sets up an altar, it marks the spot, it raises its Ebenezer, and says, "Hitherto the Lord hath helped me?" And in proportion to the greatness of the help that God has given ought to be the greatness of the expression; in proportion to the magnitude of the blessings bestowed ought to be the expression of gratitude, not by our lips, not by our singing, not by our prayers, but by something which shall live in the minds of the world, something that men shall behold and our children shall see, and which shall lead them to say, "Because God led our fathers thus and gave them a great inheritance, they have set up these altars to his name?"

The question then comes up: If we make an expression, what shall be its character? Now, there are many local interests which may well call out our offerings of gratitude in various localities of the Church. There are churches that may be erected; there are academies which may be builded; there are colleges which may be endowed; there is help which may be extended to Germany across the ocean, or to old Ireland, from whom we have received so many blessings. All these are specific objects which we may aid. As I listened to the very beautiful and eloquent plea in behalf of Ireland and Germany, my own heart was touched, and I thought if a New-Englander can sympathize so fully with those countries, what may some of us feel? As the bishop was speaking, I was reminded of what I was told, when in Ireland, of an Englishman who visited that country, and who was so charmed with the Lakes of Killarney that he declared if he ever was going to be born again, he would be sure to be born in old Ireland. But besides these local interests, to which we do well to take heed, it seems to me the great expression of our gratitude ought to be something which shall bind us together as a people, something that shall cement us as one body, and that can be felt to be an expression of our gratitude reaching all parts of our Church.

Now as I look at Methodism, I recognize this fact: from its birth and through its history of one hundred years, it has been struggling more and more for connectional sympathy and for connectional power. The first indication of this is in the pastorate. Unlike many other churches, we take the whole sweep of the church in our pastorate. I am not a pastor of this church, nor is my brother who occupies the pulpit here regularly. He is not the pastor of this church simply, but he is one of the pastors of Methodism. St. Paul's Church stands not alone as a congregation, but as one of the churches of Methodism, and hence the great connectional bond. We have one ministry, one pastorate, which circulates through the whole Church, thus binding us together. This is the first great idea, the first bond which distinguishes Methodism in the eyes of the world. You term it an itinerant ministry; but after all it is only this, giving to the whole Church the talents of all the ministers whom God has called to operate within the Church. But there follow other agencies, and those agencies have been from the first assimilating themselves to this great connectional thought. For instance, we take up our literature. Other churches have their literature, but to none occurred the idea of having one church literature that should spread throughout the bounds of the whole country. Though we began so feebly with but a single book or two, and a little establishment, first in Philadelphia, then in New York, struggling for years, yet the great idea was before the mind of the Church, the feeling that we ought to give to our people such reading as would develop their intellects and cultivate their moral feelings. The Church thus, as a Church, undertook to spread a religious literature among her people.

What has she done? Other churches have followed her example; other churches are now treading in the same path, but Methodism in this field is still pre-eminent. Hence have sprung up our periodicals and Book Concerns, through which our authors circulate their productions. Look at the power given to the few by the press. One million of members are interested in everything that is written by some masterminds; so that great thoughts reach not only one, two, or three thousand persons, but by means of the press a burning thought, which God has let down from some upper sphere, tells upon the hearts and consciences of multiplied thousands. The next step was, in addition to educating the children, to bind them to the Church. There is the Sunday-School Union, and I love it for its benevolent work, but the idea of making the Sunday-school a part of the Church is a Methodistic idea, not that of separate agencies, going outside of our work, but from the first making the Sunday-school part of the Church, for which also a literature is prepared. The children of the Church are educated as a

Church. We now gather in our folds not only nearly a million of members, but a full million of Sunday-school scholars. It is the connectional idea still that pervades the whole.

Then, again, there is the Missionary Society. We bring our offerings not to establish a mission here or a mission there, nor for one church to become the patron of one particular mission-field, but we look out and grasp the world in our thoughts. And here at the close of this first century, what have we accomplished? We have a Conference in Germany, of which you heard, a Conference organized in India, and schools and missionaries in China. We have swept over the wilderness of the west and have planted our Conferences up among the Rocky Mountains. God has given us a Conference in Africa, a Conference in Asia, a Conference in Europe, and multiplied Conferences in America. The world is our parish. This is the idea of Methodism, whose expansive heart is not satisfied until it lays its arms around the teeming millions of earth's population, and, so far as it may, draws them to the cross of Christ. This is the great connectional idea of Methodism, which gives it such immense power. The same thought that binds us thus together has led us to organize in the last few years a Church Extension Society, so that we shall be able to aid in the erection of edifices in the Western territories, in poor sections of the country, in the suburbs of cities, and in whatever lands are open before us, so that by a little systematic contribution to this and that church, by applying the means properly, we may stimulate the erection of churches in all parts of the land. For the churches are all one; they are houses of Methodism; they belong to the great field we are cultivating. Thus has the connectional idea pervaded all the movements of Methodism. But there remains one field not so fully connectionalized, and that is the field of education. We have our schools, colleges, universities, and theological seminaries; they are placed here and there as the Church saw fit to erect them; yet we have all mourned over this fact, that we have failed to accomplish what we ought to have accomplished in the education of our children. First, because of apathy on the part of the general Church; secondly, because neighborhoods that needed these schools were not able to found them at the proper time, and there were none to give them aid; thirdly, because schools were established in wrong places, and founded by unskilful men. Hence much of our labor has run to waste, and we have not accomplished what we ought. The question then suggests itself, Can we connectionalize our educational work? Can we at the close of the first century of Methodism do something by which we may control to such an extent our educational interests as to bring them close to the heart of the Church?

Now I need not before this audience attempt to prove the value of education. We feel it. This audience recognizes it. You educate your children, for you know that education is a power in the world. The educated men, say what we may, will govern the world, and it is simply optional with us whether our children shall be among the governors, or whether they shall be among the hewers of wood and drawers of water. God has given to developed mind this power, and this power will rule the world. I think we all feel the necessity of educating the children whom God has given us, and we are a large family. When I look at the number of children to be educated it sometimes almost makes my heart tremble. I occasionally see some rich old bachelor who has no family talking about educating the children of the land, but it gives him very little trouble and very little thought; but I see some man who has a family of half a dozen or a dozen children growing around him, with limited means, and his inquiry is, "How can I educate them? how shall these sons be prepared to be master-minds? how shall these daughters be so cultured and refined that they shall bloom in the garden of society?" This is a problem which occupies the thoughts and exercises the hearts of many of the fathers and mothers possibly in this assembly.

The Methodist Church occupies this position: God has given it a great many minds to cultivate, a large family of children, counted by hundreds of thousands, swelling up towards a million; and the question is, "How is it to educate them? Where are its means? You, sir, spoke of our means being part of the nation. I rejoice that God has given us some means; and yet sometimes (if I would not descend from the dignity of my theme) I am reminded that in some places we are a little like the poor beggar who came to plead with a rich old miser for bread for his father. Said the man, "Wherever God sends mouths he sends bread?" "Yes," said the little boy, "but he sent you all the bread and sent us all the mouths?" It sometimes seems to me that our work is so vast and overflowing in proportion to our means, I scarcely know how we shall accomplish it. The work being so vast, it requires extraordinary exertion, and the whole Church needs to rally around it.

It is therefore proposed, as an expression of our gratitude to God, that we shall throw our contributions into one fund, to be wisely vested in trustees, appointed by the General Conference, men in whom the Church can confide, partly laymen and partly ministers, who shall hold this fund and distribute its interest from year to year for the purpose of helping education. The principle is precisely the same as in the endowment of a college, an academy, or a theological school, with this single exception: this fund is not for any one school, nor for any one section, but to be distributed by the Church where it can accomplish the greatest amount of good in promoting its educational interests. This is the character of the scheme. Now I ask you to look at it for a moment. If you give to a single institution, which I hope you will do as largely as your local sympathy may prompt you, yet the fact must be remembered that that institution has but a local sphere.

Look at our swelling country; you have heard of the coming millions of population. If the old statesman stood at the summit of the Alleghany Mountains listening for the coming millions, we stand in the Mississippi Valley, or the Rocky Mountains, and on the Sierra Nevadas, listening for the footsteps of the coming tens of millions. And what will institutions located here or there do for the vast multitudes that will come hereafter? Our country is extending, and is destined to extend. God has given us a government capable of expansion, and it will expand. We ought to be in a position where we can follow the people, and do something, wherever they go, to aid them in founding their institutions of learning.

Again, there is this other thought: If you give to a single institution, valuable as the contribution is, your donation carries out its own work alone. It is valuable, and, being dead, you will yet speak; but suppose you leave a fund under the administration of wise men, who say, "If you will raise five thousand dollars, we will give you one thousand for this year; if you endow a chair in three years, we will support the professor until it is endowed, and give you his labors—what a stimulus you would furnish! And such a fund judiciously used might bring to the Church tenfold more than all the money you give. The aid you extend would be powerfully multiplied. I will give you an instance. I received a letter a few days since, pleading for three hundred dollars, telling me of a certain place where there is a church property worth seven thousand dollars, which can be bought to-day for three hundred dollars. I hope the Church will be secured. This is an instance where a little given may accomplish much. Benevolent men will combine where there is a nucleus. You give aid to an institution, and men who love education will rally round it; and this fund, thus used, may gather about it a hundredfold more in time to come. Then, again, I advocate such a fund because it is not subject to the difficulties resulting from the management of other funds. You endow a professorship, and a man may occupy the chair who is unworthy, and the local institution is unwilling to remove him. Sometimes the chairs become almost sinecures, and are almost useless for the cause of education; but if the income be annually given by the Church just where the greatest amount of good may be accomplished, there will be no sinecures, for the donation is bestowed as a premium, and as an aid to individual effort. The same money may help a school in Maine this year, and next year a school in Oregon. It

33

may to-day help a school in Michigan, and next year one in Mississippi. When our great Church in all its branches shall hereafter become united again, and Methodism shall be one from the Lakes to the Gulf, the fund which you create will exercise its influence in aiding institutions of learning, and in developing the cause of education. It is in behalf of this fund I plead with you to-night. I ask you to take it to your minds, consider it, and ask what you can do. And, while I ask you not to give the less to the institutions we now have, I ask you to give something that shall be a memento to our sons, and which the public shall recognize as a fund for the cause of general Christian education.

Would it not be glorious to take this position? If there is a single point on which the public regard us unfavorably, it is in the matter of education. They acknowledge our piety; they know our numbers; they admit our energy and enterprise; but they have not given us credit for being deeply interested in education. They do not look upon us, I think, as favorably as they ought. But if, at this time, standing at this point of our history, we put forth our energies in behalf of Christian education, the world will recognize the fact that Methodism, spiritual religion, that religion which touches the hearts, the affections, and the emotions, does not pass by the intellect, but, calling fire from heaven, kindles in the intellect the highest thoughts, and exalts its power. I look into the Methodism of the future and I recognize all this. I see a people vast in number—a people whose hearts swell with gratitude to God—a people with intellects educated, with tastes refined, artistic, lovely, energetic, and expressive—going forth preaching the Gospel in all languages, and conquering the world unto God.

This is a cause which, more than any, should engross the hearts, the affections, and the feelings of Methodists. It is not merely the general cause of education, which I love in all its bearings, but especially the training-up of strong, fervid, polished, and powerful ministers of the gospel, who shall go like bright and burning lights all over this country of ours. The need of Methodism now, at the close of the first century, is not less fire, but more learning. We want rhetoric, but we want it set on fire of God. We want a learning polished and yet sanctified, whereby we may educate the people and, at the same time, lead them upward to God. God grant that we may now do something worthy of Methodism! And when the year 1866 shall be remembered, among the years of the past, may the pen of the future historian record that among its most notable events was this: That Methodism gave its grandest efforts for the education, not of men and women of a particular locality, not for partial ends, or for personal aggrandizement, but for educating the minds of the masses all over the world.

INDEX.